Getting Ready to
Teach Math
for the New Teacher

Grade 1

by

Becky White

Published by Frank Schaffer Publications
an imprint of

 **Children's Publishing**

Author: Becky White
Illustrator: Becky J. Radtke

 **Children's Publishing**

Published by Frank Schaffer Publications
An imprint of McGraw-Hill Children's Publishing
Copyright © 2004 McGraw-Hill Children's Publishing

Send all inquiries to:
McGraw-Hill Children's Publishing
3195 Wilson Drive NW
Grand Rapids, Michigan 49544

Getting Ready to Teach Math for the New Teacher—Grade 1
ISBN: 0-7682-2931-6

1 2 3 4 5 6 7 8 9 MAL 09 08 07 06 05 04

The **McGraw·Hill** Companies

Table of Contents

© McGraw-Hill Children's Publishing   0-7682-2931-6 *Getting Ready to Teach Math for the New Teacher*

Table of Contents

0-7682-2931-6 *Getting Ready to Teach Math for the New Teacher*

Introduction

Getting Ready to Teach Math for the New Teacher will help you tackle your first year of teaching first-grade math. As a starting point, you are likely to receive curriculum materials from your school or school district. You also may be assigned a textbook or math program that includes lists of standards and benchmarks. This book is designed to support those materials. It is aligned to NCTM (National Council of Teachers of Mathematics) Standards. Content areas of study are separated into five strands: Numbers and Operations, Algebra, Geometry, Measurement, and Data Analysis and Probability. To learn math, a student must do math. Each strand includes hands-on, concept-building activities, reproducibles for independent practice, and assessment activities that evaluate conceptual understanding.

0-7682-2931-6 *Getting Ready to Teach Math for the New Teacher*

Process standards are embedded in every activity and assessment. We use problem solving as an application of skills. We invite our students to reason through math processes and make sense of their answers. We have students represent values in a multitude of ways, from pictures and symbols to fractions and decimals. Students make connections between math content areas such as addition and multiplication, and between math and other subject areas through problem-solving applications. Finally, activities encourage the students to communicate their understanding in speaking, writing, and computation.

Children and Math

Children will begin the year at different stages of readiness and core knowledge will vary from one individual to another. Because students have different styles and rates of learning, we have provided inclusion strategies throughout, as well as suggestions for integrated learning that can motivate students and help them make real-life connections. Use activities to show math skills at work in games, sports, shopping, cooking, and scheduling. To address a variety of learning styles, we have included active and engaging activities that appeal to multiple intelligences. These can be supported by observation, demonstration, and manipulatives.

National Council for Teachers of Mathematics

THE NCTM is the world's largest mathematics education organization. NCTM publishes four professional journals, including *Teaching Children Mathematics* and *The Mathematics Teacher*. For more information go to www.nctm.org

Good Advice!

Working through a single problem or two daily will keep skills fresh in a child's mind. Begin each class with a short skill review before a new skill is addressed.

National Association for the Education of Young Children

The National Association for the Education of Young Children (NAEYC) is an organization of early childhood educators (birth through third grade). You can find their Web site at www.naeyc.org

© McGraw-Hill Children's Publishing

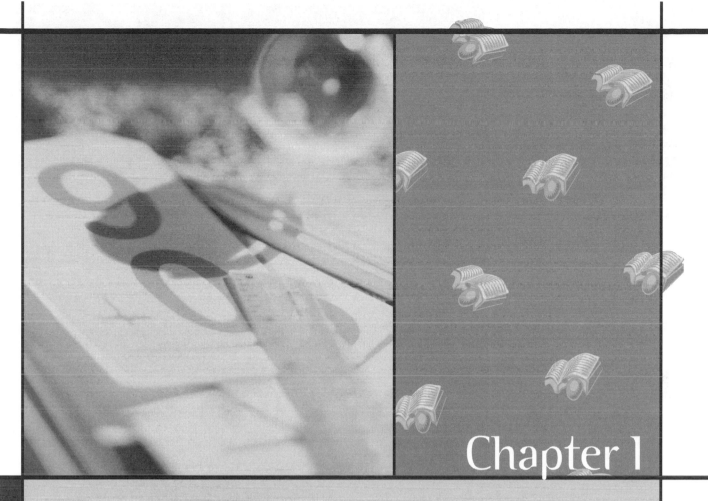

Chapter 1

Planning and Organizing: Creating a Math Environment

Long-Range Planning

Planning is essential to the success of your students. Long-range planning is the first step, with the entire school year as your time frame. Begin with the school or district's curriculum guide or course of study to ensure that students will be exposed to all required material. Use a calendar to create an overview of the year. Include special activities, holidays, short schedules, field trips, assemblies, conference times, testing times, and assessment periods. Once you have blocked out the main topics you will cover, list basic materials that you will use (such as manipulatives) that will help reinforce learning.

© McGraw-Hill Children's Publishing

0-7682-2931-6 *Getting Ready to Teach Math for the New Teacher*

Now is the time to consider a few general classroom themes that can be fun and help to motivate students. A theme is a concept used across the curriculum to connect activities and integrate learning. Something as simple and general as holidays or seasons can work well. To provide a math connection to Halloween, students could weigh and measure a pumpkin, count the seeds inside, and decorate it with geometric shapes. Observing animal populations within a spring theme can be tied in to data analysis, probability, and statistics.

Unit Planning

A unit is a combination of activities and lessons that are based on a common topic, such as operations or algebra. Follow this sequence when planning a unit. First, determine the state or district goals to address. They are the results. You must begin with the end in mind. Next, create the assessment you will use. Assessments should be aligned with the state or district goals. Block out the time needed to teach, practice, and assess each unit. Individual lesson activities and experiences can be planned within each unit with the assessment in mind . . . so the state or district goals, the assessment, and the lessons are all aligned. It's a clear pathway to success!

Lesson Planning

You must choose, schedule, and refine the lessons that will teach each skill or concept. A lesson plan book is invaluable.

Internet Resources

Check out these resources for ideas and materials to use over the school year.

- www.freestuffshop.com/teachers.htm
- www.teacherszone.com

Curriculum Connections

The Teacher's Calendar (a new one every year) is a directory to holidays, historic events, and more, by Chase's Calendar of Events (McGraw-Hill/Contemporary Books, 2003). It has a special "Curriculum Connections" section that will help you put the information to use in the classroom.

Lesson Planning Strategy

A publisher's bookmap can be useful in long range planning. On a single sheet of paper, draw one large square to represent each month of the school year. Within each square write the topics you intend to cover that month. The map can be seen at a glance. You can easily track the sequence in which each skill and concept will be taught, and you can plan to build one set of skills upon another.

© McGraw-Hill Children's Publishing

0-7682-2931-6 *Getting Ready to Teach Math for the New Teacher*

Depending on your style, you can find detailed planners at teacher supply stores or online. A notebook or 3" x 5" cards can work. Your school may even supply a planner.

Teachers Sharing with Teachers

If you would like to see how other teachers handle lessons, go to www.intime.uni.edu for a video peek.

Learning is a continuum, and each lesson should be part of a larger picture. Begin each lesson with a bridge to previously-learned concepts by clearly stating the goal of the lesson to students. This allows them to connect new information with prior knowledge. "Yesterday/last week/last year we learned __. Today we will build on that as we learn __."

The more actively kids participate in the body of the lesson, the better they will learn. Review and reinforce at the close of the lesson: *What did you learn new today? How does this fit into what you already know?* Close with a preview of how what kids learned today will be used tomorrow.

Balance lessons by using static activities that require focus to find a particular answer or solution, activities that require creative thinking that may be resolved with a variety of responses, and activities that allow movement or hands-on participation. When planning individual lessons, consider commonplace activities that may reinforce learning. Such activities can help to balance quiet and active time. Sharing a pizza can demonstrate fractions. Baking cookies helps with measurement. Planning a party can incorporate a

Lesson Preparation Strategy
You should be able to explain the purpose of each lesson or activity in one sentence. Before you assign an activity, do it yourself ahead of time to identify snags. If you require materials, order or prepare them in advance. Place instructions, support material, related books, supplies, and/or pre-made copies in a plastic tub or shoe box with a cover. Label the container with the date the lesson will be given.

great deal of math. Your goal is to help students master a combination of concepts, facts, and skills. Be realistic about the amount of time an activity will take. Be flexible, so you can shorten or extend activities as needed. Figure in extra time to check for understanding through questioning and guided practice. If you still have a few moments left, offer independent practice.

Watch for "teachable moments" that may help you drive home a point, but return to your prepared lesson or activity as soon as possible. Remember the INPUT/OUTPUT rule of lesson planning. When the teacher provides the means for students to explore, draw conclusions, find patterns, and so forth, the students do more thinking and the bulk of the work.

Questioning

Questioning serves several purposes. It can facilitate learning, encourage classroom dialogue, and address the needs of individual students. When assessing a student, asking effective questions helps you determine what the child has learned and identify areas where he or she may still have problems.

When asking questions, use phrases that include all members of the class. Suggest that they all "think together" about an answer. Give students time to think and raise their hands before calling on an individual.

Questions that can be answered with yes/no or other one-word answers are not helpful. *How or why* questions encourage thinking and stimulate class discussion. Once a student has answered, you can extend and include, by asking another question or asking for peer response. When you have other students summarize the answer or address it in some way, you insure that most students will get in the habit of listening to the dialogue. This creates an atmosphere of exchange that encourages participation and, in some cases, a little risk-taking.

Ten Steps of Planning

- Review curriculum
- Create an overall calendar
- Block out general units
- Select general materials
- Determine state or district goals for each unit
- Create assessments for each unit
- Choose general lesson plans for each unit
- Clarify individual lessons and create a weekly/daily agenda
- Choose activities to reinforce lessons
- Review lessons to reinforce inclusive concepts

© McGraw-Hill Children's Publishing

When helping an individual student, you can deepen his understanding of the lesson through questions. For example, if a student is working on a math story, ask strategic questions to guide him to the answer. Have the student read the information. Then ask questions such as:

What do you know?

What do you need to know?

Is there any information that you don't need?

Can you explain your thinking?

Have you seen a problem like this before?

Is there another way to think about it?

Can you give an example?

Do you see a pattern?

Your goal is to help the student understand the process, not simply get the right answer.

Questioning is an excellent opportunity for assessment. To determine if a student has truly mastered understanding, ask clear questions that require more than good recall to answer. Open-ended questions with more than one possible answer are excellent for this purpose.

Good Questions

1. *How did you solve the problem/find the answer? This gets at the process the students used to solve a problem.*

2. *How do you know your answer makes sense? This addresses math sense and reasoning.*

3. *Could you solve the problem another way? This addresses flexibility in thinking and making connections between mathematical ideas.*

© McGraw-Hill Children's Publishing   0-7682-2931-6 *Getting Ready to Teach Math for the New Teacher*

Assessment

Assessment Strategies

- questioning
- observation
- textbook tests
- teacher-developed tests
- rubrics
- student self-evaluation
- journal review
- portfolio review
- checklists
- conferences

The purpose of assessment is to determine what a student has learned. It is based on the curriculum, but it encompasses more. It should vary to fit the multitude of styles you are likely to find in your classroom. Formal written assessments should include multiple choice, constructed responses, and performance-based elements. The assessments in this book include a mix of these approaches. In addition to formal assessments, ongoing informal assessment should be part of everyday instruction. This includes listening to students' responses to questions and observing students at work.

At the beginning of the school year, do a baseline assessment of each student. To do this, watch students in a variety of situations, such as at lunch, on the playground, in line, in group activities, and during individual work. An early assessment should include factors such as social (communication and cooperation), behavioral (confidence and self-control), and academic (organization and work habits). Use the assessment pages in this book as quizzes, homework, or review. Remember that there are many ways in which students should be evaluated.

0-7682-2931-6 *Getting Ready to Teach Math for the New Teacher*

An important math assessment tool is a portfolio for each student, which can be as simple as a manila folder. Date all of the child's math work. Allow the student access to it for review. To help with assessment, make evaluations and clip them to student worksheets. Keep the work together until the end of each report period to answer parents' questions about their child's evaluation. Make copies of any papers that highlight particular progress or concerns, and return the originals to the student to take home. Keep the most important copies on file until after the beginning of the following school year, in case the child's next teacher would like to review them.

Modeling

Have students model math problems by using manipulatives or drawing pictures. Have them talk about what they learned, and how it relates to what they already know. Check their work.

Assessment Rubric

3 The student's performance or work sample shows a thorough understanding of the topic. Work is clearly explained with examples and/or words, all calculations are correct, and explanations reflect reasoning beyond the simplicity of the calculations.

2 The student's performance or work sample shows a good understanding of the topic. There may be some errors in calculations, but the work reflects a general knowledge of details and a reasonable understanding of mathematical ideas.

1 The student's performance or work sample shows a limited understanding of the topic. The written work does not reflect understanding of the mathematical ideas, and examples contain errors.

0 The student's performance or work sample is too weak to evaluate, or nonexistent.

Women in Math

Some girls may still be getting the message that boys are better than girls in math. An Internet search using key words "women mathematicians" will provide several sites that can be inspirational to the girls in your class. Two possible sites are:

http://camel.math.ca/Women/BIOG/Biographies

http://womenshistory.about.com/cs/sciencemath/

Differentiation

As you begin assessing your students, it soon becomes apparent that several levels of understanding are represented in your class. Students who cannot do the work may be frustrated, while others are bored because the material is not challenging enough. Each lesson should offer some success for every student. You may have to modify some assignments by breaking them into sections that can be completed at different rates. Include activities that address various styles of learning. When possible, offer choices for completing assignments, such as making a model or a poster. Keep in mind that every student brings special talents to the classroom.

Continuing to engage students who are having difficulty can be a challenge. Since it is your responsibility to deliver the on-grade level curriculum, you may be faced with the challenge of teaching the prerequisite skills required for success on a particular topic. For example, to add fractions with unlike denominators, students need to understand how to identify the least common denominator, find equivalent fractions for the denominator, and simplify the resulting sum. If a student cannot add fractions with unlike denominators, revisiting one or more of the above mentioned prerequisite skills may be necessary. Make time to remediate in

0-7682-2931-6 *Getting Ready to Teach Math for the New Teacher*

small groups with students who are not ready to move on to new or more complex lessons. Have challenged students write short and long term goals for math. Celebrate reaching each goal.

When evaluating an assignment, an evaluation of 19/40 on a page of addition problems may not give the correct picture. You might consider showing two evaluations on such a paper. Put the number of problems finished over those that were not completed to show that element. Let's say 20/40. Looking at the completed problems only, put the number of correct answers over the number completed. Let's say 19/20. This gives a much better evaluation of this student.

Some students will be bored because the material is not challenging enough. These students need stimulation and more difficult material. This can take many forms. You can offer enrichment ideas, such as problem formulation or real-life problem applications of the concepts they already know. Another option is teaching a more sophisticated version of the concept. To return to the fraction example, students could add three or more fractions or add mixed numbers with unlike denominators.

Rich with Resources

Having a great library of resources will enrich your own enthusiasm for teaching math! Here's a gem for you: *Big Math Activities for Young Children* by Overholt, White-Holz, and Dickson published by Delmar. This resource provides a wide selection of activities and investigations for young children. Multilevel activities provide increasingly-advanced skills for pre school through third grade and have been designed to promote mathematical reasoning, communications, and problem-solving skills.

Teacher Resources
Download the Help! They don't speak English Starter Kit at http://www.ael.org/page.htm?&index=58&pd=1. It is from the Institute for the Advancement of Emerging Technologies. The site offers a wealth of resources for Native American, Mexican American, and migrant students. It also addresses issues in rural education, with a special focus on mathematics achievement in rural schools.

0-7682-2931-6 *Getting Ready to Teach Math for the New Teacher*

No matter what level of understanding students may have, they will benefit from clear directions. When explaining an assignment, have students clear their desks and keep their eyes on you. Keep it simple. Tell the students what they will do and why they will do it. Demonstrate if necessary. Write the instructions on the board and have students repeat them and write them down. Answer any questions. You can even tape-record the instructions and keep the tape player on your desk for students who need to hear them again.

Tip *Celebrate Uniqueness*
To celebrate each student, create a paper treasure chest and make it the center of a bulletin board display. Learn something unique about each student and write it on a paper coin with his or her name. Perhaps a student plays chess, draws, sings, or raises guinea pigs. Pin the coins to the board around the treasure chest.

Suggested Math Period
5   minutes: Warm-up and bridge
5   minutes: Goal setting
20   minutes: Focus lesson on the day's main concept
25   minutes: Small group follow-up instruction. This may include prerequisite skills with strugglers or enriching/extending "high flyers."
5   minutes: Close and preview for tomorrow

0-7682-2931-6 *Getting Ready to Teach Math for the New Teacher*

Math Centers

Learning centers are a great way to differentiate instruction in the classroom. In addition, they promote independence and challenge students to reinforce ideas and extend learning on their own. Math centers should address a mix of formats to accommodate different learning styles. Once an instructional unit is taught, students can be invited to complete learning center activities independently to clarify concepts. Small group activities are helpful when students need additional skill practice. Centers can provide multi-level opportunities. For example, you may begin an activity at the instructional level, then enrich or extend it to address students' needs. Many of the math concepts in this book can be taught during class and the activities used for independent learning.

Math centers should include manipulatives, opportunities for critical thinking and analysis of concepts, writing prompts, games, and other activities. You don't need a lot of space to set up a center. You can keep materials and supplies in plastic see-through tubs or shoe boxes in cubbies or on shelves. Manipulatives and other small supplies may be stored in plastic bags and clipped to a clothesline with clothespins. File folders in an open-topped storage bin or box are ideal for storing reproducibles by topic. Make use of wall space with bulletin boards, instructional posters, and a magnetic whiteboard with magnetic letters and numbers.

0-7682-2931-6 *Getting Ready to Teach Math for the New Teacher*

Multiple Intelligences

- verbal-linguistic
- logical-mathematical
- visual-spatial
- bodily-kinesthetic
- musical-rhythmic
- interpersonal
- intrapersonal
- environmental-naturalist
- existentialist

Howard Gardner developed his groundbreaking theory of multiple intelligences in the early 1980s. He has since described nine ways that people may process information and learn. Most use a combination of the intelligences. Learning centers are the ideal area to address this concept. The classic math intelligence is logical-mathematical, but a student who learns through movement may be bodily-kinesthetic. An environmental-naturalist will love a lesson conducted outside involving plants or animals, while an interpersonal intelligence can benefit from peer tutoring and group work.

Making a School-to-Home Connection

Encourage parents to demonstrate to children the relevance of math in everyday life. Ask them to point the mathematical

applications when shopping, cooking, following directions, reading schedules, driving a car, etc. When parents recognize the math they use everyday and verbalize that to their children, students will see its relevance. These real-world applications help students comprehend the concepts on a personal level.

To strengthen the school-home connection, keep parents informed of the concepts students are learning in class. Send

0-7682-2931-6 *Getting Ready to Teach Math for the New Teacher*

home vocabulary words and skills lists so parents can understand and help reinforce concepts at home. Home math projects help students explore the content of their world, discover new things, organize their thinking, communicate with others, and summarize what they have learned. This allows your students to become full participants and investigators in the world around them.

Avoid calling the math that students are required to do at home *homework*. Instead, use terms such as: *home challenges, daily puzzles, special questions,* or *family projects*. These assignments can be written on the board or sent home on slips of paper. Occasionally, a small prize might be given to students who, with assistance from parents, arrive at a correct answer.

School-to-Home Activity Ideas

Motivate students to explore math concepts through the use of parent-assisted projects. Follow up with activities using the projects in class.

At home:	In class:
▶ Write family recipes.	Use recipes to create dishes and/or reproduce all the favorite recipes and create a class cookbook.
▶ Cook and record outcome.	Share information and/or food.
▶ Bake desserts.	Divide a whole apple crisp into equal-sized pieces or two dozen cookies into enough parts for the whole class.
▶ Measure specifics around the house, such as number of trees in yard, length of driveways, etc.	Compare figures by creating class graphs.

Stages of Critical Thinking
- explore
- discover
- organize
- communicate
- summarize

0-7682-2931-6 *Getting Ready to Teach Math for the New Teacher*

At home:

▶ Record distances traveled in family car.

▶ Draw house plans or floor plans.

▶ Draw maps of the neighborhood.

▶ Check, record, and compare prices of a specific item at different markets, such as red delicious apples.

▶ Graph family-gathered data, such as favorite color, animal, etc.

In class:

Use figures to write story problems.

Draw plans for dream homes, vacation cabins, houseboats, etc.

Create a giant map of the neighborhood on a bulletin board, incorporating the figures and measurements on student maps.

Decide where to go for the best buy on a specific product.

Combine data to create new graphs.

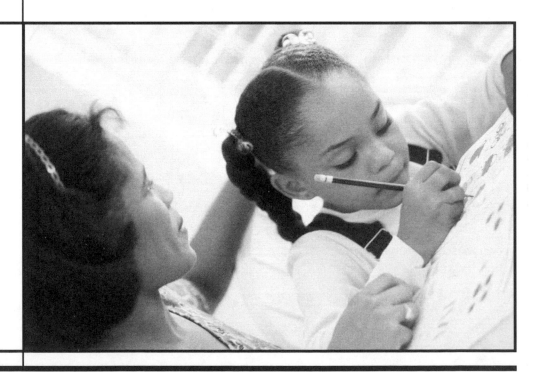

0-7682-2931-6 *Getting Ready to Teach Math for the New Teacher*

At home:

▶ Create time lines and family trees that include dates.

▶ Play card games such as "Rummy."

▶ Play dominoes.

▶ Estimate, then count large quantities, such as jelly beans in a bag.

▶ Compute change when shopping.

▶ Compute discounts in clothing stores.

In class:

Have students create time lines of their lives.

Create card games to practice math facts that can be shared during game time at home.

Make up math games that can be played with dominoes. Example: Play "War." Each player turns over a domino. The one who has the highest total keeps all the faceup dominoes.

Fill a jar with candy (pennies, marbles, shells, stones, etc.). Estimating the total might be an ongoing game. Whoever guesses correctly first or is nearest at the end of a given time period, wins the jar or another prize.

Use prices in catalogs and ads to write and solve story problems.

Use sale ads to figure discounts.

0-7682-2931-6 *Getting Ready to Teach Math for the New Teacher*

At home:	In class:
▶ Help pay the bills, estimate tips at restaurants, etc.	Figure how much it costs to buy a meal ticket for a week, month, or the school year.
▶ Record patterns in nature, such as the phases of the moon.	Keep weather graphs (rainfall, high/low temperatures, barometer readings, etc.).
▶ Solve challenging puzzles.	Share the solutions families devised to solve puzzles.
▶ Create a working sundial and/or thermometer.	Use devices to measure time and temperature.
▶ Build and construct kites, paper airplanes, or crafts that float.	Share constructions and explain the steps used in building.

0-7682-2931-6 *Getting Ready to Teach Math for the New Teacher*

Chapter 2

Number and Operations Activities

First graders are naturally active and resourceful. They will construct, modify, and integrate ideas by interacting with the physical world. At play, they begin to form connections that clarify and extend concepts introduced in the classroom. Games and activities that incorporate mathematical terms will provide concrete models and help students develop number sense. Most six-year-olds have acquired a wide range of mathematical understanding. Interviews and observations will be your best guide to assessing their level of knowledge.

In first grade, building mathematical knowledge through **problem solving** should involve situations that arise in the classroom. The more practical and connected to the child's world you can make math, the more motivated they will be to find the answers. Mathematics should emphasize problem solving so students can investigate and understand mathematical content; formulate problems form everyday situations; develop and apply strategies to solve problems; and acquire confidence in using mathematics meaningfully.

0-7682-2931-6 *Getting Ready to Teach Math for the New Teacher*

Communication

To make assumptions and test ideas, students must be able to **communicate** their thoughts. Language is as important to learning mathematics as it is to learning to read. It is important for students to hear the language of mathematics in meaningful context. To optimize mathematical thinking, create and structure a mathematics-rich environment for your students. Exploring their ideas will give them practice in thinking coherently and communicating ideas clearly to peers, teachers, and others. Presenting, discussing, reading, writing, and listening are vital parts of learning and using mathematics.

Reasoning and proof are fundamental aspects of mathematics that require young learners to make assumptions and to investigate whether their ideas are sound. For students to test their ideas, manipulatives are essential. First-grade students can learn to use models to understand physical, social, and mathematical phenomena. Manipulatives provide practice adding more objects and taking away objects to test addition and subtraction facts.

When students learn to create and use **representations** to organize, record, and communicate mathematical ideas, they will be able to solve more complicated problems and make predictions. Students who learn to problem solve, reason to prove, communicate mathematical ideas, make connections, and use representation to interpret mathematical phenomena, will know more than simple numbers and operations. Mathematics will become the key to understanding their universe and how everything in it relates to everything else.

© McGraw-Hill Children's Publishing

Skills List

Skill levels for your first graders will vary. The following list covers the basic expectations for Number and Operations in primary grades. Use it as a guide for lesson planning and for determining whether your students are developing and learning math skills as expected.

▶ count with understanding and recognizes "how many" in sets of object

▶ match numerals (1 to 12) to the quantities they represent and their number words

▶ match various physical models and representations to numerals

▶ write numerals 1 to 100 on a number chart

▶ use multiple models to demonstrate place value and base ten number system

▶ recognize a penny as 1¢, nickel as 5¢, dime as 10¢, quarter as 25¢, half-dollar as 50¢

▶ understand that a tens rod equals ten ones blocks

▶ understand relative position and magnitude of numbers and their connections

▶ understand *equal to*, *more than*, and *less than* and use signs to make number connections

▶ understand even and odd numbers

▶ skip count by 2s and 5s

▶ use ordinal terms *first*, *second*, *third*, and *fourth* in sets of objects

▶ understand commonly used fractions: $\frac{1}{2}$, $\frac{1}{3}$, $\frac{1}{4}$, $\frac{1}{6}$, $\frac{1}{8}$

▶ understand that "+" and addition mean joining sets

▶ understand that "−" and subtraction mean comparing sets

▶ use a number chart to solve addition and subtraction problems

▶ know basic number fact families for addition and subtraction

Learning to Count

Many first graders know the numerals 0 through 12 and their quantities. Some, but not all, will be able to count to 100. While using a number chart, it's a good time to introduce even and odd numbers, counting by 2s, 5s, and 10s, and place value.

One Hundred Game Board

Create a bulletin board-sized "One Hundred Game Board" where students can play a variety of counting games.

Directions:

1. Use the illustration below as a model.
2. Cover a square bulletin board with white paper.
3. Measure and divide it into ten equal columns and ten rows.
4. Outline the columns and rows with yarn pinned at the top/bottom and along the edges.
5. Cut 100 squares of heavy paper slightly smaller than each grid space and write numerals 1 through 100 on them.
6. Use a hole punch to place a hole in the top of each number card.
7. Place a pin at the top center of each of the 100 sections on the bulletin board so that a number card can be hung within the yarn boundaries.

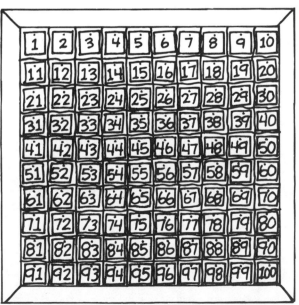

0-7682-2931-6 *Getting Ready to Teach Math for the New Teacher*

Hundred Game Board Activities

Use the "One Hundred Game Board" (page 26) for these activities.

▶ Remove the number cards and mix them up. Time small groups to see how long it takes each group to hang all 100 cards sequentially.

▶ With all number cards in place, ask students to close their eyes. Mix up two cards. When they open their eyes, see who is first to name the two cards out of sequence.

▶ Each day, remove three number cards. Students list the numbers that are missing.

▶ Remove the last card in each row. As a group, count from 1 to 100 saying the missing numbers, too.

▶ Skip count by removing even or odd number cards. As a group, have students whisper the numbers that are on the board and say aloud those that are missing.

▶ Remove the cards divisible by 5. Have students list the missing cards. Read the list together. Explain that this is counting by fives.

▶ Remove all the cards from the board. Shuffle them and deal two or three to each student. Count as a group while students hurry to the board in relay fashion to hang number cards in order. Repeat each day for a week and see how much more quickly they can complete the activity.

27

Number Words

Write the number words (one to ten) on flash cards. Hold up a word and have students count that many. Then have students make a set of their own number words on 5" x 8" index cards. For self-checking, place the appropriate numeral on the back of each card.

One Hundred Chart Activities

Use the *One Hundred Chart* (page 43) to play a variety of number games.

▶ Have students point to each number as they count aloud from 1 to 100.

▶ Begin counting at any number. Say four numbers. Wait for students to respond with the number that follows.

▶ As a group, count aloud the even numbers and whisper the odd numbers.

▶ Ask:

1. *How many numbers between 1 and 100 have the digit 7 in them?*

2. *How many numbers between 1 and 50 are even?*

3. *How many numbers between 1 and 100 have two digits that total 9?*

▶ Ask sequencing questions.

1. *What number comes after 46?* (one more than)

2. *What number comes just before 88?* (one less than)

3. *What number comes between 76 and 78?* (consecutive numbers)

4. *What number is directly under 88?* (adding tens)

5. *How many numbers between 1 and 100 come after 96?*

▶ Have students use their hundred charts like number lines.

1. *What is six and ten more?* (moving forward—addition)

2. *What is 19 and five less?* (moving backwards—subtraction)

0-7682-2931-6 *Getting Ready to Teach Math for the New Teacher*

Using the One Hundred Grid

Use the *One Hundred Grid* (page 44) to review numbers and solve puzzles. Give each student a copy of the grid. Begin by having them fill in each square with the appropriate number. Then look for number patterns by coloring according to directions.

Examples:

▶ Beginning with 2 (or 1), color every other square to show the even (odd) numbers.

▶ Color all squares with a number that ends with 5 or 0. (counting by 5s)

▶ Color all squares with twin digits. (counting by 11s)

▶ Color square 3. Skip two squares. Color the next square. Repeat until you reach 99.

▶ Color the squares containing a 2, red; containing a 5, blue; containing a 7, green. Look for patterns.

Money Matters

▶ Use paper coins and bills (page 138) to teach place value.

▶ Use the *One Hundred Chart* (page 43). Have students put ten pennies in the top row. When they have placed all ten, explain that they can remove the ten pennies and put a dime on the 10. Next put a dime on the 10, 20, 30, etc. When students get to 100, explain that they can remove the ten dimes and fold a dollar bill and place it in the last space.

▶ Use coins and bills to show ways of making given amounts.

1. 10¢—Discuss the variety of ways and list on board. (ten pennies, two nickels, five pennies and one nickel).

2. 25¢—Discuss the variety of ways and list on board.

3. 50¢—Discuss the variety of ways and list on board.

4. $1.00—Discuss the variety of ways and list on board.

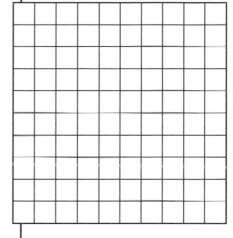

1	2	3	4	5	6	7	8	9	10
11	12	13	14	15	16	17	18	19	20
21	22	23	24	25	26	27	28	29	30
31	32	33	34	35	36	37	38	39	40
41	42	43	44	45	46	47	48	49	50
51	52	53	54	55	56	57	58	59	60
61	62	63	64	65	66	67	68	69	70
71	72	73	74	75	76	77	78	79	80
81	82	83	84	85	86	87	88	89	90
91	92	93	94	95	96	97	98	99	100

29

Place Value Money

Use the *One Hundred Chart* (page 43). Have students find the place that equals:

1. one penny
2. one nickel
3. one dime
4. one quarter
5. one half-dollar
6. one dollar

Creating Tens Counters

To create a visual aid to help understand base ten and ten's place value, give each student ten craft sticks. Have students glue ten beans to each stick. When glue is dry, count the beans on a stick. Count the sticks by tens. Remind students that a craft stick with ten beans is like a dime (worth 10 pennies).

Hands for Counting

As a group, use hands with fingers stretched out in front for tens and single fingers for ones.

Examples:

▶ 21—Hold out all fingers and say, *Ten*. Close them and open. Say, *Twenty*. Close and show one index finger and say, *One*. Repeat more quickly: *Ten, twenty, one*.

▶ 45—Hold out all fingers and say, *Ten*. Repeat and say, *Twenty*. Repeat and say, *Thirty*. Repeat and say, *Forty*. Show five fingers and say, *Five*. Repeat more quickly: *Ten, twenty, thirty, forty, five*.

© McGraw-Hill Children's Publishing

0-7682-2931-6 *Getting Ready to Teach Math for the New Teacher*

Number Relationships

As students learn to count, the next logical step is to make connections between numbers. How do numbers relate to other numbers? Is a number equal to, greater than, or less than another? Does a number come before or after another number? Which number is first or last in a sequence? The *One Hundred Chart* (page 43) is an excellent visual for showing connections between numbers. As students look at their charts, play these guessing games:

Teaching Strategy

When using worksheets, make certain students understand what you want them to do. Read the directions aloud once or twice. Do an example on the board so students can see the steps in solving the problem. Have students work problems on the board so that others can see the step-by-step solutions.

- **Which Comes First?**—Name two numbers. Students tell which comes first on the chart.

- **Which Comes Last?**—Name two numbers. Students tell which comes last.

- **What's in the Middle?**—Name two consecutive even or odd numbers. Students tell which number comes between them.

- **What Comes After?**—Name a number. Students tell which number follows in sequence.

- **What Comes Before?**—Name a number. Students tell which number comes immediately before it.

- **Name That Order**—Write three numbers on the board. Use consecutive numbers, but change the order. Ask, *Which number is first, second, or last in the sequence?*

- **Skip Counting Even Numbers**—Students begin counting with 0 and skip every other number. Play Skip Counting Odd Numbers by beginning with 1.

 0-7682-2931-6 *Getting Ready to Teach Math for the New Teacher*

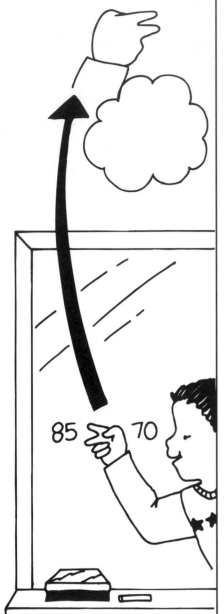

More Than, Less Than, and Equal To

Introduce the mathematical signs for more than (>), less than (<), and equal to (=) on the board where everyone can see them. Draw cartoon figures on the board. The one with the big mouth, who can eat the most, is named "more than." The one with the beak can only peck and doesn't eat much. His name is "less than." Challenge students to use the signs to make up a story with pictures. Share the stories with the class.

more than   less than

Signing Math

Use index and middle fingers, spread apart to make the more than (right hand) and less than (left hand) signs. Write two numbers on the board and let students come up and use their fingers to place the appropriate sign between the numbers. When students get used to using fingers for the signs, play a game. Name two things and students indicate how they relate with a show of fingers.

Examples:

1. car   airplane
2. school bus   bicycle
3. motorcycle   computer
4. truck   scooter
5. tree   flower
6. hippopotamus   pig

0-7682-2931-6 *Getting Ready to Teach Math for the New Teacher*

First, Second, Third, Fourth, and Last

Write each of the positions, *first, second, third, fourth,* and *last* in bold letters on a sheet of 11" x 8½" paper. Have five students stand in front of the group, each holding one of the position words. Move students to mix up the order. Ask another student to come up and put them back in order. Repeat with other groups of students.

For a variation of this activity, give verbal commands for students to follow: *I want Leroy, James, Luke, Kevin, and Paul to stand in a row. James first, Kevin second, Paul third, Leroy fourth, and Luke last.* Repeat the instructions only once. Remind students that if each person remembers his own position, it will be easier to follow the directions.

Name That Fruit

To practice positions first, second, third, fourth, and last, draw five fruits on the board—or use real fruit.

Ask questions:

▶ *What position is the apple?*

▶ *Which fruit is second?*

▶ *If I eat the apple, then which fruit will be third?*

▶ *If I shift the pear to the front of the row, then which fruit will be last?*

© McGraw-Hill Children's Publishing

Introducing Fractional Parts of Sets

Teaching Strategy

To demonstrate the difference between dividing a whole and a set into fractional parts, cut an apple into halves and then quarters. Next, divide four apples into two groups of two (half) and four groups of one (quarters).

Explain that fractions tell how many parts are in the whole and refer to a part of the total. A good way to introduce fractions of a set is to count off the number of children in the class. On the board, write that number as the denominator. Then have the girls count off. Write that number as the numerator. Explain that this shows the fractional part of the class that is girls. Do the same with the boys.

Introducing Fractional Parts of a Whole

Use an oral guessing game to give students the opportunity to think of dividing wholes into fractional parts and naming them. Draw pictures on the board as you ask the questions.

Say:

1. *(Name a student) baked a pie and cut it into eight slices. She ate a slice. What fraction of the pie did she eat? What fraction of the pie was uneaten?*

2. *(Name a student) baked a cake. He cut it into sixteen pieces. Friends ate seven pieces. What fraction of the cake was eaten? What fraction of the cake was uneaten?*

3. *(Name a student) had a collection of 25 marbles. Ten marbles were cat-eyes. What fraction of the collection was cat-eyes? What fraction was not cat-eyes?*

0-7682-2931-6 *Getting Ready to Teach Math for the New Teacher*

Using a Fraction Bar

Give each student fraction bars. (You can use the top half of page 54.) Students study the bars and answer the following questions:

1. Which is greater, $\frac{1}{2}$ or $\frac{1}{3}$?
2. Which is greater, $\frac{1}{4}$ or $\frac{1}{6}$?
3. Which is greater, $\frac{1}{4}$ or $\frac{2}{6}$?
4. Which is greater, $\frac{2}{8}$ or $\frac{1}{2}$?
5. Which is greater, $\frac{1}{6}$ or $\frac{1}{8}$?
6. Which is greater, $\frac{1}{3}$ or $\frac{2}{6}$?
7. Which is greater, $\frac{5}{8}$ or $\frac{5}{6}$?
8. Which is greater, $\frac{1}{4}$ or $\frac{2}{8}$?
9. Which is greater, $\frac{4}{8}$ or $\frac{1}{2}$?
10. Which is greater, $\frac{4}{4}$ or $\frac{8}{8}$?

Adding and Subtracting with Manipulatives

An easy way to show addition is to ask students to use blocks, balls, string wooden beads, etc., and group items into two sets to be joined or compared.

Examples:

1. How many red beads on the string? How many blue beads? How many beads in all?

2. Arrange a set of three blocks and four blocks. Ask, *How many?* Rearrange into two blocks and five blocks. Ask, *All together, how many now?* Again rearrange the seven blocks into two sets of one and six and ask again, *All together, how many blocks now?* Addition fact families are easy to remember when introduced in this fashion. It also provides students with practice in reasoning and proof.

0-7682-2931-6 *Getting Ready to Teach Math for the New Teacher*

Face-Off

To play this addition game, two students stand facing each other, and both put their hands behind their backs. To begin the game, they count in unison to 3. Then they both show a number of fingers. The first person to call out the total of fingers showing, wins the round. When a player has won three rounds in a row, he is the winner of that game. That winner goes on to play the winner of another face-off. To find the Face-Off class champion, play this game round-robin tournament fashion.

Domino Addition

Divide students into small groups of three or four. Give each group a set of dominoes. Place all the dominoes facedown in a pile. Each player draws a domino and writes the total on paper. Repeat five more times. After six rounds of play, students find their grand totals. The player with the largest sum is the winner.

Subtraction Dice

Divide students into small groups of three or four. Give each group a pair of dice. Students take turns rolling the dice, subtracting the smaller number from the larger number, and recording the difference. At the end of ten rolls, each player finds the sum of his points. The player with the smallest sum is the winner.

0-7682-2931-6 *Getting Ready to Teach Math for the New Teacher*

How Many Do You Have?

Name two things and ask students to answer in unison when giving the total.

Examples:

1. ears and eyes
2. legs and toes
3. fingers and feet
4. knees and elbows
5. knuckles and ankles
6. noses and toes

How Many Do They Have?

For this game, students respond by writing an addition equation on paper.

Examples:

1. Bears have how many paws and heads? $4 + 1 = 5$
2. Dogs have how many legs and ears? $4 + 2 = 6$
3. An octopus has how many arms and heads? $8 + 1 = 9$
4. Snakes have how many legs and heads? $0 + 1 = 1$

How many fingers and feet?

12

Show Me

Divide students into groups of three or four. Give each group a piece of chalk and a place to work at the board. Present a challenge and let the groups work it out by drawing a picture. Ask each group to explain its picture and how it represents the math story. Repeat.

1. Draw a picture of birds to prove what 18 take away 5 equals.
2. Draw a picture of worms to prove what 27 plus 10 equals.
3. Draw a picture of snakes to prove what 19 minus 11 equals.
4. Draw a picture of tens bars and ones blocks to prove the sum of 31 and 42.

    0-7682-2931-6 *Getting Ready to Teach Math for the New Teacher*

Math Fact Rummy

Students can learn and review basic math facts by playing "Math Fact Rummy." Use index cards to make a deck of cards for the game. Write a number sentence on each card. Cards can be all addition, all subtraction, or a combination. Create decks of cards to reflect addition or subtraction facts students are learning currently or need to review. You will need at least four cards with the same answer. For example, one set of four cards could include 2+3, 3+2, 6–1, and 7–2. All have the same answer: 5. Make at least ten sets of four.

To play, divide students into groups of three or four. Shuffle the cards and deal four to each player. Students draw and discard in an attempt to get four cards with the same total. If players go through the discard pile before someone gets a rummy, shuffle the cards and place them facedown again. Play continues until one player gets a set of four cards with the same answer. These cards can also be used as flash cards for practicing addition and subtraction facts.

Inclusion Strategy

Most students enjoy writing on the board. However, when asked to perform in front of a large group, some students may feel uncomfortable. When you want students to use the board, arrange the assignments so that small groups or pairs of students are working and using the board at the same time.

0-7682-2931-6 *Getting Ready to Teach Math for the New Teacher*

Practice Time

Directions: Write each numeral three times and each word one time.

0 zero _____

1 one _____

2 two _____

3 three _____

4 four _____

5 five _____

6 six _____

0-7682-2931-6 *Getting Ready to Teach Math for the New Teacher*

Practice the Numerals

Directions: Write each numeral three times and the number word one time.

7 seven _____

8 eight _____

9 nine _____

10 ten _____

11 eleven _____

12 twelve _____

© McGraw-Hill Children's Publishing

0-7682-2931-6 *Getting Ready to Teach Math for the New Teacher*

How Many?

Count the number of animals in each set.
Write the number.

1. 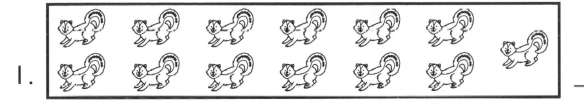 _____

2.  _____

3.  _____

4.  _____

5. 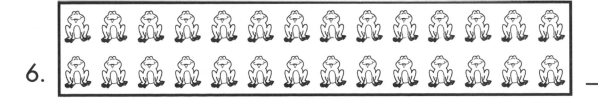 _____

6. _____

 0-7682-2931-6 *Getting Ready to Teach Math for the New Teacher*

Make the Connections

Draw lines to connect each set of dots to its numeral and its word name.

1	●●●	four
2	●●●●	one
3	●●●●●	five
4	●	two
5	●●	three
6	●●●●●●●	six
7	●●●●●●	ten
8	●●●●●●●●●	seven
9	●●●●●●●●	eight
10	●●●●●●●●	nine

© McGraw-Hill Children's Publishing

0-7682-2931-6 *Getting Ready to Teach Math for the New Teacher*

One Hundred Chart

1	2	3	4	5	6	7	8	9	10
11	12	13	14	15	16	17	18	19	20
21	22	23	24	25	26	27	28	29	30
31	32	33	34	35	36	37	38	39	40
41	42	43	44	45	46	47	48	49	50
51	52	53	54	55	56	57	58	59	60
61	62	63	64	65	66	67	68	69	70
71	72	73	74	75	76	77	78	79	80
81	82	83	84	85	86	87	88	89	90
91	92	93	94	95	96	97	98	99	100

0-7682-2931-6 *Getting Ready to Teach Math for the New Teacher*

One Hundred Grid

Directions: Write the numbers in order from 1 to 100.

1									
									100

0-7682-2931-6 *Getting Ready to Teach Math for the New Teacher*

Name _____ Date _____

What's It Worth?

Directions: Use the tens bars and ones blocks to find the values. The first one has been done for you.

1.  = __12__

2. 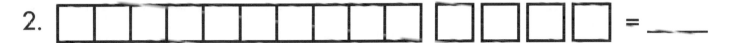 = __ __

3. 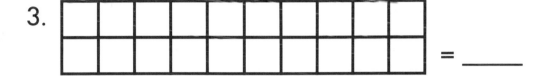 = _____

4. 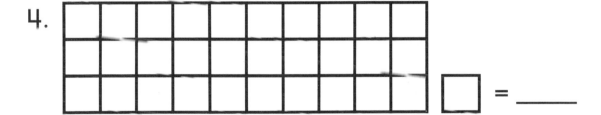 = _____

5. 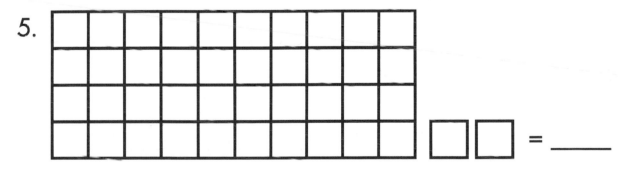 = _____

6. 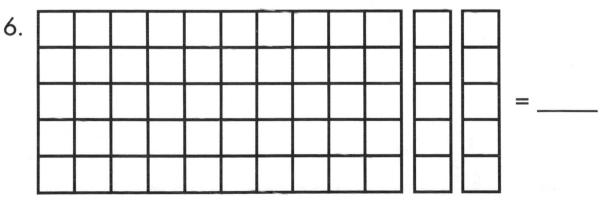 = _____

0-7682-2931-6 *Getting Ready to Teach Math for the New Teacher*

Drawing the Values

Directions: Draw one coin that equals each row of coins.

1.	(five pennies)	=
2.	(two nickels)	=
3.	(five nickels)	=
4.	(two dimes, one nickel)	=
5.	(five pennies, two dimes)	=
6.	(five dimes)	=
7.	(two quarters)	=

0-7682-2931-6 *Getting Ready to Teach Math for the New Teacher*

Missing Numbers

Directions: Write the missing number in each row.

1.	1	2	3	4	5	____	7
2.	73	74	75	76	____	78	79
3.	41	42	43	____	45	46	47
4.	94	95	96	97	98	99	____

Write the number that comes next.

5. 10   ____

6. 28   ____

7. 77   ____

8. 99   ____

Write the number that comes before.

9. ____   9

10. ____   21

11. ____   74

12. ____   100

0-7682-2931-6 *Getting Ready to Teach Math for the New Teacher*

Name _____   Date _____

At the Animal Races

Directions: Follow the directions.

1. Color the first animal blue. Color the second animal red. Color the third animal green. Color the fourth animal orange. Color the last animal any color you choose.

2. Pay attention to the way the animals are walking. Which animal is first in line? Color the fourth animal in the parade purple. Color the first animal pink. Color the third animal green. Color the last animal yellow. Color the second animal your favorite color.

3. Draw a parade of animals. Draw a snake in first place. Draw a worm in second place. Draw a bird in third place. Draw a dog in fourth place. Draw your favorite animal in last place.

48

0-7682-2931-6 *Getting Ready to Teach Math for the New Teacher*

Skip Counting

Directions: 1. Color the lamb. Don't color the dog.
Then color every other animal.

2. Begin with two. Circle every other number.
(skip, circle, skip, circle) Those are even numbers.

1 2 3 4 5 6 7 8 9 10 11 12 13 14 15
16 17 18 19 20 21 22 23 24 25 26 27 28 29 30

3. Begin with one. Circle every other number.
(circle, skip, circle, skip) Those are odd numbers.

1 2 3 4 5 6 7 8 9 10 11 12 13 14 15
16 17 18 19 20 21 22 23 24 25 26 27 28 29 30

4. Begin with five. Circle every fifth number.
This is counting by fives.

1 2 3 4 5 6 7 8 9 10 11 12 13 14 15
16 17 18 19 20 21 22 23 24 25 26 27 28 29 30

0-7682-2931-6 *Getting Ready to Teach Math for the New Teacher*

Equal To

Directions: Draw the animals needed to make the sets and numerals equal.

1. 6 =

2. 13 =

3. 16 =

4. 20 =

5. 31 =

6. 17 =

7. 11 =

0-7682-2931-6 *Getting Ready to Teach Math for the New Teacher*

More, Less, or Equal?

Directions: Use the signs **=** (equal to), **>** (more than), or **<** (less than) to complete each number sentence.

1. ▢ 9

2. ▢ six

3. ▢ 14

4. ▢ eight

5. ▢ ten

6. ▢

7. ▢ twelve

8. ▢ 11

© McGraw-Hill Children's Publishing   0-7682-2931-6 *Getting Ready to Teach Math for the New Teacher*

Name _____ Date _____

Farmer John

Directions: 1. Farmer John has 5 sheep. 4 are white. 1 is black.

What fraction of the sheep are white? _____

What fraction of the sheep are black? _____

2. Farmer John has 12 pigs. 6 have spots. Give 6 pigs spots.

What fraction is spotted? _____

What fraction is not spotted? _____

3. Farmer John has 8 horses. 5 are brown and 3 are gray.
Color the horses.

What fraction is brown? _____

What fraction is gray? _____

4. Farmer John has 10 cows. 7 cows give milk. Color them brown.
Color the cows that do not give milk black.

What fraction of Farmer John's cows give milk? _____

What fraction of Farmer John's cows do not give milk? _____

     0-7682-2931-6 *Getting Ready to Teach Math for the New Teacher*

Pie Party

Directions:

1. Justin baked a berry pie. He cut it into 3 large slices. He ate 1 slice. Use your red crayon to color the slice Justin ate.

What fraction of the pie did Justin eat? _____

What fraction of the pie is uneaten? _____

2. Maggie baked a blueberry pie. She cut it into 4 slices. She gave away 3 slices. Use your blue crayon to color the slices she gave away.

What fraction of the pie did Maggie give away? _____

What fraction of the pie is left? _____

3. Max baked a lemon pie. He cut it into 6 slices. He and a friend each ate one slice. Use your yellow crayon to color the slices Max and his friend ate.

What fraction of the pie was eaten? _____

What fraction of the pie was uneaten? _____

4. Eric baked an apple pie. He cut it into 8 slices. He and 4 friends each ate a slice. Use your green crayon to color the slices Eric and his friends ate.

What fraction of the pie was eaten? _____

What fraction of the pie was uneaten? _____

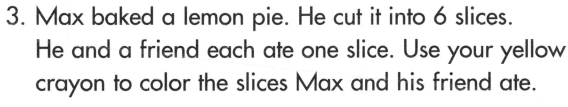

© McGraw-Hill Children's Publishing   0-7682-2931-6 *Getting Ready to Teach Math for the New Teacher*

Name _____ Date _____

Comparing Fractions

Directions: Use the fraction bars to help you write the signs. Use = (equal to), > (more than), or < (less than) to complete each fraction sentence.

1 whole							
$\frac{1}{2}$				$\frac{1}{2}$			
$\frac{1}{3}$		$\frac{1}{3}$			$\frac{1}{3}$		
$\frac{1}{4}$		$\frac{1}{4}$		$\frac{1}{4}$		$\frac{1}{4}$	
$\frac{1}{6}$	$\frac{1}{6}$	$\frac{1}{6}$		$\frac{1}{6}$	$\frac{1}{6}$		$\frac{1}{6}$
$\frac{1}{8}$	$\frac{1}{8}$	$\frac{1}{8}$	$\frac{1}{8}$	$\frac{1}{8}$	$\frac{1}{8}$	$\frac{1}{8}$	$\frac{1}{8}$

1. $\frac{1}{2}$ ☐ $\frac{1}{4}$

2. $\frac{1}{4}$ ☐ $\frac{1}{8}$

3. $\frac{1}{3}$ ☐ $\frac{2}{6}$

4. $\frac{2}{4}$ ☐ $\frac{1}{2}$

5. $\frac{1}{6}$ ☐ $\frac{1}{8}$

6. $\frac{1}{3}$ ☐ $\frac{1}{4}$

7. $\frac{5}{8}$ ☐ $\frac{5}{6}$

8. $\frac{1}{2}$ ☐ $\frac{2}{6}$

9. $\frac{4}{8}$ ☐ $\frac{1}{2}$

10. $\frac{3}{3}$ ☐ $\frac{6}{6}$

0-7682-2931-6 *Getting Ready to Teach Math for the New Teacher*

Name _____ Date _____

Can You Prove It?

Directions:

1. Draw two sets of to prove that 11 + 2 = 13.

2. Draw two sets of to prove that 13 + 2 = 15.

3. Draw two sets of to prove that 4 + 11 = 15.

4. Draw two sets of to prove that 12 + 12 = 24.

5. Draw two sets of to prove that 18 + 6 = 24.

6. Draw two sets of to prove that 19 + 8 = 27.

0-7682-2931-6 *Getting Ready to Teach Math for the New Teacher*

Name _____ Date _____

Can You Picture That?

Directions:

1. Draw 11 and cross out to prove that 11 − 7 = 4.

2. Draw 10 and cross out to prove that 10 − 9 = 1.

3. Draw 14 and cross out to prove that 14 − 7 = 7.

4. Draw 10 and cross out to prove what 10 − 5 equals.

5. Draw 24 and cross out to prove what 24 − 12 equals.

6. Draw 30 and cross out to prove what 20 − 12 equals.

 0-7682-2931-6 *Getting Ready to Teach Math for the New Teacher*

Name _____ Date _____

Again and Again

Directions: Use the pictures of the animals. Write an equation and solution for each question. The first one is written for you.

1. How many legs on six ducks? $2 + 2 + 2 + 2 + 2 + 2 = \underline{12}$

2. How many horns on two cows?

3. How many legs on three frogs?

4. How many wings on six hens?

5. How many ears on four pigs?

6. How many tails on seven foxes?

7. How many eyes on five worms?

8. How many legs on four hippos?

0-7682-2931-6 *Getting Ready to Teach Math for the New Teacher*

Name _____ Date _____

They All Add Up

Directions: Count how many of each animal. Use the numbers to write an equation and solution for each question.

🐸 = _____   🦊 = _____   🦢 = _____

🦋 = _____   🐿️ = _____   🦫 = _____

🐫 = _____   🐤 = _____   🦝 = _____

1. 🐤 + 🦋 + 🐸 = _____

2. 🐤 + 🐫 + 🐿️ = _____

3. 🦫 + 🐤 + 🦊 = _____

4. 🦢 + 🐤 + 🐫 + 🐿️ = _____

5. 🦢 + 🦝 + 🦋 + 🦫 = _____

0-7682-2931-6 *Getting Ready to Teach Math for the New Teacher*

Small Sums

Directions: Follow the coloring directions.

1. Color red the sections with the sum of 1.
2. Color blue the sections with the sum of 2.
3. Color yellow the sections with the sum of 3.
4. Color green the sections with the sum of 4.

$1 + 1 =$

$2 + 0 =$

$1 + 3 =$

$0 + 3 =$

$3 + 0 =$

$0 + 4 =$

$2 \\ + 2$

$2 + 2 =$

$0 + 1 =$

$1 + 0 =$

$2 + 1 =$

$1 + 2 =$

$3 + 1 =$

$0 + 2 =$

$1 + 1 =$

0-7682-2931-6 *Getting Ready to Teach Math for the New Teacher*

Add and Subtract

Directions: Write two addition equations and two subtraction equations for each domino. The first one is done for you.

1.

4 + 1 = 5
1 + 4 = 5
5 – 1 = 4
5 – 4 = 1

2.

_____
_____
_____
_____

3.

_____
_____
_____
_____

4.

_____
_____
_____
_____

5.

_____
_____
_____
_____

6.

_____
_____
_____
_____

0-7682-2931-6 *Getting Ready to Teach Math for the New Teacher*

That's Some Total!

Directions: Add.

1. $0 + 7 =$ _____   2. $5 + 2 =$ _____   3. $4 + 3 =$ _____

4. $1 + 6 =$ _____   5. $2 + 5 =$ _____   6. $3 + 4 =$ _____

7. $6 + 1 =$ _____   8. $7 + 0 =$ _____   9. $0 + 8 =$ _____

10. $1 + 7 =$ _____   11. $2 + 6 =$ _____   12. $3 + 5 =$ _____

13. $4 + 4 =$ _____   14. $5 + 3 =$ _____   15. $6 + 2 =$ _____

16. $7 + 1 =$ _____   17. $8 + 0 =$ _____   18. $0 + 9 =$ _____

19. $1 + 8 =$ _____   20. $2 + 7 =$ _____   21. $3 + 6 =$ _____

22. $4 + 5 =$ _____   23. $6 + 3 =$ _____   24. $7 + 2 =$ _____

25. $8 + 1 =$ _____   26. $9 + 0 =$ _____   27. $5 + 4 =$ _____

0-7682-2931-6 *Getting Ready to Teach Math for the New Teacher*

Missing Addends

Directions: Addition is the opposite of subtraction. To find out what number is missing in each math sentence, subtract.

1. 6 + ☐ = 12

2. 8 + ☐ = 10

3. 9 + ☐ = 11

4. 7 + ☐ = 12

5. 6 + ☐ = 11

6. 8 + ☐ = 12

7. 9 + ☐ = 12

8. 4 + ☐ = 12

9. 8 + ☐ = 11

10. 6 + ☐ = 10

11. 7 + ☐ = 11

12. 5 + ☐ = 10

13. 7 + ☐ = 10

14. 9 + ☐ = 10

15. 4 + ☐ = 11

16. 5 + ☐ = 12

0-7682-2931-6 *Getting Ready to Teach Math for the New Teacher*

Name _____ Date _____

Number and Operations

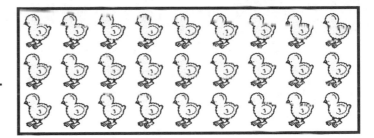

1. How many in this set? _____

2. Which is more?

      or   eight

_____

3. Fill in the missing numbers.

57 58 59 _____ 61 62 63 _____ 65 66 67 68 69 _____

4. Which number comes before 63? _____

5. Which number comes after 89? _____

6. Draw a coin that equals

7. How many one-dollar bills equal a ten-dollar bill? _____

8. What's it worth?

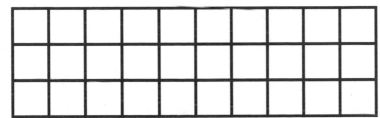  = _____

© McGraw-Hill Children's Publishing   0-7682-2931-6 *Getting Ready to Teach Math for the New Teacher*

Number and Operations

9. Color the first and last bird red.
   Color the third bird green.

10. Circle the even numbers.

    1 ② 3 4 5 6 7 8 9 10 11 12 13 14 15

11. Use the < or > sign to complete the math sentence.

12. Use the < or > sign to complete the math sentence.

     ☐ ten

13. Farmer Jones has 6 horses.
    Five are brown and 1 is gray.
    What fraction of the mules is gray? _____

14. Color $\frac{5}{8}$ of the pie purple.

15. Write two addition equations
    and two subtraction equations
    for the domino.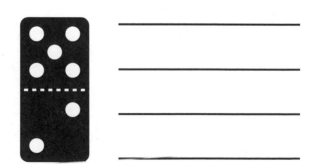

    _____
    _____
    _____
    _____

16. Fill in the missing addend. 7 + ☐ = 11

0-7682-2931-6 *Getting Ready to Teach Math for the New Teacher*

Chapter 3

Algebra Activities

An introduction to algebra at the first-grade level includes exploring patterns, relations, functions, and models to represent and understand quantitative relationships. Don't rely primarily on workbooks or paper-and-pencil learning activities to practice these concepts. Children learn math language and thinking skills best when they interact with a wide range of materials and people. Keep lessons game-like and offer students opportunities to be creative in their explorations.

Sorting

Children love to sort! They begin sorting as toddlers and with practice they become proficient. Give students plenty of opportunities to play sorting games. Encourage sorting by providing a variety of manipulatives:

▶ use colorful wooden beads to sort by color and string with repeated color patterns

▶ use buttons to sort by size, shape, and color

▶ use blocks to sort by size or shape and build "trains" of repeated patterns

0-7682-2931-6 *Getting Ready to Teach Math for the New Teacher*

- use wallpaper cut-outs to sort by pattern or shape of cut-outs
- sort stuffed toys by size, color, texture, or kind
- sort books by size, thickness, color of cover, shape, topic
- sort leaves by size, shape, texture

Name a Category

Help students practice grouping according to similar attributes with this game. Name things that belong in a specific category: fruits, round things, things with four legs, things that squeak, things that fly, purple things, etc. Students try to identify the categories. Encourage more than one answer; for example, rabbit, marshmallow, pillow—soft things, white things, round things.

Variation: Divide students into groups of three or four. Name a category. Have students brainstorm and draw pictures or make a list of objects that fit the category. Bring the group back together to compare answers.

1. Which objects were only listed by one group?
2. Which objects were listed by all the groups?
3. Which group thought of the most items for the category?

Teaching Strategy

After completing sorting tasks, ask the student to tell you how they classified each set. Then ask, *Is there another way we can sort these same objects?* Set up situations where students explain to each other how they have sorted objects.

Store It

For easy storage of attribute blocks, keep each set in an envelope with the student's name on it.

The National Council of Teachers of Mathematics

NCTM recommends teaching qualitative changes by measuring and recording each student's height in the fall. Mid-year, and at the end of the school year, measure again. Use numbers to talk about how much each student has grown.

0-7682-2931-6 *Getting Ready to Teach Math for the New Teacher*

Sound Patterns

Patterns can be distinguished in ways other than visual. Intricate sound patterns fill our world. Reinforce distinguishing sound patterns. Give each student a simple musical instrument, such as bell, horn, stick, drum, triangle, etc. Have students take turns making simple sound patterns.

Examples:

◗ three rings of a bell, pause, repeat

◗ four drum beats, pause, two drum beats, pause, repeat

◗ two horn toots, pause, repeat

Ask students to name sound patterns that could occur in nature (animal sounds, rain, etc.).

Have students verbalize the sound patterns they hear.

Multiple Intelligences: Auditory Learners

Enhance the experience of auditory learners. Make sound patterns such as three whistles followed by a pause. Have students duplicate the sound pattern.

Multiple Intelligences: Kinesthetic Learners

Moving the body in rhythmic patterns is nothing strange or new—we call it "dancing!" Your students will enjoy moving in repeated ways to choreograph patterns. Have youngsters take turns demonstrating a repeated pattern while the others watch and then try to repeat it. You may give a few examples first.

Examples:

1. Tap right foot five times. Tap left foot three times. Repeat.

2. Clap hands five times. Pause. Repeat.

3. Stomp right foot three times. Put feet together and pause. Repeat.

0-7682-2931-6 *Getting Ready to Teach Math for the New Teacher*

Skills List

The following skills list covers the basic expectations for algebra in first grade. Use it as a guide for lesson planning or for determining each student's progress.

▶ sort, classify, and order objects by size, number, and other properties

▶ recognize, describe, and extend patterns that involve sounds and movements

▶ analyze how both repeating and growing patterns are generated

▶ continue simple number patterns

▶ recognize and describe patterns that involve size, colors, and shapes

▶ make predictions about patterns

▶ sort and classify objects by attributes

▶ sort, classify, and order objects into appropriate subsets (categories) based on one or more attributes, such as size, shape, color, or thickness

▶ analyze simple patterns and make predictions

▶ identify two or more attributes at the same time

▶ create and describe a repeating or growing pattern using manipulatives, geometric figures, or numbers

▶ describe qualitative changes, such as growth of a plant or person

Touch and Tell

When asked to describe similarities and differences, students must have a clear understanding of what you mean. Do the objects look alike? Smell alike? Feel alike? Are they both round, but different colors? With first graders, a good place to begin making these kinds of distinctions is with a kinesthetic game called "Touch and Tell."

Place six food items such as an apple, banana, orange, lime, carrot, and potato in a large bag. One at a time, blindfold students. Place one of the foods in the student's hands and give her about ten seconds to feel it. Take it away and replace it with another food or the same one. The student says if it is the same or different. Play the

Teaching Strategy

Encourage ideas for comparing foods—shape, texture, aroma, flavor quality, how it is cooked, how it grows, how it is served, where it is kept, sound it makes when dropped or chewed, etc. Praise original ideas.

0-7682-2931-6 *Getting Ready to Teach Math for the New Teacher*

game again without the blindfold. This time have students verbalize comparisons. If you gave a student an apple and a potato, he might say they are the same because they are round in shape, but different because one is smooth and the other is rough. The banana and carrot are the same because they are long and narrow, but different because one is curved and one is straight. The orange and lime are the same shape and texture, but different sizes. The carrot and orange are the same color, but different shapes.

Common Attributes

This game stimulates creative thinking and reinforces recognition of similar attributes. Name two objects. Students take turns naming ways the two things are similar. Brainstorm as many common attributes as possible, and list them on the board. Praise innovative connections.

Suggestions:

1. Compare a book and computer: Both are used in classrooms, give information, have corners, are kept on desks, and are seen in libraries.

2. Compare a garbage truck and wheelbarrow: Both are used to transport things, have wheels, need a driver, move on wheels, and are kept in garages.

3. Compare a light bulb and a pear: Both are smaller at one end, have a stem, are about the same size, and can be bought in a store.

4. Compare a pizza and deck of cards: Both are kept in a cardboard box, used at parties, have multiple pieces, and are colorful.

5. Compare wind and potato chips: Both are very light, have a pleasant aroma, and can be noisy.

Use Relevant Examples

When choosing objects to use as examples in class, ask yourself if they relate to the children's lives. For example: A plow might be a good object to use if your students live on farms, but students who live in a large city may never have seen one.

69

Leaf Collections

To help children practice careful observation, take a walk and have each child find six large fallen leaves. Encourage students to select leaves that are as different as possible. Have students glue each leaf to a sheet of paper and number them 1 through 6. Ask students to use the numbers to record their answers to your questions.

Possible Questions:

1. *Which of your leaves is the largest?*
2. *Which two leaves are the most similar in size?*
3. *Which two are the closest to being the same shape?*
4. *Which two are most different in shape?*
5. *Which two are nearly the same color?*
6. *Which two are most different in color?*
7. *Which ones have similar markings?*
8. *Which two are nearly the same texture?*
9. *Which two have the most different texture?*

Patterns and Relationships

A strong recognition of patterns benefits students in learning mathematics. When students comprehend patterns, they can organize information and transfer that information to similar mathematical problems. As students learn to recognize, describe, and extend very simple patterns of shapes and numbers, they sharpen their problem-solving skills.

0-7682-2931-6 *Getting Ready to Teach Math for the New Teacher*

Attribute Block Patterns

Attribute blocks are handy tools for teaching students to sort, draw, and classify common geometric shapes: squares, circles, triangles, and rectangles (see patterns on page 78). Begin by reproducing the page in three colors (red, blue, and yellow) for each student. Students can cut out the 24 shapes in the set. Use Attribute Blocks to reinforce learning and to play games.

▶ Have students use their paper shapes to build trains with adjacent shapes having no common attributes. Repeat with shapes having only one or more than one common attribute

▶ Hold up an attribute block. Ask students to hold up one with two common attributes. (Alike in two ways and different in one way.)

▶ Hold up a block. Ask students to name blocks that have one and only one common attribute. List these on the board. For example, you hold up a large red square, and students name the small red rectangle, triangle, circle, and square.

Using Mathematical Models

The more tactile experiences you can give youngsters, the quicker they will learn. Have students find and name similarities and differences between:

- coins (penny, nickel, dime)
- socks, hats, or other clothing
- fruit (color, size, shape)
- toys
- wooden blocks
- leaves, shells, stones

Computer Resource

A particularly colorful and interesting Web site for students to use for creating, describing, and analyzing patterns; for recognizing relationships and making predictions; and for extending pattern understandings is provided by the National Council of Teachers of Mathematics at: standards.nctm.or/document/examples/chap4/4.1/Part3.hum

© McGraw-Hill Children's Publishing 0-7682-2931-6 *Getting Ready to Teach Math for the New Teacher*

Color the Twins

Directions: Find the matching animals and color them the same colors.

0-7682-2931-6 *Getting Ready to Teach Math for the New Teacher*

What's Different?

Directions: Look at the numbers in the top box.
What is different in the bottom box?

Which numbers are missing? _____ and _____.

Which numbers are listed more than once in the bottom box?

_____ and _____

13	3	2	15
6		1	8
20 10		4	18
7		9	
19	11		16
5	14	12	17

13	3	2	10
6		1	8
20 10		4	18
7		9	
19	1		16
5	14	12	17

0-7682-2931-6 *Getting Ready to Teach Math for the New Teacher*

Name a Way

Directions: Name a way that each animal pair is alike and different.

		Alike	**Different**
1.		<u>stripes</u>	<u>size</u>
2. 		_____	_____
3. 		_____	_____
4.		_____	_____
5. 		_____	_____
6. 		_____	_____
7. 		_____	_____
8.		_____	_____

0-7682-2931-6 *Getting Ready to Teach Math for the New Teacher*

Name _____ Date _____

They're the Same

Directions: Draw a line to connect the number pairs with the same sum.

1. 8 + 2 = _____

2. 9 + 2 = _____

3. 4 + 5 = _____

4. 6 + 2 = _____

5. 10 + 2 = _____

6. 5 + 2 = _____

7. 3 + 3 = _____

8. 0 + 5 = _____

A. 4 + 4 = _____

B. 6 + 6 = _____

C. 5 + 5 = _____

D. 6 + 5 = _____

E. 3 + 6 = _____

F. 1 + 5 = _____

G. 4 + 1 = _____

H. 3 + 4 = _____

0-7682-2931-6 *Getting Ready to Teach Math for the New Teacher*

Name _____ Date _____

What's Next?

Directions: At the end of each row, draw the picture needed to continue the pattern.

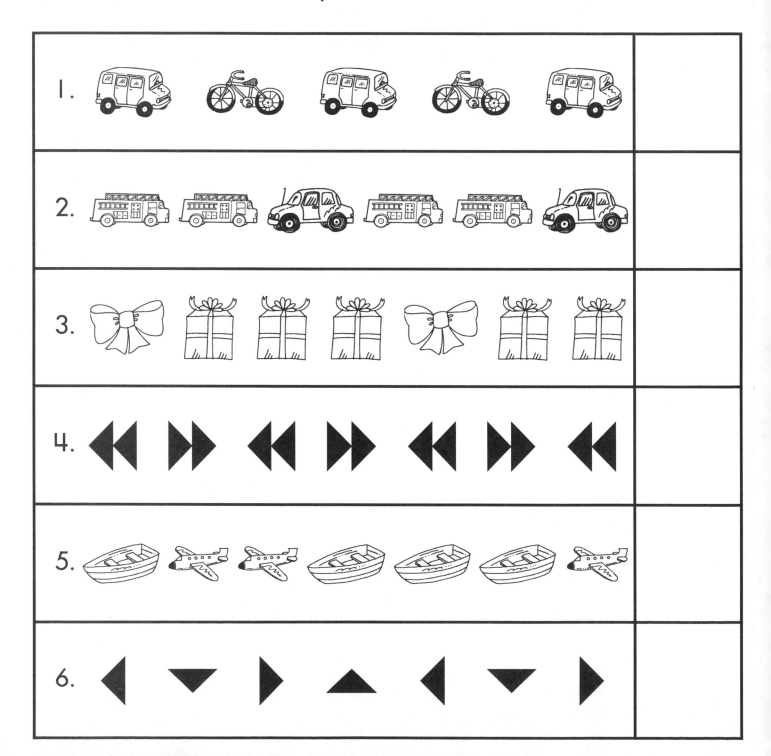

0-7682-2931-6 *Getting Ready to Teach Math for the New Teacher*

Number, Please

Directions: Write the next number in the pattern.

1. 1   2   1   2   1   ____

2. 10   8   7   10   8   ____

3. 5   5   6   5   5   ____

4. 11   10   8   7   5   ____

5. 7   7   7   12   7   ____

6. 1   2   3   5   8   ____

0-7682-2931-6 *Getting Ready to Teach Math for the New Teacher*

Attribute Block Patterns

0-7682-2931-6 *Getting Ready to Teach Math for the New Teacher*

Something in Common

Directions: Follow the directions.

1. Draw the same shape. Make it a different color and size.

2. Draw a different shape. Make it a different size, but the same color.

3. Draw a different shape. Make it a different color, but the same size.

4. Draw the same shape. Make it a different color and size.

5. Draw a different shape. Make it the same color, but a different size.

0-7682-2931-6 *Getting Ready to Teach Math for the New Teacher*

One and Only One

Color the shapes as directed. Then circle the ways they are alike—shape, size, or color.

1. 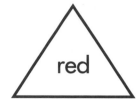 blue   red   shape   size   color

2. red   red   shape   size   color

3. yellow   blue   shape   size   color

4. red   blue   shape   size   color

5. red   blue   shape   size   color

Name _____ Date _____

Nothing in Common

Directions: After each shape, draw and color a shape that has no common attributes with the first—not the same color, not the same size, and not the same shape.

1. red

2. yellow

3. red

4. 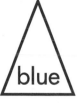 blue

5. yellow

6. red

0-7682-2931-6 *Getting Ready to Teach Math for the New Teacher*

Name _____ Date _____

•Assessment•

Algebra

1. Cross out the animal that is different.

2. Color the animals that are the same.

3. Color the bird with a middle-sized beak.

4. Color the animal that will grow to be the largest.

5. Draw a picture to continue the pattern.

6. What number is next?

11   9   7   5   3   ____

7. What parts are the same? Circle them.

red   red   shape   size   color

Chapter 4

Geometry Activities

An introduction to geometry includes exploring spatial relationships: *inside, outside, above, under, near, far, close by, below, above, up, down, beside*, and *next to*. Using manipulatives to demonstrate math stories gives students practice in spatial relationships. Stories allow students to hear the language, while manipulatives give them practice seeing and arranging objects in various positions. Math manipulatives to teach geometry should:

- be interesting
- be in sight, to promote the likelihood of students requesting the materials
- be varied, giving children choices
- be set up so students do not require assistance in using them
- be designed to stimulate creativity and communication skills

0-7682-2931-6 *Getting Ready to Teach Math for the New Teacher*

Geometry involves ideas about shape, size, space, position, direction, and movement. Traditional activities provide practice in these interactions.

▶ Familiarize children with common three-dimensional shapes and allow students opportunities to explore the properties of figures using colorful building blocks.

▶ Through art activities, give children the opportunity to explore filling of two-dimensional space with notions about position, movement, and direction of movement through art activities.

▶ Give students practice filling three-dimensional space with manipulatives such as tablespoons, cups, liters, etc., using sand, rice, or water.

Geometry Skills List

▶ understand terms of spatial relationships: *inside, outside, above, under, near, far, close by, below, above, up, down, beside,* and *next to*

▶ name common two- and three-dimensional shapes

▶ identify and draw two-dimensional shapes: square, circle, rectangle, triangle, oval, diamond

▶ describe the properties of triangles, squares, and rectangles, including the number of sides and corners

▶ recognize and apply slides, flips, and turns

▶ recognize and create shapes that have symmetry and create patterns with them

▶ identify examples of symmetry in nature, art, and architecture

▶ identify shapes that have symmetry using paper-folding, mirrors, tracing paper, and pattern blocks

▶ draw line(s) of symmetry (horizontal, vertical, diagonal) for different figures

▶ describe, name, and interpret relative positions in space and apply ideas about relative position

▶ investigate and predict the results of putting together and taking apart two-dimensional shapes

▶ explore and make different three-dimensional shapes with blocks

▶ compare and contrast geometric figures by size and shape

 0-7682-2931-6 *Getting Ready to Teach Math for the New Teacher*

- create circles, triangles, squares, rectangles, diamonds, and ovals using various methods, including body movements
- identify solid geometric shapes: sphere, pyramid, cube, cylinder, cone
- create mental images of geometric shapes using spatial memory and spatial visualization
- recognize and represent shapes from different perspectives

Teacher, May I?

Introduce students to describing, naming, and interpreting relative positions in space and applying those ideas about relative position. To explore spatial relationships, *inside, outside, above, under, near, far, close by, below, up, down, beside,* and *next to,* play a version of "Mother, May I?" Address each student with a spatial relationship direction. Have students ask, "Teacher, may I?" If a player forgets to ask, he does not get to follow the directions.

Possible directions:

1. Jacob, will you please go stand beside Michael?
2. Emily, please go stand under the window.
3. Matthew, put your hands inside your pockets, please.
4. Hannah, please place this book outside the classroom door.
5. Joshua, please clap your hands above Madison's head.
6. Christopher, put this book under your desk, please.
7. Ashley, will you please go stand near the window?
8. Nicholas, without leaving the room, please stand as far away from the door as you can.
9. Daniel, will you please come stand close to me?
10. Jessica, please go stand below the world map.
11. Andrew, hold your arms up in the air, please.
12. Elizabeth, will you please sit down at your desk?
13. Alexis, please look up.
14. Lauren, go stand next to Sydney, please.
15. Haley, will you please pretend you are walking down a steep flight of stairs?

85

It's a Zoo

To complete this activity, each student needs a copy of *It's a Zoo* (page 91) and crayons in primary and secondary colors. Allow plenty of time for answering each question—at least thirty to sixty seconds. If a student isn't finished coloring when it is time for the next instruction, explain that he can go back at the end and complete each picture.

1. Use your red crayon to color the animal above the butterfly.
2. Use your blue crayon to color the animal inside the circle.
3. Use your yellow crayon to color the animal below to the starfish.
4. Use your green crayon to color the animal inside the triangle.
5. Use your purple crayon to color the animal farthest away from the cow.
6. Use your orange crayon to color the animal under the snake.
7. Use your red crayon to color the animal next to the horse.
8. Use your blue crayon to color the animal inside the rectangle.
9. Use your yellow crayon to color the animal between the porcupine and snail.
10. Use your green crayon to color the animal above the alligator.
11. Use your purple crayon to color the animal inside the square.
12. Use your orange crayon to color the two animals near to but outside the square.
13. Use your red crayon to color the animal between the starfish and alligator.
14. Use your blue crayon to color the animal under the rhino.

Shape Recognition

Students should be able to name, build, draw, compare, and sort two- and three-dimensional shapes. Use the tangram on page 95:

- as patterns for making multiple copies of the shapes
- attached to a coat hanger with string to create shape mobiles
- to place on mirrors to explore doubling the size of shapes
- overlapped to discover how the shapes relate in size

0-7682-2931-6 *Getting Ready to Teach Math for the New Teacher*

Geometric Exercises

Using the whole body is a kinesthetic way to learn shapes. Have students try some of these exercises:

1. Use hands to make a small circle.
2. Use legs to make a big triangle.
3. Use a finger to draw an small oval (circle, triangle, square, diamond) in the air.
4. Use a foot to draw a large square in the dirt.
5. Lying down, use your whole body to make a big oval.
6. Curl into a small ball.
7. Use chest, arms, and hands to make a big square.
8. Use hands to make a small diamond.
9. Run in small (large) circles.
10. Use arms to make a big triangle.
11. Put feet together to make a small rectangle.
12. Hold hands with a friend and make a big circle with arms.
13. Use one finger and thumb to make a little circle (oval).
14. Put fingertips of both hands together, spread fingers, and make a small sphere.
15. Use upraised arms to make a big circle.

Sweet Ways to Reinforce Two-Dimensional Shapes

1. Bend licorice whips to form circles and ovals.
2. Put a variety of shapes of candies in a bowl. With eyes closed, students pick one, and, by feeling, name its shape.
3. Break rectangular chocolate bars into squares and eat.
4. As students brainstorm, list types of candies and their basic shapes on the board.
5. Sugar-coated cereals come in many shapes. Make necklaces by stringing round sweet cereals onto licorice whips in patterns of colors or shapes. Discuss the patterns and shapes as the students work.
6. Use cookie cutters to cut basic shapes from sandwich bread. Spread with different flavored jams. Discuss the shape and color of the open-face sandwiches.

0-7682-2931-6 *Getting Ready to Teach Math for the New Teacher*

Shapes Within Shapes

Once students can describe the properties of circles, squares, triangles, and rectangles, including the number of sides and corners, they will be able to see these shapes within other shapes. On the board, draw a diamond, parallelograms, and a hexagon. Ask,

1. *How many triangles are in a diamond?*

2. *How many triangles are in a parallelogram?*

3. *How many triangles are in a hexagon?*

After discussing each shape, draw in the triangles so students can see them.

Play Clay

Help students make play clay and use it to create three-dimensional shapes: spheres, cubes, cylinders, pyramids, and cones. For each four students, you will need a large bowl, 3 small bowls, 1 cup of salt, 1 cup flour, $\frac{1}{4}$ cup shortening, water, food coloring, waxed paper, rolling pin, and plastic serrated knife.

Directions:

1. Mix together salt, flour, and shortening in a large bowl.
2. Squash with hands until completely mixed.
3. Add water to the mixture, one spoonful at a time, until the consistency is right. The dough should not be too sticky.
4. Divide dough into three bowls.
5. Add two drops of red, blue, or yellow food coloring to each bowl.
6. Knead the dough until it is a solid color, then work the dough into three-dimensional figures.

Note: Students also get practice following directions and measuring as they prepare the clay.

0-7682-2931-6 *Getting Ready to Teach Math for the New Teacher*

Bubble Geometry

Using bubbles is a fun way to experience three-dimensional figures. Experiment with bubble shapes. Create bubble wands out of found objects such as straws, pipe cleaners, strawberry baskets, and coat hangers, and have a bubble festival. Who can create a cube bubble? Who can catch a bubble? The secret is the soap solution. Try catching a bubble with a dry hand versus a wet hand. Which lasts longer? What could you use to make lots of tiny bubbles? How could you measure a bubble? Why do bubbles fall toward the ground?

Mirror Exercises

Mirrors are excellent tools for exploring symmetry in shapes and designs. Small rectangular mirrors work well for placing along the edges of shapes. Students can use the tangram shapes (page 95) and mirrors to investigate and predict the results of putting together and taking apart two-dimensional shapes.

Symmetrical Designs

To reinforce symmetry, reproduce the tangram shapes on page 95. Help students cut out the seven shapes. Use the shapes to complete these activities. Students can:

▶ Fold each shape down the middle and explore the shapes within shapes. Try folding vertically, horizontally, and diagonally. Which shapes are symmetrical?

▶ Place a small mirror along each of the edges of shapes to see how they change. Place the mirror on the center fold to see how it looks.

▶ Draw line(s) of symmetry (horizontal, vertical, diagonal) for each of the figures.

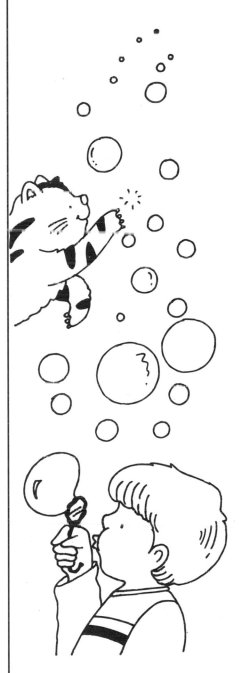

89

Discover Shapes in Nature

Our world is filled with many different shapes. Symmetry is all around us in nature, art, and architecture. Ask students to name objects in nature that are symmetrical. Let students go outside and draw pictures of natural and man-made shapes. How many shapes can they find? Look for examples of symmetry in:

❱ leaves	❱ buildings	❱ flowers
❱ flowers	❱ bridges	❱ insects
❱ spider webs	❱ paintings	❱ sidewalks

Tangrams

A tangram is a seven-piece Chinese puzzle. It is a square cut into seven pieces: five triangles, a square, and a rhombus. The Chinese name for the puzzle is Chi-Chiao, which has been translated into English as "The Seven Clever Pieces" or "The Seven Wisdom Puzzle." Tangrams help students discover interesting ways of putting pieces of a square into other shapes.

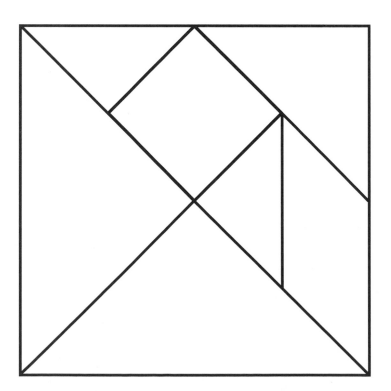

0-7682-2931-6 *Getting Ready to Teach Math for the New Teacher*

Name _____ Date _____

It's a Zoo

0-7682-2931-6 *Getting Ready to Teach Math for the New Teacher*

Name _____ Date _____

The Shape of Things

Directions: Draw pictures or write words to answer each question.

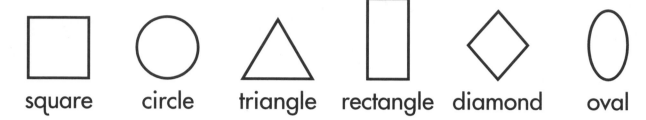

square   circle   triangle   rectangle   diamond   oval

1. Which two shapes have four equal sides?

2. Which shape has three sides?

3. Which shape has four sides and is taller than it is wide?

4. Which shapes have no straight sides?

5. Which shape is most like a circle but is not a circle?

6. Which shape is most like a square but is not a square?

7. If you divide them in half, which shapes could make two triangles?

© McGraw-Hill Children's Publishing   0-7682-2931-6 *Getting Ready to Teach Math for the New Teacher*

Coloring Hidden Shapes

Directions: Use the color code to color each shape in the design the appropriate color.

red   blue   yellow   green   purple   orange

0-7682-2931-6 *Getting Ready to Teach Math for the New Teacher*

Name _____ Date _____

Name That Figure

Directions: Write the letter of the correct shape on the line.

A.
sphere

B.
cube

C.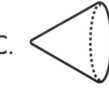
cone

D.
cylinder

1. A cardboard box is most like figure _____.

2. A clown's cap is most like figure _____.

3. A can of coffee is most like figure _____.

4. An oatmeal carton is most like figure _____.

5. An ice cream cone is most like figure _____.

6. A megaphone is most like figure _____.

7. Dice are most like figure _____.

8. A globe is most like figure _____.

0-7682-2931-6 *Getting Ready to Teach Math for the New Teacher*

Tangrams

Directions: Reproduce the tangram puzzle on light cardboard or heavy paper. Cut along lines.

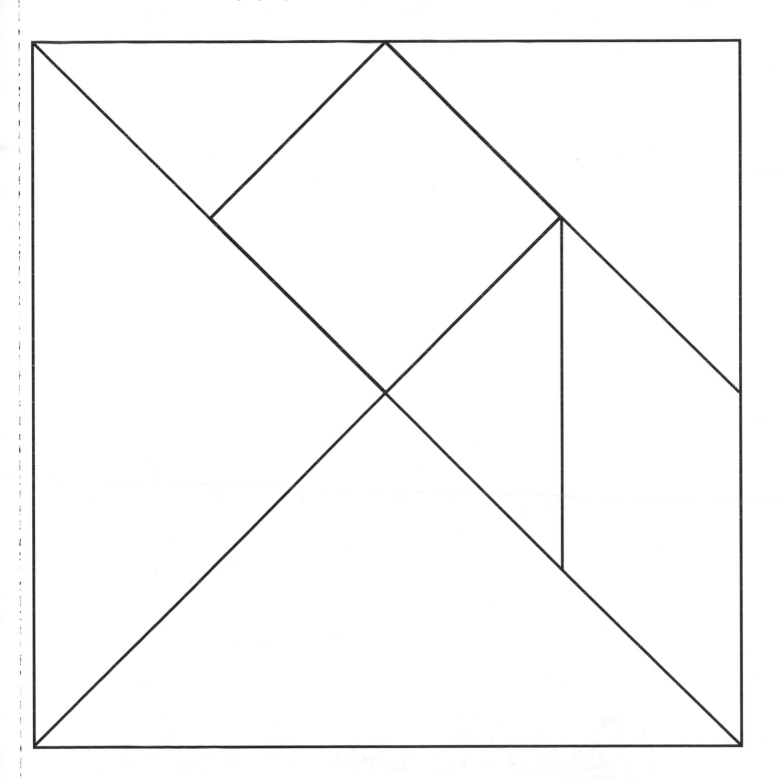

   0-7682-2931-6 *Getting Ready to Teach Math for the New Teacher*

Name _____ Date _____

Put It Back into the Box

Directions: Cut out the seven pieces. Put them all into the box. None can overlap. When you complete the puzzle, glue the pieces in place.

0-7682-2931-6 *Getting Ready to Teach Math for the New Teacher*

Name _____ Date _____

Other Challenges

Directions: Try to make these animal shapes with tangrams. You must use all seven pieces. None can overlap.

1. rabbit

2. dog

3. goose

4. bear

5. swan

6. cat

7. kangaroo

8. camel

0-7682-2931-6 *Getting Ready to Teach Math for the New Teacher*

Name _____ Date _____

Double the Shape

Directions: Draw the mirror image of each shape.
Write the answers.

1.

Two squares
can make a

_____.

2.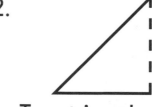

Two triangles
can make a

_____.

3.

Two triangles
can make a

_____.

4.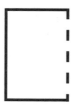

Two rectangles
can make a

_____.

5.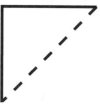

Two triangles
can make a

_____.

6.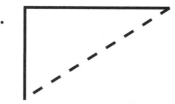

Two triangles
can make a

_____.

0-7682-2931-6 *Getting Ready to Teach Math for the New Teacher*

Name _____ Date _____

Half the Shape

Directions: Follow the directions. Answer each question with the name of a shape.

1. Draw a line across the square to divide it into equal halves.

   What are the two new shapes? _____

2. Draw a line corner to corner to divide the square into equal halves.

   What are the two new shapes? _____

3. Draw a line up and down to divide the rectangle into equal halves.

   What are the two new shapes? _____

4. Draw a line corner to corner to divide the rectangle into equal halves.

   What are the two new shapes? _____

5. Draw a line to divide the triangle into two equal shapes.

   What are the shapes? _____

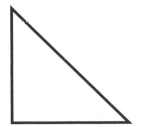

0-7682-2931-6 *Getting Ready to Teach Math for the New Teacher*

A Closer Look

Directions: Write the letters to answer the questions.

A.   B.   C.    D.    E.

1. Which figures look most like ◯ from another angle?

_____ and _____ and _____

2. Which figures look most like ▢ from another angle?

_____ and _____

3. Which figures look most like ▯ from another angle?

_____ and _____

4. Which figure looks most like △ from another angle?

_____

5. Which figure is ▱ from another angle? _____

6. Which figure is ▱ from another angle? _____

7. Which figure is △ from another angle? _____

0-7682-2931-6 *Getting Ready to Teach Math for the New Teacher*

Name _____ Date _____

Geometry

1. Use your blue crayon to color the animal nearest to the hen.

2. Use your red crayon to color the animal beside the box.

3. Use your yellow crayon to color the animal farthest from the mouse.

4. Use your purple crayon to color the animal inside the circle.

5. Circle the name of this shape.

   square   circle   triangle

6. Circle the name of this figure.

   cylinder   cube   sphere

7. Color the shape that is most like a circle.

0-7682-2931-6 *Getting Ready to Teach Math for the New Teacher*

• Assessment •
Geometry

8. Draw and color a shape that has no common attributes with the figure—not the same color, size, or shape.

9.

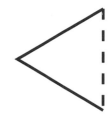

Two triangles can make a

_____ .

10. Draw a line corner to corner to divide the square into equal halves.

What are the two new shapes? Color the shape of the halves.

11. Color the figure that looks most like a △ from another angle.

0-7682-2931-6 *Getting Ready to Teach Math for the New Teacher*

Chapter 5

Measurement Activities

Learning to measure begins with comparing the size of objects, followed by using tools to make precise measurements. Students need to learn to compare the size of common objects and use nonstandard and standard tools for measuring. Comparing the size of objects is not only good math practice, it also develops language and thinking skills. Provide students with a variety of measurement opportunities. They could measure with multiple copies of units of the same size, such as paper clips laid end to end. They can use repetition of a single unit to measure something larger than the unit; for instance, measuring the length of a room with a meterstick, foot, or strides. Students should develop common referents for measures to make comparisons and estimates.

0-7682-2931-6 *Getting Ready to Teach Math for the New Teacher*

Which Is Longer?

When comparing the size of objects that are not physically present, students must use their visual memories. Name two objects. Ask students to tell which is longer. (Note: Answers may vary—explore interesting answers.)

Examples:

1. spaghetti or macaroni?
2. bird's tail or turtle's neck?
3. light bulb or snake?
4. frog or tadpole?
5. cow or calf?
6. eyelash or fingernail?
7. finger or toe?
8. TV remote or pencil?
9. giraffe's leg or neck?
10. rabbit's ears or legs?

Measurement Skills List

▶ compare the size of objects
▶ identify largest/smallest
▶ understand how to measure using nonstandard units
▶ measure using thumb as tool
▶ measure using pretzel sticks/miniature marshmallows/paper patterns
▶ measure using standard units—ruler, meterstick
▶ understand volume

0-7682-2931-6 *Getting Ready to Teach Math for the New Teacher*

Measure Like an Ancient Egyptian

Measure each student's height. Tie a knot at one end of a piece of string. Cut it to match the student's height and tie a knot at the other end. The knots keep the strings from unraveling. Let students use their "height strings" for measuring distances and large objects. This is what the ancient Egyptians did!

Have children work together in pairs to measure items such as a room, a door, a parking space, etc. (The results will be more dramatic if you pair up students who are several inches different in height.) One student holds one end of the string while the other stretches it out. When the second student has a firm grip, the first student lets go and continues measuring by going "end over end." Have each pair of students measure each item twice, using both height strings. Ask them why they found different answers.

Pretzel-Stick Measuring

Ask, *Do we all have the same size body parts? How can we show the length of our feet, legs, hands, and arms using pretzel sticks?*

Divide students into groups of three to four. Give each group a handful of pretzel sticks. Allow time for students to help each other line up enough pretzels to match the lengths of their arm (fingertip to elbow). Ask:

1. *Did any of you have the same size arm?*
2. *What was the most common arm measurement?*
3. *What was the longest arm measurement? Shortest?*
4. *How many different sizes of arms do we have?*

On another day, let students take off their shoes and socks and use paper clips to measure the length of each toe and their feet. Record the measurements with pictures and numbers. Discuss the results.

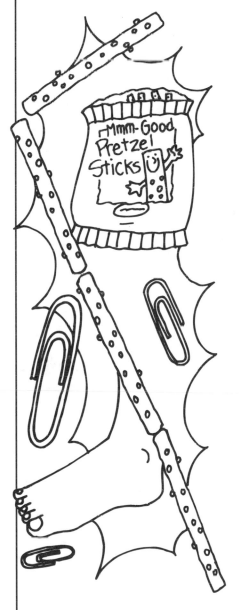

0-7682-2931-6 *Getting Ready to Teach Math for the New Teacher*

Personal Measurements

The more personal you can make measuring, the more likely your students are to be enthusiastic about the process. The length of a hand, foot, out-stretched arms, or stride are good ways to measure because we always have those measuring instruments with us.

Which Was My Tool?

Line up three items on a table, such as a banana (about 6" long), a marshmallow (about 2" long), and a small carrot (about 3" long). Name objects and their lengths (in bananas, carrots, or marshmallows). Students must figure out which tool you used to measure.

Examples:

1. This book is three units long.
   Did I use the banana, marshmallow, or carrot to measure?

2. My arm is about five units long.
   Which food did I use to measure?

3. My hand is about three units long.
   Which food did I use to measure?

Other foods that make interesting measuring tools include:

◗ pastas, such as spaghetti
◗ celery sticks
◗ pretzel sticks
◗ licorice whips
◗ apple
◗ square or rectangular cracker
◗ graham cracker

0-7682-2931-6 *Getting Ready to Teach Math for the New Teacher*

Measurement with Standard Units

Part of learning to measure is assessing the appropriateness of tools to use to make accurate measurements. In first grade, students should begin to understand standard units of measure and be able to name the correct tool needed to measure. Gather objects needed to answer the questions: clock or watch, stopwatch, calendar, ruler, meterstick, measuring tape, and scale. Also include a few not needed for answers, like a measuring cup, a shoe, a piece of string, etc. As you ask the following questions, students take turns choosing and holding up the appropriate measuring tool.

1. *What do you need to find out the date in three weeks?*
2. *What do you need to know how long before school starts?*
3. *What do you need to measure how many pounds of bananas you have?*
4. *What do you need to measure how long your foot is?*
5. *What do you need to measure how many centimeters long a cardboard box is?*
6. *What do you need to measure the length of a large room?*
7. *What do you need to find out what next month will be?*
8. *What do you need to accurately measure who wins a running race?*

Telling Time

Teach students to tell calendar- and clock-time by recording the day and date on the board each day and mentioning the time often during the day. Example: "It is 11:30. We will be going to lunch now." Let students make paper plate clocks to practice telling time to the hour and half-hour.

© McGraw-Hill Children's Publishing   0-7682-2931-6 *Getting Ready to Teach Math for the New Teacher*

Animal Lengths Patterns

Directions: Cut out the animals. Use them to measure things.

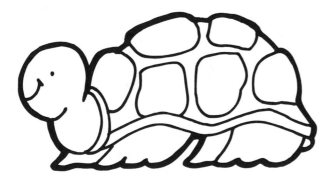

0-7682-2931-6 *Getting Ready to Teach Math for the New Teacher*

Measuring in Animal Lengths

Directions: Use the animals on page 108 to measure.

1. How many fish long is the arrow? _____

2. How many turtles long is the arrow? _____

3. Which is longer, the snake or the arrow? _____

4. How many snails long is the arrow? _____

5. How many snails long is the snake? _____

6. Which is longer, five snails or two fish? _____

7. Which is longer, two fish or a snake? _____

8. Which is longer, the arrow or four turtles? _____

0-7682-2931-6 *Getting Ready to Teach Math for the New Teacher*

Thumbs Up

Directions: Use the width or length of your thumb to measure.

1. How many thumbs wide is the length of your hand? _____

2. How many thumbs wide is your wrist? _____

3. How many thumbs long is your arm from fingertip to elbow? _____

4. How many thumbs long is your foot? _____

5. How many thumbs wide is the length of your thumb? _____

6. How many thumbs wide is your desk? _____

7. How many thumbs long is your leg from ankle to knee? _____

8. How many thumbs tall is your best friend from head to toe? _____

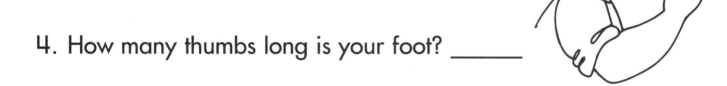

0-7682-2931-6 *Getting Ready to Teach Math for the New Teacher*

Name _____ Date _____

How Many Inches?

Directions: Use a ruler to measure. Circle your answers.

1. How long is the arrow?

   1"   2"   3"   4"

2. How many inches long is the snake?

   1"   2"   3"   4"

3. From nose to tip of tail, how long is the cat?

   1"   2"   3"   4"

4. Approximately how long is your foot?

   3"   4"   5"   6"   7"   8"   9"   10"   11"

5. Approximately how long is your arm from fingertip to elbow?

   8"   9"   10"   11"   12"   13"   14"   15"   16"

6. Approximately how long is your hair?   less than 1"
                                 1"–3"
                                              4"–6"
                                              7"–12"
                                              longer than 12"

0-7682-2931-6 *Getting Ready to Teach Math for the New Teacher*

Name _____ Date _____

How Many Centimeters?

Directions: Use a ruler to measure the length of each animal in centimeters.

1.

_____ cm

2.

_____ cm

3.

_____ cm

4.

_____ cm

5.

_____ cm

6.

_____ cm

0-7682-2931-6 *Getting Ready to Teach Math for the New Teacher*

Take It Outside

Directions: Measure with a meterstick. Write the number of sticks long for each object.

1. Approximately how many meters long is a car? _____

2. Approximately how many meters tall is a big bush? _____

3. Approximately how many meters wide is a window? _____

4. Approximately how many meters tall is a small tree? _____

5. Approximately how many meters tall is a friend? _____

6. Approximately how many meters wide is the door? _____

7. Approximately how many meters wide is a sidewalk? _____

8. Approximately how many meters is it from your classroom door to the playground? _____

0-7682-2931-6 *Getting Ready to Teach Math for the New Teacher*

Name _____   Date _____

Comparing Volume

Which Holds More?

Directions: Color the object that holds more.

1.

2.

3.

4.

5.

6.

114

© McGraw-Hill Children's Publishing   0-7682-2931-6 *Getting Ready to Teach Math for the New Teacher*

How Many Will It Hold?

Directions: Cut out the square centimeters at the bottom of the page. Glue squares inside the shapes. Count and write the number.

1.

_____

2.

_____

3.

_____

4.

_____

© McGraw-Hill Children's Publishing   0-7682-2931-6 *Getting Ready to Teach Math for the New Teacher*

Name _____ Date _____

How Many Will It Hold Now?

Directions: Cut out the square centimeters at the bottom of the page. Glue squares inside the shapes. Count and write the number.

1.

_____

2.

_____

3.

_____

4.

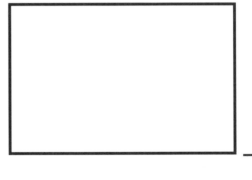

_____

0-7682-2931-6 *Getting Ready to Teach Math for the New Teacher*

Name _____ Date _____

Measurement

1. Which is longer or  ? _____

2. Which weighs less or ? _____

3. Which is farther? Circle the letter.

    A. From one end of the field to the other end of the field

    B. From your house to school

    C. From the library to the cafeteria

4. How many inches long is the first arrow? _____

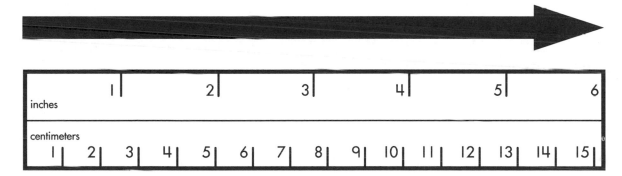

5. How many centimeters long is the next arrow? _____

6. Which is more—5 inches or 17 centimeters? _____

   0-7682-2931-6 *Getting Ready to Teach Math for the New Teacher*

Name _____ Date _____

Measurement

7. Which holds more? Circle it.

8. Circle the one that holds more.

9. Circle the one that holds less.

10. How many inch squares inside the rectangle? _____

1"			

11. How many centimeter squares

inside the square? _____

1cm			

0-7682-2931-6 *Getting Ready to Teach Math for the New Teacher*

Chapter 6

Data Analysis and Probability

Explain to students that graphing is a way to organize information from the real world. Instead of doing math as an isolated set of skills unrelated to reality, students can see data as a vibrant study of the world in which they live. The numbers tell a story about aspects of their own lives. When students gather data and put it on a graph, they can see relationships, patterns, and trends. Asking students simple questions such as, "What do you want for snack—raisins, crackers, or juice?" and graphing the answers can show a variety of information, such as how many of each snack is needed, which snack is the most popular, and how the popularity of the snacks compare.

© McGraw-Hill Children's Publishing

0-7682-2931-6 *Getting Ready to Teach Math for the New Teacher*

Data Analysis and Probability Skills List

▶ read a graph to get data
▶ pose questions, gather data, and organize data on a graph
▶ use a graph to show data
▶ represent data using concrete objects and pictures
▶ sort and classify objects according to their attributes and organize data about the objects
▶ discuss events related to students' experience as likely or unlikely
▶ understand if something is possible or impossible

Board Graphs

Introduce graphing with a class discussion and demonstration. Begin by talking about how everyone has similarities and differences, such as eyes, hair, and clothes. Draw a bar graph and explain that we use graphs to show information in an organized way. Draw this graph on the board.

Hair Color

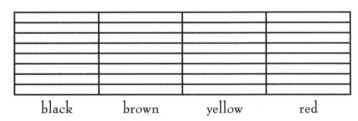

| | | | |
| black | brown | yellow | red |

Ask each student to name his or her hair color. Fill in the graph for each answer. When all the data is recorded, talk about what hair color most students have and other information shown on graph. On other days, make graphs with topics such as:

▶ eye color
▶ hair—short and straight, short and curly, long and straight, long and curly)
▶ color of shoes
▶ color of shirt/blouse/top

▶ favorite sport/hobby
▶ favorite pet
▶ birthday month
▶ favorite holiday

0-7682-2931-6 *Getting Ready to Teach Math for the New Teacher*

Weekly Favorites: Bulletin Board Graphs

Reinforce graphing by setting aside a section of the bulletin board for a "Weekly Favorites" graph. Make a master graph form on a large sheet of paper by drawing a grid, five or six columns wide and 10 to 15 units high. Leave room at the top for a title. Number the units in each column on the left side, beginning with one in the bottom row. Leave room along the bottom to write the options.

Each week, pose a "favorites" question to the class. Give five or six options and ask students to name their favorites. Label the graph with a title "Our Favorite _____" and list the options along the bottom.

As each student names a favorite, color in one square in the appropriate column. Use the completed graph to discuss which item was the most or least favorite with the group, how many students liked the first and second options best, how much difference there was between the most favorite and least favorite choice, etc.

Suggestions for topics include favorite pet, color, book, movie, song, subject in school, flower, bird, insect, place to visit, game to play, TV show, Web site, type of weather, day of the week, and month of the year. Let students suggest topics for the weekly poll. As they become more familiar with graphing, collect the data with tally marks and let students take turns creating the graphs.

Gathering Data

After students understand simple graphing and data collecting, make a copy of the bar graph on page 124 for each student. Ask them to take their graphs home over the weekend and ask friends and family members to answer the same "Favorites" question that they answered in class that week.

On Monday, discuss the differences between the class favorites and what students found on their own. Repeat frequently during the school year.

Teaching Strategy

When graphing questions that require addition or subtraction, do the math on the board. Write an equation on the board and see who can explain what question the equation answers. Example: $8 + 9 =$ number of students who choose dogs and cats.

Possible or Impossible?

For six-year-olds, deciding whether something is possible or impossible can be difficult. Plenty of discussions and opportunities to think through questions will help students comprehend these terms.

Thumbs Up, Thumbs Down

When posing questions of *possible* or *impossible*, you may be surprised at what some students think is possible! Because of TV, computer games, etc., some students will have a difficult time making the distinction between *possible* and *impossible*. When introducing this concept, don't put students on the spot by having them answer individually. Ask them to answer as a group, with thumbs up for *possible* and thumbs down for *impossible*.

Ask, *Possible or impossible:*

1. raining cats and dogs
2. flying turtles
3. carrot soup
4. talking rabbits
5. singing birds
6. chocolate-covered popcorn
7. hot ice cream
8. apples as big as pumpkins
9. a tree that moves around
10. a cat that climbs telephone poles

Possible for Whom or What?

Things that are possible for some are impossible for others. For a trapeze artist, leaping from one trapeze bar to another is possible; for most people, it is impossible. Many things that are possible for adults are impossible for children. Many animals can do things that humans cannot do, and the reverse is also true. To stimulate thinking skills, name some events and have students name who or what could do it.

Examples:

1. swimming along the bottom of the sea for two hours (sharks)
2. running as fast as a car (jaguar)
3. eating nothing except warm milk in a bottle (a baby)
4. building a house (carpenter)
5. flying to the moon (astronaut)
6. jumping from treetop to treetop (monkeys)
7. riding a small bike (children, not adults)
8. jumping out of an airplane (skydiver)
9. fixing a car (mechanic)
10. flying (birds, bats)

0-7682-2931-6 *Getting Ready to Teach Math for the New Teacher*

Likely and Possible

Help students distinguish between *likely* and *possible* with this activity. Name something and then ask two questions: *Is it likely? Is it possible?* When an event is not likely but possible, ask students to name the circumstances where it becomes a possibility. Although it is unlikely to see a dog dressed up in clothes, it is possible at a circus.

		Likely?	Possible?
1.	seeing a dancing dog?	no	yes
2.	finding a pig in the classroom?	no	yes
3.	seeing a unicorn on the roof?	no	no
4.	seeing triplets at the park?	no	yes
5.	feeling an earthquake at school?	no	yes
6.	finding a book in the library?	yes	yes
7.	watching a clown drive a car?	no	yes
8.	seeing a cow with wings?	no	yes (cartoon)
9.	seeing a hot air balloon on the roof of a building	no	yes

More Likely?

To reinforce the concept of *likelihood*, name two things and have students decide which is *more likely*. There may be more than one correct answer. Encourage creative thinking and verbalization of ideas by asking, *Why do you think so?* Praise all ideas.

Ask, *Which is more likely:*

1. seeing a full moon or seeing snow?
   (depends upon time of day and time of year)
2. seeing a shooting star or lightning and thunder?
   (depends upon time of day and weather)
3. hearing laughter in the library or crying in the movie theater?
4. seeing a purple car or a black blimp?
5. seeing a red sunset or a flying bat?

Likely or Unlikely

Explain that *likely* is not the same as *possible*. Some very unlikely things are possible: a dancing bear is an unlikely sight, but in a circus one might see a bear that has been trained to dance. At the same time, unlikely is not the same thing as impossible. It is unlikely to see a dancing bear, but it is not impossible to see one. Helping young children understand the difference will take time, patience, and lots of discussions.

0-7682-2931-6 *Getting Ready to Teach Math for the New Teacher*

Bar Graph

_____
(Title)

Data: _____

_____

_____

_____ _____ _____ _____

0-7682-2931-6 _Getting Ready to Teach Math for the New Teacher_

Favorite Sweets

Directions: Look at the graph. Count how many.

1. How many picked pies? _____

2. How many picked ice cream? _____

3. How many picked cake? _____

4. How many picked cookies or candy? _____

5. How many picked something other than pie or cake? _____

6. What was the most popular sweet? _____

7. How many picked doughnuts or candy? _____

8. How many picked something other than

   cake, pie, or ice cream? _____

0-7682-2931-6 *Getting Ready to Teach Math for the New Teacher*

Name _____ Date _____

Picking Fruit

Directions: Use the graph to write a number sentence and answer for each question. The first one is written for you.

1. All together, how many chose either apples or pears? $8 + 1 = 9$
2. All together, how many chose either watermelon or peaches?
3. How many more chose apples than bananas?
4. All together, how many chose either peaches or pears?
5. Which was the least popular fruit?
6. How many more chose apples than watermelon?
7. All together, how many chose either apples or bananas?
8. Which was the most popular fruit?

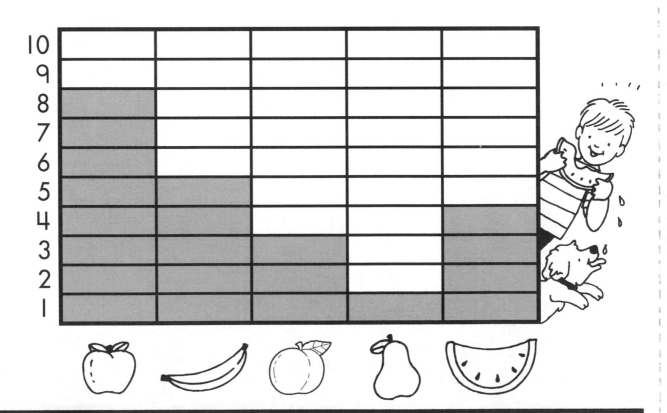

0-7682-2931-6 *Getting Ready to Teach Math for the New Teacher*

Name _____ Date _____

MacDonald's Farm

Directions: Use your crayons to make a circle graph showing the number of each kind of animal on MacDonald's Farm.

Data: All together, Farmer MacDonald has 24 animals.
He has 10 cows, 7 pigs, 4 lambs, 2 chickens, and a cat.

1. Use your blue crayon to color the spaces to represent cows.
2. Use your red crayon to color the spaces to represent pigs.
3. Use your yellow crayon to color the spaces to represent lambs.
4. Use your pink crayon to color the spaces to represent chickens.
5. Use your purple crayon to color the spaces to represent cats.

0-7682-2931-6 *Getting Ready to Teach Math for the New Teacher*

Favorite Pastimes

Directions: Use crayons to record the data on the bar graph.

Data: 10 children said that sports was their favorite hobby.
8 chose reading. 7 chose dance. 6 chose art.
5 liked spending time on a computer.

1. Use red to show how many students liked reading best.
2. Use yellow to show how many chose computers.
3. Use purple to show how many chose art.
4. Use green to show how many chose dance.
5. Use blue to show how many chose sports.

sports	reading	dancing	art	computers

0-7682-2931-6 *Getting Ready to Teach Math for the New Teacher*

Name _____ Date _____

Favorite Colors

Directions: Ask twenty people which of the five colors they like best. Record each response on the graph. When your graph is complete, use it to answer the questions.

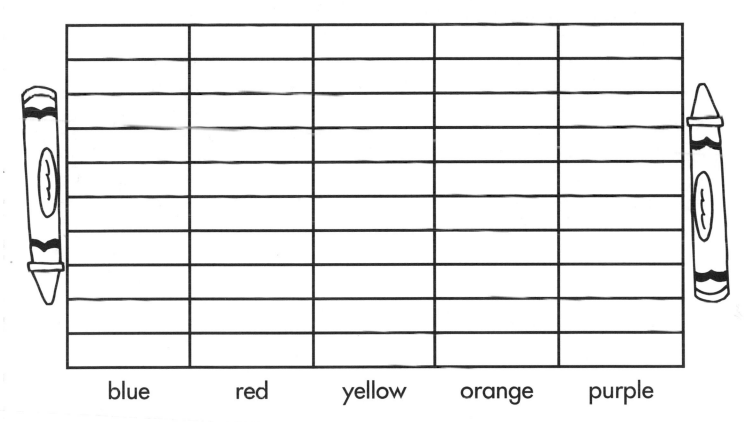

blue   red   yellow   orange   purple

1. Which color is the most popular? _____

2. Which color is the least popular? _____

3. All together, how many people chose either the most popular or least popular color? _____

4. All together, how many people chose either yellow, orange, or purple? _____

5. How many people chose a color other than red? _____

 0-7682-2931-6 *Getting Ready to Teach Math for the New Teacher*

The Eyes Have It

Directions: Look at 12 people's eyes. Make a tally for each one's eye color. After gathering the information, record it on the circle graph. Use your graph to answer the questions.

Data:

blue:_____

green:_____

brown:_____

gray:_____

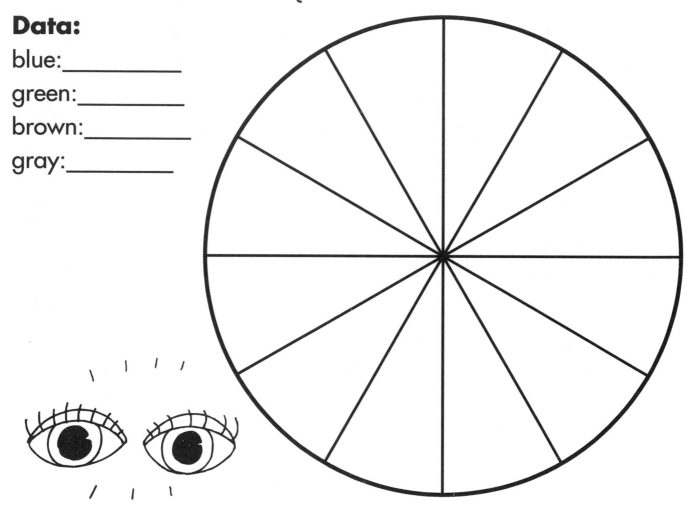

1. Do more people have blue or gray eyes? _____

2. Do more people have green or brown eyes? _____

3. What color eyes do the most people have? _____

4. What color(s) eyes did no one have? _____

0-7682-2931-6 *Getting Ready to Teach Math for the New Teacher*

Name _____ Date _____

Yes or No?

Directions: Read each statement. Decide if it is possible or impossible. If it is possible, circle **yes**. If it is not possible, circle **no**.

Possible?

1. A flute-playing ?   yes   no

2. A tree-climbing ?   yes   no

3. A dancing ?   yes   no

4. A talking ?   yes   no

5. A flying ?   yes   no

6. A purple- and orange-stripped ?   yes   no

7. An egg-laying ?   yes   no

8. A singing ?   yes   no

    0-7682-2931-6 *Getting Ready to Teach Math for the New Teacher*

Name _____ Date _____

Can You Do It?

Directions: Read each question. Circle the appropriate word.

1. Can you fly to the moon?   possible   impossible

2. Can you build a treehouse?   possible   impossible

3. Can you cook dinner for your family?   possible   impossible

4. Can you invent a cure for a disease?   possible   impossible

5. Can you ride on the back of a camel?   possible   impossible

6. Can you learn to play the piano?   possible   impossible

7. Can you bend steel rods with your
   bare hands?   possible   impossible

8. Can you climb the highest mountain
   on the planet?   possible   impossible

0-7682-2931-6 *Getting Ready to Teach Math for the New Teacher*

On the Way Home from School

Directions: What do you see on your way home from school? Do you ever see an alligator? Look at each picture and decide if it is likely that you would see it on your way home from school. If it is likely, circle **yes**. If it is not likely, circle **no**.

1.   yes   no

2.   yes   no

3.   yes   no

4.   yes   no

5.   yes   no

6.   yes   no

7.   yes   no

8.   yes   no

0-7682-2931-6 *Getting Ready to Teach Math for the New Teacher*

A Likely Pet?

Directions: Look at the pictures of animals. Decide if each one is a likely pet. If it is a likely pet, circle **yes**. If it is not a likely pet, circle **no**.

1. yes no	2. yes no
3. yes no	4. yes no
5. yes no	6. yes no
7. yes no	8. yes no

0-7682-2931-6 *Getting Ready to Teach Math for the New Teacher*

What Are the Chances?

Directions: Read each sentence. Decide if it is something certain, possible, or impossible. If you absolutely would see it, circle **certain**. If you probably would see it, circle **likely**. If you would never see it, circle **impossible**.

1. The chances of seeing a school bus in my neighborhood are:

   certain   likely   impossible

2. The chances of seeing a dinosaur in my neighborhood are:

   certain   likely   impossible

3. The chances of seeing a circus clown in my neighborhood are:

   certain   likely   impossible

4. The chances of seeing a snake in my neighborhood are:

   certain   likely   impossible

5. The chances of seeing a snowman in my neighborhood are:

   certain   likely   impossible

6. The chances of seeing a woman walking a dog in my neighborhood are:

   certain   likely   impossible

7. The chances of seeing a snail crawling on the ground in my neighborhood are:

   certain   likely   impossible

8. The chances of seeing a man skiing in my neighborhood are:

   certain   likely   impossible

© McGraw-Hill Children's Publishing   0-7682-2931-6 *Getting Ready to Teach Math for the New Teacher*

Name _____ Date _____

Data Analysis and Probability

Directions: Use the "Favorite Pet" graph to answer the questions.

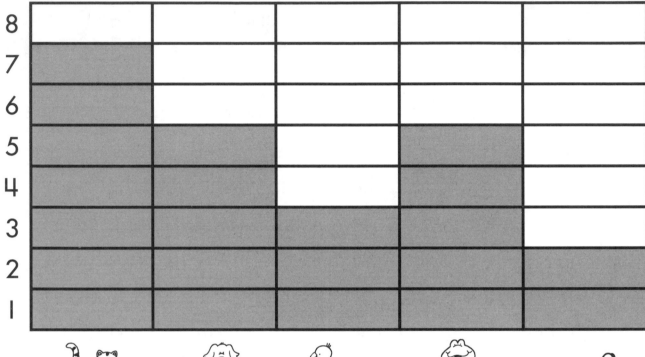

1. What is the most popular pet? _____

2. What is the least popular pet? _____

3. How many choose dog or bird as a favorite pet? _____

4. How many choose a pet other than a frog? _____

5. Which two pets had the same number of votes? _____

6. How many children took the Favorite Pet Survey? _____

0-7682-2931-6 *Getting Ready to Teach Math for the New Teacher*

Data Analysis and Probability

7. Draw pictures or write words to show the data on the circle graph.

Data:

Four children own a dog.
Two children own a cat.
One child owns a bird.
One child owns a turtle.

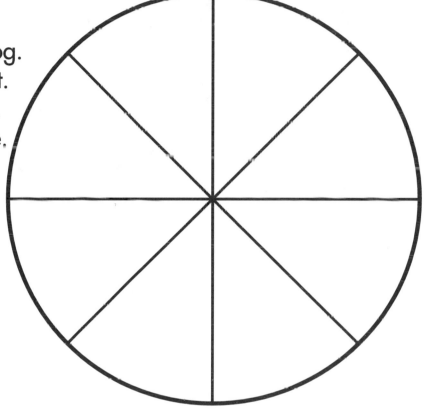

8. Is seeing a dancing dog likely or unlikely? _____

9. Is seeing triplets at the park possible or impossible? _____

10. Is finding a dollar-bill on the ground possible or impossible?

_____

11. Is a bird flying to the moon possible or impossible? _____

12. Is a mother cat having kittens likely or unlikely? _____

    0-7682-2931-6 *Getting Ready to Teach Math for the New Teacher*

Money

0-7682-2931-6 *Getting Ready to Teach Math for the New Teacher*

How Many?, Page 41
1. 13
2. 16
3. 27
4. 24
5. 18
6. 28

What's It Worth?, Page 45
1. 12
2. 14
3. 20
4. 31
5. 42
6. 60

Drawing the Values, Page 46
1. nickel
2. dime
3. quarter
4. quarter
5. quarter
6. half-dollar
7. half-dollar

Missing Numbers, Page 47
1. 6
2. 77
3. 44
4. 100
5. 11
6. 29
7. 78
8. 100
9. 8
10. 20
11. 73
12. 99

At the Animal Races, Page 48
1. blue lion, red elephant, green dog, orange cow, alligator (any color)
2. pink fox, bird (any color), green squirrel, purple raccoon, yellow pig

Skip Counting, Page 49
2. 2, 4, 6, 8, 10, 12, 14, 16, 18, 20, 22, 24, 26, 28, 30
3. 1, 3, 5, 7, 9, 11, 13, 15, 17, 19, 21, 23, 25, 27, 29
4. 5, 10, 15, 20, 25, 30

More, Less, or Equal?, Page 51
1. <
2. <
3. >
4. =
6. <
7. <
8. >

Farmer John, Page 52
1. $\frac{4}{5}, \frac{1}{5}$
2. 6 spotted, $\frac{6}{12}, \frac{6}{12}$
3. $\frac{5}{8}$ brown, $\frac{3}{8}$ gray, $\frac{5}{8}, \frac{3}{8}$
4. $\frac{7}{10}$ brown, $\frac{3}{10}$ black, $\frac{7}{10}, \frac{3}{10}$

Pie Party, Page 53
1. $\frac{1}{3}$ red, $\frac{1}{3}, \frac{2}{3}$
2. $\frac{3}{4}$ blue, $\frac{3}{4}, \frac{1}{4}$
3. $\frac{2}{6}$ yellow, $\frac{2}{6}, \frac{4}{6}$
4. $\frac{5}{8}$ green, $\frac{5}{8}, \frac{3}{8}$

Comparing Fractions, Page 54
1. >
2. >
3. =
4. =
5. >
6. >
7. <
8. >
9. =
10. =

0-7682-2931-6 *Getting Ready to Teach Math for the New Teacher*

Again and Again, Page 57
1. 2 + 2 + 2 + 2 + 2 + 2 = 12 legs
2. 2 + 2 = 4 horns
3. 4 + 4 + 4 = 12 legs
4. 2 + 2 + 2 + 2 + 2 + 2 = 12 legs
5. 2 + 2 + 2 + 2 = 8 ears
6. 1 + 1 + 1 + 1 + 1 + 1 + 1 = 7 tails
7. 2 + 2 + 2 + 2 + 2 = 10 eyes
8. 4 + 4 + 4 + 4 = 16 legs

They All Add Up, Page 58
frogs = 7
foxes = 3
swans = 9
butterflies = 6
squirrels = 2
hippos = 5
camels = 4
birds = 4
raccoons = 8
1. 4 + 6 + 7 = 17
2. 4 + 4 + 2 = 10
3. 5 + 4 + 3 = 12
4. 9 + 4 + 4 + 2 = 19
5. 9 + 8 + 6 + 5 = 28

Add and Subtract, Page 60
1. 4 + 1 = 5, 1 + 4 = 5, 5 − 1 = 4, 5 − 4 = 1
2. 5 + 1 = 6, 1 + 5 = 6, 6 − 1 = 5, 6 − 5 = 1
3. 6 + 1 = 7, 1 + 6 = 7, 7 − 1 = 6, 7 − 6 = 1
4. 3 + 2 = 5, 2 + 3 = 5, 5 − 2 = 3, 5 − 3 = 2
5. 4 + 2 = 6, 2 + 4 = 6, 6 − 2 = 4, 6 − 4 = 2
6. 5 + 2 = 7, 2 + 5 = 7, 7 − 2 = 5, 7 − 5 = 2

That's Some Total!, Page 61
1. 7
2. 7
3. 7
4. 7
5. 7
6. 7
7. 7
8. 7
9. 8
10. 8

11. 8
12. 8
13. 8
14. 8
15. 8
16. 8
17. 8
18. 9
19. 9
20. 9
21. 9
22. 9
23. 9
24. 9
25. 9
26. 9
27. 9

Missing Addends, Page 62
1. 6
2. 2
3. 2
4. 5
5. 5
6. 4
7. 3
8. 8
9. 3
10. 4
11. 4
12. 5
13. 3
14. 1
15. 7
16. 7

Assessment—Number and Operations, Page 63
1. 27
2. eight
3. 60, 64, 70
4. 62
5. 90
6. nickel
7. 10
8. 32

© McGraw-Hill Children's Publishing   0-7682-2931-6 *Getting Ready to Teach Math for the New Teacher*

Assessment—Number and Operations, Page 64

9. first and last bird red; third is green
10. 2, 4, 6, 8, 10, 12, 14
11. >
12. <
13. $\frac{1}{6}$
14. $\frac{5}{8}$ purple
15. $5 + 2 = 7$, $2 + 5 = 7$, $7 - 5 = 2$, $7 - 2 = 5$
16. 4

What's Different?, Page 73

missing: 11, 15
twice: 1, 10

Name a Way, Page 74

(Answers will vary.)
1. Both have stripes; different sizes
2. Both lay eggs; make very different sounds
3. Both live in water; move differently
4. Both have rough, tough skin; one has a horn and the other does not.
5. Both live on farms; cows give milk, pigs do not.
6. Both are colorful and can fly; parrots talk and butterflies do not.
7. Both crawl on the ground; snakes eat mice and snails do not.
8. Both carry people and objects; camels have a hump or two, mules do not.

They're the Same, Page 75

1. C = 10
2. D = 11
3. E = 9
4. A = 8
5. B = 12
6. H = 7
7. F = 6
8. G = 5

What's Next?, Page 76

1. bike
2. fire truck
3. present
4.
5. jet
6.

Number, Please, Page 77

1. 2
2. 7
3. 6
4. 4
5. 7
6. 13 (add last two digits)

Something in Common, Page 79

1. Any circle that is not red
2. Any blue shape
3. Any shape, same size, not yellow
4. Any triangle not red
5. Any blue shape, different size

One and Only One, Page 80

1. shape
2. color
3. shape
4. size
5. shape

Nothing in Common, Page 81

Drawings will vary.

Assessment—Algebra, Page 82

1. third one is different
2. first and third are the same
3. duck has middle-sized beak
4. elephant
5.
6. 1
7. color

It's a Zoo, Page 91

1. red lamb
2. blue snail
3. yellow mule
4. green butterfly
5. purple lion
6. orange dog
7. red rhino
8. blue porcupine
9. yellow zebra
10. green cat
11. purple starfish
12. orange swan and mouse
13. red alligator
14. blue snake
15. yellow hen

0-7682-2931-6 *Getting Ready to Teach Math for the New Teacher*

The Shape of Things, Page 92

1. square and diamond
2. triangle
3. rectangle
4. circle and oval
5. oval
6. diamond
7. square, triangle, rectangle, diamond

Name That Figure, Page 94

1. B.
2. C.
3. D.
4. D.
5. C.
6. C.
7. B.
8. A.

Put It Back into the Box, Page 96

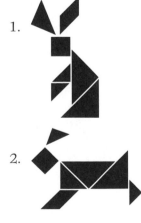

Other Challenges, Page 97

1.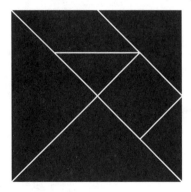

2.

3.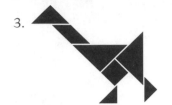

4.

5.

6.

7.

8.

Double the Shape, Page 98

1. rectangle
2. triangle
3. diamond
4. square
5. square
6. rectangle

Half the Shape, Page 99

1. rectangles
2. triangles
3. squares
4. triangles
5. triangles

A Closer Look, Page 100

1. A., C., E.
2. B., D.
3. D., E.
4. C.
5. B.
6. D.
7. C.

0-7682-2931-6 *Getting Ready to Teach Math for the New Teacher*

Assessment—Geometry, Page 101

1. blue mouse
2. red rhino
3. yellow snake
4. purple hen
5. square
6. cube
7. oval

Assessment—Geometry, Page 102

9. diamond
10. triangle
11. cone

Measuring in Animal Lengths, Page 109

1. 3 fish
2. 2 turtles
3. arrow
4. 6
5. 5
6. 5 snails
7. 1 snake
8. 4 turtles

Thumbs Up, Page 110

Answers will vary.

How Many Inches?, Page 111

1. 3"
2. 4"
3. 3"
4.–6. Answers will vary.

How Many Centimeters?, Page 112

1. 5 cm
2. 6 cm
3. 3 cm
4. 8 cm
5. 2 cm
6. 1 cm

Take It Outside, Page 113

Answers will vary.

Which Holds More?, Page 114

1. tablespoon
2. mug
3. pint jar
4. carton
5. wagon
6. dump truck

How Many Will It Hold?, Page 115

1. 4 square centimeters
2. 16 square centimeters
3. 9 square centimeters
4. 25 square centimeters

How Many Will It Hold Now?, Page 116

1. 8 square centimeters
2. 12 square centimeters
3. 15 square centimeters
4. 24 square centimeters

Assessment—Measurement, Page 117

1. cat
2. butterfly
3. B.
4. 6"
5. 2 cm
6. 17 cm

Assessment—Measurement, Page 118

7. tablespoon
8. mug
9. small square
10. 4
11. 16

Favorite Sweets, Page 125

1. 5
2. 2
3. 3
4. $3 + 2 = 5$
5. 8
6. pie
7. 3
8. 6

0-7682-2931-6 *Getting Ready to Teach Math for the New Teacher*

Picking Fruit, Page 126

1. $8 + 1 = 9$
2. $4 + 3 = 7$
3. $8 - 5 = 3$
4. $3 + 1 = 4$
5. pear
6. $8 - 4 = 4$
7. $8 + 5 = 13$
8. apples

MacDonald's Farm, Page 127

1. blue 10
2. red 7
3. yellow 4
4. pink 2
5. purple 1

Favorite Pastimes, Page 128

1. red, 8
2. yellow 5
3. purple 6
4. green 7
5. blue 10

Yes or No?, Page 131

1. no
2. yes
3. yes
4. yes
5. yes
6. no
5. yes
6. no

Can You Do It?, Page 132

Answers may vary.

On the Way Home From School, Page 133

1. no (possible if you live in Florida)
2. yes
3. yes
4. yes
5. yes
6. no (possible if you go past a zoo)
7. yes
8. yes (not likely if you live in a desert area)

What Are the Chances?, Page 135

Answers will vary.

Assessment—Data Analysis and Probability, Page 136

1. cat
2. snake
3. 8
4. 17
5. dogs and frogs
6. 22

Assessment—Data Analysis and Probability, Page 137

7. 4 dog, 2 cat, 1 bird, 1 turtle
8. unlikely
9. possible
10. possible
11. impossible
12. likely

© McGraw-Hill Children's Publishing

0-7682-2931-6 *Getting Ready to Teach Math for the New Teacher*

Why Do You Need This New Edition?

If you're wondering why you should buy this new edition of *Effective College Learning*, here are 6 good reasons!

1. A new Appendix from a psychology chapter, entitled "Memory," will help you to better understand how memory, learning, and studying are related.

2. A new excerpt from a technology textbook that focuses on computer memory, along with new examples, will show you how to apply the strategies you've learned in this textbook to a variety of disciplines.

3. A new Appendix from a History textbook, focusing on the Great Depression, will be timely and interesting to read, since the world is struggling economically.

4. A new feature, "Did You Know?," will help you learn how to acquire new words and increase your vocabulary.

5. The chapter-opening assessments will provide you with opportunities for writing and reflecting, as you assess your own strengths and weaknesses.

6. A new design will engage you and be more conducive to your learning.

PEARSON

The Authors

JODI PATRICK HOLSCHUH

Jodi is an associate professor in the Department of Curriculum and Instruction at Texas State University. For more than fifteen years, Jodi has been involved in helping students make the transition from high school to college learning. An award-winning teacher, Jodi teaches courses to help students learn effective and efficient study habits as well as courses for graduate students and instructors on how to teach reading and learning at the college level. She has presented many conference papers both nationally and internationally and has written many articles, book chapters, and books on the topic of helping students learn in college. Her research interests include students' beliefs about learning, making the transition from high school to college learning, strategies for academic success, and motivation. When she is not writing, teaching, or researching, Jodi loves rediscovering the world as her son and daughter learn new things. She also loves to read good books and travel to new places.

SHERRIE NIST-OLEJNIK

Sherrie is a professor emeritus at the University of Georgia. Prior to retiring, she was the director of the Division of Academic Enhancement at the University of Georgia. Before becoming director, she taught reading and studying courses to college students in the same division. Dr. Nist received both her master's and doctoral degrees from the University of Florida. It was as a graduate student that she first became interested in how students learn, particularly concerning the factors that seem to influence a smooth transition from high school to college, and the academic struggles that first-year students seem to face. Sherrie has published more than eighty articles, textbooks, textbook chapters, and other professional pieces all related to how college students learn and study. She has presented the results of her research in more than 100 national and international professional meetings, and she has received honors and awards for her contributions to both teaching and research. She continues to be active in her field by writing books and consulting. Sherrie loves traveling, cooking, and, of course, reading and learning new things.

Effective College Learning

SECOND EDITION

JODI PATRICK HOLSCHUH

Texas State University

SHERRIE L. NIST-OLEJNIK

Professor Emeritus University of Georgia

Longman

Boston   Columbus   Indianapolis   New York   San Francisco   Upper Saddle River
Amsterdam   Cape Town   Dubai   London   Madrid   Milan   Munich   Paris   Montreal   Toronto
Delhi   Mexico City   São Paulo   Sydney   Hong Kong   Seoul   Singapore   Taipei   Tokyo

DK Education
Publisher and Managing Director: **Sophie Mitchell**
Design Director: **Stuart Jackman**
Project Art Editor: **Clive Savage**
DTP Designer: **David McDonald**

Longman Publishers
Aquisitions Editor: **Kate Edwards**
Development Editor: **Janice Wiggins-Clarke**
Marketing Manager: **Thomas DeMarco**
Production Manager: **Ellen MacElree**
Project Coordination:
Elm Street Publishing Services
Cover Design Manager: **Wendy Ann Fredericks**
Cover Design: **Dorling Kindersley**
Cover Photos: **Gary Conner/PhotoEdit**
Photo Researcher: **Linda Sykes**
Manufacturing Manager: **Mary Fischer**
Printer and Binder: **Courier Kendalville**
Cover Printer: **Coral Graphic Services**

For permission to use copyrighted material, grateful acknowledgment is made to the copyright holders on pp. 327-328, which are hereby made part of this copyright page.

Library of Congress Cataloging-in-Publication Data
Nist-Olejnik, Sherri
Effective college learning / Sherrie L. Nist-Olejnik, Jodi Patrick Holschuh.—2nd ed.
p. cm.
Includes bibliographical references and index.
ISBN 0-205-75013-3
1. College student orientation—United States. 2. Study skills—United States. 3. Active learning—United States. I. Holschuh, Jodi. II. Title.
LB2343.32.N573 2011
378.1'70281—dc22

2009036750

1 2 3 4 5 6 7 8 9 10-CRK-13 12 11 10

Longman
is an imprint of

www.pearsonhighered.com

ISBN 10:   0-205-75013-3
ISBN 13: 978-0-205-75013-9

Dedication

FOR JODI
To my family—
my husband Douglas,
my daughter Maia,
and my son Samuel.

FOR SHERRIE
To my family—
my husband Steve Olejnik,
my daughter Kama,
and my parents,
Roy and Charlene Miller.

Brief Contents

Detailed Contents

Detailed Contents

Detailed Contents

Detailed Contents

Detailed Contents

Detailed Contents

Detailed Contents

Detailed Contents

Detailed Contents

Preface

"It is important that students bring a certain ragamuffin, barefoot irreverence to their studies; they are not here to worship what is known, but to question it."

—Jacob Bronowski

Effective College Learning has been given a face lift in the second edition with the focus being on design and a widening of the content areas we expose students to. The design of the book has been streamlined so as to be more student friendly and less cluttered. In addition, we have included additional readings on which students can practice strategies. In the second edition we continue to focus on helping students become active, engaged, and flexible learners who take responsibility for their own learning. We believe this new edition not only has a new look, but also a new feel that will inspire confidence in students' abilities to be successful in and out of the classroom.

What's New in the Second Edition? There are two keys changes to *Effective College Learning*, Second Edition. The first is the overall visual design of the book. Although the second edition retains visual elements that are attractive and engage the reader, the new design is more conducive to learning and is less cluttered. The strategy examples have been enlarged so that students can better focus on them, while many of the color photographs have been reduced in size or taken out altogether. Figures are used when they aid in comprehension. In addition, the headings and subheadings have been reworked so that students can better follow the flow of each chapter and see how ideas are related. Each chapter still begins with an assessment followed by two vocabulary features and the "Research Into Practice" feature.

The second key change is the chapters and chapter excerpts in the appendices. All of the text pieces from the first edition have been changed, although the biology excerpt still covers digestion and nutrition. The other new excerpts include: (1) a psychology chapter titled "Memory," which helps students better understand how memory, learning, and studying are related; (2) a history excerpt titled "The Great Depression and the New Deal," which focuses on the Great Depression, a topic that is very timely as the world once again struggles economically; and (3) an excerpt from a technology textbook titled "Hardware Basics," which focuses on computer memory. With these new chapters come new examples that show students how to apply the strategies taught in *Effective College Learning*, Second Edition, to a variety of disciplines.

There are also several pedagogical changes that are an improvement on the first edition. First, the "Word Wise" feature, which introduces several vocabulary words that can be found in each chapter, is now at the beginning rather than at the end of the chapter. It made more sense to expose students to the words before rather than after reading the chapter. Each "Word Wise" is followed by a new feature called "Did You Know?," which also expands students' knowledge of how to go about learning more new words. Based on research that has been conducted on vocabulary learning, this feature helps students understand what it means to truly "know" a word and creates an awareness of the many ways students can increase their vocabulary.

Second, students will have the opportunity to write and reflect more often. Each assessment is followed by some questions for students to answer as they assess their strengths and weaknesses. This activity also gives them time to reflect so that as they read the chapter, they can pay more attention to using their strengths to improve their weaknesses.

Third, instructors who used the first edition of *Effective College Learning* will notice that several of the features have been condensed to reduce redundancy. We attempted to streamline the material to help the readers focus on important concepts.

CONTINUING FEATURES FROM THE FIRST EDITION

Effective College Learning, Second Edition, continues to expose students to a wide range of research-based learning strategies and studying behaviors that lead to academic success, and therefore it is the book for students who want to be at the top of their academic game. Because we believe that college students are adults capable of making wise choices, we have designed *Effective College Learning*, Second Edition, so that students can try out different strategies using a variety of chapters and excerpts, identify which are a "fit," and then modify them based on the texts, tasks, and how they learn best. *Effective College Learning*, Second Edition, takes the premise that learning is not something that is done to students. Rather it is a process in which they must participate, be involved in, and think about in order for learning to be maximized. Nor is learning just the memorization of facts. Real learning requires the ability to synthesize, analyze, and think critically.

Because of the general philosophy of *Effective College Learning*, we have retained many of the features from the first edition. These features include:

Self-Assessment An assessment at the beginning of each chapter. Each assessment has been broadened to involve students in writing a brief self-assessment that summarizes their strengths and weaknesses of the targeted skill.

WORD WISE This feature builds vocabulary by presenting three or four new words that are used in the chapter.

RESEARCH INTO PRACTICE This feature summarizes current research to help students think about the implication of issues important to studying and learning.

Monitor Your Learning This sidebar helps students examine themselves as learners and gives them an opportunity to reflect on key topics.

NETWORKING This sidebar focuses on using technology to learn.

Reality Check This sidebar also helps students monitor their learning by thinking about and evaluating their own experiences.

BEYOND THE CLASSROOM This feature is targeted at students who are older than the traditional college-aged student. Many of these tips focus on time management, balancing work, school, and family, and other issues that, in reality, affect all college students.

Real College Each scenario features a college student who has a problem related to what students have learned in the chapter. By helping these college students, students will gain further insight into their own strengths and weaknesses.

Add to your Portfolio In this feature, students are asked to try out different strategies that are presented in each chapter.

Lengthy text excerpts These text pieces serve as common vehicles for students to practice the strategies presented in ECL. Additionally, we have used these chapters for our example strategies throughout the book.

To be an effective learner means that students play a key role in the process regardless of how good or bad their professors happen to be. It involves the ability to engage all of the senses—in listening, writing, reading, talking—because the more senses students use, the better they learn and remember. Learning rarely occurs in a precise step-by-step process, nor are there any "magic beans." In short, *Effective College Learning*, Second Edition, communicates that learning is complex, thus requiring work and effort, but that there is a big payoff for those willing to go down this path.

TO STUDENTS

"What we have to learn to do, we learn by doing"

—Aristotle

The focus of *Effective College Learning*, Second Edition, is rooted in the importance of your becoming actively involved in, and responsible for, your learning. In other words, you learn by doing. Learning is a complex process, yet effective learning can be mastered with diligence and practice. *Effective College Learning* presents this complexity through discussing four key factors that interact to maximize learning: (1) your own learning characteristics; (2) the tasks that you must complete; (3) strategies that help you read, understand, and remember; and (4) the texts that you use. We present strategies that involve reading, writing, listening, talking, and doing. We help you discover your own learner characteristics. We also encourage you to be a flexible learner and to modify strategies as a way of personalizing learning, by practicing the strategies and finding out what elements work best for you.

In short, *Effective College Learning* assumes that to become an efficient and effective learner, you must view yourself as central to the learning process. Just as you participate in campus clubs and organizations, you must also recognize the importance of participating fully in each course you take and every academic experience you have. What this translates to is using active reading and study strategies, rehearsing as you prepare for exams, taking organized lecture notes and reviewing them, giving daily attention to your work, monitoring your learning, and a variety of other strategic approaches for studying. Studying actively means using all of your senses to learn—you write, you hear, you listen, you speak. You have a variety of strategies that you can use, and you know the appropriate time to use them. *Effective College Learning* presents strategies to assist you in becoming an active learner and helps you understand when and how to apply them. Just as the basketball team has a playbook outlining a variety of plays, it is important for you to know a variety of strategies so you can be prepared for the wealth of academic tasks that come your way.

USING *EFFECTIVE COLLEGE LEARNING,* **SECOND EDITION**

"Practice doesn't make perfect. Perfect practice makes perfect."

—Vince Lombardi

Effective College Learning, Second Edition, was designed not only to get you reading about what it takes to learn actively but also to start you thinking and talking about it. Thus, the self-assessment at the beginning of each chapter, the sidebars throughout each chapter, and the exercises at the end of each chapter ask you to discuss important questions with classmates, to think about issues, or to reflect on your learning. While passive learners study by merely skimming or reading over materials, active learners read, write, listen, discuss, and visualize, interacting with information in a variety of ways. Active learners plan, set goals, make conscious choices about the strategies they use, and monitor their learning. This activity—this *doing*—leads to academic success.

Effective College Learning, Second Edition, has several important features. First, you will complete a self-assessment at the beginning of each chapter. These assessments give you an idea of the ways you currently approach learning so that you can make changes for the better. After you have completed the assessment, we ask you to reflect by writing about your strengths and weaknesses. This will help you make the connection between the strategies and your own learning experiences. Second, the "Word Wise" and "Did You Know" features will help you improve your vocabulary. "Word Wise" culls out words from the chapter that you may not know, and "Did You Know" provides tips and strategies for improving your vocabulary on a daily basis. Third, "Research into Practice" segments present current research in a practical way. These segments are meant to help you think about how the implications of important research in the field of studying and learning translate into application. Fourth, you will find "Real College" scenarios located near the end of each chapter. Each scenario features a college student who has a problem that is related in some way to what you have learned in that chapter. By helping these college students solve their problems, you can further apply the ideas and strategies you have learned. We believe that you may see part of yourself in many of the scenarios which, by the way, are based on real issues that our students consistently face as they work toward becoming effective learners.

Finally, each chapter ends with an "Add to Your Portfolio" feature, which asks you to try out and evaluate the strategies presented in the chapter. As you build your portfolio over the course of the term, you will see how far you have come. The expectation is that by the end of the term, you will have a notebook or folder that shows you have practiced all of the strategies presented in *Effective College Learning,* Second Edition. We suggest that as you try out the strategies for your portfolio, you select courses for which many of the strategies would be appropriate, such as history, biology, sociology, chemistry, or the like, rather than courses that require little interaction with texts, such as a computer application course.

TO INSTRUCTORS

"The illiterate of the twenty-first century will not be those who cannot read and write, but those who cannot learn, unlearn, and relearn."

—Alvin Toffler

We have based *Effective College Learning*, Second Edition, on many years of experience of interacting with college students as well as on our own research focusing on how college students study. From our interactions with students, we have learned that: (1) Even students who have been successful in high school often enter college unprepared to meet the studying demands placed on them. (2) College students are sometimes overwhelmed with the reading and studying demands that college can bring, and can become frustrated when they believe they are "working hard" but not seeing their efforts pay off. (3) It takes more than knowledge of a few strategies for students to achieve academically. (4) Students benefit from learning about their own personal learner characteristics. And, perhaps most important, we have learned that (5) students can be taught how to study effectively, and in most cases, they are eager to learn new skills that will help them be successful in college.

We have based *Effective College Learning*, Second Edition, on a strong theory and research foundation. Many first-year experience and study-skills books tout study methods that are based only on conventional wisdom, but are not necessarily grounded in learning theory and what the research shows about learning and studying. In preparation for writing this book, we went back and reread some of the studies that influenced our own work and influenced the field of college studying in general. We also read the most up-to-date research to present the most effective strategies for learning in college. Our review of the literature reinforced our belief that being an active learner included many factors that all had to interact in order for learning to be maximized.

The second edition also reflects the wisdom of the reviewers of the first edition—instructors who are "in the trenches" on a daily basis and teach a variety of different types of students. These reviewers provided a great deal of input that makes this edition much stronger. We incorporated many of their design and content suggestions that has resulted in a final product that is more student-friendly and strategy-focused.

Not only does *Effective College Learning* provide a cutting edge to academic success in college but also it was designed visually with learning in mind. In a partnership between Pearson Education and Dorling Kindersley, the visual elements that make *Effective College Learning* are attractive but they are also there to engage the reader. For example, the assessments at the beginning of each chapter can get students thinking about themselves as learners, and the different writing and discussion activities throughout each chapter reinforce the importance of using all of the senses to learn. In addition, the "Add to Your Portfolio" feature allows students to track their progress over an entire semester.

THE ANCILLARY PACKAGE

Available for adopting instructors.

The Instructor's Manual/Test Bank (0-205-75014-1)

Accompanies *Effective College Learning* and offers teaching insights, sample syllabi, schedules, activities, and tests. Please ask your Longman sales representative for a copy.

In addition to this book-specific supplement, many other skills-based supplements and testing packages are available for both instructors and students.

The Longman Developmental English Package

Longman is pleased to offer a variety of support materials to help make teaching reading easier on teachers and to help students excel in their coursework. Many of our student supplements are available at a greatly reduced price when packaged with *Effective College Learning*, Second Edition. Contact your local Longman sales representative for more information on pricing and how to create a package.

Acknowledgments

"It takes a village to raise a child."

—African Proverb

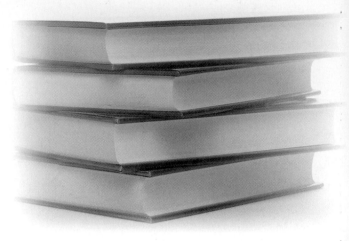

There are many individuals who contributed either directly or indirectly to the contents of *Effective College Learning*, Second Edition. Certainly it is important for us to acknowledge the students that we have had the privilege to teach. As is always the case, our students help to ground our writing in reality—the reality of the many pressures currently faced by today's college students and the reality of just how important lifelong learning has become. We were especially struck as we wrote the second edition of the importance of understanding and using technology to learn and how rapidly technology applications change. Today's students are expected to know and keep abreast of new technological advances that can enhance learning.

In addition to our students, our thanks also goes out to the numerous professors and graduate students at the University of Georgia and beyond who have willingly shared their concerns and their expertise about learning in their particular disciplines. A special thanks to Denise Pinette Domizi, Eleanor Pardini, Daniel Forbes, and Gretchen Pettis for their insightful suggestions and willingness to share the parallel note-taking strategy in *Effective College Learning*. Thanks to Audrey Haynes for the use of Web-notes from her political science class and to the many students in Dr. Holschuh's classes who shared their strategies with us. This text would have not been nearly as effective without their valuable insights.

Certainly *Effective College Learning*, Second Edition, has been enhanced by the constructive and insightful comments and suggestions made by the content consultants who reviewed every chapter of this book. Their valuable feedback enabled us to further understand the needs of a variety of college students and provided suggestions that helped to improve the book. A big thank you goes out to:

Sonya Armstrong, Northern Illinois University
Ann Ho Becks, University of Florida
Doralee Brooks, Community College of Allegheny County
Dr. Mary Jane Farley, Dyersburg State Community College
Karen Fenske, Kishwaukee College
Gara B. Field, Ph.D., University of Georgia
Betty Fortune, Houston Community College
Barb Grady, Gateway Community College
Deborah Miller, The Ohio State University at Newark
Marilyn Rice, Collin County Community College
Paige Sindt, Arizona State University
Dr. Lynda Villanueva, Brazosport College
Carla Young, Community College of Allegheny County

We would be remiss if we failed to acknowledge all of the assistance we received from those we have worked with at Pearson Education. We especially thank Kate Edwards, our acquisitions editor, for the major support she gave to us on this project. We can't say enough about Kate. She listened to our ideas and was always sensitive to the vision that we had for the second edition. We appreciate her patience and her willingness to explore new ideas.

Likewise, we thank Janice Wiggins-Clarke, our development editor, who assisted greatly when we got down to the nuts and bolts of completing the second edition and helped us make sense of the technical side of publishing this book. We thank Ellen MacElree, production manager, for working behind the scenes to keep the book on track and help make *Effective College Learning* something we can be proud of. We also thank the design team at Dorling Kindersley who created a beautiful, interactive, and reader friendly text. Our thanks to Heather Johnson, and others at Elm Street Publishing Services, who tightened up our language and worked their magic throughout this book. As always, they were a pleasure to work with.

Finally, we acknowledge our respective families— our spouses, in particular—who always offered their continuous support, as we worked to complete this edition of *Effective College Learning* within record time. We appreciate their understanding, support, and advice as the writing of this text seemed to take over our lives at times. Their support allowed us the time to create what we believe is an excellent book.

JODI PATRICK HOLSCHUH

SHERRIE L. NIST-OLEJNIK

Effective College Learning

SECOND EDITION

Chapter 1

You Have Arrived: A Primer on College Life

Read this chapter to answer the following questions:

- How does studying in college differ from studying in high school?

- What special situations can you expect to encounter in college, sooner or later?

- How do you make a positive impression on your professors?

- How do you ask a professor for help?

- How do you take full advantage of the resources your college has to offer?

Self-Assessment

DIRECTIONS: On a scale of 1 to 5, with 1 being "strongly disagree," 3 being "somewhat agree," and 5 being "strongly agree," respond to each of the statements below. Although you may not have firsthand experience with some of these issues, you probably do hold some preconceived notions of what college will be like. Your responses to these items should give you a good idea about how much you think your college experience will differ from what you experienced in high school.

	Strongly disagree 1	2	Some what agree 3	4	Strongly agree 5
1. My college professors will expect much more of me.		X			
2. My college classes will move at a faster pace.			X		
3. My college classes will require more than just memorization.			X		
4. My college classes will not give me chances to earn extra credit.		X			
5. My college classes will require me to spend more time studying.			X		
6. My college professors will give fewer exams.		X			
7. I will have more freedom in college.			X		
8. I will often feel anonymous in college.					X
9. I will experience motivation problems in college.				X	
10. Managing my time effectively will be more challenging in college.			X		
11. It will be more difficult to get to know my teachers in college.			X		

Now add up your score. The higher your score, the more differences you believe you will experience in making the transition to college. The more differences you experience, the more time it may take you to make the adjustment. But don't despair. The skills you will learn in *Effective College Learning* will help you make this transition.

Before reading the chapter, reflect on your responses to the self-assessment. What types of information will you need to find out to make your transition to college smooth? What do you feel confident about?

That they do give you time

Before You Begin

WORD WISE

In each chapter you will notice two to four words that appear in bold. These are your "Word Wise" words. As you read, try to construct the meaning of the words through the context of the paragraph or sentence. This section will define the words for you and provide you with a brief context so that when you encounter the word in your reading, you will have some familiarity with it.

1. **Presumably** (adv., p. 5) — by reasonable assumption; can be taken for granted.
*She bought a ticket for the concert, so **presumably** she will go.*

2. **Ancillary** (adj., p. 5) — supplementary; extra; material that is subordinate to something else.
*The handout was **ancillary** to the textbook, so the professor impressed on the class the importance of not losing it.*

3. **Proactive** (adj., p. 7) — acting in advance; anticipatory actions.
*By studying a little every day, the student took **proactive** steps to maintain her excellent grades in the class.*

4. **Inevitably** (adv., p. 9) — is a way that is certain; impossible to avoid or prevent; by necessity.
***Inevitably**, our final exams will occur in May.*

DID YOU KNOW?

You may have heard that the best way to learn new words is to figure out what they mean by the way they are used in a sentence. This is known as "getting the meaning through context." It is certainly not a bad idea for a beginning point of learning a new word, but rarely is it enough. Research shows that using context alone works only if the context provides a very clear definition of the word. However, this is usually not the case. So, if you run across a word in the course of your reading that you don't know and the context is weak, use your dictionary or ask someone to clarify the meaning for you.

RESEARCH INTO PRACTICE

Friendsickness and Adjusting to College

In this study, researchers examined the role of friendsickness in adjusting to college life. They define *friendsickness* as concern about losing old friends and/or worries about making new friends in college. The results indicated that more than 50 percent of their participants experienced moderate to high levels of friendsickness as they transitioned to college. Students who experienced these levels of friendsickness showed difficulty in making the transition to college. They reported feeling lonely, had poor self-esteem regarding the ability to make new friends, and felt that their social life in college was not what they expected. The researchers suggested several ways to overcome friendsickness. First, students should consider this transition a process, during which time they will begin to learn new coping skills.

Second, students who are friendsick need to realize that they are grieving. Grief or loss education, often available at campus counseling centers, can help them develop productive coping strategies. Third, the researchers found that it is helpful for students to create a balance between working on building and strengthening college friendships and realizing that their relationships with precollege friends will change. This research is important because many students realize that they are homesick but may not consider the role that friendsickness can play in the adjustment to college.

Source: E. L. Paul and S. Brier, "Friendsickness in the Transition to College: Precollege Predictors and College Adjustment Correlates," *Journal of Counseling and Development* 79 (2001): 77–89.

How Is College Different from High School?

Starting college! You may feel as if you have been preparing for this day forever. You've taken a college preparatory curriculum in high school, you've talked with friends or siblings who are already in college, and you may have visited several campuses before deciding which school to attend. Or you may be returning to college after several years of working, having already gone through careful life assessment and financial budgeting. Regardless of your situation, **presumably** you are excited about what the next few years have in store for you. And, for a variety of reasons, some of you may even be a little wary and unsure of yourselves as you begin down the college path.

In this chapter, we will discuss some of the ways in which college differs from high school. In addition, we will present nine situations that you are sure to encounter in college sooner or later and will offer suggestions about how you might deal with them. We will also talk a little about college professors and how your relationship with them can influence your college success. Keep in mind as you read this chapter that campuses differ in size and in the expectations they have of students. For example, students attending a large university may have experiences very different from those of students attending a local community college. Students starting or returning to college after working for a couple of years will have still different experiences. In this chapter, we will discuss a variety of generalizations and solutions, many of which will apply to your particular situation.

How many times have you heard one of your relatives say something like this: "Oh, (insert your name)! Enjoy these college years. They will be the best of your life." Although this statement may be true—college is enjoyable and memorable—it is also demanding and, in many instances, just plain

different from high school. It's a time in your life when you will go through many changes as you prepare for the world of work that follows. In this section, we will discuss some of the reasons why high school and college differ.

Reality Check

Transitioning to College
We often ask students what they wished they had learned in high school about making the transition to college. Surprisingly, many students tell us that they wish that teachers didn't scare them so much about professors. They are often told in high school that professors won't care about them or get to know them at all, but our experience says that this is really not the norm. With a little effort, you can get to know your professors, and most of us are pretty nice folks. Think about your own experience. What do you wish you had learned about the transition to college? How do you feel so far about your interaction with your professors?

Good discussion topic!

What have students noticed about professors

1. COLLEGE REQUIRES GREATER INDEPENDENT LEARNING

Your high school teachers may have been willing to give you lots of test preparation help. They may have prepared study guides or even provided the exact questions that would be asked. Although college instructors also want you to be successful—we have never met a professor who wanted students to fail—they don't give students as much study help. Sure, most professors will answer questions about course content and things you don't understand, but they rarely provide you with a variety of **ancillary** learning materials and they certainly will not give you exact test questions. They also expect that you know effective and efficient study strategies; and if you don't know how to study for their courses, they expect you to learn how.

2. COLLEGE COURSES MOVE AT A FASTER PACE

If you ask first-year college students about the differences between high school and college, one of their most common responses would be that college courses move much faster than high school classes. What might have taken a full year to cover in high school will probably be covered in a semester in college. It's not uncommon for college professors to move through three, four, or more chapters in a week, expecting you to keep up. In addition, topics are generally covered in greater detail. However, college professors may go into detail on just a few points and expect you to fill in the rest of the details on your own.

3. COLLEGE COURSES REQUIRE CRITICAL THINKING

In your high school classes, perhaps you were required to memorize lots of facts for exams. You may even have been discouraged from questioning either your high school textbooks or your teacher. But as you proceed through college, you will find yourself in classes where your professors want you to do more than memorize. You might have to critique an essay on literary theory, read and respond to a historian's view of the Vietnamese conflict, or compare and contrast conflicting scientific theories. All of these tasks require you to think critically because you need to go beyond memorization to applying or synthesizing the information.

4. COLLEGE CLASSES HAVE FEW SAFETY NETS

Usually on the first day of a college class, your professor will give you a syllabus. The syllabus outlines the course requirements and also generally tells you how your grade will be determined. Something that will become clear as you read your syllabus is that many of the safety nets that you had in high school, such as extra credit assignments or other bonuses to improve your grade, have all but disappeared. This means your course grade will be determined by the grade you earn on a limited number of tests or papers; you'll need to give every assignment your best effort.

5. COLLEGE REQUIRES YOU TO STUDY LONGER AND MORE EFFECTIVELY

You will probably find out pretty quickly that both the amount of time you put into studying and the way you study in college will have to change if you want to earn high grades. Many of our students tell us that they really didn't have to study in high school. "Studying" was reading over a study guide or skimming class notes for about a half hour. Some students begin college without ever having had to read their texts, and others have never taken essay exams. It is important to realize that studying in college requires not only more time, but also a variety of study strategies. In fact, you will soon realize the strategies that work for you in English literature will not work for you physics.

6. COLLEGE PROVIDES FEWER CHANCES FOR EVALUATION

When you were in high school, it may have seemed as though you were always taking tests or writing papers. Chances are you were tested on small amounts of material (only one or two chapters) and you had numerous chances for evaluation. If you did poorly on one test, you could usually make it up on the next one. In college, on the other hand, you will probably have fewer chances to be evaluated. At first, the idea of taking fewer tests per course in a term may seem appealing. But think about the big picture. If you have only three exams, you are going to be held responsible for much more information at one time than you were in high school. What at first seems to be an advantage—fewer tests, homework that goes unchecked, a longer period of time between exams—may actually work against you, unless you know how to stay on top of things.

7. COLLEGE GIVES YOU GREATER FREEDOM AND GREATER RESPONSIBILITY

In college, no one makes you stay on top of your schoolwork or keeps track of your comings and goings or checks to see that you have done all of your reading and studying before heading out for a night on the town. This freedom comes with a tremendous amount of responsibility. It is your responsibility to prioritize the tasks you have to do against the things you want to do. This applies to all students, no matter what your age when you begin college. If you're like most students, you will love the freedom part and not be so fond of the responsibility part.

8. COLLEGE PROVIDES GREATER ANONYMITY

If you attend a moderate to large college or university, you will be faced with being somewhat anonymous, and in some cases, very anonymous. This is an issue for community college students as well because most two-year institutions are commuter schools with little or no on-campus lodging. By *anonymous* we mean that you can become just another face in the crowd. Think back to high school, especially those of you who attended small schools. Most of you probably got to know your teachers and your classmates fairly well. Your teachers not only knew your name, but also were concerned about whether or not you were learning and understanding the information presented in their classes. For the most part, you don't get to know most of your college professors that well. All is not lost, however. Most of the time, students are anonymous only if they want to be, regardless of how large or small their campus may be or how old they are. You can become more than a "face" to your professors by making appointments to talk with them. You can join clubs that have faculty sponsors. You can take part in a variety of campus activities with other students who share your interests.

9. COLLEGE REQUIRES YOU TO BE PROACTIVE

Being **proactive** means that it's your responsibility to take the initiative in a variety of situations. In high school, either your teachers or your parents may have insisted that you get help if you were having problems with a particular course. And you may have followed their advice reluctantly. In college, however, it becomes your responsibility to know the resources that are available on your campus, so that if you do run into difficulties or need the services of some office, you'll know how to find the information you need or where to go to get assistance. If you are proactive and find out a little about them before you need their services, it will

save you time in the long run. Some of these services include:

The Library In addition to providing resources, the library is a great place to study, to do research online, or to meet your study group. Most campuses have library orientations that help students learn to navigate large and complex systems. Although much of what you need from the library will be online, there will be times when you will have to use the bricks-and-mortar library, so it's a good idea to familiarize yourself with it early on.

The Learning Center The campus learning center can be an excellent source of assistance, because most offer a variety of services—from academic counseling to help with writing, studying, and mathematics.

Tutorial Services Like learning centers, most campuses offer tutorial services for a broad range of courses. Generally, tutoring is provided by undergraduate students who earn top grades in the areas that they tutor. This tutoring is usually free, but appointments are often necessary. Individual departments—particularly those in languages, mathematics, and sciences—may also offer tutoring or group reviews. Find out which departments on your campus offer such tutoring services.

Learning Disability Services These centers provide a resource for students requiring classroom accommodations because of a variety of learning disabilities. They also often provide comprehensive assessments for students. If you have been diagnosed with a learning disability or think you may have one, it is a good idea to use their services as soon as you get to campus.

Health Services Because getting sick enough to need the services of a doctor is inevitable, know where your campus health facility is and what the rules are to be able to see a medical professional. Don't wait until you feel as if you're on your deathbed. Find out where to go and what to do early on.

Counseling Center More and more students are enlisting the help of trained professionals from their campus counseling centers. If you find that you have problems that are getting in the way of your academic success, you should seek out help. Sometimes talking with a friend works. If it doesn't, find out more about the services offered through the counseling center.

Office of Diversity Many campuses house offices of ethnic and racial diversity where students can find workshops, lecturers, and even faculty mentors. The aim of these offices is to foster an understanding for and respect of cultural differences in the campus population and to promote equity for all students at the institution.

Student Center or Student Union On most campuses, the student center is the hub of the campus where you can meet friends, but most also offer a wealth of resources. Sometimes campus organizations and clubs have offices in the student center. Social event and concert tickets can be purchased there. General information about campus such as bus schedules, campus maps, and event schedules can be obtained. Often, the campus bookstore is located in or near the student center. When you don't know where else to turn, the student center is a good place to start if you need information about your campus.

Monitor Your Learning

✳ Use as in-class discussion

DIRECTIONS: Now that you have read about some of the ways that college requires you to think differently, analyze your own experiences and respond to the following questions.

✳ Suppose you had a teacher or a professor you did not like. How would you deal with the situation? What suggestions do you have for others who might be in the same predicament?

_____

_____

_____

✳ What are the advantages of going to class each day? Think about advantages for both students and professors.

_____

_____

_____

Think about a time when your motivation to learn was low. What caused you to lose motivation? What did you do to restore it? How do you know when you're losing motivation?

_____

_____

_____

_____

Eight Situations You Can Expect to Encounter Sooner or Later

Now that you have seen some of the ways in which high school and college differ, let's examine the transition from another perspective. Let's examine eight situations that most college students will **inevitably** encounter and how you might cope with or handle each situation. All of these situations will be addressed again throughout this text so you will be able to explore these ideas in greater detail.

In a perfect world, none of the following situations would occur. All students would go to class every day, distribute their study time over several days, stay on top of their reading, and make the dean's list every term. However, the world of college is an imperfect place. So, let's discuss some of the situations that you might encounter in college, some for which you might not be prepared. As you read each section, think about how you might handle the situation and what additional information might help you cope better.

1. PROFESSORS WHO TAKE ROLL

Someone may have told you that the only time you really *have* to show up for classes in college is on test days, or that if you can get the information on your own, professors don't really care whether you are in class. Although many professors don't take attendance, eventually you will run across one who does; and, in reality, most actually do want you present in class. Many professors truly believe that attending class will help you learn. We believe this as well, so even if your professor does not take roll, it's still a good idea to attend class. We will talk more about the role of professors later in this chapter.

What about for online classes? Have students share their thoughts about online courses & how often they should attend.

BEYOND THE CLASSROOM

Many returning and commuting students can feel unconnected to their college campuses. It may be because they are going to school part-time and don't spend a lot of time on campus, because they are older than many of their classmates, or because of a variety of other reasons. Yet, research has indicated that students who feel associated with their campuses tend to do better in their classes and graduate at higher rates. So, even if you are very busy and on campus only a few hours each week, get to know your campus—the facilities, the supports, the culture. You will be glad you did.

Discuss campus activities (maybe, give as an additional assignment)

2. EARLY MORNING CLASS

Most traditionally aged college students (as well as many who are of nontraditional age) are not morning people. In fact, there's even scientific evidence to indicate that the biological clocks of young people are preset to stay up late at night and to sleep late in the morning. However, the college officials who determine the times of class periods evidently are unaware of this research.

Unfortunately for most college students, a time will come when you will have to take an early morning class. If you do have that early class, try to juggle the rest of your schedule so that you can go to bed earlier than usual. Additionally, try to take one that meets only two or three days a week, thus allowing you a little more flexibility on other days. In Chapter 2, we will discuss additional ways to manage your time so you can make it to your classes.

3. A COURSE OR PROFESSOR YOU DON'T PARTICULARLY LIKE

It's perhaps sad, but true: there will be courses you don't like and professors with whom you will fail to connect. Even if you have a wide range of interests and you can get along well with almost everyone, at some point you'll probably have to make it through a rough class. You can take one of two routes when this happens:

Route A

You can think of every excuse imaginable not to do the work or go to class. You can blame your attitude on the professor or the boring material that you are expected to learn.

↓

Consequences of Route A

A poor course grade, feeling bad about yourself, and having to work doubly hard in another course to bring up your overall grade point average.

Route B

Acknowledge that you really don't care much for the course or the professor. It's one course, however, and you can make it through. Study with someone who seems to like the course. Try to motivate yourself with small rewards. Tell yourself that this is temporary and the course will soon be over.

↓

Consequences of Route B

Perhaps you will not earn an A in the class, but you will emerge with your ego and your grade point average intact.

We will talk more in Chapter 3 about the role of attitude on learning.

4. CRAMMING FOR A TEST

Imagine that you have a big test in a couple of days (or worse yet, tomorrow) and you've done very little preparing. Now it's *cram time*! Personally, we've never met a student who didn't have to cram at some time. And cramming occasionally probably isn't a horrible thing, but it shouldn't become the way you live your academic life. If you have to cram occasionally, try to use the strategies you'll learn in this book to study to your advantage. And, as soon as possible, regroup so that you don't have to cram again. We will discuss a variety of ways to prepare for exams in Chapters 10–13.

5. DIFFICULTY MAINTAINING MOTIVATION FOR ACADEMICS

Most college students experience motivation problems at some time or another. This usually doesn't last long, but for some students the decline in motivation is long enough and severe enough to interfere with their schoolwork. Other students

experience a lull in motivation in just one class, generally a class with which they may be experiencing difficulty. Still others begin the term with good intentions, yet quickly develop general motivation problems in every class. If you are having motivation problems, try setting some specific, reachable goals. Whether your lack of motivation is concentrated in one particular course, occurs at a specific period of time (such as around the midpoint of a semester), or is generalized across all your academic courses, goal setting can help you stay focused and improve your motivation to learn. We will discuss motivation in more depth in Chapter 3.

6. PERSONAL PROBLEMS AND/OR ILLNESS

No one plans on getting sick or having serious personal problems, but at some point you will likely experience both predicaments. However, there are some things you can do to salvage even a bad situation. First, as you plan your schedule for the term, build in some flexibility, just in case. If everything goes according to plan, the worst thing that can happen is that you'll have some extra time to study, work, or play. Second, as mentioned earlier, use the services that are available on your campus. Third, develop a set of reliable peers or count on family members who can be there for you in times of illness or other problems. Often, knowing that some other person can help you out makes all the difference in the world. We will talk about these issues in Chapter 5.

7. FRUSTRATION

It's a given that you will experience frustrations and stressful situations, but it's how you deal with them that makes the difference. Try not to let things build up to the point where you can't cope. As much as possible, deal with frustrations as they

Have students share what motivates them.

arise. Evaluate all the alternatives. And try not to become stressed by things you have no control over. So . . . take a walk. Go work out. Spend a few minutes venting to a friend. In time, it will work out. See Chapter 5 for more suggestions on managing stress and frustration.

8. JUGGLING TOO MANY RESPONSIBILITIES

College students tend to be busy people—going to class, studying, attending meetings, working, exercising, taking part in campus organizations, and the list goes on. Add to all of this family responsibilities, social interactions, and some good old time to play, and you can easily become over committed. Although you certainly want to get the most out of your college experience, try to think about how new responsibilities will affect you. Remember that if you are in college full time, your primary job is to be a student. If you are a part-time student, you have at least two roles to fill. Then you can ask yourself: "What other kinds of responsibilities can I take on?" Will you have so much to do a month from now that you will constantly feel stressed out and frustrated? If you can think about this in advance and learn to say "No" when you find yourself maxing out, you will be able to keep all those balls in the air and be a much happier student. We will talk in Chapter 2 about ways to manage all you have to do.

Feeling Comfortable With Your Professors

College can be intimidating at times. Sometimes it's easy to find yourself in situations where you want to initiate conversations but you are simply too scared to follow through. This uncomfortable feeling can be especially painful if you feel like the new kid on the block. One situation that seems to make many college students uneasy, particularly first-year or returning students, is approaching professors. Whether it's to ask for assistance, to clarify a reading assignment, or to discuss a grade on a paper or an exam, talking with your professor doesn't have to be threatening.

Students are often unsettled about talking with professors because they believe that the professor is the only one who determines their grade. Many students fail to acknowledge that grades are earned, not given, and therefore they see the professor as the power person in the classroom. Because they view the professor as having all of the control, they see little they can do in the way of talking to professors to influence their grades. What they don't realize is that knowing how to interact in a positive way with their professor can go a long way toward helping them *earn* a better grade. Notice that we didn't say that just because the professor knows who you are and gets the impression you are trying, he will give you a better grade. No professor that we know gives a student a grade just because the student has gotten to know him. But knowing *how* to talk with your professor can go a long way toward making a positive impression and helping you feel more relaxed with that professor—and other professors—in the future.

HOW PROFESSORS ARE RANKED?

Most professors have what are called *advanced degrees*. The degree required generally depends on the type of post-secondary institution in which an individual teaches. For example, a community college may require each of their teachers to have a master's degree, while a university might expect a doctorate degree. A person can have a doctor of philosophy degree in botany, English literature, history, or just about any other discipline you can think of. Usually it takes an individual three or more years after earning a master's degree to earn a doctorate.

When a professor is hired, she will normally begin at the *assistant professor* level. Each new assistant professor receives institutional guidelines that outline what she must do in order to get promoted to the next level, which is *associate professor*. Depending on the type of post-secondary institution, the criteria for promotion may be weighted heavily on the professor's ability to teach, but it might also be on the research she publishes, the committees she serves on, and the service projects in which she participates. It takes anywhere from four to seven years to reach the associate level.

The next rank, *full professor*, is reserved for those who are able to sustain exemplary teaching, research, and/or service records for another several years, because college teachers usually must hold the rank of associate professor at least five years before being promoted to full professor. Full professors generally have high status because they have an extended track record.

We believe that it is important for students to be familiar with this ranking system so that they can better appreciate how much work their college professors must invest in order to be promoted. Some college students believe that all professors have to do is to sit in their offices and wait for students to come and ask them questions. Nothing could be further from the truth. Certainly, most professors enjoy interacting with students and enjoy teaching, but regardless of the type of institution, they have expectations and responsibilities that extend beyond the classroom. The point here is that college professors, no matter what kind of college they teach at, are busy people.

A good opening question is How grades are assigned

Some General Tips About Interacting with Professors

"The first impression is a lasting one" holds true when interacting with professors as much as it does with other people. Recall the first time you met someone with whom you eventually became friends. What was your first impression of him or her? Chances are that you liked that person right from the beginning. You didn't become best friends overnight, but there was something about the person that made a good impression on you and made you want to get to know him or her better. Because first impressions don't change dramatically over time, it's important to make a good impression on your professor right from day one. How can you do that? Several general tips may help you out.

Sit Up Front in Class When you are up front, you are more likely to stay alert and focused on the lecture, especially if you are in a class with lots of other students. If you can't get a seat up front, at least try to sit in the professor's line of vision. If you have to sit in the back, sit in the center, not off to one side where it's more difficult to focus on the professor.

Ask Questions Professors may begin or end each class with a question-and-answer period. Some professors use the first few minutes to answer questions about the previous lecture or reading assignments. Others will take questions near the end of the lecture period. Still others will tell students to raise their hands at any time during the lecture if they have questions. And more and more professors are taking questions via e-mail. When you ask *well-thought-out questions*, you make a good impression because professors sense that you are interested and that you are keeping up with the course material. Notice that the questions should be phrased in such a way that the professor understands the clarification you need and that she doesn't need to repeat something she just said a minute ago.

Ask For Help Sooner Rather Than Later
Nothing makes a worse impression than waiting until the day before the test or, worse yet, five minutes before the test to ask a question about course material that was presented a week earlier. This is especially true if it's a rather large chunk of material that is giving you trouble. As soon as you realize that you are having trouble, make an appointment to see your professor, a tutor, or some other person designated to provide assistance.

Read the Syllabus The syllabus contains a wealth of information and should always be your first

---

NETWORKING

Professors' Web Pages

As a way of learning a little more about one of your professors, check to see if he or she has a Web page. You can begin by looking at the professor's department Web page. For example, if you want to see if your botany professor has a Web page, you could first find the Web page for the botany department. Department Web pages generally list each faculty member, with links to their individual pages. At smaller colleges, which may not be large enough to have a botany department, look for the science department instead, or perhaps life sciences. Once you have found the Web page for your professor, look to see the information that is included. For example, does your professor include a syllabus, additional information about tests and assignments, or other material that would be helpful to you in the class? Some professors even include their notes on the Web or post example test questions. After you have checked out the Web page, consider sending your professor an e-mail if you have any questions about the syllabus or course.

Ask Dr. Hill about this or create my own on Google

13

source when you have questions about grading, course pacing, or expectations. For example, if your professor hasn't discussed in class how your course grade is determined, before you ask him to explain it, check your syllabus. If it's not on there and he hasn't explained it in class, then ask. In addition, refer to your syllabus often. It's not a document that you read only at the beginning of the term. Professors often revise their syllabi over the course of the semester. If this happens in your class, you need to be sure you are following the most current version.

Know and Follow the Class Rules Most professors have pet peeves about something. For example, we don't know of any professors who are fond of cell phones ringing during class. One faculty member we know explained this very clearly to students during the first class session and reminded them of his policy during the second session. "If your phone goes off, it's mine for a week, and trust me, I will keep it for a week." During the third class session, a student's phone rang right in the middle of his lecture. Embarrassed, the student quickly silenced it, but the professor kept his word and took the phone. In addition to violating class rules, this

student did not make a good impression at all. It's important for students to know what rules are in place and to follow them. Don't be the student that the professor uses as an example of inappropriate behavior.

Talk with Your Professors via E-mail More and more professors are encouraging students to communicate with them through e-mail. In fact, some professors require students to interact with them using e-mail at several points over the term. In addition, many professors have Web pages where you can view the syllabus, download class notes, and obtain additional information about both the course and the professor.

Make an Appointment to Talk with Your Professor Sometimes students feel intimidated about talking with their professors, but it can be a positive experience if approached in the right manner. To make a good impression, be sure to arrive on time for your appointment, be able to clearly explain why you made this appointment, and, if you are there to get help, take notes on your professor's advice. If you follow these simple guidelines, you will make a good impression.

Real College

TAMARA'S TRANSITION

DIRECTIONS: *Read the following scenario and respond to the questions, based on the information you learned in this chapter.*

Tamara was so excited about going to college. She was ready for the friends, the parties, and the fun! Although her older sister warned her about some of the difficulties of getting off on the right foot, she really didn't pay much attention. Tamara's lack of attention was, in part, because she had been an excellent student in high school without ever cracking open a book, and she expected to do the same in college.

Tamara has several problems as she tries to adjust to college. First, she has an 8:00 a.m. class. Out of three classes the first week, she has only made it to one. Second, her professors seem to expect much more of her than her high school teachers did. She is already behind in her reading, especially for her 8:00 class. Third, it isn't that easy to make friends, so she really doesn't have anyone to hang out with; she feels alone and isolated. She likes her roommate and would like to get to know her better, but her roommate knows a lot of people already and she's not around much. It seems so hard to make new friends. Finally, she feels very intimidated by her English professor and knows she won't feel comfortable asking him for help. Even though it's only the end of the first week of class, she worries that she is just not cut out for college.

What can Tamara do?

1. What advice do you have for Tamara?

_____

_____

_____

2. What could she do to help herself academically? Socially?

_____

_____

_____

3. What might she do so that she doesn't feel so intimidated by her English professor?

_____

_____

_____

Add to Your Portfolio

1. Sometimes professors can seem intimidating, especially when you first begin college, but most college teachers are personable people who enjoy interacting with students. In order to get to know one of your professors a little better, make an appointment to talk with him or her. You might discuss course expectations, ask for studying pointers, or discuss your past successes or problems with similar courses. Write up a one-page summary of your conversation.

2. Listed below are the services discussed in this chapter. Complete the information for your campus services and use it as a convenient way to have access to important information.

LIBRARY

Location _____

Telephone number _____

Hours _____

LEARNING CENTER

Location _____

Telephone number _____

Hours _____

TUTORIAL SERVICES

Location _____

Telephone number _____

Hours _____

HEALTH SERVICES/COUNSELING CENTER

Location _____

Telephone number _____

Hours _____

STUDENT CENTER OR STUDENT UNION

Location _____

Telephone number _____

Hours _____

BOOKSTORE

Location _____

Telephone number _____

Hours _____

OTHER IMPORTANT SERVICES _____

(Have students list available student organizations)

_____

_____

_____

_____

Chapter 2

Getting Things Done: Organizing Yourself and Your Time

Read this chapter to answer the following questions:

- Why do I need to manage my time?
- What is self-management?
- How can I create a schedule I can live with?
- How do I plan time to study for finals?

Self-Assessment

DIRECTIONS: On a scale of 1 to 5, with 1 being "not at all effective," 3 being "somewhat effective," and 5 being "very effective," respond to each of the statements below. This evaluation should give you a good idea of your current time-management system.

	Not at all effective		Some-what effective		Very effective
	1	**2**	**3**	**4**	**5**
1. How effective is your current system for managing time?					
2. How effective is your current system for balancing your school, work, and social obligations?					
3. How effective is your ability to get things done in an organized way?					
4. How effective is your use of short periods of time (such as the time in between classes) to get things done?					
5. How effective is your use of a planner, to-do list, or other means of keeping a written account of your work?					
6. How effective is your ability to avoid procrastinating on academic work?					

Think about your scores. The more 5s you have, the more you feel comfortable with your current time-management skills. The lower your score, the more you will need to make some changes to how you manage your time.

Before reading the chapter, reflect on your responses to the self-assessment. What are you doing that is helping your time management? What do you need to work on?

_____

_____

_____

_____

_____

_____

_____

_____

Before You Begin

WORD WISE | As you read the rest of the chapter, be on the lookout for the following Word Wise vocabulary words.

1. **Formidable** (adj., p. 21) — difficult to undertake; arousing dread; inspiring awe.
*Preparing for five final exams all at once is a **formidable** challenge for college students.*

2. **Ostensibly** (adv., p. 21) — presumably; apparently but not necessarily true; it seems as such.
*Although the new law **ostensibly** appeared to help the poor, it ended up cutting many benefits.*

3. **Heuristic** (n., p. 23) — a rule of thumb, relating to a guide or technique for problem solving; an algorithm that usually, but not always, gives the correct answer.
*One **heuristic** for finding your lost keys is to think of where you last saw them.*

4. **Tangible** (adj., p. 25) — real or concrete; able to touch; possible to be treated as fact.
*The jury was convinced because the prosecution had provided **tangible** evidence of the defendant's guilt.*

DID YOU KNOW? What do you do when you are reading and you come across a word you don't know? Most likely you skip over it, and actually that is not a terrible thing. If you stopped to look up a word in the dictionary every time you found one you were unsure of, it could make your overall comprehension suffer. Instead, find your "need-to-know moments." That is, when the word you don't know enters your consciousness—you read it in a book, hear it on TV, see it on a Web page—look it up. You are more likely to remember the word's meaning when you have this need to know.

RESEARCH INTO PRACTICE

Time Management and College Success

In this study, Dr. William Kelly sought to determine if "time use efficiency" was related to college students' grade point averages. He defines time use efficiency as consisting of three components: (1) an awareness of the passage of time (and being able to use that awareness to plan); (2) an awareness of the tasks that fill time (and the ability to allot sufficient time to complete those tasks); and (3) having cognitive and behavioral ability, such as self-discipline and attention, to stay focused on completing a task. To explore this idea, Dr. Kelly compared student responses to a time use efficiency questionnaire with their grade point averages. He found that the higher the scores on the questionnaire, indicating higher time use efficiency, the higher the GPA. This study is interesting because it highlights the effects of understanding time on a student's grades. Students who keep the three components of time use efficiency in mind by planning their time, knowing how they spend their time, and developing self-discipline will do better in college.

Source: W. E. Kelly, "As Achievement Sails the River of Time: The Role of Time Use Efficiency in Grade-Point-Average," *Educational Research Quarterly* 27 (2003): 3–8.

The Basics of Self-Management

Managing yourself and your time may be one of the most difficult challenges for you as a college student. If you are a returning student who has been in the workforce for a while, or if you are raising a family or holding a full-time job while attending college, you will face new challenges in juggling your many responsibilities. For example, you may take all of your courses at night or on the weekends. You may also find that you need to refocus your priorities to account for all of the work involved in college life. All of this poses a **formidable** challenge for most college students.

If you are a recent high school graduate, you are probably used to having most of your time managed for you. Your teachers and parents were responsible for setting a good deal of your daily schedule—you were in classes most of the day, and after school you probably had some family obligations that were planned for you, or perhaps you had a part-time job. But in college, you are in class for fewer hours each day, which leaves you with big blocks of time to manage, and you have the added responsibility of being in charge of managing yourself as well. You need to get to class on time, set your priorities, and plan your days.

For most students, this freedom is thrilling. You have a new social life, may live in a new town or state, and are experiencing new opportunities each day. However, some students become overwhelmed by the abundance of freedom they have and end up not managing themselves or their time at all. The trick is to start out with a plan and not have to scramble to make up for lost time. This chapter will present ways to create a plan that will help you maximize your time so you can get everything done without falling behind. Before reading the rest of the chapter be sure you have read the "Research into Practice" section, which discusses the relationship between time management and college grades.

Before you can manage your time effectively, you have to be able to manage yourself. One aspect of self-management is being able to organize and keep track of all the things that you have to do. College life is very hectic; you have class assignments, roommates to deal with, tests to prepare for. You may also have a full-or part-time job or daily family obligations. The secret to getting organized is to create a balance among school, home, work, and social life. Sometimes people who give advice about time management seem to forget that an important part of the college experience is social. In the past, you may have been taught about time management with an approach that suggested giving up your social life to focus only on studying. However, this is not our viewpoint. We believe that you should also have fun in college. We want you to be able to hang out with your friends, but we also want you to be able to get the work done for your classes so that you can be academically successful and *stay* in college.

The following four principles will help you create a balance between all the things you have to do and all the things you want to do.

1. TREAT COLLEGE LIKE A FULL-TIME JOB

If you are a full-time student, academic work should take up about 40 hours each week. So, for the next several years, college is **ostensibly** your full-time job. You might be in class only 15 hours per week, but the other 25 hours should be spent studying and preparing for class. If you break it down, you will see that it is not so bad. Each day, you will spend three to four hours in class and four to five hours reading, studying, and preparing for your assignments. The rest of the time is left for social activities and your part-time job (if you have one). If you already have a full-time job, you are most likely familiar with the pressures of a 40-hour workweek. But if you are going to college full-time and working full-time, you are essentially looking at an 80-hour workweek. You might want to consider taking a reduced course load or planning most of your studying for evenings and weekends in order to accomplish everything.

The good news is that, unlike a full-time job, in college you have more control over when you want to schedule your classes and your study time. No one says that your studying must take place between 9:00 and 5:00 Monday through Friday; you are free to study whenever you want—early in the morning, late at night, or on weekends.

2. SCHEDULE YOUR CLASSES FOR YOUR MOST ALERT TIMES

Think about when you are at your mental peak. Are you a morning person? A late-afternoon person? An evening person? Are you up with the sun or lucky to be awake by noon? If you know you will never make it to an 8:00 a.m. class, avoid scheduling a class for that time, if possible. Likewise, if you are totally useless in the afternoon, try to schedule your courses so that they are over before lunchtime.

Many students don't consider class times as an issue to think about when making their course schedules, but when you have the luxury of creating your own schedule, you should try to tailor it to your alert times. But sometimes classes fill up so quickly that you may be able to register only for classes that meet during your least attentive times. If that is the case, try to schedule a course that you think you will really like for your least alert time, because you will be more likely to stay attentive and awake during the class if you find it interesting.

You should also plan to study during your alert times and take breaks if you find you are losing concentration. This topic will be discussed further in the next section.

3. GO TO CLASS

Although many professors don't take attendance in their courses, most still believe that going to class is a very important part of learning. Research shows that students who go to class do better in college. You wouldn't skip your full-time job just because you were up too late or because there was a good afternoon movie on cable. College is your full-time job for the next few years; the same rules apply.

Students who skip a lot of classes miss out on the important information that they can get only from going to class. Suppose a professor assigned a paper that was mentioned only in class. You would be responsible for turning in the paper, but the only way you would know that would be if you were in class. Also, as an added bonus, by going to class each day, you know what the professor emphasized, which will help you know what to focus on when you study. So do yourself a favor and go to class everyday.

4. DON'T PROCRASTINATE

Procrastination is intentionally putting off work that should be done. This problem may actually be the toughest part of self-management for some students. Because you are in control of your own time, it is tempting to put off work until later. The trouble is that you can quickly become overwhelmed by the amount of work you need to do when you continually neglect your work. Almost everyone has a friend who has procrastinated until the last minute and must read an entire novel and write a five-page English paper all in one night—a virtual impossibility. Procrastination tends to become a bad habit and a way of life for some students. Sometimes students tell us that they work best under pressure, that they have to have a clean room before they can get work done, that they like the challenge or thrill of doing school-related tasks at the last minute. However, these students also often complain about feeling stressed out or find that their grades are suffering. Such students may find that it is difficult to get back on track. The strategies in the next section should help you stay on top of things.

Reality Check

Figuring Out Your Reading Load
Many students do not realize just how much reading is assigned for them each week. To figure out your current reading load, you will need your syllabus, your texts, and your class notes. For this week, figure out how many pages were assigned for each class (if your syllabus just says "read Chapter 5," you will need to consult the textbook to see how many pages Chapter 5 contains) and add it all up. Chances are it is a lot more than you might imagine. Time yourself on each of your textbooks to find out how many pages you can typically read in 10 minutes. This will help you estimate how long it will take you to complete your reading.

The AT Heuristic of Time Management

Most students believe they could use some improvement in the area of time management. When thinking about time management, it is helpful to use the AT **heuristic** to determine two important pieces of information: 1. What do I need to **accomplish**? (A) 2. How can I keep **track** of what I need to do? (T)

THE *A*–FIGURE OUT WHAT YOU NEED TO ACCOMPLISH

The first step in managing your time is figuring out what you need to do. How many classes do you have to attend? What is your work schedule? How many social commitments and family obligations do you have? What assignments do you have to finish this week? This month? This term? How long will it take to complete everything? One of the most difficult time-management challenges is figuring out how much time an assignment will take. For example, when writing a paper, you have to know if it will take you one hour or several trips to find what you need in the library. Can you do most of your research using online resources? Will you be able to write your paper in two days or will you need a full week? Some of the ability to know how long things will take comes with experience, but the following general rule may help you plan your time:

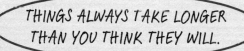

THINGS ALWAYS TAKE LONGER THAN YOU THINK THEY WILL.

Given this basic rule, try to plan more time than you think you will need in most situations. If you rush to get an assignment completed—whether it is studying for an exam, writing a paper, or finishing a lab—you will probably get frustrated or angry when things take longer than planned. You may even give up without completing the assignment. It is much better to be left with some extra time than to be rushing to get an assignment completed at the last minute.

THE *T*–HAVE A TRACKING SYSTEM

The second part of effective time management is creating some kind of system for keeping track of what you have to do. Most people who manage their time successfully say that they can't live without their schedule book or daily planner. You can use a traditional paper calendar or an online calendar. You can even use the calendar feature on your cell phone. Just be sure that whatever method you use suits your needs. Use your planner to keep track of appointments, assignments, social commitments, and even important phone numbers. Carry your planner with you to class so you can be sure to mark down any changes to your assignments. By writing down when things are due, you will be better able to keep track of all of the things you need to accomplish each day. But writing it down is only half the battle—you have to make a habit of consulting your planner every day to see what you need to do.

Keeping a schedule book is a good start to managing your time. But to be really effective, you also need to schedule in exactly when you will study for your classes. You might think of it as making an appointment with yourself to study. It's similar to making an appointment to get your hair cut or go to the dentist. You schedule those appointments and know in advance that the time is taken. Scheduling specific appointments or times to study is no different. So plan your study sessions along with the rest of your responsibilities—and keep those appointments. Some students are able to keep an hour-by-hour schedule in their schedule books, but many prefer to keep a separate daily or weekly study schedule. In the rest of this chapter, we will discuss ways to keep a weekly schedule and follow it.

Creating a Personalized Schedule

Creating a schedule that works is a challenge. Many students start out with good intentions but ultimately end up with an unworkable schedule for a number of reasons. Some students create a schedule that is so rigid that they don't have the flexibility they need; others create a schedule that is not detailed enough to be useful. Still others create a good schedule but don't consult it daily and so forget what they need to do. To avoid falling into one of the time-management pitfalls, consider the following tips as you create your own schedule.

PLAN TO STUDY WHEN YOU ARE MOST ALERT

If you find that you are very tired or you are having trouble concentrating as soon as you sit down to study, you probably are not studying at your most alert time. Some students use caffeine to help them concentrate and stay awake when studying. Although a cup of coffee or tea or a glass of soda may give you a temporary burst of energy, too much caffeine can actually lower your ability to concentrate. Instead of relying on caffeine to keep you awake, find blocks of time that are naturally best for you. Try out several times of the day and night to find out when you are the most ready to study. Try times that you might not initially think are your best times of day—you just may surprise yourself and be a morning (or night) person after all.

SPEND SOME TIME EVERY DAY ON EACH COURSE YOU ARE TAKING

Even when you don't have an assignment due, plan some time each day to read the text, review your notes, and prepare for the next class. If you are taking classes such as math or chemistry that require problem solving, it is a good idea to work some problems each day. If you are taking a language class, plan to review new vocabulary or work on verb conjugation every day. By spending some time every day, you should not have to cram for exams because you will always be caught up.

BE SPECIFIC

The more specific you can be when planning your study schedule, the better, because you will know exactly what you need to do each time you study. Just as you would not just write "appointment" on the calendar when you have a doctor's appointment, when you create your schedule, don't just write down "study." It is much more effective to write "Read psychology text, pgs. 219–230." By creating a schedule that lists specific tasks, you are more likely to accomplish all of your assignments in a timely fashion.

NETWORKING

Wasting Time Online

It is becoming more and more common for students to spend hours online each day. Some students go online to "warm up" for studying. However, this is usually a recipe for procrastination. They may be chatting with friends, checking Facebook or IMs again and again, or simply going to favorite Web sites. Although these are fine activities, they can get in the way of getting things done. One suggestion is to use computer time as a reward—don't go online until *after* you have kept all of your studying appointments.

MAKE A READING SCHEDULE FOR EACH CLASS

One of the simplest, yet most effective, ways to manage your time and to stay on top of your reading assignments is to make a reading schedule for each class. To make a reading schedule, simply add up the number of pages you need to read in the next week (some students prefer to add the pages in between each exam rather than weekly) and divide that number by five (or six or seven if you will read during the weekend). For example, Samuel has the following reading assignments this week:

Political Science	Read Chapters 2–3	65 pages
Precalculus	Read Chapter 5 Complete 15 practice problems	27 pages
Sociology	Read Chapter 4	39 pages
Literature	Read 6 chapters of novel	90 pages
Biology	Read Chapters 8 and 11	29 pages

Figure 2.1: Example of a Reading Schedule No change to text

This equals 250 pages of text reading, which, according to surveys of various four-year colleges, is about average. If Samuel falls behind on his reading this week and he has another 250 pages of reading next week, you can see how the work would snowball quickly. Thinking about reading 250 pages is overwhelming, but when he divides the reading over five days, he sees that he has only 13 pages of political science, 6 pages of pre-calc (and 3 practice problems), 8 pages of sociology, 18 pages of literature, and 6 pages of biology to read each day. And that sounds a lot more manageable. If he spreads it out over six or seven days, his daily reading load is cut even more.

To create your own reading schedule, survey the reading assignments (usually found on your syllabus) and divide up the reading in a way that makes sense. Write it down in your planner or to-do list to make it seem more **tangible**. Use section breaks or headings to help you determine how to divide the readings so that you are not stopping in the middle of a concept.

PRIORITIZE

When you make your schedule, it is helpful to prioritize what you have to do. You might want to label your assignments as "high," "medium," or "low" priority. For example, reading your biology text before the lab might be a high priority, but starting on your history research paper that is due in three weeks might be a lower priority. In general, start with high-priority tasks so that you are sure to get them done. But don't ignore the medium and low priorities. That history research paper may be low priority now, but if nothing gets done in the next three weeks, it will quickly become high priority.

MAKE TO-DO LISTS

Sometimes when students begin to study, they start to think about all the other things they need to do—call home, get a haircut, cancel a dental appointment. All of these thoughts are distracting. To keep yourself on track and to avoid procrastination, make to-do lists and keep them in your planner. Write down all the things you think of, including course work, household chores (such as laundry, phone calls, e-mails to answer), and so forth. Check items off as you complete them. Your to-do list might look something like the list on the next page.

KEEP EVERYTHING IN ONE PLACE

Sometimes students keep separate calendars for school, family, and social events. They may write deadlines on scraps of paper, notebook covers, or even the palms of their hands. Because they have so many places to consult, they may schedule two things for the same time. They may also let things fall through the cracks if they forget to check every scrap of paper. It is much more effective to use one planner or calendar book for everything you need to do. Your to-do list might look something like the list in Figure 2.2 on the next page.

Date: Oct 2 What do I need to do?	Priority (high, medium, low)	Completed? (yes, no)
1. Finish revising English paper	high	yes
2. Doctor's appointment @ 1:45	high	yes
3. Read Math pp. 81–97 and do the problems	medium	yes
4. Call home	medium	no
5. Plan spring break trip	low	no
6. Think about topic for final history paper	low	not completely

Figure 2.2: Example of a To-Do List

BORROW TIME—DON'T STEAL IT

If you decide to go out for a pizza instead of spending an hour reading your psychology chapter, it's no problem—as long as you don't steal that time. If you decide to go out instead of following your schedule, be sure to add the activity you missed (that is, reading your psychology chapter) to your schedule (or to-do list) for the next day so that you can make up that time. In other words, if you cancel your studying appointment, you have to make another one. By having a schedule that is very specific, you'll know exactly what you have to do to catch up and make up for the lost time.

USE THE TIME BETWEEN YOUR CLASSES

Many times, students don't know where all of their time goes—an hour between classes, two hours between school and work, 15 minutes before classes begin. All of this time adds up and it is useful for getting your work done. You could read for one of your classes during hour breaks, review your notes while you are waiting for class to begin, use the time between lunch and class to review, or even study with a partner in the laundromat. Plan to use your short periods of time when making your schedule so this time does not get "lost."

SCHEDULE BREAKS IN YOUR STUDYING

If you plan to study for more than an hour at a time, schedule a 10-minute break for each hour of study. You should also plan short breaks when switching from one topic to another to give yourself time to refocus. But be careful that your short breaks don't turn into long breaks. Some students find it helpful to set a timer to keep themselves on track.

BUILD SOME FLEXIBILITY INTO YOUR SCHEDULE

Don't have your schedule so tightly planned that if an issue comes up you go into meltdown. Everyone gets sick, has car problems, or experiences personal or family troubles they must deal with. If your schedule lacks flex time, you will have difficulty managing unanticipated problems. No matter how many hours you work or how many other responsibilities you have, you should keep this in mind as you build your schedule.

TAKE SOME TIME OFF

Many students feel guilty when they take time off because they are always thinking about the things they "should be doing." But when you have an effective schedule, you will be able to reward yourself by taking time off without guilt, knowing that you have planned time to get all of your assignments completed. Then, after you have completed your work, relax and enjoy yourself. You deserve it. In fact, we suggest that you plan some free time when creating your schedule.

DON'T SPIN YOUR WHEELS

Seek help from a tutor, a professor, or a friend if you are having problems with a course you can't seem to get a handle on. There is nothing that gets in the way of managing your time more than wasting it! In addition, if you find that your schedule is not working for you, do a reality check. Evaluate why your schedule isn't working. It may be that you simply need to shift some things around, or it could be that your schedule needs a compete overhaul. It's important to stay on track so that you don't fall behind.

BEYOND THE CLASSROOM

If you are a returning student or a student who works more than 25 hours a week, using the time between classes is absolutely essential. For example, if you have an hour between two of your classes, you can review your lecture notes, go online and do research for a paper, meet with a study group, or prepare for your chemistry lab. If you learn to use this time effectively, you will find that you can get a lot done in a short amount of time and perhaps also have a bit more free time.

Planning for Midterms and Finals

Every principle of time- and self-management discussed in this chapter usually goes into warp speed when you are preparing for midterms and finals. Generally, you will need to rethink your entire schedule to cope with the added pressures of preparing for midterms and finals. During these periods, you might even need to put in a few hours of overtime on your 40-hour workweek, but don't despair. By following the techniques outlined in this chapter, you should get through it without going crazy. In addition to the strategies discussed in this chapter, we add the following important points to help you cope with exam crunch time:

IT'S IMPORTANT TO PLAN AHEAD

Cut down on work and other commitments. If you work part-time, ask for some time off or for fewer hours at your job, and make sure that your friends and family understand that you will be extra busy. In addition, start to rehearse and review your notes and the texts before exam week so that you can cut down on your workload for the week. If you work full-time, begin even earlier. Starting early is especially important for classes in which you have cumulative exams that hold you responsible for everything you have covered through the midpoint or the entire term because there is so much information to review.

IT'S IMPORTANT TO GET ENOUGH SLEEP

Cramming all night for a big exam rarely pays off. Instead, try to create your schedule for exam week in a way that leaves you adequate sleep time. You won't do well on an exam if you are falling asleep while taking it.

IT'S IMPORTANT TO MAINTAIN MOTIVATION

We have seen many students lose their motivation at midterms and finals because they feel overwhelmed by all that they have to do. If you start to feel swamped, it might help to remind yourself that midterms and finals happen only once each semester. Tell yourself that you can get through it, and plan a nice reward to look forward to once you have completed your exam week.

IT'S IMPORTANT TO STUDY WITH OTHERS

Misery loves company and this is never truer than during midterms and finals. By the time midterms roll around you probably will have found a study group that works. Study with your group or study partner to keep each other on schedule and motivated to work.

IT'S IMPORTANT NOT TO PANIC

Midterms and finals are really just exams. The world will not stop and does not end because of midterms and finals. But if you find that the pressure is getting to be too much, readjust your schedule to allow more break time and try to really relax during those breaks. If you find that you have excessive anxiety, get some help before it becomes a stumbling block to doing well.

In this chapter, you have learned some tips for managing yourself and your time. Try to make a schedule and follow it strictly for one week. Then make adjustments to suit your needs. Even if you do not consider yourself a "schedule person," you should find that knowing what you need to accomplish and keeping track of what you need to do really helps you organize and take control of your college career.

What time of day do you find that you get the most work accomplished?

_____

_____

_____

_____

What is working well in your current studying schedule?

_____

_____

_____

_____

What adjustments do you need to make to your current schedule?

_____

_____

_____

_____

Real College

STEPHANIE'S SCHEDULE

DIRECTIONS: *Read the following scenario and apply what you have learned about time management to help Stephanie organize her time.* Stephanie is a first-year student at a small local college. She is taking five classes, which she thought would be interesting, but she did not expect so much work. She is reading five novels in her literature class, at least one chapter a week in chemistry, one long history chapter every other week, and one short but difficult chapter of accounting each week. Her sociology class does not have a textbook. Instead, she has to rely on her instructor's lectures, which often seem to ramble. Her reading assignments each week are more than she had in a month in high school. She is having trouble keeping up and often goes to class feeling unprepared.

In addition, she is working 20 hours a week at a local restaurant, which is taking a lot of her time, but she needs the money and really can't consider quitting. Luckily, her hours are pretty flexible and she can work mostly on weekends.

Another reason that she is falling behind is that her old high school friends are always stopping by. Many of them are not going to college and think she should be able to hang out as much as she used to. She knows she should be getting more work done but has a hard time saying no.

What can Stephanie do?

Using the strategies you've learned about time- and self-management, what advice would you give Stephanie to help her manage herself and her time?

_____

_____

_____

_____

_____

_____

_____

_____

_____

Help Stephanie create a plan to stay organized. Consider all of her obligations, including class time, work, and other commitments.

	Monday	Tuesday	Wednesday	Thursday	Friday	Saturday	Sunday
7 a.m.		Account. 140		Account. 140			
8 a.m.							
9 a.m.							
10 a.m.	Chem. 120		Chem. 120		Chem. 120		
11 a.m.	Soc. 130	Hist. 100	Soc. 130	Hist. 100	Soc. 130		
12 p.m.							
1 p.m.	Amer. Lit 160		Amer. Lit 160		Amer. Lit 160		
2 p.m.							
3 p.m							
4 p.m.						Work	Work
5 p.m.	Chem. 120 Lab				Work	Work	Work
6 p.m.					Work	Work	Work
7 p.m.					Work	Work	Work
8 p.m.					Work	Work	Work
9 p.m.					Work	Work	Work
10 p.m.					Work	Work	Work
11 p.m.							
12 a.m.							
1 a.m.							

Add to Your Portfolio

Consider the recommendations and tips discussed in this chapter as you create a schedule for the upcoming week. Use either your planner or the chart on the following page. Before filling in the schedule, take a minute to jot down what you need to accomplish this week. For example, what course assignments do you have to complete? What personal goals do you want to work on? Then use this information to help you track your schedule.

Fill in the schedule in the following order and then evaluate it using the questions below.
1. Enter your class and lab times.
2. If you commute, enter the time it takes to travel to and from campus.
3. Enter your work schedule.
4. Enter your meal times.
5. Enter all of your weekly personal activities (clubs, athletics, exercise).

6. Schedule your study times for each class. Include time for the following:
   • Reviewing your notes
   • Reading the text
   • Preparing for exams, writing papers, working on projects, etc.
7. Schedule 10-minute study breaks if you plan to study for longer than one hour.
8. Keep some time open to allow for flexibility in your schedule.
9. Add any other things that you have to do this week.

EVALUATING YOUR SCHEDULE

1. How many hours per week are scheduled for study time?

_____

_____

2. How many hours per week are scheduled for social obligations?

_____

_____

3. Is your schedule too tightly packed? Did you leave room to be flexible?

_____

_____

4. Is your schedule too free? Is there a lot of time when you do not have anything scheduled? If so, that time will most likely be wasted.

_____

_____

	Monday	Tuesday	Wednesday	Thursday	Friday	Saturday	Sunday
7 a.m.							
8 a.m.							
9 a.m.							
10 a.m.							
11 a.m.							
12 p.m.							
1 p.m.							
2 p.m.							
3 p.m.							
4 p.m.							
5 p.m.							
6 p.m.							
7 p.m.							
8 p.m.							
9 p.m.							
10 p.m.							
11 p.m.							
12 a.m.							
1 a.m.							

Now, create a to-do list of what you would like to accomplish today.

Date _Oct 23_	What do I need to do?	Priority (high, medium, low)	Completed? (yes, no)
1.			
2.			
3.			
4.			
5.			
6.			

Chapter 3
Learning About Your Motivation, Attitudes, and Interests

Read this chapter to answer the following questions:

- What motivates people to learn?

- How do you get and stay motivated?

- How do attitudes and interests influence learning?

- How can you maintain a positive attitude?

- How can you develop interest, even for topics you dislike?

Self-Assessment

DIRECTIONS: On a scale of 1 to 5, with 1 being "not at all true of me," 3 being "somewhat true of me," and 5 being "very true of me," respond to the following statements as honestly as you can. This assessment should give you a good idea of your motivation, attitudes, and interests.

	Not at all true of me		Some-what true of me		Very true of me
	1	2	3	4	5
1. I feel motivated for college learning.					X
2. I am more motivated to succeed in college than most of my peers.				X	
3. I set and reach reasonable goals.				X	
4. I am aware when I have reached my goals.				X	
5. I have a positive attitude about attending college.				X	
6. I have a positive attitude about most of the courses I am taking this term.				X	
7. I tend to have a wide range of interests.					X
8. I can motivate myself even in courses I find uninteresting.					X
9. I know why I am attending college.					X
10. I am motivated to learn in all courses, not only in those I find interesting.				X	

If you scored mostly 5s, you probably have a positive attitude and are motivated for college learning. If, on the other hand, you scored mostly 1s, you may want to pay careful attention to the strategies discussed in this chapter.

Before reading the chapter, reflect on your responses to the self-assessment. What are you doing that is helping your motivation to learn? What do you need to work on?

to stay motivated to stay wanting to succeed in life
to keep my eye on the ball
stay focused.

WORD WISE As you read the rest of the chapter, be on the lookout for the following Word Wise vocabulary words.

Research shows that the vast majority of words are learned from context. To improve your context skills pay close attention to how words are used. Doing a search on a word using Google.com groups (for searching newsgroups) will give you many examples of how that word is used in context.

1. **Optimal** (adj., pg. 38) — most favorable or desirable.
*Doctors recommend exercising three times a week for at least 30 minutes for **optimal** health benefits.*

2. **Squander** (v., pg. 47) — to waste; to fail to take advantage of; to lose a chance for.
*He **squandered** his chances to get the job by failing to fill in the application completely.*

3. **Propensity** (n., pg. 49) — an inclination do to something; a disposition to behave in a certain way.
*Her **propensity** to oversleep and miss her morning classes was directly related to her tendency to staying up late.*

DID YOU KNOW? Why should one increase his or her vocabulary? Some would argue that the more words you know, the more fully you experience the world. It might be because when people have a richer vocabulary to describe or interpret events, they have an enhanced perception of them. Or perhaps it might be because people's ability to express themselves is limited by their knowledge of words. In either case, having a larger vocabulary is an asset in college where one of your primary goals is to able to express your ideas both in writing and in speech.

RESEARCH INTO PRACTICE

Motivation and Procrastination

In this study, the researchers explored the impact of intrinsic and extrinsic motivation toward academic work on procrastination in college students. They chose this area of research because they noted that procrastination is common in college students even though that behavior leads to lower grades and increased stress and anxiety. Procrastination is a persistent delay of the start or completion of a task and for many students it becomes a chronic habit. One reason may be that procrastinators have trouble setting appropriate goals for themselves and they often find they run out of time for any given academic task. Most procrastinators fall into one of three categories: (1) procrastination because of a fear of failure, (2) procrastination because of unnecessary perfectionism, and (3) procrastination because of a desire to avoid tasks that are perceived as difficult.

The researchers found that students who do not procrastinate are motivated by both intrinsic and extrinsic forces. This means that students are motivated both by an internal drive or interest and by external factors such as grades, money, or extra credit. Students who procrastinate tend to be motivated by extrinsic forces and attribute their successes to external forces (such as luck or a good professor). This indicates that they do not believe that they are responsible for their achievements; such beliefs can lead to a loss of motivation for academic work. These findings are important because they show that students who lack intrinsic motivation for learning are more prone to procrastinate on their academic work.

Source: S. Brownlow and R.D. Reasinger, "Putting Off Until Tomorrow What Is Better Done Today: Academic Procrastination as a Function of Motivation Toward College Work," *Journal of Social Behaviour and Personality* 15 (2000): 15–34.

What Is Motivation?

You may have already noticed that motivation, attitudes, and interests are tied together. It just makes sense that you will be more motivated to learn in courses that seem relevant or that interest you. Let's separate these three important factors to define what they are and how they interact to promote active learning and success in college. We'll begin with motivation.

In college, you have probably noticed that the term *motivation* is used in many different ways.

"I really have to motivate myself to learn history."

"Professor Jones is a lot more motivating than Professor Smith."

"I am very motivated to make good grades this year."

"I am more motivated to learn chemistry than literature."

"I am always more motivated at the beginning of the term."

"I am much less motivated to study on nice days."

These statements seem to say that motivation is something that drives you from within, something encouraged by a professor, something that depends on what you are learning, and something that depends on the time of year or the weather. How can the same word have so many meanings? Part of the reason is that people use the word *motivation* to stand for many different things, and that may be because motivation, like learning, is complex. In addition, the term *motivation* is often a catch-all term that is used to describe a student's ability to stick with it . . . or not. Parents, in particular, are apt to account for their student's success this way: "Bill is highly motivated to go to law school, so he does well in his undergraduate studies. He's very focused." Likewise, parents may also blame their student's lack of success on motivation: "Jenny is very bright, but because she doesn't know what kind of career she wants to purse, she's not motivated academically at all." In both instances, motivation is used as a sweeping term to describe a complexity of actions.

Think about any class that you are currently taking. Even during a one-hour class period, you may have several changes in motivation. As the class begins, you may be motivated to take good notes, to listen attentively, and to make good grades. But as the hour wears on, you might start looking at the clock and thinking about your next class or what to have for lunch. Then the instructor might say something that piques your interest, which motivates you once again. Your motivation is always changing, depending on the situation. When you move on to your next class, one you dislike, you may be motivated enough to go to class, but you take minimal notes, procrastinate on keeping up, daydream when you should be listening, and avoid reading the text. But you love your third class of the day, even though it's your most difficult. It's the first thing you study, you pay attention and ask good questions, and your're always on top of the material. Why can't you be that motivated in all of your classes? That's what makes the concept of motivation so complex. It involves much more than simple wanting or not wanting to do something.

However, even though motivation may mean different things to different people, in general, students who are motivated are more successful in college. They approach each course with a positive attitude and are in college for more than just grades—they are there to learn. Think of motivation to do well academically as "academic energy"; the more energy you have, the more successful you will be. Just as some people are highly motivated to lose weight, to quit smoking, to get fit, or to run a marathon, students must be highly motivated to learn—to have an abundance of academic energy. The remainder of this chapter discusses what motivation is, how to get motivated, and ways to stay motivated. Be sure you have read the "Research into Practice" section on motivation and procrastination before proceeding.

What Influences Motivation?

Motivation is a combination of several factors including choice, desire for learning, value of learning, and personal control. Motivation is influenced primarily by the following four factors:

1. THE AMOUNT OF CHOICE ABOUT WHAT YOU ARE LEARNING

Sometimes your professors will offer several projects to choose from, or sometimes they will even ask you to choose the topics that will be covered. Choices like these will help to increase your motivation. However, even if you are not given choices about the class content, college offers you many choices about what you will learn. You choose your major and, to a certain extent, you choose the courses you will take and your course schedule.

2. YOUR DESIRE TO LEARN

It's likely that, because you are currently enrolled in college, you do want to learn, but sometimes you might be required to take courses that you are not particularly interested in. For example, most colleges have core requirements for all students, which means that regardless of their major, students must take courses in humanities, mathematics, and the sciences. As you probably have already noticed, the more you want to learn in a particular course, the more motivated you will be. It is a good idea to balance your course schedule by taking courses you feel motivated about along with courses that you don't feel especially motivated to take.

3. HOW MUCH YOU VALUE THE SUBJECT TO BE LEARNED

As a general rule, the more you believe the subject to be worthwhile, the easier it will be to become motivated. For example, many colleges require students to take at least one foreign language course. If you believe that it is valuable to learn another language, you will feel motivated—perhaps even enough to take a second course. However, if you do not, you may have a harder time motivating yourself to learn in your language course.

4. THE LEVEL OF CHALLENGE

As you may know, challenge plays a role in your motivation to learn. Most people find that they are motivated when the task is at the **optimal** level of challenge—not too difficult and not too easy—because they experience a personal level of accomplishment. When the task is too difficult, people are not motivated because they do not believe they can complete the task; when it is too easy, people become unmotivated because they may not value the achievement as much as that of a challenging task. Think about the classes you have liked the best. Chances are they were the more challenging courses.

   In an ideal setting, you would have all of the components of motivation. However, you can learn successfully without choice, desire, challenge, and value; but such learning will take more conscious effort on your part.

Think about a time when you were motivated to learn. It can be an event that happened in school or in your personal life. Jot down as much detail as you can about the experience.

_____

_____

_____

_____

_____

_____

_____

_____

Compare your response to the four components of motivation: choice, desire, challenge, and value. How many were present in your own experience? What does this say about what motivates you?

_____

_____

_____

_____

_____

_____

_____

_____

_____

_____

What Motivates People?

You may not realize it, but you are always motivated. No matter where you are or what you are doing, *you are always motivated to do something,* even if it's just sleeping. Focusing your motivation on learning, however, may sometimes be challenging.

It's important to understand that you are responsible for your own motivation, even in courses that you don't like. The current thinking on motivation can be summed up by saying that motivation is not something that is done *to* you; in other words, no one can motivate you but you. Others can provide stimuli, explaining, for example, the reasons why it is important to learn biology even though you plan to major in literature; but in the end, the motivation must come from you. Thus, although an interesting instructor makes it easier for you to stay motivated, no one can directly motivate you to learn. But given that you are always motivated to do something and that you are primarily responsible for your motivation, there are some differences between students who are motivated to learn and students who are not.

You may have heard the terms *intrinsic* and *extrinsic*, especially as they relate to motivation. Intrinsic motivation occurs when the activity is its own reward. For example, some people read for the sheer enjoyment, others like to calculate numbers for the pleasure of it, and still others like to conduct experiments for the thrill of discovery. Think of intrinsic motivation as doing something you choose to do for the pleasure, challenge, or simply because it interests you.

Extrinsic motivation, on the other hand, occurs when your incentive is a reward, such as grades or praise or even money. Did your parents ever pay you for good grades on your report card? Money can be a very strong extrinsic motivator, as can automobiles, new clothes, or spring break trips. You can think of extrinsic motivation as trying to "get it done" for some external reward rather than for the sake of learning. For example, you may be doing poorly in organic chemistry, but when the professor offers an extra credit assignment, you decide to do it even though you are not motivated to learn in the course. In this case, you are extrinsically motivated to earn extra credit points that can boost your course grade rather than by learning organic chemistry for its own rewards.

In general, most people accomplish more when intrinsic motivation is present, even though extrinsic rewards may initially seem more appealing. Thus, the more you are intrinsically motivated to learn, the easier learning will be for you. The key to becoming intrinsically motivated, even in classes you don't particularly like, is to find something about the course that you find motivating and try to focus on the positives rather than the negatives. It also helps to focus more on understanding the concepts to be learned rather than solely on grades.

NETWORKING

Finding Motivation

Many sites on the Internet feature tips for getting and staying motivated. Some good sources include college counseling centers or freshman-year experience sites. Try the following keywords to find at least three motivation sites: *motivation, college motivation, student motivation, or learning motivation.* What kind of information did you find that will help you become more motivated or to maintain your motivation? And how do the different Web sites compare?

Getting Motivated Through ~~Goal~~ Setting

Reality Check

Is Your Sleep Cycle Off-Kilter?

Some students tell us that their motivation is low because they have gotten their sleep cycle out of whack. These students nap for several hours each afternoon and then stay up until the wee hours of the morning. Then they sleep fairly late in the morning (or for some, mid afternoon). This cycle of sleeping during the day and then staying up most of the night leads them to miss many classes and to feel somewhat unconnected from the topics they are supposed to be learning. If you find yourself in this situation, you will need to give up that long daytime nap to get your awake/asleep cycles back on track. You may be tired for a day or two as your body readjusts, but you should find a vast improvement in your motivation for learning.

of exercising more and getting ~~in~~ shape is a good resolution to make, it is unrealistic to expect to be in great shape right away if you have not been exercising regularly. Individuals who do not set short-term goals on their way to reaching long-term goals soon find that their resolutions are not easily achievable and give up on reaching their goals.

In addition, the goals you set should be conscious and deliberate. A goal is more than a to-do list. Doing your laundry or completing your science lab tonight is a to-do list item; keeping up with your assignments by doing at least 30 minutes for each class each night is a goal. You should set and have a plan to meet your goals only after you have given them some deliberate thought. Another reason why New Year's resolutions are easily forgotten is that they are generally made with little thought. Most of the time,

we make resolutions in the middle of a party on New Year's Eve when someone says, "So what's your New Year's resolution?" We may respond with the first thing that comes into our mind, which provides very little incentive to follow through.

In order to set goals that can be achieved, your goals should be:

REALISTIC

Can the goal be achieved? If not, how can the goal be divided into smaller goals? You should try to have short-term, intermediate, and long-term academic goals. A short-term goal is one that you will achieve within the next few days, such as "I will work five statistics problems each night for the next week." Intermediate goals are ones that you will achieve within the next few weeks or months, for example, "I will compare my notes to the text material each night to prepare for my cumulative psychology exam, which will be at the end of the semester." A long-term goal is one that will take longer still—perhaps a few months or even years to achieve—such as "I will begin to learn Spanish this year by taking a summer intensive course." An even longer-term goal is, "I want to graduate with a degree in marketing." Most people make the mistake of setting only intermediate and long-term goals, but short-term goals are also important because they help you follow the progress you are making and help you stay on track. If you don't accomplish your short-term goals, you probably won't accomplish your long-term goals. In addition, it's important to think about how realistic your goal is, based on the time frame you have given yourself to achieve it.

BELIEVABLE

Do you believe that you will be able to achieve your goal? Being confident about your ability to learn is crucial to your motivation. If you think that a task is too difficult for you to achieve, your motivation will decrease and you might give up before you even try. Some students believe that they can succeed only in certain disciplines. Students will say, "I'm good at math, but I'm terrible at English" or "I can learn history, but not science." These statements tell us that the students are motivated to learn one topic but not another. If you find yourself making these kinds of statements, take a minute to reflect on how they are negatively affecting your motivation to learn in those courses. Remember, motivation is a psychological concept. If your goal is realistic and you believe you can do it, the chances are much greater that you will accomplish it.

DESIRABLE

How much do you want to reach your goal? When goals are desirable, you can provide reasons why you should work hard toward reaching the goal. Figuring out why it is important to accomplish a task helps to intrinsically motivate you. In order to succeed in reaching your goals, they should be goals that you really desire. Then, learning will be particularly rewarding or enjoyable and the goal will

be easier to achieve. We know students who were in majors they didn't really like because their parents put pressure on them. Such students often performed poorly because the goal their parents set for them was not the goal they had for themselves. So, if your goal is to graduate from college within four years and to land a good job in your choosen field, you must have the desire for success to reach that type of goal. In addition, try writing your goals in the positive. So, rather than writing "Stop wasting time," phrase it in the positive and be specific by writing, "Use my time more efficiently by . . . " Your subconscious mind is more likely to carry out positive, specific statements than negative ones.

MEASURABLE

How will you know whether or when your goal has been met? Some goals are easy to measure. If your goal is to lose ten pounds, you will know whether you've met your goal when you weigh yourself. However, learning goals are not always easy to quantify, so you need to set some standards to help you measure your progress. This may be as simple as taking a few minutes to think about what you have learned after each study session or may include a more in-depth assessment. In general, you will need more checks of your progress for long-term goals than for short-term goals.

MADE PUBLIC

Finally, it is a good idea to make your goals public. This means sharing your goals with others—those you believe will encourage you to stay on track and might even help you achieve your goals. In addition, the fact that others know your goals, in some respects, holds you more accountable. For example, if your goal is to make the dean's list, share that with your roommate, members of your study group, or your best friend. Ask them to check in with you occasionally to see if you are on track. This puts some pressure on you, to be sure, but sometimes a little pressure can be a plus in helping you work toward your goals.

Staying Motivated

Getting motivated is one thing; staying motivated is another. We rarely see students at the beginning of a term who are not motivated. Almost everyone is excited about the prospect of a new term and, in a sense, starting with a clean slate. But as the term wears on, it is easy for motivation to also wane, especially in courses you might be experiencing trouble. In order to stay motivated, you should give yourself checkpoints on the way to reaching your goals.

Just as you monitor your comprehension when you read, you should also monitor your motivation for learning. Each time you sit down to study, ask yourself about the level of motivation for what you are doing. Your internal body clock makes certain times of the day more conducive to learning than others. Pay attention to your body clock to find out when you are most motivated and try to plan your study sessions around those times. In addition, pay attention to how you feel psychologically and physically when you begin to lose motivation.

Because your thought processes tend to change when you lose motivation, you may experience less confidence in yourself and have more of a negative take on your life as a student. Physically, you may experience tiredness or an increased stress level, feelings that typically do not describe you. Being in tune with yourself can often help you recognize your slump in motivation and enable you to bounce back sooner and easier.

STRATEGIES TO KEEP YOU FROM LOSING MOTIVATION

So, what if you find yourself losing motivation? It's important to have strategies to follow in this scenario. It might help if you:

Study Your Most Difficult Subjects First Then move to the subjects that are easier or those that you enjoy more. In that way, you will be more likely to stay motivated to study the subjects you find the most interesting.

Take a Break Keep the breaks short and consistent. If you are studying for several hours in a row, study for an hour, then take a 5- or 10-minute break between each hour of study.

Switch Topics Changing direction can help you maintain motivation for longer periods. For example, if you have just spent an hour reading your psychology assignment, take a short break and come back and do the practice exercises for your mathematics class.

Work with a Study Group One key component of motivation is collaborating with others. Motivation can be contagious.

Plan to Study in a Quiet Place Try studying in the library or another quiet place, especially if you find that your social life is interfering with studying because your friends are calling you or dropping by. Find somewhere to study where you will be free from distractions and temptation.

Use the Best Case-Worst Case Scenario Technique Imagine what will happen and how you will feel if you get your work done. Focusing on that positive image may help you find your motivation. Or picture what will happen if you do not complete your task. Thinking about the poor grade—or worse, being placed on academic probation—is enough to get some students moving in the right direction.

Stand Up! If you are studying or reading and find your mind wandering, stand up immediately. You can turn away from your desk, take a few deep breaths, stretch—whatever works for you. Then sit back down and get back to work. The whole routine only takes about 30 seconds, and you will be surprised how quickly you can regain your motivation and concentration.

Sometimes students find that they lose motivation as the term goes on. Some of this is natural—people are generally more motivated at the beginning and at the end of a term. So, if you experience a slight dip in your motivation toward the middle of a term, or during the first nice spring day, you probably shouldn't be too concerned. Set some new goals to get back on track. However, losing motivation sometimes can be a sign of a bigger problem. If you think your loss of motivation may be a problem, reflect on the source of your lack of motivation. Can you pinpoint a reason for it? Or are you unsure why you are unmotivated? Sometimes students become unmotivated by poor grades in a particular course, or sometimes outside influences (for example, family, roommates, social situations, substance abuse, or health concerns) cause students to lose their motivation.

Another way to maintain your motivation is to figure out all of the tasks that you need to complete in your courses. By listing this information, you should be able to find something in the course that is motivating for you. You will also be able to determine the tasks that are setting you back, which can help you psych yourself up in advance to maintain your motivation. Any method you find to renew your motivation is great. Try a few techniques to find out what works best for you. Use the "Monitor Your Learning" activity that follows as a motivation checkpoint. It will help you discover the kinds of tasks you find particularly motivating and those that you find less motivating. You can then apply some of the techniques discussed above to achieve your goals.

DIRECTIONS: For one of your courses this term, answer the following questions.

What do I need to learn? What is the task (exam, paper, presentation, discussion, etc.)?

_____

_____

_____

_____

What sources will I need to use (text, labs, lecture, discussion, etc.)?

_____

_____

_____

_____

What are my goals for completing this project? (Include short-term, intermediate, and long-term goals.)

_____

_____

_____

_____

What is my level of motivation for completing the task (high, medium, low) and why?

_____

_____

_____

What, if any, adjustments do I need to make to reach my learning goals?

_____

_____

_____

Changing Attitudes and Interests

Now that you understand the role that motivation plays in active learning, let's turn to attitudes and interests. As you read this portion of the chapter, reflect on how all three of these concepts relate to one another.

How many times have you dealt with a clerk in the grocery store, a family member, your advisor, a server in a restaurant, or even your best friend, and walked away thinking, "Now there's a person with a bad attitude"? Everyone probably has a bad attitude about something at some time, which suggests that attitude, like motivation, is situational. Rarely are people positive about everything, nor are they negative about everything. Likewise, interest is situational. Students generally aren't interested in everything. In most cases, individuals tend to show great interest in a limited number of areas, moderate interest in a greater number of topics, and low or no interest in many more. Everyone knows people who have a strong passion for something—video games, skiing, music, drawing, writing, baseball, politics. And more often than not, these passions are reflected in majors that students select and the careers they ultimately choose. Interests can't help but influence academic decisions that students make and how actively they pursue certain goals.

Like motivation, attitudes and interests help define who you are as a learner. Moreover, each of these factors is either directly or indirectly a part of your personality, thus making them a bit more difficult to change than basic study habits.

Although everyone seems to know someone who, in general, has a bad or good attitude, attitudes can actually be thought of as emotional reactions to specific situations. Attitudes are reflexive, meaning you experience them without even thinking about it. For example, if your professor assigns you two extra chapters to read before a quiz on Friday and you already have every minute of your schedule between now and Friday planned, you may have an immediate negative reaction. However, that attitude may not be permanent. Perhaps a professor in another class cancels a test that was scheduled for Friday, or a date that you really didn't want to go on in the first place begs off, causing your initial bad attitude to mellow. The bottom line is that most students' attitudes about things change. What you have a bad attitude about on Tuesday may be seen in another light by Wednesday.

Attitudes are also elements that match your motivation. It makes sense that if you are motivated in a particular course, your attitude would be more positive than if you were unmotivated. Additionally, attitudes are often characteristics that match your behavior. If you have a bad attitude toward learning a foreign language and feel that you can't succeed no matter what, your behavior will follow suit. You won't work on the material on a daily basis, you won't say much in class, and you may even display a poor attitude toward your professor, even if she is a good teacher.

Four Types of Academic Attitudes

There are four different types of academic attitudes you will encounter in college: (1) attitude toward college, (2) attitude toward your instructors, (3) attitude toward the subject and learning environment, and (4) attitude toward yourself as a learner. As you read about each one, think about yourself as a learner and the attitudes that you have.

ATTITUDE TOWARD COLLEGE

Students begin college with different attitudes for many different reasons. Some are happy with their school choice, others aren't, and still others don't care. Obviously, it's better to begin on the right foot—with a positive attitude about the college you are attending—but also remember that attitudes change. We've known many students who started college having one perception about what they would experience, only to be either disappointed or elated later on. For whatever reason you chose to attend your current college, know that your general attitude about being in college and your expectations of what that college experience will be like will strongly influence your attitudes. Those attitudes, in turn, influence your academic performance. Such conflicts often occur when there is not a good match between your expectations and the realities of your actual college life. For example, if you have attended a small high school where you knew everyone and had small classes and lots of individual attention, you may be overwhelmed by being on a campus with 30,000-plus students. Or, if you are a returning student, you may not have realized that you would have to spend so much time away from your family and children. In addition, sometimes college just isn't what students expected it would be. Any of these things can negatively impact attitude.

ATTITUDE TOWARD YOUR INSTRUCTORS

Your attitude about your instructors also influences your academic performance. This is especially true for disciplines you don't particularly like. If you enroll in a mathematics course hating math and direct that feeling toward your professor, you are probably going to have some problems. On the other hand, if you try to have the attitude that each instructor has something unique to offer to your education, you may have a totally different experience. We suggest that students try to get to know their professors and not feel intimidated about talking with them. Try sending a message by e-mail or meeting with your professor during office hours to ask any questions you have.

ATTITUDE TOWARD THE SUBJECT AND LEARNING ENVIRONMENT

When we think about attitudes toward subject matter, it's difficult to separate attitude from interest and motivation because most students have a more negative attitude toward subjects in which they are not interested. For example, if you are strong in mathematics and science and have been successful in those courses in the past, you

will most likely enter into these courses in college with a positive attitude toward learning the material. However, if you have little interest in math and science and fail to see their relevance to your future career choice, then you may **squander** your opportunity for learning in these classes. In fact, some students try to avoid subjects they dislike until the very end of their program. We know students who have delayed taking their lab science, history, or mathematics requirements until their senior year, only to find out that the course wasn't as bad as they thought it would be. It's also important to try hard not to have preconceived notions about a course. Even though you may have had an unpleasant experience in a similar past course, try to begin each course with an open mind. An open mind can go a long way toward changing your attitude, helping you develop your interests, and maintaining motivation.

ATTITUDE TOWARD YOURSELF AS A LEARNER

The attitude that you have toward yourself as a learner may be the most important of the four because it is the sum total of your educational experiences. If you have had teachers who encouraged you, if you have experienced academic success, and if you have parents who have been actively involved in your learning at home, you probably have a positive view of yourself in learning situations. That's not to say that students who have a positive attitude never doubt themselves. They do. But they know themselves well enough to realize what and how they will have to change to make things improve.

On the other hand, if school was not challenging, if you experienced only moderate academic success, if your family had little involvement with your learning, or if you have been out of school for a while, you may have a more negative view of yourself and lack confidence academically. Students who fall into this category initially may have a more difficult time adjusting to college, but we have seen such students gain increasing confidence as they experience academic successes.

Maintaining a Positive Attitude

Few students begin college with a totally negative attitude. Thus, we suggest that your first step is to evaluate what you like about college. You may have a great roommate, you may have at least one class that seems enjoyable, or you may simply be positive about a new beginning. Whatever excites you and makes you feel positive should be what you concentrate on, especially during those first two or three weeks of a new term. Yes, things will go wrong. The new registration system touted by the registrar's office might crash just when you finally were making some progress in adding a class you wanted, the class you really need might be full, the bursar's office may have lost proof that you paid your tuition, or the lines in the bookstore may go on forever. But you have no control over these things. Take a deep breath, count to 10 (or 50, if need be), and try not to let negative happenings get in the way of your excitement and positive outlook. This can be difficult, but it's important to learn early on that you need to develop patience with things in life that you have little or no control over. Save your energy for staying on top of what you can control and do something about.

Not dwelling on past mistakes is another way that students maintain a positive attitude. For example, if writing has always been a struggle for you, telling yourself "I can't write very well" will do little to help. Rather, concentrate on the positives, such as "I'm a good learner in general, so writing should not be impossible. I can get help at the Writing Center if I need it, so I know I can do it." Everyone has strong and weak points. The secret of maintaining a positive attitude is balance. If you lack confidence in writing, for example, balance that writing course with another course that you will like and that will be less of a struggle for you. Also, try to give each

> **BEYOND THE CLASSROOM** Many students come to college with a good deal of life experiences and interests. This can put you at an advantage because you have a wealth of experience to draw on. Try maximizing your learning by trying to connect what you are learning in your classes—which can sometimes seem abstract and removed—with your past experiences and current interests.

course and each professor a chance. Enter each course with the attitude that you will do your best. In some courses, this may mean that you will not earn the best grade. There's nothing wrong with earning a C in a course that is particularly difficult for you. There is something wrong, however, in settling for a C because your attitude in that course was negative and you simply did not put in the necessary effort.

In addition, expect to learn something valuable in every course you take. That's often a difficult suggestion to follow, but if you tell yourself that parts of a course might be interesting and valuable, both your attitude and your motivation will be better. It's particularly difficult to follow this suggestion if you, like many first-year students, get stuck taking "leftover" courses or core courses on subjects that don't hold much interest for you. But no matter how uninteresting or boring you might find a course, look for the positive. Think how you might use some of the information at a later date or how it might be related to other areas that do interest you and for which you already possess a positive attitude. Imagine how you might feel at the end of the term if you do well in a class that wasn't your favorite or was one that previously made you struggle. Moreover, we have had lots of students who were in courses they started with a negative attitude, only to find that a good professor sparked something in them and turned them around. The point is, give each course and each professor a chance; you might be pleasantly surprised.

The Role of Interests

As we mentioned earlier, attitudes and interests go hand in hand. Whatever you have an interest in, you also probably have a good attitude toward. Likewise, when you don't have a **propensity** for a topic or course, you may not have a very good attitude about having to learn it.

We have found that many students lack interest in a wide variety of areas, which puts limitations on the courses they want to take. But not having a wide variety of interests doesn't mean that you can't develop them. As we suggested, every course has *something* interesting about it or people wouldn't spend their lives studying it. Students who have the most focused interests are usually those who have the most difficult time developing new interests. We have had conversations with students that go something like this:

Student: Why do I have to take this stuff—history, sociology, and drama—for goodness' sake? I'm a pre-med major and none of this is important to me. I like science and math and I just want to learn what will help me pass the MCAT and get into med school. Taking other courses just wastes my time.

Professor: Well, I understand that, but you also have to take a series of core courses—courses that help you have a well-rounded education. Besides, they can help to develop other interests. One of the reasons for a college education is to give you a broader view of the world. Don't you want to be able to talk about something other than science?

Student: (rolling her eyes) Maybe so, but I don't care about any of this. I'll do it because I have to, but I'm not going to like it.

The student shuffles off, unhappy, determined to get nothing from any course unless it is in some way related to a career in medicine. Chances are that she will get into academic trouble—trouble that may keep her out of medical school—simply because she is already convinced that there is nothing about these courses that could possibly be of interest. How different the scenario might have been if she had thought about courses as a chance to develop new interests and learn new things.

There are also students who enter college with no overriding interest in any one particular area. Many of these students have not yet selected a major and hope to find something that interests them as a result of enrolling in general core courses. The best advice we can give to such students to develop interest is to keep up with assignments. Do the reading, participate in discussion groups, study with others, befriend a professor in a course that you like and seek assistance when the going gets rough. Often, a class that starts out dull turns into an interesting course if you keep on top of things. It particularly helps if you create study groups to talk about the information, and it helps even more if at least one person in the group has more than a superficial interest in the course. You also need to keep in mind that you will never develop an interest in something if you don't put in your fair share of the work.

A final suggestion about developing and maintaining interest in courses: Don't save up all the courses you think you'll hate because they're uninteresting and boring until the end of your college career. Intersperse the good with the bad. Try to balance a course you know you'll be interested in with those you think hold little interest for you. And for those less interesting courses, try to select your instructors carefully. A good instructor can make or break your interest toward and attitude about a particular course.

It is easy to see that motivation, attitude, and interest are related to one another and difficult to separate. Unfortunately, lack of motivation, a poor attitude, and few interests are also related and difficult to separate. Still, everyone can gain from conscious efforts to develop interests, improve attitudes, and work on motivation.

Real College

MARIO'S MISERY

DIRECTIONS: *Read the following scenario and respond to the questions, based on the information you learned in this chapter.* Mario is returning to college after working for three years at a job he didn't like. He is excited to go back to school, even if it is only part time, but he is worried that he won't be able to maintain his motivation and good attitude.

When Mario arrived on campus, he immediately felt overwhelmed. The campus seemed big, he didn't know anyone, and his classes were extremely difficult. He had no choice in his courses for the first term because his schedule was set for him. He was enrolled in three courses: political science, calculus, and computer applications. Mario became miserable—fast! Political science is not at all what he expected. His professor lectures a mile a minute and doesn't even ask if the students have questions. His calculus teacher plans to cover two chapters each week, but he is finding he doesn't remember much math from high school. For the first few weeks, he tried to maintain a positive attitude and a high level of motivation, but he kept asking himself, "Why am I here? Why am I doing this?" He knew if he didn't do something fast, he was going to dig himself in a hole he couldn't get out of.

What can Mario do?

Mario is bright and has a long-term career plan of landing a job in the technology field. Based on what you have read and what you know about the role that motivation, attitudes, and interests play in learning, what advice would you give Mario to help him maintain his motivation and attitude?

_____

_____

_____

_____

_____

_____

_____

_____

_____

Add to Your Portfolio

Write down three short-term goals, two intermediate goals, and one long-term goal for the rest of this year. Before you begin working on these goals, determine if your goals are realistic, desirable, believable, and measurable. Write a one-page reflection on why you selected these goals and outline your plan of action for achieving them. Then, as the semester progresses, evaluate your goals every week or two.

Short-Term Goals

1 _____

2 _____

3 _____

Intermediate Goals

1 _____

2 _____

Long-term Goal

1 _____

Chapter 4
How Beliefs About Knowledge Impact Learning

Read this chapter to answer the following questions:

- How is your learning affected by your beliefs?
- What are the five belief components that influence learning?
- How can you change your beliefs about learning?

Self-Assessment

DIRECTIONS: Read the following scenario and answer the questions honestly to find out your personal theory of beliefs. The purpose of this scenario is to get you to think about your beliefs. Remember that there are no right or wrong responses.

Chris is a student in introductory biology. He studies hard for the class, but he has failed his first two exams. When he studies, he tries to focus on the material covered in the lectures but really doesn't read the text. He does try to memorize almost all of the bold-faced terms in the text by writing them on 3 x 5 cards and flipping through them until he has memorized the definitions. After the last exam, he tried studying with friends, but he didn't find it helpful because his friends were explaining the information in a different way than the professor, so he was not sure if they knew what they were talking about and didn't want to get confused.

Chris believes that science mainly consists of memorization and that most science problems have only one answer, so if he looks at the material enough he should do fine. Even though he doesn't spend a lot of time studying, he feels that he puts in hard work and effort and, therefore, he should be receiving high grades; but this has not been the case. Chris thinks his poor grades could be due to the new professor teaching the course. Professor Smith tries to have class discussions, despite the fact that there are 250 students enrolled in the class. Professor Smith also tries to tell the class about all sides to each issue. When there are competing scientific theories, she is sure to inform the class and discuss each one, because she wants to give an unbiased lecture each time. However, Chris knows that science is based on proven facts and finds all these theories confusing. When Chris went to her office asking which theory was the right one or which one he needed to know for the exam, she told him that all of the theories have some merit and that he must decide for himself what he will believe. Chris believes that it is the professor's responsibility to make sure that the students learn in class. However, this professor often asks exam questions about topics that were covered in the text but not during the lectures. Chris is beginning to believe that he is failing the class because he is not able to learn science.

	Strongly disagree		Some-what agree		Strongly agree
	1	**2**	**3**	**4**	**5**
1. I agree with Chris that science is based on proven facts.		X			
2. I agree with Chris that the students should only be responsible for the scientific theories that the professor discusses in class.				X	
3. Like Chris, I believe that there must be one theory that is more correct than others.			X		
4. I agree with Chris that the professor is responsible for student learning.				X	
5. I agree with Chris that if I don't do well on my biology exam it, is because I am not able to learn science.				X	
6. Like Chris, I believe that I don't have to read the text as long as I listen in class, because the professor goes over all of the important information.				X	

	Strongly disagree 1	2	3	4	Strongly agree 5
7. I agree with Chris that learning competing science theories is too confusing for students.			X		
8. I agree with Chris that there is usually only one right answer to a science problem.		X			
9. I believe that some people will do fine in Chris's class because they are good learners, but others have a limited ability to learn science.			X		
10. Like Chris, I believe that I will only do well in this class if I can learn information quickly.		X			
11. Chris's plan of taking good notes and trying to memorize facts should be all it takes to get a good grade in introductory biology.			X		
12. Chris will be able to understand the complex processes involved in biology if he memorizes definitions.			X		
13. If Chris tried to understand every theory, it would take him too much time to read a chapter.			X		
14. Like Chris, I believe that no matter how much time and effort is put in to it, some people will never be able to learn biology.		X			
15. I believe that if I am going to understand my biology text, it will make sense the first time I read it—rereading will not help me understand any better.			X		

To find your personal theory, add your scores to the following questions together. See page 56 for an explanation of each of these componets.

Component 1—Certain Knowledge: 1 _____ + 3 _____ + 8 _____ = _____

Component 2—Simple Knowledge: 7 _____ + 11 _____ + 12 _____ = _____

Component 3—Responsibility for Learning: 2 _____ + 4 _____ + 6 _____ = _____

Component 4—Speed of Learning: 10 _____ + 13 _____ + 15 _____ = _____

Component 5—Ability: 5 _____ + 9 _____ + 14 _____ = _____

Assessing Your Personal Theory
Look at where your scores fall for each component (scores for each can range from 3 to 15). The higher your score on a component, the more strongly you hold a belief that may get in the way of your academic success. The lower your score on a component, the more strongly you hold a belief that research has shown should lead to academic success. Because no one is completely consistent in his or her beliefs, chances are you hold a strong belief on some components (as indicated by either high or low scores) but are more in the middle on other components. Before reading the chapter, reflect on your responses to the self-assessment. How are your personal beliefs helping you learn? What do you need to work on?

Source: Adapted from Holschuh, J. P. "Assessing beliefs: The epistemological scenario." *Academic Exchange Quarterly*, 10(2) (2006): 172–175.

WORD WISE

1. **Consolidate** (v., pg. 58) — to unite into one system or whole; combine.

Claudette's goal was to consolidate everything she would need for her first semester of college into the trunk of her car.

2. **Futility** (n., pg. 58) — the quality of having no useful result; uselessness.

As the hurricane raged on, rescue workers knew it was an exercise in futility to sandbag the seawall because the water surge was predicted to be twenty feet.

3. **Derogatory** (adj., pg. 59) — belittling; tending to detract or diminish.

Politicians are known for the derogatory remarks about those outside their party who have differing beliefs.

4. **Synthesize** (v., pg. 60) — to combine; to form or produce by combining; to integrate from multiple sources

When considering the nature of the electoral process, the political science professor expected students to synthesize information from textbooks and lectures.

DID YOU KNOW?

What does it mean to know a word? If you have ever realized you really didn't understand a word, you probably realize that knowing a word involves more than a definition. To know a word, you need both depth (often called the *denotation* of a word)—knowing the definition(s), being able to use the word appropriately, recognizing the meaning when others use the word—AND breadth (often called the *connotation* of a word)—knowing how the word is connected to other words and ideas. Some would say that the breadth is the most important part because it means you have a good understanding of the context of the word. SMSU

RESEARCH INTO PRACTICE

First-Year College Students' Beliefs About Instructional Practices

In this study, Professor Barbara Hofer examined how students perceive beliefs about knowledge differently, depending on the class and the instructor. The study focused on two chemistry classes, each taught by professors with very different beliefs about how they defined their disciplines and learning. Dr. Hofer drew conclusions about the simplicity, certainty, source, and justification of knowledge.

Concerning simplicity of knowledge, she found that the types of tests students had in their courses gave them an idea of whether knowledge was simple or complex. She also found that students who thought knowledge was simple struggled when the way a professor taught suggested knowledge was simple but his exams indicated that learning was complex.

Concerning certainty of knowledge, Dr. Hofer found that students in both chemistry classes accepted all opinions and theories equally, thus struggling with the idea that each had its own strengths and weaknesses.

Concerning the source of knowledge, students seemed to hold views that both the professor and

the text were the authorities, but there were distinct differences in how the two chemistry professors approached the construction of knowledge and the students' role in that construction.

Finally, concerning the justification for knowing, or how students evaluate their own knowledge and that of others, Dr. Hofer found that students in both classes fell short. They had little knowledge of scientific processes and appeared to need more instruction and practice to evaluate research.

The main importance of this study may be in the finding that how teachers teach can have a big effect on changing students' belief systems. Given guidance, it appears students begin to change their own beliefs when they have professors who communicate more sophisticated ways of knowing.

Source: B. K. Hofer, "Exploring the Dimensions of Personal Epistemology in Differing Classroom Contexts: Student Interpretations During the First Year of College," Contemporary Educational Psychology 29 (2004): 129–163.

The Five Components of Beliefs That Influence Learning

Many different kinds of beliefs affect your life every day. People have different religious beliefs, moral beliefs, political beliefs, and so on. You may have thought a lot about those kinds of beliefs, but have you ever thought about your beliefs about learning? Have you ever considered how you gain knowledge or what knowledge is? If you are like most students, you probably haven't thought much about where knowledge comes from, but your beliefs about knowledge do impact what and how you learn.

As you read this chapter, consider your own beliefs about learning. Where do your beliefs fall? How might these beliefs affect your learning in college courses? Remember that to get off on the right foot in college, you may need to reevaluate your beliefs and the role they play in your academic success.

The Five Components of Beliefs		
Component 1	Certainty of Knowledge	Can range from the belief that knowledge is fact, to the belief that knowledge is continually changing
Component 2	Simple Knowledge	Can range from the belief that knowledge is made up of isolated bits of information, to the belief that knowledge is complex
Component 3	Responsibility for learning	Can range from the belief that it is the professor's responsibility to ensure that students learn, to the belief that it is the individual's responsibility to learn information
Component 4	Speed of Learning	Can range from the belief that learning happens fast or not at all, to the belief that learning is a gradual process that takes time
Component 5	Ability	Can range from the belief that the ability to learn is fixed, to the belief that people can learn how to learn

Adapted from: M. Schommer, "An Emerging Conceptualization of Epistemological Beliefs and Their Role in Learning," in eds. R. Garner and P. A. Alexander, *Beliefs About Text and Instruction with Text* (Hillsdale, NJ: Erlbaum, 1994): 25–40.

Figure 4.1: The Five Components of Beliefs

COMPONENT 1: CERTAINTY OF KNOWLEDGE

Some students believe that knowledge is continually changing based on current information. When they are in class, they may change their beliefs about a topic by adding new information to what they already know. For example, a student might enter a physics class believing that when a bullet is shot from a gun, it falls to the ground faster than a bullet that is simply dropped. However, she might change her beliefs based on new information after learning about the laws of gravity.

Other students believe that there are absolute answers and there is a definite right or wrong solution to every problem. These students approach learning by trying to find the truth in all situations. In the same physics class, another student may have trouble understanding that scientists believe that physics is based on theories, not truth, and that these theories are in a constant state of change based on new research. Even though experts are continually reassessing what they know, students are often encouraged to look only for the facts in their textbooks. They may approach reading history by looking strictly for names, dates, and places because that was what was important in their previous experience. But most college courses require you to do more than learn facts. Professors tend to view their disciplines as dynamic and constantly changing; therefore, to memorize only facts would be a waste of time. Instead, most professors want you to understand what is currently known and also want to prepare you for future learning. Professors expect students to question what they read and be willing to live with the idea that there may not be a solution or definite answer to every problem or question.

COMPONENT 2: SIMPLE KNOWLEDGE

Some students believe that knowledge is complex and consists of highly interconnected concepts, but others believe that knowledge consists of a series of unrelated bits of information. Students who believe that knowledge is complex look for relationships between ideas as they learn. They try to see the big picture and the relationships among the small pieces of information within that big picture.

On the other hand, students who have a strong belief that knowledge is simple tend to break information down into very small isolated parts and never put it back together. Although breaking information into smaller chunks is a great strategy for some tasks, such as memorizing the periodic table of the elements, students who learn only isolated pieces of information will miss the big ideas. If a student in history class memorized only dates and names, she would be unprepared for an essay question that asked her to compare and contrast ideas about the larger concepts. Likewise, a student who memorizes bold-faced terms in biology would not be able to explain more complex science processes. Because most of your assignments will require application of what you have learned, you need to go beyond memorizing small bits of information and begin to see how information is connected.

COMPONENT 3: RESPONSIBILITY FOR LEARNING

Beliefs about knowledge also depend on your perception about who is responsible for your learning. Some students believe that it is the professor's responsibility to ensure that all students learn the information. Others believe that although the professor guides their learning, they are ultimately responsible for their own learning. Before college, your teachers probably took a lot of the responsibility for your learning in class. You most likely had little choice in the subjects you studied, what you learned, or the way you were assessed (e.g., tests, papers, labs, etc.). In fact, your teachers may have even gone over all of the relevant information in class, which left you little to learn on your own. However, you have probably already noticed that college professors have different assumptions about who is responsible for learning. Professors expect students to take responsibility for a good deal of their own learning. They expect students to be able figure out information on their own, and they also may expect students to **consolidate** information from a variety of sources.

BEYOND THE CLASSROOM

If you are a student who has worked for a while before beginning college or if you are returning to college after finishing your degree, you may find yourself having different beliefs about learning and knowledge than more traditionally aged college students. Regardless of where you are in your life when you enter college, you can count on your beliefs about learning to change because of your new college experiences. Being aware of where you are now—and where you need to go—can help you learn more effectively.

COMPONENT 4: SPEED OF LEARNING

Some students believe that learning is a gradual and ongoing process, but other students believe that learning happens quickly or not at all. That is, some people believe that most things worth knowing take a long time to learn, but others think that if they don't "get it" right away, they never will. Students who believe that learning takes time are better prepared for college tasks, because few things you learn in college have immdiate results. However, students who believe that learning should happen quickly are often frustrated when they are faced with complex information. Many of these students believe that learning should happen quickly because of their past learning experiences.

Most every student has had the following experience at one time or another: The teacher asks a question, no one immediately raises his hand, and everyone just sits there, usually looking down at his desk. What happens next? The teacher answers her own question because the few seconds of silence makes everyone uncomfortable. In this case, even the teacher expects learning to be fast.

In addition, research has shown that in high school mathematics classes, most problems that students answered could be solved in less than two minutes. It's no wonder that many students are unprepared for more demanding tasks in college and why some get frustrated or view solving challenging problems an exercise in **futility**.

Now that you know a little more about the different dimensions of beliefs, go back to the Self-Assessment at the beginning of the chapter and review your results. Think about which components you might like to work on based on these results.

COMPONENT 5: THE ROLE OF ABILITY

Some students believe that people can learn how to learn or how to do new things, but others believe that the ability to learn is fixed and that they are naturally good at some things but will never be able to do other things. For example, a student may say, "I am good at math and science, but not history or English." Students who believe that the ability to learn is fixed tend to talk to themselves in a **derogatory** way and often use their perceived inability as an excuse for either not doing well or not trying at all. For example, a student may say, "I will never be able to do this" or " I am too dumb to learn that," when in fact the student may just be giving up too easily. In a sense, when students believe they can't do something and then they perform a task poorly, they are experiencing a self-fulfilling prophecy. Many students who perceive that they are terrible at writing, for example, will just not put any effort into it at all. Then when they earn a low grade on a paper, they simply say, "See, I told you I can't write." It's much easier for students such as these to do little or nothing and be unsuccessful. At least they can't blame their failures on trying and not succeeding.

On the other hand, students who believe that people can learn how to learn tend to view difficult tasks as challenges that can be met. Instead of giving up, these students will try different strategies for learning and will ask for help from the professor or others if they need it. Certainly there are people in your classes who make learning look easy, but students who appear to learn "naturally" probably spend time and effort in activities—such as reading and reflecting—that promote academic success. Most students are not born geniuses! Good students work at being good students. They have confidence, knowing how to study smart and understanding that some tasks

Reality Check

Taking Time to Learn

Most students hold beliefs about how long it should take to complete a task. For example, the student who has only encountered math problems that could be solved in two minutes would likely believe that all mathematics problems can be solved that quickly. When this student encounters a math problem that requires more time, he or she will quickly get frustrated after trying to solve the problem for two minutes. Students have similar beliefs about how long it should take to read a textbook chapter, write a paper, study for an exam, and so forth. However, these time frames may not be an accurate assessment of how long it should take, because the tasks in college are different than those they experienced in high school. The next time you find yourself unmotivated or frustrated in your classes, think about your own beliefs about the speed of learning. Are your expectations holding you back from giving the task the time it requires? Are you being realistic in determining the amount of time it should take you to learn something or accomplish other studying tasks?

and subjects will be easy for them to grasp, while others will take more effort.

Based on what you have read about beliefs, it should be clear that they can impact academic achievement. Students who believe that knowledge is changeable, that knowledge consists of interrelated concepts, that learning is under the control of the student, and that learning may take time and effort will be expected to have more success in college than students who hold the opposite beliefs.

Modifying Your Beliefs

After evaluating your personal belief theory using the scale at the beginning of this chapter, you may have found that you have some beliefs that need to be altered because they may negatively affect your success in college. This section will present some strategies for promoting change.

Your beliefs about learning influence the strategies you use to study, which is part of the reason why beliefs are related to college performance. For example, if you believe that knowledge is simple, then you will select a strategy that reflects your belief, such as making flash cards to memorize definitions of key terms even when your professor expects you to integrate ideas. Thus, when you have all of the terms memorized, you will feel prepared for the exam. If you do not pass the exam, you may not understand what you did wrong, because according to your beliefs about learning, you were adequately prepared. The question, then, is: If you currently hold beliefs that may make academic success more difficult, how do you go about changing those beliefs?

Be Aware of Your Beliefs If you have beliefs that are getting in the way of your learning, consider changing them. However, before you can change a belief, you must first be unsatisfied with your current beliefs about learning. For example, when you find yourself giving up on an assignment too quickly or trying to merely memorize when the task requires you to understand and apply difficult concepts, you can reflect on your beliefs, rethink your approach, and take the time to really learn the information.

Look for the Big Picture Instead of just memorizing a lot of separate facts, make a conscious effort to relate ideas to what you already know and to other ideas discussed in class. Many of the strategies you will learn in *Effective College Learning* will enable you to integrate and **synthesize** ideas as you read.

Learn to Live with Uncertainty It is sometimes difficult to accept that there are no right answers to some questions. For example, in a statistics class, you may want to know the "right" way to solve a problem, and although there are some ways that are better than others, chances are that if you ask three statisticians how to solve the problem, you will get three different answers

Don't Compare Your "Ability" with That of Others Worrying that you are not as good as your roommate in math will not get you anywhere. Focus instead on how to improve your ability to learn in the subjects that you find difficult. You can find a tutor to work with or form a study group to help you learn. It may take you longer to get there, but remember that college learning is more like an endurance sport than a sprint.

NETWORKING

Deciding What to Believe

You may have noticed that some information that you find on the Internet seems to contradict other information. Your personal theory of beliefs will influence how you decide which information to believe. Find three sites that give you different perspectives about the same topic.

For example, you might look at three reviews of the same movie or three political essays about an issue from a Democratic, a Republican, and an Independent perspective. Consider how you decide which one to believe. How do your beliefs about knowledge affect your decision?

Realize That Learning Takes Time This is true for most disciplines. If you begin your assignments with the expectation that they will take time to fully understand and complete, you are likely to experience less frustration and more understanding. Don't expect to learn complex concepts the first time you encounter them. Instead, plan to spread out your study time so you can review difficult material several times.

Tune In to Your Professor As you read in the "Research into Practice" section, your professors' beliefs not only have a lot to do with how you should approach learning, but they also have a great deal to do with how he approaches teaching. As you go from course to course and discipline to discipline, try to be aware of the beliefs your professor is trying to communicate.

Now that you know about how beliefs affect your learning, you can begin to examine your own beliefs in the many learning situations you encounter. Depending on your age and maturity level, your beliefs will fall in different places along the belief continuum.

Monitor Your Learning

What have you observed about your own beliefs that may make learning easier for you?

_____

_____

What have you observed about your own beliefs that may make learning harder for you?

_____

_____

How are your beliefs affecting how you approach and carry out the tasks in your courses?

_____

_____

Are your beliefs leading you toward academic success? Why or Why not?

_____

_____

_____

What are some ways you can tune in to your professors' beliefs? How can you determine their views of learning?

_____

_____

_____

61

Real College

COLLEGE KNOWLEDGE

DIRECTIONS: *In the following scenario, you will read about four college students. Use what you have learned in this chapter about beliefs about knowledge to consider their beliefs and respond to the questions at the end of the section.*

Lucy is taking political science only because it is required. She is uninterested in anything dealing with politics. In addition to the fact that she doesn't like the course, she finds that the professor often asks exam questions about topics that were not covered in class. Lucy thinks this is unfair because she doesn't know what to study if the professor doesn't tell her what is important.

Lenny believes that he will be successful in chemistry because he wants to be a veterinarian and because he has always done well in science classes. He believes that a scientist, if he or she tries hard enough, can find the "correct" answers to almost anything. One problem Lenny is encountering in chemistry is that his professor tries to tell the class about too many science theories, which he finds confusing.

David is returning to college to finish his degree after working for three years. He wants to get his degree in English because he was good in English in high school. He was always able to quickly understand the concepts and didn't need to spend a lot of time on homework. When he started his literature class, the readings were familiar and he didn't really spend much time outside of class reading or studying. However, he found that he did not do well on the first essay exam and that the new concepts were confusing. He still believes that he should be able to learn the information quickly and is unsure why he is having so much trouble.

Misha is sure that she will never "get" math. She believes that some students just seem to "get it" because they are naturally good at math. To compound the problem, Misha was recommended to begin her math requirements in a remedial math course, which further confirmed her view that she can't do math. She wishes that the college would understand that some people just can't learn math and that it shouldn't be a requirement for all students.

What can they do?

Answer the following questions, then discuss your responses with a partner or small group.

1. How are these students' beliefs similar to yours? How do they differ?

_____

_____

_____

2. How do you think these beliefs will affect the students' performance in their classes?

_____

_____

_____

3. What advice would you give these students?

_____

_____

_____

Add to Your Portfolio

1. Reflect on your self-assessment scores from pages 53-54 at the beginning of the chapter. Write a one-page reflection on your results. Is this an accurate reflection of you? Why or why not? Which components of beliefs do you think are negatively impacting your academic career? Brainstorm and write down three changes you can make this semester to these components.

_____

_____

_____

_____

_____

2. At the end of this semester, retake the self-assessment. Write a one-page reflection on your results. Have your beliefs changed since you first took the assessment? If so, how? What experiences have helped you make those changes?

_____

_____

_____

_____

_____

3. Reflect on the three changes you sought to make. Write a one-page reflection on your progress. How successful have your efforts been? What do you think you still need to work on in the future?

_____

_____

_____

_____

_____

Chapter 5
Identifying and Handling Stress

Read this chapter to answer the following questions:

- What are common sources of stress?
- How does stress affect you?
- What is academic stress?
- How can you control or reduce academic stress?

Self-Assessment

Take the following assessment of stressful situations to determine your current stress level. Remember, some stress is necessary for everyday life. But if you are experiencing an overwhelming amount of stress, look for ways to reduce it and seek help if necessary.

Student Stress Scale

Directions: Check those events you have experienced in the past six months or those you are likely to experience in the next six months.

Event		Score
1. Death of a close family member		100
2. Death of a close friend		73
3. Divorce between parents		65
4. Jail term		63
5. Major personal injury or illness		63
6. Marriage		58
7. Fired from job		50
8. Failed important course		47
9. Change in health of a family member		45
10. Pregnancy		45
11. Sex problems		44
12. Serious argument with a close friend		40
13. Change in financial status	✓	39
14. Change of major		39
15. Trouble with parents		39
16. New girlfriend or boyfriend		38
17. Increased workload		37
18. Outstanding personal achievement		36
19. First quarter/semester in college		35
20. Change in living conditions		31
21. Serious argument with instructor		30
22. Lower grades than expected		29
23. Change in sleeping habits		29
24. Change in social activities		29
25. Change in eating habits		28
26. Chronic car trouble	✓	26
27. Change in the number of family get-togethers		26
28. Too many missed classes		25
29. Change of college		24
30. Dropped more than one class		23
31. Minor traffic violations		20

TOTAL _____

Add your scores. A total of 300 or higher indicates an extremely high-stress life; a score of 200 to 299 indicates a high-stress life; a score between 100 and 199 indicates a moderate-stress life; and a score below 100 indicates a low-stress life. NOTE: If you find that you are having a very high-stress life, you might want to seek help from a counselor, friend, or family member.

Before reading the chapter, reflect on your responses to the self-assessment. How much stress do you currently have? How do you currently deal with stress? If your stress level is high, what can you do to better control it?

not much, listen to music

Sources: K. DeMeuse, "The Relationship between Life Events and Indices of Classroom Performance," *Teaching of Psychology* 12 (1985): 146–149; T. H. Holmes and R. H. Rahe, "The Social Readjustment Rating Scale," *Journal of Psychosomatic Research* 11 (1967): 213–218; P. Insel and W. Roth, *Core Concepts in Health*, 4th ed. (Palo Alto, CA: Mayfield Publishing, 1985).

Before You Begin

DID YOU KNOW?

Many students believe that if they know root words, they can unlock the meaning of unknown words. Although knowing roots can help you, building your vocabulary exclusively by learning Greek and Latin roots probably won't increase your word knowledge. This approach only works well if you already have a fairly large vocabulary to begin with. So, our advice to you is to use multiple methods. Use the dictionary and context, coupled with learning roots. Using this approach will maximize both the depth and breadth of your vocabulary.

RESEARCH INTO PRACTICE

Stress and College Life

In this study, Ranjita Misra and Michelle McKean examined the relationship among academic stress, time management, and leisure satisfaction in college students. They found that students with poor time-management skills had high academic stress, especially when students did not feel that they were in control of their time. The lack of time management did not relate to satisfaction of leisure activities, which means that students were still enjoying their free time even when they did not feel in control of their time.

In addition, Misra and McKean found that there were gender differences. Females had more effective time-management skills but also experienced greater academic stress. Males reported greater satisfaction with leisure activities. Interestingly, freshmen and sophomores reported greater stress levels than juniors and seniors. This could be because freshmen and sophomores don't have the strong social groups or strategies to cope with college stress that juniors and seniors rely on. The authors state that developing both social support networks and cognitive strategies for dealing with stress is important for students in their freshman and sophomore years.

Source: R. Misra and M. McKean, "College Students' Academic Stress and Its Relation to Their Anxiety, Time Management, and Leisure Satisfaction," *American Journal of Health Studies* 16 (2000): 41–51.

Six Major Sources of Stress

When you are under a lot of pressure, you might tell your friends that you are "stressed out." Usually we think of stress as something to be avoided, but actually that's not always true. Stress is **ubiquitous,** and much of the stress you experience in college is helpful and stimulating—without stress we would lead a rather boring existence. The problem comes when you experience too much stress.

Believe us when we say that as a college student you will experience many different types of stress, including social pressures, financial burdens, and academic competition. In fact, stress levels in college tend to ebb and flow—you might feel more stress at the beginning of a term when everything is new, less stress in the middle of the term (until midterms, of course), and more stress again at the end of the term when you take final exams. In this chapter, you will learn about the sources of stress you will experience in college, strategies for coping with and reducing stress, and four common types of academic stress. Before reading the rest of the chapter, be sure you have read the "Research into Practice" section on the previous page.

Although at times it may feel as if there are infinite sources of stress, generally college stress stems from six main sources: prior academic record, social influences, family, finances, career direction, and situational problems (such as illness or drug problems). Most students think that stress is caused by outside factors. They might say that a test, a professor, or a paper is "stressing them out." But stress is really an internal process. For example, suppose your friend fails her first mathematics exam. She may think that she will flunk out of college, not be able to get a good job, or not find success in life. She may even consider dropping out.

Obviously, your friend is overreacting to the situation, but that is the way stress can work. Your friend needs some strategies for dealing with her stress in order to put her reaction into a realistic perspective. As you read about the six sources of stress, remember that stress is natural, it is internal, it is often an overreaction to a specific situation, and it can be controlled.

1. ACADEMIC RECORD

Your previous academic success can affect your current level of stress. Students who have "shaky" academic pasts may think that they can't succeed in college. On the other hand, students who have 4.0 averages may feel stress to maintain their stellar grade point averages. Either way, your past history as a learner affects your stress level.

2. SOCIAL INFLUENCES

Dealing with others can often be stressful. A fight with your roommate, breaking up with a boyfriend or girlfriend, meeting new people—all of these situations can be stressful. In fact, even situations considered to be positive social factors—such as falling in love or socializing with really good friends— can cause stressful reactions. Overall, however, having good friends and social support will actually reduce your stress levels because you have people to confide in.

3. FAMILY

Your family relationships can cause you to feel stress in several ways. You may feel pressure to do well in college in order to make your family proud, you may feel stress because you have moved away from your family, or you may feel stress because of family crises that arise. Some students feel stress because they are away from family; others are stressed because they feel the pressure of being the first or the last child in the family to attend college. Still others feel stress because they have families of their own and find that college work takes away from family time. Alternatively, family can be an excellent source of support to help you when you experience a lot of stress.

4. FINANCES

With the cost of a college education increasing every year, financial stress seems to be increasing among college students. Financial stress usually begins in college because to pay for their education students take out loans, get or maintain jobs, or have to achieve a certain grade point average to keep their scholarships. In addition, many college students get their own credit cards, which can lead to great financial stress if they are used excessively. We know many college students who have graduated college not only with a diploma but also student loans and a **myriad** of credit card debts. College students are also usually responsible for paying bills and are gaining responsibility for their financial security. Students returning to college after working for several years may feel the financial stress of paying tuition or making less money while taking college courses.

5. CAREER DIRECTION

"So what's your major? Oh, what are you going to do with that?" You may have heard similar comments from friends and relatives. Everyone (perhaps yourself included) wants to know what you will do with your life after college. More and more often, college students are expected to know their career choice as soon as they enter college. The less sure you are about your career direction, the more stress you might feel about it. You may even be concerned that you'll never find your direction. On the other hand, students who have decided on a career might also feel stress. If you have already decided on a career, you might be concerned about achieving your goals. For example, a student who has decided to go to veterinary school might feel anxious about doing exceptionally well in college because she knows that very few applicants are accepted each year at the school she has chosen.

6. SITUATIONAL PROBLEMS

Certain stresses are unexpected and sometimes devastating. You may become ill during the term, experience the death of someone close to you, or

realize that you have a drug or alcohol problem. As with all of the categories of stresses, if you feel overwhelmed by situational problems, seek help from a counselor on campus or from someone you can talk to about these concerns. Also keep in mind that it is better to get help sooner rather than later. Problems such as these generally to not take care of themselves.

BEYOND THE CLASSROOM

Returning students often face the same six sources of stress in different ways. You may feel stress because you have not taken any exams in a while. Cutting back on your hours at your job to fit in course work may cause financial worries. Working full-time while taking classes can lead to stress if it seems as though every minute of your time is committed. You may feel stress because of time away from your family or because family relationships changed once you returned to school. To begin to cope with these new stresses, try to be aware of what is causing stress for you. Talk with family members or friends about your feelings and read the rest of the chapter for suggestions on dealing with increases in stress levels.

How Does Stress Affect You?

How does stress impact you? Stress can affect both your body and your mind. Have you heard of the "fight or flight" response? This is an automatic warning system our bodies have had since our primitive days that triggers a release of hormones to allow us to react to perceived threats. However, in modern life such threats can be psychological as well as physical. We rarely fight or run away from such stresses, so our bodies cope with stress differently.

In general, people exhibit stress in one or more of four different ways, and different types of stress can cause different types of responses. For example, a student may get a headache every time she opens her accounting book because she is concerned that she does not understand it, which is a physical reaction to stress. This same student may exhibit a behavioral reaction, such as arguing with her boyfriend, after doing badly on a test. Thus, it is a good idea to keep track of your reactions to different stressful situations. To help you learn how to cope with the stress in your life, use the list below to look for a pattern to your responses to stress.

1. EXHIBITING STRESS THROUGH THOUGHTS

Some people may speak negatively to themselves when faced with a stressful situation: "I'll never be able to do this," "I am so stupid," "Why am I even in college anyway?" Often this type of stress is in response to something that a person anticipates happening rather than something that has actually occurred.

2. EXHIBITING STRESS THROUGH FEELINGS

Some people may be moody, angry, depressed, or feel like crying when they are stressed out. They may even experience mood swings while under pressure. If you find yourself experiencing mood

Reality Check

Stress and Illness

Have you had a cold or other illness that you just can't shake? Are you getting frequent headaches? Have your sleeping patterns been out of whack? Have you felt moody, especially with those close to you? Consider that these behaviors may be a reaction to stress. It may be your body's way of telling you that you are under too much pressure and need to do something to bring your stress level down.

swings after stressful situations, you may be exhibiting stress through your feelings. Usually, this happens when people keep their stress "bottled up" and fail to deal with individual stressful situations in constructive ways.

3. EXHIBITING STRESS THROUGH BEHAVIORS AND "ACTING OUT"

Some people may sleep too much or too little, eat too much or too little, or use drugs or alcohol when stressed. They might purchase things that they can't afford, gamble (something that is becoming much more common among college students), or get into physical fights or verbal arguments with others. Often these behaviors cause additional stress because they have their own negative side effects such as credit card debt, exhaustion, or weight gain or loss.

4. EXHIBITING STRESS PHYSICALLY

Some people may feel sick all the time, get migraines, headaches, or stomachaches; or they may experience "butterflies in the stomach" or dry mouth. These physical reactions to stress are often situational. A student may feel great until he enters a classroom to take an exam, and suddenly the stress hits. Then he may feel nauseated or get a headache; when he finishes the test and leaves the classroom, he feels fine once again.

Strategies for Reducing Stress

Now that you know what stress is, what causes stress for most students, and what the effects of stress are, you will be happy to know that there are many ways to control or even reduce your stress levels. Before you start feeling overwhelmed, consider the following strategies for reducing stress.

RELAX

You should plan to make relaxation a regular part of your day. If you don't know how to go about relaxing, there are numerous self-help books available that offer great techniques and advice. You might also ask your doctor or the health center for some advice. At the very least, try deep breathing or meditation each day to help you unwind. If you find yourself stressing out, stop whatever you are doing, close your eyes, and focus on your breathing for a few minutes. This should help you relax so that you can return to what you were doing, feeling in more control of the situation.

EXERCISE

A great way to reduce stress is to work out. Physical activity helps take your mind off of your worries, with the added benefit that the chemicals your body releases during exercise actually boost your ability to handle stressful situations. If you are feeling especially stressed, try taking a walk or a jog to clear your head.

TAKE CHARGE

You are in control of your own situation and you have to accept that responsibility. By taking charge, you can control the amount of stress you feel by remembering that stress is an internal reaction to situations and is often an overreaction. However, when stress gets out of control, you can also take charge of the situation by seeking help.

BE PROACTIVE

For some students, academic stress is a way of life because they are constantly reacting to events in their lives. They go from crisis to crisis—usually centered around exam dates. However, when you are proactive about your schoolwork, you manage your time effectively and stay on top of things. You incorporate fun and relaxation into your schedule rather than getting to the point where stress is in control.

PUT PROBLEMS IN PERSPECTIVE

Sometimes it helps to talk to a good friend or a parent who has been in a similar situation, to help you put your problems in a more realistic light. Don't allow yourself to get carried away imagining all the things that could go wrong in a situation—instead, focus on the positives. Try not to live in the past or the future; stay in the present. For example, if you fail an exam, instead of saying, "I'll never pass this course because I've always been terrible in English," tell yourself that "I can and will pass the course—it was only one test after all."

NETWORKING

Surfing for Stress

Many colleges and universities offer advice for stressed out college students. Use the following keywords to search for at least three Web sites dealing with stress management: stress, stress management, college stress, student stress, test anxiety, math anxiety, writing anxiety. What kind of useful information did you find about the causes of stress or about stress management? How will this information help you cope with your own stress?

BE FLEXIBLE

Everyone makes mistakes, and learning from your mistakes will help reduce your stress levels. But if you are too set in the way you do things or the way you view the world, you may end up causing yourself additional stress. For example, sometimes students are afraid to change the way they study, even if their methods are no longer working. By being inflexible about their study strategies, these students are putting themselves in a stressful situation come exam time.

DEVELOP INTERESTS

Join a club on campus, meet with others who share similar interests, or find some new interests on your own. By having interests outside of schoolwork, you will be able to enjoy yourself and relax during your time off from studying. Developing new interests also helps you in the classroom because you tend to do better in subjects that interest you.

SEEK HELP

Find support resources—friends, family, counseling centers. Seek out campus resources to help you through stressful times. In fact, it is a good idea to seek out the people and places that can support you *before* you need them. We touched on the idea in Chapter 1 of seeking out help if you need it, but it doesn't hurt to repeat that advice here. Often, problems can be solved easily if you ask for assistance before a problem balloons into a catastrophe.

ENJOY YOURSELF

Take a walk, read a good book, see a movie, call a friend. Do something you like to do before you start feeling overwhelmed. We don't recommend this often, but sometimes it's better to relax before you settle down to study if you feel stressed. Doing something you like first can be helpful in reducing stress and prepare you for the things you have to do.

DIRECTIONS: Now that you have read about stress and what it can do to your body, think about your own experiences and respond to the following items.

List three to five sources of stress that you are currently experiencing.

1. _____

2. _____

3. _____

4. _____

5. _____

When you are feeling very stressed out, what do you generally do to reduce your stress level?

_____

_____

_____

_____

_____

How can the strategies for reducing stress discussed in this section help you reduce your current stress level?

_____

_____

_____

_____

_____

How effective are you in dealing with friends who are stressed out? What do you do to help? How might some of these strategies work for you?

_____

_____

_____

_____

_____

Self-Assessment

DIRECTIONS: On a scale of 1 to 5, with 1 being "rarely," 3 being "sometimes," and 5 being "most of the time," evaluate how active you are as a learner.

	Rarely		Some-times		Most of the time
	1	**2**	**3**	**4**	**5**
1. When I read my texts, I can make connections with what I have read earlier in the course.	X				
2. After I read my texts, I can restate the key ideas in my own words.			X		
3. After lectures and when I am finished reading my texts, I can clearly state what I do and do not understand.			X		
4. I can take meaningful and organized notes for a full class period without losing concentration.		X			
5. When I prepare for tests, I use my time wisely.				X	
6. I seek out help when I am having problems understanding the material presented in a course.			X		
7. I use different strategies for learning, depending on the course and the type of exams.				X	
8. If information I hear or read does not fit with what I already know, I try to examine the issue from a variety of viewpoints.			X		
9. When I enter a testing situation, I have a good idea of how I will do.					X
10. I am motivated to learn in most of my classes.				X	

Add up your score. The higher your score, the more active you are as a learner. The lowest score you can receive is 10; the highest score is 50. Your score gives you an overall picture of how much work you have to do and which areas of active learning you need to work on.

Before reading the chapter, reflect on your responses to the self-assessment. What reading and studying strategies are you using that help you learn? What kinds of things do you need to do to become a more active learner?

_____

_____

_____

WORD WISE

1. **Lethargic** (adj., p. 83) — characterized by sluggishness and inactivity.
*On hot summer days, it is easy to become **lethargic** after working outside.*

2. **Synonymous** (adj., p. 84) — having the same or similar meaning.
*For people who like to garden, playing in the dirt is **synonymous** with relaxation.*

3. **Plausible** (adj., p. 85) — seemingly valid, likely, or acceptable; credible.
*Although the reason Carla gave for getting to work late seemed **plausible**, her supervisor had no choice but to dock her pay.*

4. **Fallible** (adj., p. 90) — capable of making an error; likely to be incorrect.
*Because memory is **fallible**, everyone has made errors at one time or another when recounting past events.*

DID YOU KNOW?

Did you know that all dictionary definitions are not equally helpful? In fact, sometimes dictionary definitions can confuse you more than they help. This is because some definitions are considered to be "strong," meaning that by reading them, it is easy to determine what the words mean. Other definitions, however, are termed "weak," meaning that if you have no idea what the word means, the dictionary definition will help you very little. Many weak definitions tend to define the word in question with another equally difficult word or with another version of the word itself. The message here is that if you can't figure out the definition by what's in the dictionary, take another approach.

RESEARCH INTO PRACTICE

What Aspects of Memory Are Important to College Students?

This research examines memory from the perspective of college students. The researcher, a professor who teaches a psychology course on improving memory, wanted to know what kinds of information college students were most interested in remembering. He also was interested in learning if there were differences between genders, majors, or grade point averages in the information these students deemed as important to remember.

The students were asked to respond on a scale of 1 to 10 to possible reasons why they were taking a memory improvement course. Not surprisingly, the results indicated that college students ranked as most important memory tasks related to schoolwork. Study skills, remembering what they read, and remembering facts and details were ranked as most important. Also ranked highly was remembering names and faces. This makes sense as well, because college students meet many new people and therefore have a lot of new names to remember. The researcher also found that there were no gender, major, or grade point average differences. That is, males and females responded in similar ways to the questionnaire, as did those with differing majors and grade point averages. This research indicates that college students understand the importance of improving their memories as a way of adding to their success in college, both academically and socially.

Source: K. L. Higbee, "What Aspects of Their Memories Do College Students Most Want to Improve" *College Student Journal* 38, no. 4 (2004): 552–556.

Characteristics of Active Learners

Successful learners share certain characteristics and employ various strategies and techniques to ensure that they continue to do well in their courses. This chapter considers how people learn, theories about memory and learning, and factors that influence learning. Use of the senses to enhance learning also is discussed. Before reading the chapter, be sure you have read the "Research into Practice" section on the previous page.

You hear it all the time, read about it in magazines and newspapers, and even watch television programs dedicated to the theme: Activity! Don't be **lethargic**! Be active, exercise, get involved. It's good for your health, both mental and physical. It seems as though everywhere you turn there's another piece of research or another claim about the importance of being active. Let's take the premise that you are tired of being out of shape. You take the big step and join a fitness club or gym so that you can work yourself back into good condition. Such good intentions! But what if you went to the gym and merely watched other people exercise? Would you become fit? Of course not, because you would not be an active and involved participant. Learning works in the same way. If you don't participate in learning, you won't become mentally fit, nor will you maximize your performance in the classroom. To define active learning, we'll discuss the eight characteristics of active learners. Then we will contrast those characteristics with those of passive learners.

ACTIVE LEARNERS:

Read with the Purpose of Understanding and Remembering
We'd bet that no one deliberately sits down to read with the purpose of not understanding the text. However, we're certain that you have been in situations where you "read" an assignment, closed the text, and thought, "What in the world was that about?" When you respond to a text in that manner, you are reading passively. Active readers, on the other hand, set goals before they read and check their understanding as they read. When they finish, they can explain the main points and know that they have understood what they have read. Think about something you have read for pleasure — a book or magazine about a hobby or something you have a great interest in. Most likely, you automatically read such information with the purpose of remembering. The trick in college is to apply this skill to reading information that you may not find as highly engaging.

Reflect on Information and Think Critically
Being reflective is an important part of active learning because it means that you are thinking about the information. You may make connections between the new information and what you already know, identify concepts that you don't understand very well, or evaluate the importance of what you are reading. An active learner reflects constantly. In contrast, uninvolved learners may read the text and listen to lectures, and even understand most of what is read and heard, but they do not take that crucial next step of actively thinking about it.

Listen Actively by Taking Comprehensive Notes in an Organized Fashion
We are always amazed at the number of students who engage in activities other than listening and note taking in their lecture classes. We've seen students read the campus newspaper, do assignments for other classes, work crossword puzzles, or chat with a classmate. Perhaps the all-time winner for passive learning, however, was a student who regularly

came to class with a pillow and blanket and fell asleep on his girlfriend's shoulder. Unlike these students, active learners are engaged learners. They listen actively by paying attention to the professor for the entire class period, and they write down as much information as possible.

Know That Learning Involves More Than Simply Putting in Time

Most students know about the importance of having good time-management skills and expect to invest time in studying in order to be successful. But just putting time into studying is not enough. It is the quality of that time—what you actually do with it—that makes the difference. In college, effort does not count; performance does.

Get Assistance When They Experience Problems

Because active learners constantly monitor their understanding, they know when their comprehension breaks down and they ask for help before they become lost. In addition, active learners can often predict the courses (or even particular concepts within courses) that may give them trouble. They have a plan in mind for getting assistance should they need it. They may even hire individual tutors, take advantage of free peer tutoring, or seek assistance from their professors. Although passive learners may seek help at some point, it is often too little, too late. In addition, because passive learners do not reflect and think critically, they often don't even realize that they need help.

Accept Much of the Responsibility for Learning

Active learners understand that the responsibility for learning must come from within themselves, while passive learners often blame others for their lack of motivation, poor performance, time-management problems, and other difficulties. When active learners don't perform as well as they'd hoped, they evaluate why they didn't do well and change those studying behaviors. Passive learners, on the other hand, often approach every course in the same manner and then blame their own professors or study partners when their own performance is poor. It is only when students accept the responsibility for their own learning that they can truly be called active learners.

Question Information

Active learners question information that they read and hear, while passive learners accept both the printed page and the words of their professors as "truth." Active learners don't question *everything*, but they do evaluate what they read and hear. When new information fails to fit with what they already know, they may differ from others in the conclusions they draw or in the inferences they make.

Understand the Role That Memorization Plays in Learning

To be sure, active and involved learning does require some memorization, but it is much more than that. When asked the question, "What is learning?" passive learners will often reply, "Learning is memorization." Although memorization plays a role in some types of learning, learning and memorization are not **synonymous**. Think of memorization as the building blocks for further learning. Memorization builds a solid foundation for the rest of the learning you will need to do. Involved learners go beyond memorization; they analyze, synthesize, and elaborate to make sense of information.

Understand That Attending College Is a Choice

Unlike elementary or high school requirements, there are no state or federal mandates requiring people to go to college. Active learners understand that they have chosen to attend college, and they plan to work to get the most out of it. If you begin to feel that college is a chore instead of a choice, it may help to reflect on what helped you make the choice to go to college.

The Role of Memory: Two Theories

Have you ever heard a student comment that she doesn't do well on tests because she has a bad memory? Why can you remember some things very easily, while other information needs to be pounded into your head? The answers to these questions have something to do with the way memory works. No one knows for sure exactly how memory operates, but scientists do know that certain sections of the brain are responsible for certain types of memories. Two theories that we briefly present here involve two different ways that researchers look at memory. These theories are presented in greater detail in the psychology chapter in Appendix A. As you read about the theories, keep in mind that they are just that—**plausible** explanations about how memory works.

The Parts Theory

According to what we will call the "parts theory," there are three different types of memories, or what we will refer to as "parts." It is easiest to think of memory as something that might look like the flowchart you see here:

The first part of memory, the **sensory store**, serves as a kind of filter. That is, your senses are often bombarded with information, much of which you can't remember. For example, if you are looking up a number in the telephone book, you don't look at every number. You find the number you want and then you process that piece of information in some way. For the most part, you probably have no recollection of the other numbers that were in that column. Your sensory store has filtered that information for you.

Although your sensory store can never be "filled up," it can overload. You may have been in a situation where you tried to study for a history exam but your roommate had the TV on, your next-door neighbor was listening to loud music, and dogs were barking in the distance. When there's just too much vying for your attention, it's difficult for the filter to function properly. Under normal circumstances, however, when you identify a piece of information that you want, your sensory store filters out what you don't need and you are actually not even aware of the process.

What happens to the information that you need to remember? Your **short-term memory (STM)** takes over. STM is the part where information is held for a brief period of time—less than thirty seconds, unless you do something to retain it. STM can only hold a small number of items—anywhere from five to nine pieces of information, sometimes referred to as 7±2 pieces of information.

In order to increase the amount of time information can stay in STM, you can either rehearse the information by saying it several times or writing it down, or you can "chunk" the information to reduce the number of pieces you have to remember. When you chunk information, you group it together so that you are learning fewer items. For example, separating the numbers in a phone number into two groups—555-2958 rather than thinking of it as seven separate numbers (5-5-5-2-9-5-8)—makes it easier to remember and helps hold the information in STM.

What if you need to remember the information longer than a minute? Your **long-term memory (LTM)** takes over. LTM has an unlimited capacity; it never gets "filled up," which is why you can remember things that happened when you were a small child. To get information into LTM (like information that you need to learn for an exam), you have to rehearse. Just as rehearsal will help you hold information in STM, it also helps you put information into LTM so you can remember it for an indefinite period of time. Therefore, if you write it, repeat it several times, listen to it over and over again, and/or talk it through with someone, you will be able to remember it later.

Think for a minute about how this theory of memory applies when you are taking a test. For example, if you have a multiple-choice exam, as you read the questions, your sensory store must filter out all the distractions such as the hum of the air conditioner or the person behind you with

Reality Check

Cramming and STM

The next time you think about cramming for an exam rather than spreading your learning out over several days, remember about the capacity of STM. Since STM only holds five to nine pieces of information only for a brief period of time, cramming is not a very good option. How can you use what you know about how memory works to learn and remember test information?

a persistent cough. Then, your STM must hold the question while you think about the correct answer. Finally, you must be able to retrieve the information you need from your LTM to answer the question. This process repeats for each test question.

Levels of Processing Theory

Not all psychologists agree that the parts theory explains how memory works because they do not believe that there are separate systems in the brain. Another plausible explanation is the levels of processing theory. This theory states that the degree to which you can remember and retrieve information depends on the "level" or depth to which information is processed. According to the levels of processing theory, it's not important to process everything at a deep level. In fact, if we did that, in many instances we would be wasting our time. For example—returning to the phone number example—if you wanted to remember the phone number just long enough to call the health center, repeating the number several times or writing it down in an attempt to process it deeply would be a waste of time. You would still need to rehearse the information a bit, just long enough to make the call. This type of rehearsal is called *maintenance rehearsal*—engaging in just enough repetition to process the information shallowly so that you can use it for a brief period of time and then "forget" it. This is not the kind of rehearsal you would want to use when studying for an exam.

If it were important for you to remember that telephone number, you would need to engage in *elaborative rehearsal*—making the information meaningful and rehearsing it so you can remember it later. For example, you might note that the last four digits are the same as your grandmother's address. If you were studying for an essay exam in history, it would be important for you to use elaborative rehearsal in order to have access to the information at test time. Elaborative rehearsal usually leads to deep processing and includes writing the information in an organized way, repeating the material, or personalizing it in some way to make it easier to remember.

Regardless of which theory you believe better explains how memory works, it is obvious that the theories have a key commonality: Remembering and learning information requires you to be actively involved. You must interact with it by saying, writing, or doing something. In fact, given how memory works, your participation in the learning process is crucial if you want to be an efficient and effective learner. In the next section, we discuss four key factors that influence your learning.

Four Factors That Influence Active Learning

Remembering and learning are complex processes. Part of the complexity of learning is caused by the many factors that you have to consider. Cognitive psychologists—those who study how people learn—suggest that there are four key factors that influence learning:

• Your own characteristics as a learner

• The tasks your professors ask you to do

• The texts with which you interact

• The strategies you select

We briefly cover each of these factors here, but will discuss each factor in greater detail in later chapters.

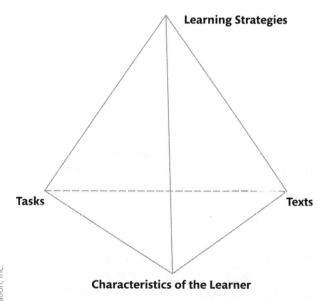

Learning Strategies

Tasks

Texts

Characteristics of the Learner

Figure 6.1: The Tetrahedral Model of Learning

Adapted from John D. Bransford, *Human Cognition: Learning, Understanding, and Remembering* (Belmont, CA: Wadsworth, 1979).

FACTOR 1: YOUR UNIQUE CHARACTERISTICS

As a student, you bring a variety of unique characteristics to each learning situation. These characteristics play a key role in how well you will perform, your interest in the material, and the strategies you will select to learn and remember the course content.

Motivation Motivation is one of the most important characteristics you can bring to a learning situation. As we discussed in Chapter 3, without motivation you would find it hard to get out of bed each morning. General interest in the topic being studied helps, but if you are open to learning new things and expanding your interests, you will be more successful.

Your Background Knowledge The more you already know about a topic, the easier it is to learn. This means that it might be a good idea to select at least some courses during your first semester or two that you know something about.

Your Ability to Concentrate How well you can concentrate on what you are reading or studying also affects your learning. Everyone has times when his mind wanders and concentration is difficult. But if you frequently leave class or finish reading a chapter feeling that you got little or nothing out of it, learning may be difficult.

Your Beliefs About Knowledge and Learning This is a characteristic that is rarely discussed, but is very important. What do you believe knowledge is? Do you believe that knowledge consists of information that is transmitted from your professor to you? Or do you believe that you can be a part of creating knowledge? How you answer questions such as these influences the way you learn. One thing is for sure: The more you believe that you are a key part of the learning process, the more effective a learner you will be.

FACTOR 2: THE TASKS FOR YOUR COURSES

Simply put, tasks are what your professors ask you to do. You can think of them as daily tasks, such as reading your text before you attend lectures, or larger tasks, such as preparing for various kinds of tests or writing papers. Most professors are pretty clear about what the tasks are. They will let you know the number of tests you will have and the kind of tests they will be (for example, essay or multiple choice), as well as their expectations about papers, lab participation, or library work.

But some professors may not be clear in defining course tasks; others may even give you conflicting messages. Therefore, it is important to try to get your professor to be as specific as possible about the tasks you must undertake. If you don't know what is expected of you, you can't select the proper learning strategies or the most effective way to approach your texts. We discuss issues relating to tasks in many of the chapters in this book, but most directly in the next chapter.

FACTOR 3: THE TEXTS YOU USE

Texts are crucial to learning in college. In fact, it has been estimated that 85 percent of all college learning involves reading. Students often think of texts as simply textbooks, and certainly textbooks are a major source of information in many of your college classes. But texts also come in other forms. Periodicals, newspapers, novels, and essays are printed texts. Another type of text that is being used more often on university campuses is computer text, sometimes called *nonlinear* or *hypertext*. You may be required to view films or documentaries, which are visual texts. In addition to textbooks, lecture notes are the other most frequently used type of "text" that college students must use.

Whatever types of text you are expected to use, you should know how the particular text is organized. In most textbooks, each chapter is organized in the same fashion. In addition, your professor's lectures probably follow the same pattern each day. Even visual texts have organizational patterns. Once you have determined how your text is organized, learning the material becomes a much easier task. Like learner characteristics and tasks, texts are an important part of the learning puzzle.

FACTOR 4: THE LEARNING STRATEGIES

The final, and perhaps the most complex, factor that influences learning is the strategies that you choose. It is important to realize that strategies should be chosen based on the other three factors: your characteristics as a learner, the tasks you have to do, and the texts used. Thus, a large portion of *Effective College Learning* is devoted to learning strategies.

The first two sections of this chapter discussed the importance of active learning and memory and why learning is more than simply memorizing information. Certainly, learning involves memory. Without it, we could not retain information or retrieve it again for an exam. However, it is also easy to see that in order to make sense of information, we must understand ourselves as learners, know how to interact with texts, be aware of course tasks, and then select the appropriate strategies. Strategies for active learning have several features in common, including:

You Can Use Them on Your Own Once you learn them, you can use all of these strategies by yourself. Because studying is mostly a solitary activity, it is important to be able to use strategies without guidance from someone else—a professor or a friend, for example.

They Have a Self-Testing Component These strategies have specific underlying processes that research has consistently shown lead to better performance. For example, all of the strategies you will learn have a self-testing component, which helps you monitor your learning by immediately letting you know whether or not you understand the information.

They Help You Think Critically The strategies require participation on your part in the form of critical thinking and reasoning. They will help you think beyond the text and analyze, synthesize, and apply the information. In other words, the strategies will help you go beyond memorization.

They Are Flexible Strategies should not be a rigid system or a lockstep process. In other words, you can modify learning strategies according to your own learning preferences, the tasks, and the texts.

DIRECTIONS: Think about how the four factors—your unique characteristics, tasks, texts, and learning strategies—relate to your own learning by responding to each of the questions below. Then compare your responses with those of your classmates.

Which of these factors have you consciously considered in your own learning? In what ways have you considered them?

_____

_____

_____

_____

_____

_____

_____

_____

For those factors that you have not thought about, how might you begin to consider them in your courses this term?

_____

_____

_____

_____

_____

_____

_____

_____

_____

Using Your Senses for Effective Learning

So far, we've discussed the characteristics of active learning, the importance of memory in learning, and the four factors that influence learning. We turn now to how you can use your senses to become a more effective learner.

Thinking About How You Learn Best

When students talk to us about their difficulty remembering information, they often mention learning styles as a reason why memory sometimes breaks down. One student might say, "I can't learn from my history teacher because all he does is lecture and I don't learn very well through listening. I like to do things to learn." Another might say, "I can't grasp the material without charts, tables, and diagrams. Reading just words doesn't work for me." When we use the term *learning styles*, we are referring to how students learn best. Researchers who study this issue suggest that there are three main kinds of learners.

VISUAL LEARNERS

Visual learners tend to learn best by watching or seeing. They like to be shown how to do things and often learn best through diagrams or by using imagery. If you are a visual learner, if someone asks you how to spell a word, you probably have to write it down first rather than simply trying to spell the word in your head or out loud. Such learners also gravitate toward using imagery and written rehearsal strategies—particularly concept maps, diagrams, flow charts, and the like.

AUDITORY LEARNERS

Auditory learners tend to learn best by listening or speaking. They can learn easily through listening to lectures or by talking information over with a peer. If you are an auditory learner, you probably rarely miss a class lecture and you may participate in study groups for many of your courses. You may rehearse information by repeating it, either to yourself or out loud. However, sometimes auditory learners may not learn very well from course lectures but do learn well from small group interactions with their peers. In addition, auditory learners may have a difficult time taking notes, so they try to rely on their memory to reconstruct the nature of the lecture. And as we all know, no matter how well you listen, memory can be **fallible**.

KINESTHETIC LEARNERS (ALSO CALLED *TACTILE LEARNERS*)

Kinesthetic learners tend to learn best by touching or movement. They generally prefer writing or even typing things out. If you are a kinesthetic learner, you may rehearse information by writing it several times. You may also enjoy lab courses where there is a hands-on approach to learning. In addition, when learning a new skill—such as tennis, for example—kinesthetic learners like to be shown how to do everything.

Engaging All of Your Senses

Although somewhat helpful, we believe these three categories of learners oversimplify the complex task of college learning. Sometimes in study skills classes, instructors will have students take a learning styles inventory to find out how they learn "best." As a result of these tests, students are often pigeonholed into one of the three categories and then given suggestions for learning and studying based only on one particular style. Students can feel trapped when their preferred mode cannot be used in a particular course. For example, it is hard to be kinesthetic in a philosophy course. Additionally, even in this day of technology, the fact remains that most colleges rely primarily on the traditional classroom structure where students must read their texts, listen to lectures, take notes, and take exams. Therefore, you need to tap as many of the learning methods as possible if you are to be successful in college. That is why we suggest that, rather than relying on one particular learning style that may actually impede your learning, you use strategies that incorporate them all. We call this "learning through your senses".

Many students use a "one trick pony" approach. That is, they prepare the same way for all of their classes, regardless of the type of test they'll have. They study biology the same way they study history. However, in college, it is important to use a variety of strategies and all of your senses to learn. In history, for example, you would want to read your text, listen actively to the lectures, and take a good set of notes. In that way, you would use your senses to begin to get the information into your memory. You would have a record of the important information to study from and you would be actively engaged. As test time approaches, you might study with a group of other students, make time lines as a way of outlining major historical events, and predict and answer essay questions. You would be listening, reading, discussing, and writing as a way of engaging all of your senses. Contrast that approach with simply attending all the lectures. Which method do you think would help a student remember more come test time?

Although we encourage you to use all of your senses to learn, we also realize that many students prefer one mode of learning over another. That's fine. We encourage students to go with their strengths, but at the same time realizing that they can use strategies and approaches that are related to their weaker modes. In fact, most tasks in college make it necessary to approach learning by using multiple senses. For example, in the sciences, there are generally diagrams to learn and understand. You can't ignore that task just because you aren't a visual leaner. Likewise, if you learn best visually, you must still attend lectures and listen actively.

In Chapters 8, 9, and 10, we will present a variety of strategies that will assist you in learning and remembering information. We have divided these strategies according to the three major types of learners.

BEYOND THE CLASSROOM

We have observed that when people return to college after working for a few years or delay beginning college after high school graduation, they often struggle with and fear math courses more than anything else. If you fall into this category, you might look into taking a course to help you brush up on your math skills before taking your first required class. You can also seek out tutoring or get assistance with math test anxiety.

Learning Through Technology

Most of your college professors will incorporate technology (specifically computers and the Internet) into their classes, thus expecting you to learn in yet another way. But expect to find a wide range in the level of integration. Some professors will be old school, low-tech holdouts who won't even have an e-mail account. Other professors will use high-tech presentations during class and will expect you to have a high level of technical knowledge. Most professors fall somewhere in the middle and use technology where they find it to be most beneficial for explaining course content and supporting classroom instruction. You can expect to see many or all of the following uses of learning through technology as part of the tasks in your college courses. And you will probably find several other ways that professors incorporate technology into their course tasks as new tools become available.

Computerized Class Presentations Such As PowerPoint Many professors use computer slides to outline their lectures. They may use overheads of diagrams or show video clips to emphasize points. They may also display Web pages or other Internet sources of information during class.

Computerized Notes It is becoming more common for professors to put their notes on the Web. Web notes are best used as a supplement or as a guide for taking your own notes in class (see Chapter 8 for strategies on using Web notes

effectively). You may also find yourself in a classroom equipped with computers or computer hookups that allow you to take notes on a laptop. Such classrooms are equipped with the latest technology. This is a wonderful service that we suggest you take advantage of if it is available on your campus.

Computer Modules or CD-ROM Supplements Some professors place sample questions or problems on the Web so that students can evaluate their understanding of the course material as they prepare for exams. Other professors (especially in the sciences) provide supplementary material on CD-ROMs. These CDs generally contain information that cannot be depicted in a text format—such as a video of a chemical reaction—but enhances the information discussed in a lecture or in the text.

Computerized Course Management Systems (Such As WebCT or Blackboard) Professors using these course management systems are often quite firm in their belief that such systems add another dimension to helping you learn the course material. They may place their syllabi, quizzes, assignments, practice exams, and other course information there. They may also post student grades or have virtual chats with the class. We even know a professor who conducts exam reviews online. If your professor uses one of these

---

NETWORKING

Learning Styles Inventories on the Web

If you have never taken a learning styles assessment, you might want to. The Internet is loaded with them. You can find questionnaires that assess learning styles in the visual, auditory, and kinesthetic ways we have discussed. You can also find out about multiple intelligences. And you can take a personality inventory designed to help you figure out how you learn best—you can even find out about the learning style of your dog. But remember to take the results with a grain of salt. Don't try to base your entire approach to studying in college on such assessments.

systems, plan to visit the site often to keep up with new assignments and important information.

Course Exams Some courses will require you to take exams by computer. Many mathematics courses are moving toward computerized exams. In addition, English professors may require students to write and submit essays via computer and then provide feedback on papers using computerized mark-up systems. Taking an exam by computer is a bit different from the old paper and pencil type. But you should not abandon your traditional test-taking strategies. Continue to read each question carefully and answer the items you know first. However, you should find out whether you can return to a question or if you must answer each item before moving on to the next one. Some students say that having exams on computers takes some getting used to, but once you have some experience, it is just like taking any other test.

Readings Your professors may assign readings that can only be found online. They may be from Web-based journals supplied by the campus library's online service or from any number of other sources. If you find you have trouble reading online, as many people do, we suggest you print the reading out in advance.

E-mail Assignments Professors may require you to submit assignments over e-mail. If it is a short assignment, typing your response straight into the e-mail message is generally acceptable. If, however, you are required to turn in a longer assignment (more than one page), it is best to type it in a word processing program and send it as a file attachment. Be sure to use the file type requested by your professor. If you do not know how to do this, go to the nearest computer lab to get some help.

Group Presentations At some point in your college career, you will probably find yourself in a course that requires a group presentation that has a technology component. Some professors require a Web-based presentation or one that utilizes several types of media. We suggest that you meet with your group early and often and experiment with the technology several times to work out any problems before presenting it in class.

Discussion Groups and Listservs These supports are used to generate discussion outside the class. Some professors even require each student to post a certain number of messages each week to ensure that the listserv is used. To gain multiple perspectives, you can ask questions or see what other people are thinking about the course information.

Real College

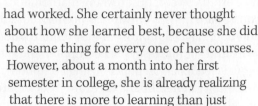

MELISSA'S MEMORY

DIRECTIONS: *Read the following scenario and respond to the questions based on what you have learned in this chapter.*

Melissa has always viewed herself as having a good memory. When she was in high school, she would memorize information slumped over a bowl of Fruit Loops on the morning of a test. Cramming and memorization were synonymous to Melissa. She would dutifully memorize detailed lists, dates, and formulas; she could usually remember most of the information she crammed into her head at least long enough to do fairly well on her exams. Even when she couldn't remember everything, she did well enough to get by. Melissa never thought much about how to learn differently because what she did

had worked. She certainly never thought about how she learned best, because she did the same thing for every one of her courses. However, about a month into her first semester in college, she is already realizing that there is more to learning than just memorizing and that she needs to do more than her "Fruit Loops" routine if she wants to remain a college student. She made an appointment at the Learning Center because she heard they could help with this sort of problem. Ms. Lawton, one of the professional staffpeople, had Melissa take a couple of assessments to gauge her learning style. Melissa was surprised at how much Ms. Lawton could tell from the assessments. She said that Melissa learned equally well from all of her senses and that she wasn't being an efficient or effective learner with her current approach to studying.

What can Melissa do?

What are some suggestions for helping Melissa become a better learner?

_____

_____

_____

_____

How might she use the assessments to change her approaches to studying and learning?

_____

_____

_____

_____

Add to Your Portfolio

1. Think about yourself as a learner and identify the learning style that seems to best fit you. You can take one of the online assessments or, better yet, assess your own learning style by writing a one-page reflection about how you think you learn.

_____

_____

_____

_____

_____

_____

_____

2. For one of your classes this semester, think about how the four factors of learning will impact your performance. Write a summary of your learner characteristics, and list the course tasks and text(s). Then think about the learning strategies that will work best in the course.

_____

_____

_____

_____

_____

_____

_____

_____

Chapter 7
Figuring Out the Task

Read this chapter to answer the following questions:

- What do we mean by "task"?
- How is the task communicated?
- How can you figure out what your professor expects?
- What types of technology might professors incorporate into their courses?

Self-Assessment

DIRECTIONS: Rate the following tasks. Place an *E* beside the tasks you consider the easiest, an *M* beside the tasks you consider to be at a middle level of difficulty, and a *D* beside the tasks you consider the most difficult.

1. _M_ Taking a matching exam in history

2. _M_ Analyzing a chemical process for a chemistry lab

3. _E_ Writing a persuasive essay for English class

4. _D_ Evaluating and drawing a conclusion about several articles presenting conflicting accounts of an event for political science class

5. _D_ Taking a multiple-choice exam over two psychology chapters

6. _M_ Taking an exam over the bold-faced terms for a biology class

7. _E_ Debating a controversial issue in sociology class

8. _E_ Giving an informational speech for a speech communications class

9. _D_ Solving calculus problems on a mathematics exam

How you rated these tasks probably had something to do with your own personal background and interests. For example, if you love mathematics, you might think solving calculus problems is easy. However, there are some overarching ideas that make numbers 1 and 6 the easiest; numbers 2, 5, 8, and 9 somewhere in the middle; and numbers 3, 4, and 7 the most difficult tasks. You'll learn why in this chapter.

Take a few minutes and reflect on some of the tasks you have been asked to do in your classes. How do go about figuring out what your professors expect from you? What kinds of tasks are easy for you? What kinds of tasks tend to be more difficult? Why?

_____

_____

_____

_____

_____

_____

_____

_____

Before You Begin

RESEARCH INTO PRACTICE

A Case Study of How Students Determine Task

In this article, Drs. Simpson and Nist followed and interviewed ten students enrolled in a large-lecture introductory history course over an entire term. Some of these students performed very well, some were average, and some were below average in their test scores. The researchers were interested in determining the factors that enabled some of the students to earn As and Bs while others failed. Although they found that the high-performing students used more efficient and effective study strategies, the more important finding was that they understood what their professor expected from them. They correctly interpreted the task—to write essay answers that called for synthesis and analysis in a well-structured format—and selected their strategies for studying *after* they had determined the task. In other words, their task definition drove their strategy choice, not vice versa. Drs. Simpson and Nist concluded that:

". . . when we reflected on the congruency between the professor's and students' perceptions of task, we concluded that Dr. Stack [the professor] did communicate the task to students in a variety of explicit and implicit ways . . . The HPG [high-performing group] had little problem in determining what it was that Dr. Stack wanted them to do. . . .

However, the LPG [low-performing group] . . . failed to 'accommodate' Dr. Stack and his communication about the task."

Drs. Simpson and Nist's finding about the importance that task interpretation plays in learning and studying in college is an important one. If you don't know precisely what it is your professor expects from you, you are doomed to struggle—at best becoming frustrated and at worst making low grades. Simpson and Nist found that students in history, for example, often defined the task as memorizing names, dates, and facts, much as they had done in high school. But their college professor looked at history as more analysis and synthesis. Students who held fast to their high school model of memorizing to study history struggled all term with the course. Some, who never figured out the task, actually failed. The implications of this study for you, the student, are clear: Figure out the task and figure it out early in the term. Then select the strategies that will best fit your professor's expectations.

Source: M. L. Simpson and S. L. Nist, "Perspectives on Learning History: A Case Study," *Journal of Literacy Research* 29 (1997): 363–395.

What Is "Task"?

In Chapter 6, we introduced the idea that there are four factors that impact learning and briefly discussed the role that task understanding plays in being an active learner. We will talk about task understanding here in greater detail because much of your success as a college student rests on your ability to interpret the tasks in your courses. There's more to studying and being an effective student than meets the eye. And "studying hard" is not always "studying smart." Your ability to understand what your professor wants you to do and the way you are supposed to do it

goes a long way toward making you a more efficient and effective student. Why? To answer this question, we'll explore two important aspects of task: What we mean by "task" and how you go about figuring out what the task is. Although the specific tasks in your courses will vary depending on the content, the professor, and the discipline, the task for any course consists of two parts:

1. The type of activity in which you engage
2. The level of thinking required as you engage in the activity

Part One: The Type of Activity

The activity you will be asked to complete for a class is usually a test, a paper, or a project that your instructor will use to evaluate you. But knowing what the activity is isn't enough information to be able to carefully select an appropriate approach to the task.

TESTS

First, you need to know the *type* of test you will take. Is it
• an objective exam, which includes multiple-choice, true/false, or matching items?
• a subjective exam that requires answering essay, short answer, or identification questions?
• a combination of both types?

   Because you will approach studying for multiple-choice tests differently than you will approach studying for essay tests, it's very important to know right from the beginning the basic type of test you will have. As we will discuss in greater detail later in the book, the kind of reading you do, the way you think about the material, and the strategies you select all have a bearing on the kinds of tasks you are asked to complete in a course.

   The importance of precisely knowing the task can be explained by describing a situation that occurred to students enrolled in a large-lecture history course. For each test, students were told that they would have "objective items" and two essay questions. On the first four exams, these objective items were always multiple-choice. However, when it came time for the final exam, the professor **reiterated** that they would have a test that was part objective and part essay; they assumed that they would once again have multiple-choice questions. Imagine their surprise when the tests were distributed and the objective items were fill-in-the-blanks. Many students were outraged and went to see the professor when they discovered that they had done poorly on the test. But the professor wouldn't budge. His definition of task for objective items included fill-in-the-blank as well as multiple-choice. The point here is clear: Get as much specific information as possible about the test. Ask the right questions. Just knowing that you will have an objective test is likely to be insufficient information.

yo-yo

PAPERS OR PROJECTS

If the task in a course consists of papers or projects rather than exams, the same advice about precisely knowing the task holds true. Talk with your professor about specific aspects of a paper, especially if the requirements seem unclear. In political science courses on our campus, for example, students must do a project that consists of several different pieces. First they select a political issue to follow throughout the term. They must subscribe to the *New York Times,* read it daily, and find a minimum of thirty articles, concerning their issue. For each article, they must write a brief summary. At the end of the term, they complete two additional tasks. First they write a policy statement, and then they write a memo to an influential political figure about the issue. Students who fail to understand how to carry out the numerous pieces involved in this task have severe problems in doing well on a long-term project that is 30 percent of their grade.

Before reading the next section, be sure you have read the "Research into Practice" segment. This piece of research suggests that students who do well understand the task and select the appropriate strategies to carry out that task.

BEYOND THE CLASSROOM

Returning students who have not been part of the technology loop may feel somewhat intimidated if their campus is high-tech or if most of their professors incorporate technology into their courses. If you find yourself in this situation, see if your campus offers either a formal course or workshops to help get you up to speed. More and more campuses are offering what are **generically** referred to as IT (information technology) literacy courses to teach students how to effectively use technology to learn.

Part Two: The Level of Thinking

Once you have identified the specific activities your professor expects, you're halfway there. The other part of task identification—perhaps the more important part—is knowing the level of thinking that is required to carry out the task. There are many types of thinking that a professor may want you to engage in. Knowing the level of questions your professor asks can help you choose appropriate learning and study strategies.

An understanding of *Bloom's Taxonomy*, a classification system that provides a way to categorize the kinds of questions that students typically encounter in their classes, can be valuable in determining what you need to do for a course. Bloom discusses six levels of questioning: knowledge, comprehension, application, analysis, synthesis, and evaluation. Each is briefly touched on below.

Knowledge includes knowledge of dates, events, major ideas, bold-faced terms.
* *Question Words*: list, define, describe, identify, match, name, what, who, when, where
* *Examples*: What happened on Black Tuesday? What are collar cells?
Define *peristalsis*.

Comprehension includes grasping the meaning, explaining or summarizing, grouping, predicting outcomes, or inferring.
* *Question Words*: summarize, describe, interpret, distinguish, defend, explain, discuss, predict
* *Examples*: Explain the two different theories that explain how we remember information.
Describe the major components of Hoover's New Deal.
Discuss the role of the small intestine in the digestion process.

Application requires the ability to use the material in a new context, to solve problems, or to utilize rules, concepts, or theories.
* *Question Words*: apply, demonstrate, calculate, illustrate, show, relate, give an example of, solve
* *Examples*: If a plant with the genotype BbCcDd was crossed with a plant that was BBCcdd, what

are the chances of producing a plant with the genotype BbCcDd?
Apply what you know about how the brain organizes information to how the computer organizes information.

Analysis involves understanding organization of parts, clarifying, concluding, or recognizing hidden meaning.
* *Question Words*: analyze, explain, compare and contrast, select, arrange, order
* *Examples*: Compare and contrast the events leading up to the Great Depression to those leading up to the global economic downturn in the late 2000s.
Select the most appropriate method for solving this calculus problem.

Synthesis involves creating new ideas, relating knowledge from several sources of information, predicting, drawing conclusions.
* *Question Words*: combine, create, design, formulate, compose, integrate, rewrite, generalize
* *Examples*: Rewrite the play *The Cherry Orchard* as if it were written by Ibsen.
If someone has a poor memory, how might they improve it?

Evaluation relies on the ability to make choices based on evidence, to support a stance with reasoning, to recognize subjectivity, to assess value of theories.
* *Question Words*: support, judge, discriminate, assess, recommend, measure, convince, conclude
* *Examples*: How successful would the proposed federal income tax cut be in controlling inflation as well as decreasing unemployment?
Do you agree with the way Hoover tried to help the county get out of the Great Depression? Why or Why not?

Source: Bloom, B., Englehart, M. Furst, E., Hill, W., & Krathwohl, D. (1956). Taxonomy of educational objectives: The classification of educational goals. Handbook I: Cognitive domain. New York, Toronto: Longmans, Green.

Many objective exams will have questions at each of these levels. Thus, you need to think about this part of the task and concentrate your studying efforts differently depending on the knowledge level required. Some students believe that objective exams don't involve higher-level thinking. That is, they think that multiple-choice and true/false tests are basically memorization tasks. However, on most objective tests, some of the questions will be factual in nature, some will ask for examples, and some will require you to synthesize and analyze. Most essay questions require the highest level of thinking, but other subjective exams—such as identification items—could ask for just factual information. We can summarize thinking about task in this way: If the task is a matching exam with a low level of thinking required, you will simply have to memorize. If the task is a multiple-choice exam with a medium level of thinking, you will need to analyze. And if the task is to write an essay or responses to short-answer questions and it requires a high level of thinking, you will need to synthesize. Remember: Unless you know the task and the types of thinking expected, you will have a difficult time selecting the appropriate study strategies.

NETWORKING

Using the Web to Understand Task

Find the Web page of one of your professors and look for information concerning task. For example, if you have multiple-choice exams, look to see whether your professor has put any example test items on the site. Also check out online information about the course. Sometimes rather than putting material concerning tests and other course requirements on their personal Web pages, professors will have a separate page for each course they teach. These pages can provide a wealth of information to help you better understand the task.

Most college students do not consciously sit down at the beginning of the term and say to themselves, "Gee, before I start doing my reading and studying for this class, I'd better figure out the task!" For students who intuitively understand that it is important to figure out the course demands, it's more of an unconscious effort. Think about yourself as a learner, and then respond to the following questions as a way of monitoring your learning about your knowledge of the tasks for your classes:

Have you taken time this term to figure out the task in each of your classes? If not, how might you begin to gather that information this term and in future terms?

_____

_____

_____

_____

Have you ever been in a class where you had a very difficult time understanding what the professor's expectations were? How did you handle that situation? What might you do differently now?

_____

_____

_____

_____

Can you think of any other sources that might be able to give you task information?

_____

_____

_____

_____

How might you organize your notes to draw attention to task information?

_____

_____

_____

_____

_____

How Is the Task Communicated?

Now that you understand how important it is to know the task for each of your classes, you might ask the obvious question: How do I figure out how to carry out the task? Because few professors will state the task precisely and completely, it becomes important for you to be able to piece together bits of information from a variety of sources in order to paint the whole picture for yourself.

ATTEND CLASS EVERYDAY

The best place to begin, of course, is with what your professor says in class, especially in the early part of the term. Some professors **delineate** the task very neatly and clearly on the first day when they go over the syllabus. Others will give you a big picture of the task early in the term and then fill in the details as the course progresses. Still others—and perhaps most college professors fall into this category—give you a combination of implicit and explicit cues and expect you to pick up on those cues.

WRITE IT DOWN

It's just as important to take notes concerning what's expected of you as it is to take notes on the content. Students often think that they will remember how to structure an essay or the types of questions that will be on their exams. However, they may discover two or three weeks later that they have only a faint recollection—or worse, no recollection at all—of some important piece of information that the professor had discussed in class. Go to class, listen carefully, and write down in your lecture notes what your professor says about the task.

CONSULT YOUR SYLLABUS

Read your syllabus carefully at the beginning of the course, and then return to it on a regular basis. Look for any statements that tell you about course expectations. Examine your syllabus for the following information:

☐ The number of tests you will have or papers you will have to write, and the approximate dates tests will be given or papers will be due

☐ Your professor's office hours and phone number (or e-mail address) so that you know how to make an appointment to talk with her

☐ Your professor's policies on make-up work or the consequences of missing an exam or another deadline

☐ Your professor's attendance policies (if any)

☐ Your professor's philosophy on the course, which can give you insight into how your professor will approach the content and can go a long way in helping you define the task

☐ The course objectives. Reading these statements will tell you what the professor hopes you will learn in the course.

All of these factors either directly or indirectly relate to task. Thus, it is important not only to read your syllabus carefully at the beginning of the term, but also to refer to it often as the term progresses.

ASK YOUR PROFESSOR TO SHOW SAMPLE QUESTIONS

Sample questions can give you information about the level of thinking and the types of questions your professor tends to ask. Some professors even make old exams available to students. If so, avoid using them as a study guide, because the professor will write the same *types* of questions on future exams, but will not ask the same exact questions.

ASK FORMER STUDENTS

Students who have already taken a particular course will be able to give you details about the course and the professor. But make sure that you ask former students the right questions. For example, asking someone, "Are Professor Smith's tests difficult?" is not the best way to pose the question, because what is difficult to one person may not be difficult to another. Better questions would be: "What kind of tests does Professor Smith give?" "Can you remember examples of some questions?" "What kind of structure does he expect for essay questions?" "Does he give you much guidance?" Questions such as these give you answers about the task.

GO ONLINE

When professors use an online component in the class, such as a course management system (e.g., WebCT or Blackboard) or a Web site where assignments and grades are posted, they often post a wealth of information about the tasks as well. Check these sites for writing guidelines, model essays, sample test questions, and so forth. Many of the course Web sites that professors use also have a discussion forum that can be an excellent place to post questions about course tasks.

Reality Check

When All Else Fails

If you have exhausted all efforts to figure out the task in a course, go see your professor—especially if you have already taken one test and performed poorly. Starting a conversation with your professor by explaining what you are doing and asking her for advice about how to study may give you a lot more information about how she wants you to think about the course information. If you ignore the fact that you are in the dark about the task and continue doing poorly in the course, you will only become frustrated.

Real College

TANYA'S TASK

DIRECTIONS: *Read the following scenario and respond to the questions based on the information you have learned in this chapter.*

Tanya decided that she could no longer put off getting her lab science requirement out of the way, especially because she has to endure two semesters of it once she makes her selection. She "hates science with a passion," and would much rather simply pursue her major courses in creative writing. It's not that she hasn't done well in science. In fact, because her grades in high school biology classes were quite good, she decided that she would go ahead and take biology in college rather than chemistry, which gave her nightmares in high school. She sees herself as a good memorizer, and because her high school biology experience involved lots of memorization of terms and labeling of diagrams, she tended to make good grades. But the fact remains: She just doesn't like science of any type, plain and simple.

As Tanya looks over her class schedule for the term, she thinks about skipping the first class or two. From her perspective, two fewer biology classes to go to would be a good thing. But her roommate, who has already taken the course, advises her to attend every class—even the first one. Tanya reluctantly takes the advice and actually thought the professor was engaging and humorous.

Obviously, in order to earn a good grade in this course, Tanya is going to have to figure out what the tasks are. On the first day, the professor said that there would be three objective exams, lab reports, and a cumulative final, but he didn't say much else about the tasks.

What can Tanya do?

Think about Tanya's situation and respond to the following questions:

1. What additional information do you think Tanya needs so that she can have a clearer idea of the task?

_____

_____

2. How should she go about gathering the necessary information?

_____

_____

3. How will Tanya's dislike of science influence the way she might approach this course?

_____

_____

Add to Your Portfolio

For each of your classes this term, answer the following questions related to task:

1. What is the task for this course? Start by looking at the syllabus, e-mailing the professor, or talking to a TA.

Course 1 _____

Course 2 _____

Course 3 _____

Course 4 _____

2. Write down the specific tasks and how you figured out what the professor expected from you.

Course 1 _____

Course 2 _____

Course 3 _____

Course 4 _____

3. What clues did the professor give that helped you figure it out?

Course 1 _____

Course 2 _____

Course 3 _____

Course 4 _____

4. Finally, think about how you will approach each course based on the task. How should you approach studying for each exam?

Course 1 _____

Course 2 _____

Course 3 _____

Course 4 _____

As the term progresses, reread your assessment of what you thought the tasks were and see if you were correct.

Chapter 8
Note Taking: Your Task in Class

Read this chapter to answer the following questions:

- Why is it important to take good lecture notes?
- What should I do before, during, and after class to take good notes?
- How can I match my note taking to the tasks of the class?
- How can I use my notes to self-test?

Self-Assessment

DIRECTIONS: Examine your notes from one of your classes and evaluate them on a scale of 1 to 5, with 1 being "hardly ever" and 5 being "almost always."

	Hardly ever		Some-times		Almost always
	1	**2**	**3**	**4**	**5**
1. My notes are organized.			X		
2. My notes distinguish main points from details.			X		
3. My notes include examples.			X		
4. I take notes over class discussions.				X	
5. I test myself over my notes.					X
6. My notes accurately reflect the content of the class.				X	
7. My notes contain abbreviations.				X	
8. I review my notes as soon after class as possible.	X				
9. I read my text assignments before lectures.				X	
10. I compare my notes to the text when I study.				X	

The more 5s you've marked, the better. Many students find that they need more efficient strategies for note taking. Read on to find out how to improve your note-taking skills.

Before reading the chapter, reflect on your responses to the self-assessment. How is your current note-taking system helping you learn? What do you need to work on?

need to get more detailed

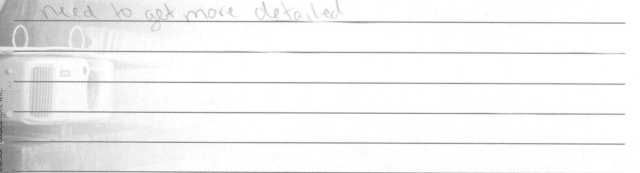

Before You Begin

WORD WISE

1. **Impede** (v., p. 110) — to obstruct the progress of; to be a hindrance to.
*Her lack of training **impeded** her ability to complete the marathon.*

2. **Soporific** (adj., p. 112) — inducing, or tending to induce, sleep.
*Many find that eating turkey during Thanksgiving dinner has a **soporific** effect.*

3. **Capricious** (adj., p. 126) — characterized by impulse; lacking a rational basis; likely to change suddenly.
*He was a **capricious** boss—I never knew how he would react.*

DID YOU KNOW?

Did you ever have a professor who lectured using $5.00 words? Sometimes it might seem like you need to have a dictionary with you the entire time just to understand what he is saying. How do you take notes when you don't understand the vocabulary the professor is using? We recognize that it can be a challenge, but you can use a few tricks to make the task more manageable. First, read the textbook before the lecture so you have some understanding of the topics. Second, make friends with a classmate to compare notes with each week. Third, compare your notes to the text to help you figure out which words are content-specific (those words that are important to the discipline you are studying) and which are general vocabulary words.

RESEARCH INTO PRACTICE

Note-Taking Systems to Fit the Task

In this study, Dr. Michael Ryan examined students' conceptions of note taking to see how those conceptions related to efforts to improve note-taking practices. Students responded to a questionnaire containing metaphors for note taking that fell into six different categories to see which metaphors they found most appealing: 1. absorbing ("note taking is like being a sponge"), 2. recording ("taking notes is like being a tape recorder"), 3. translating ("note taking is like being a court stenographer), 4. decoding ("taking notes is like being a code breaker"), 5. integrating ("taking notes is like being a reporter to get at the truth"), 6. organizing ("taking notes is like marking a trail like an explorer on an expedition").

The students also responded to questions about their own note-taking practices. Dr. Ryan found that the metaphors for note taking that students found appealing correlated with their own methods for note taking. For example, students who thought about note taking like a reporter tended to quote sources completely and look for clues to integrate different sources. This is important because the choice of metaphors may give a clue to the way students perceive the task demands of lecture note taking. In some cases, these perceptions may **impede** learning. The results also suggest that no single system of note taking may be sufficient for the variety of note-taking tasks that undergraduates encounter. In addition, students who are attempting to learn more effective note-taking practices may first need to modify their conceptions of note taking that underlie the way they currently take notes.

Source: M. P. Ryan, "Conceptual Models of Lecture Learning: Guiding Metaphors and Model-Appropriate Notetaking Practices," *Reading Psychology* 22, (2001): 289–312.

The Importance and Characteristics of Good Lecture Notes

Whether you are attending a large university, a small liberal arts college, or a community college, a large percentage of information will be conveyed to you through lecture. In the traditional lecture format, professors explain information that they believe is important for you to learn in the class. Most professors expect you to take notes in an organized fashion so that you can study and review the notes throughout the course. Note taking isn't too difficult if you have a professor who speaks slowly, clearly, and lectures in an organized fashion. Unfortunately, many professors do not lecture in this way. Therefore, students should be able to supply their own organization, to get down the important points, and to fill in the gaps when necessary.

It's important to be able to take good lecture notes for a variety of reasons:

• They serve as a record of what goes on in class each day. Without a complete record, it's difficult to have all the information you need to prepare for subsequent classes or exams.

• When your notes are organized, they can help you identify patterns in your professor's lectures. Once you see patterns, you get a better idea of what your professor believes is important.

• They help you spot overlap between your text and the professor's lecture. These overlaps are fertile ground for test questions.

This chapter addresses note taking, discussing the characteristics of good notes, how it should be done, how to match it to course tasks, and how to self-test with notes. But before reading this chapter, be sure you have read the "Research into Practice" section that discusses students' views of note taking.

Characteristics of Good Notes

What distinguishes good notes from poor notes? As you will see, good notes are more than just readable.

Good Notes Are Organized Good notes use organizational strategies such as underlining the main points, indenting details, noting examples, and numbering lists of ideas. This differs dramatically from incomplete notes. Incomplete notes—those that are inadequate as well as imprecise—occur most frequently in courses that students find uninteresting or **soporific**. In these notes, it is often difficult to tell where one idea ends and another begins or what is a main point and what is a detail.

Good Notes Distinguish Main Points from Details Every lecture has both main points and details. The main points might be reasons, characteristics, or theories. Details include information that supports or explains the main points. It's important to write your notes in such a way that the main points are distinguishable from the details. If the information runs together or if you have only written down the main points and excluded the details, your notes will be less useful for studying.

Good Notes Include Examples Often when professors get to the point in the lecture at which they are giving examples, students are nodding off or thinking about what they plan to have for lunch. But examples often surface on exams, so it's crucial to write down every example of a particular main point that the professor provides. These examples should stand out in some way so that you can tell what they illustrate as you study.

Good Notes Clearly Indicate Lecture Patterns Most professors use the same pattern in all of their lectures. The two most common are the *deductive* pattern and the *inductive* pattern. Deductive lectures begin with a generalization ("There are three main reasons for . . .") and then fill in the reasons, details, and examples. Inductive lectures do the opposite. They progress from the specific to the general. For example, an inductive lecturer would provide a series of reasons or characteristics and conclude with a statement such as "So, all of this means . . ." This concluding statement is the generalization that helps make sense of the lecture. It is generally easier to follow lectures when they are presented in a deductive manner. Moreover, different disciplines may lend themselves better to one type than the other. The style your professor uses should become apparent to you after the first few class sessions, and your notes will need to reflect this lecture pattern.

Reality Check

Using Supplemental Notes
It is becoming more common for professors to put their notes on the Web or to have students purchase copies of their notes to follow during the lecture. These alternatives are useful as long as you continue to take a good set of notes yourself. Simply using someone else's notes (even if they are the professor's) rather than taking your own does not maximize your learning. Many students find that they tune out when they don't take their own notes, causing them to miss important points. A better approach is to take your own notes and then compare them with the Web notes.

Good Notes Allow for Self-Testing Students don't usually consider that the way they take notes will influence the way they study. Most students merely "read over" their notes. However, this approach often gives them a false sense of knowing the information when, in fact, they do not. Instead, try writing questions or key words—called annotations—in the margin of your notes to help you test yourself. These questions will help you monitor your knowledge of the material. (We will discuss self-questioning of lecture notes, or self-testing, in more detail later in the chapter.)

Good Notes Stand the Test of Time Because your notes are a record of what is said in class each day, they should make sense to you long after class is over. You should be able to read through your notes and annotations two days, two weeks, or two months later and find that they are still understandable. Because of the way memory works, you will be unable to remember everything your professor says in class every day. That's why you take notes to begin with. It's important, then, to be sure that your notes are organized in such a way that they will make sense down the line and that they include as much detail as you can reasonably get on paper.

Good Notes Use Abbreviations Because most professors speak faster than you can write, it's important to use abbreviations that make sense to you. For example, if your professor is lecturing on the Industrial Revolution, it would be too time consuming to write both words out every time they were mentioned. Using *Ind. Rev.* or even *IR* saves a considerable amount of time. It is also a good idea

to develop a series of abbreviations for common and high-use words. Here are some suggestions:

Abbreviation Examples

&	and
$	money, wealth
b/c	because
/	the
<	less than
=	means, definitions, is equal to
>	greater than
↑	increased
↓	decreased
w/i	within
∴	therefore
+	in addition to, positives
*	very important
-	negatives

Taking Good Lecture Notes

Taking good notes involves active listening, attentiveness, concentration, and the ability to synthesize and condense a considerable amount of information on the spot. Effective note takers know that a lot of thinking goes on during note taking. Most students probably enter the lecture situation with every intention of staying alert, paying attention, and taking good notes. But for a variety of reasons, many students do not prevail.

From our observations, it seems that several factors enter into students' abilities to take good notes—class size, a professor's lecture style, time of day, and student health.

1. CLASS SIZE

The larger the class size, the easier it is to become unconnected with what the professor is saying. In addition, the further back or to the side that students sit in a classroom, the worse the problem tends to become. That's why it's important to stay in the professor's line of vision, sitting either close to the front or in the middle section of the room.

2. A PROFESSOR'S LECTURE STYLE

When professors are not entertaining, or if they tend to speak in a monotone, it is hard to stay focused. Professors who are difficult to follow, or those who tend to speak rapidly, can cause students' minds to wander rather than to stay actively involved in listening. We have also found that when professors put notes on the Web (we discuss strategies for using Web notes later in this chapter) or read directly from their overheads, students tend to pay less attention.

3. TIME OF DAY

Interestingly, students are most likely to fall asleep in an early morning class, presumably after they have had several hours of uninterrupted sleep. Granted, many students would consider themselves "night people" whose body clocks resist going to

bed before the wee hours of the morning and also resist getting up prior to noon. If you count yourself in these numbers, try to avoid scheduling an early morning class. Some students also seem to have trouble paying attention right after lunch (because they are full and sluggish) or during the late afternoon hours (when they feel hungry and tired). If you have a class immediately after lunch, try to eat a light meal; if a late afternoon class is on your schedule, try eating a healthy snack before class to keep up your energy level.

4. HEALTH (BOTH EMOTIONAL AND PHYSICAL)

Breaking up with your boyfriend or girlfriend, family problems, sick children, illness, or taking prescription medication can all influence your attentiveness in class. Everyone experiences problems at one time or another, and no one can expect to be perfectly attentive all the time. But when emotional or physical problems become constant barriers to learning, it's time to think about a course of action to get back to health.

BEYOND THE CLASSROOM

Do you feel that your note-taking skills are rusty? Are you uncertain that you are getting all of the key information? If you have not been in school for a while, you may be concerned that you are not getting all of the necessary information in class. In addition to following the advice in this chapter, we suggest you go to the source—visit your professor during office hours and ask him if you are getting the information in enough depth and detail for the course tasks. While you are there, ask your professor for any note-taking tips he may have.

General Note-Taking Guidelines

Let's begin our discussion of how to take good lecture notes with some general guidelines that tend to work for every type of lecture, regardless of class size. If you can get into the habit of routinely following these suggestions, you will find that you stay more engaged during the lecture, thus remembering more information that the professor presents.

Sit Front and Center Students who sit in the front of the classroom or in the professor's line of vision tend to be more attentive and listen more actively than those who sit in the back. This holds true in both larger and smaller classes. In small classes, students who sit in the front tend to ask more questions and get to know their professors better. Also, research indicates a significant relationship between students' grades and seat location. That is, the closer they sit to the front, the higher their grades tend to be.

Adjust Your Note Taking to the Professor Every professor lectures a bit differently. Some are well organized and taking notes from them is a breeze. Others are unorganized, provide few transitional cues, and get off the topic very easily. Whatever your professor's lecturing habits seem to be, you need to figure them out early in the term and make the appropriate adjustments in your note taking.

Listen, Think, and Write Students who try to write down everything the professor says tend to miss many key points because they can't keep up. Rather than trying to write down every word, listen first, think about what the professor is saying, and then write that thought, as much as possible, in your own words. Because professors tend to repeat information or say it a couple of times in different ways, it's important to listen and think before you write. Your intent should be to understand the concepts rather than get down every word.

Paraphrase Sometimes professors speak so quickly and try to cram so much material into a lecture that it is virtually impossible to get down all of the key points. If you find yourself getting more half thoughts than complete thoughts in your notes, or if you read over your notes and find that you can't piece together the important parts of the lecture, then you probably need to begin to do some serious paraphrasing. Paraphrasing, in this case, means getting down key concepts in your words and then filling in the details after class with information from the text. Look at Figure 8.1, which shows notes a professor might use for a lecture on the Tonkin Gulf incident. Then, in the same example, you will see how a student's paraphrased notes might look.

Professor's Lecture Notes	Student's Paraphrased Notes
	Tonkin Gulf Incident

Steps leading to:

In 1964, President Lyndon Johnson took several steps to show the United States' commitment to defend South Vietnam. In February, Johnson ordered the Pentagon to prepare for air strikes against the North. In May, his advisers drafted a resolution that authorized the military to escalate action. In June, General Maxwell Taylor, who was a strong proponent of more U.S. involvement in the war, was appointed ambassador to Saigon. And, in early August, patrol boats from the North supposedly clashed with two U.S. destroyers in the Gulf of Tonkin. Evidence of a real attack was skimpy at best. Johnson stated, "For all I know, our navy was shooting at whales out there." Nonetheless, Johnson announced on national television that Americans had been victims of "open aggression on the high seas." Withholding the fact that the U.S. ships had been assisting the South Vietnamese commando raids against two North Vietnamese islands in a secret operation planned by American advisors, the president condemned the attacks as unprovoked.

- *Feb. 1964—LBJ ordered Pentagon to prepare for air strikes against N. Vietnam*

- *May 1964—LBJ's advisors draft resolution to increase military action*

- *June 1964—Taylor (a strong supporter of greater involvement in Vietnam) becomes ambassador to Saigon*

August—Tonkin Gulf incident occurs—"assault" on American ships in Gulf; little evidence that it happened; LBJ says U.S. has been a victim of aggressive acts that were unprovoked.

He ordered retaliatory air strikes against the North for the first time and called on Congress to pass the previously drafted resolution giving him the authority to "take all necessary measures to repel any armed attack against the forces of the United States and to prevent further aggression." Assured by the president that this meant "no extension of the present conflict," the Senate passed the so-called Gulf of Tonkin Resolution 88 to 2; the House vote was 416 to 0. Johnson had not only signaled America's determination to stand by its allies, but also stymied Goldwater's effort to make Vietnam a campaign issue. He also now had a resolution that he likened to "grandma's nightshirt—it covered everything." His attorney general would soon describe the resolution as "the functional equivalent of a declaration of war," and the president would consider it a mandate to commit U.S. forces to Vietnam as he saw fit.

Results:

1. Retaliatory air strikes against N. Vietnam
2. Congress passes the Tonkin Gulf Resolution = give LBJ authority to use "all necessary measures" to prevent further aggressions;

passed Senate 88–2 and House 416–0

3. Stymied Goldwater's attempt to make Vietnam a campaign issue

4. LBJ could, in effect, do anything he wanted to escalate U.S. involvement

Figure 8.1: A Professor's Notes and a Student's Paraphrased Notes

Getting Ready to Take Notes

Learning how to take good lecture notes is an integral part of being a successful college student and an active learner. Like approaching textbook reading, taking good notes and using them as a successful study aid involves preparing to take notes, being an active listener during the lecture, and then rehearsing and self-testing after the lecture. You need to do some preparation before you begin to take notes. Engaging in pre-note-taking activities can make the difference between being an active and a passive listener. In order to get ready to take notes, you should:

Do the Assigned Reading Most professors expect you to be somewhat familiar with the topics they will lecture on by reading the appropriate text chapters before you come to class. Reading before the lecture gives you the advantage of making connections between the text and lecture. You will also be able to follow the "listen, think, write" rule better, because being familiar with the lecture topic will allow you to take down the key points in a more organized fashion. If you run out of time and can't read the text in its entirety, at least skim the chapter(s) to give you some idea of the key points that will be covered in the lecture.

Review Your Notes from the Previous Lecture Spend five or ten minutes before class to read through your notes from the previous lecture. By reviewing, you are refreshing your memory and getting your mind ready to become actively involved in learning. In addition, when you review, you can be sure that you understand the information that has been presented. Because many professors begin each class by answering student questions, you can get unclear information explained.

Have the Extra Edge Try to get to class with plenty of time to spare. Plan to use this time to review. Get out your notebook, get your paper ready (we'll talk more about this later), and, of course, sit in the front.

Staying Active During Note Taking

In this section, we discuss not only the format and organization of good notes, but also the kinds of information that you should include in your notes. By following these suggestions, you will be able to remain alert and active throughout the class.

FORMAT AND ORGANIZATION

If you were to examine the notes of five different college students, you would probably see five different formats. No matter what your format, you should have notes that are organized and easy to read. You want to be able to look at your notes and spend time with them. Neatness counts! As you take notes, use the following guidelines:

Use a 3-Ring Binder Rather Than a Spiral-bound Notebook A binder allows you to include class handouts, easily remove your notes, and insert notes with ease if you are absent from class.

Take Notes in a Simple Bulleted-List Form Do not use a tightly structured outline form. Outlines cause many students to get hung up on the outline format rather than focusing on the content of the lecture.

Leave Spaces Between Ideas and Underline Key Points This enables you to see where one idea stops and another begins and helps to distinguish between the key points and the details.

Try to Make Your Notes Inviting to Review

Neatness and organization count; you will not want to spend much time with your notes if they are difficult to read and review.

Indent and Mark Details and Examples

Indenting helps you know what information is related. If your notes all run together, it's difficult to tell what is a key point and what is supporting information.

Number Lists
When your professor lists reasons, characteristics, types, and so forth, number them in your notes. Numbering items in lists shows you at a glance how many factors on the list you need to remember.

Use abbreviations Whenever Possible
Abbreviating saves time and can distinguish certain kinds of information. For instance, an example can be indicated by "ex.," a definition by "def.," important information with a *, and so forth.

Active Listening

Becoming an active listener takes time, especially for classes in which you have little interest. It's not too difficult to pay attention in classes that you like or in ones where you have a professor who is dynamic. It's much more difficult in courses that are, in some way, less appealing. If you are an active listener and take organized notes for the entire class period, studying and learning the course material will be a much easier task. It's not only important to know how you should take and organize your notes, but it is also important to be aware of the kinds of information you should include. Of course, the kinds of information you should put in your notes vary from class to class. For example, although you may include names, dates, and events in your history notes, your psychology notes will probably be more focused on research and theories than on key events. Listen for the following cues that your professor may give as a way of figuring out what is important to note:

Lists Lists of things begin with cues such as "There were three major reasons why President Johnson committed more troops to Vietnam." "Short-term memory has five characteristics." "Mitosis progresses through eight stages." Anytime you hear a number followed by several factors, stages, characteristics, and so forth, make sure you write the number of points along with the explanation. In other words, don't just write "the stages of mitosis" in your notes. Write down what happens in each stage as well.

Cause-and-Effect Relationships When you hear your professor discuss causes and effects, be sure to write them down. Cause/effect cues are common in history and political science. For example, there might be an event that caused a president to make a certain decision, and this decision, in turn, had numerous effects on other events and decisions. In science, cause/effect can deal with concepts such as diseases or digestion.

Definitions Your professor might cue you by saying something as basic as "Malnutrition can be defined as . . . " It's a good idea to get definitions written in your notes precisely. If you only get down a portion of a definition or aren't sure that you have it exactly right, check your text or with your professor as soon after class as possible.

Examples Definitions are quite frequently followed by examples, yet students often see "example time" as an occasion to tune out. But examples discussed in class make for prime test questions. If you have to choose, we believe that it's actually more important to get examples in your notes than definitions (you can get the definitions from your textbook).

Reality Check

The Forgetting Curve

The forgetting curve describes the amount of information we forget once it's heard. It is based on a one-hour lecture.

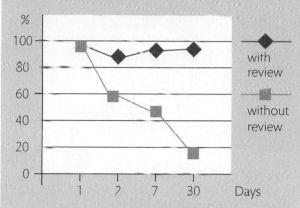

Notice that without review, you remember less than 20 percent after thirty days. But if you review your notes within one day of taking the notes and then spend some time with your notes each week, you can raise the curve to remembering almost 100 percent again.

Extended Comments When the professor spends a lot of time explaining something, you can be sure that it is important information. Try to stay connected with the lecturer during extended comments and take down as much of the information as possible. Essay, short-answer, and higher-level multiple-choice items often come from such extended comments.

Superlatives Anytime a professor describes something with words such as "most important," "best explanation," or "least influential," be sure to write it down. For example, there may be several explanations as to what constitutes intelligence, but your psychology professor might believe that one explanation is the "best." These are the kinds of things professors love to ask about on exams.

Voice or Volume Change When professors think something is important or they want to stress it, they generally speak louder and slower. A change in voice can be a clear indication that something important is being said.

Process Notes Process notes consist of information the professor gives about tests, how to study, when study or review sessions are held, how to think about the information, or how he wants an essay structured. Process notes can also include clues about the information that might be on the exam and other hints related to task. Process notes often come right at the beginning of class, before some students are ready to take notes, or at the end of class, when some students are packed up and ready to leave. Sometimes professors will even say something like "Hmmm . . . Wouldn't this make an interesting essay question?" during a lecture. This is all vital information that should be written down in your notes.

NETWORKING

Using Online Resources

Professors are using course management systems such as Web CT for many creative things. They may place their syllabi, quizzes, assignments, and other course information there. They may also post student grades or have virtual chats with the class. We even know a professor who conducts exam reviews online. If your professor uses one of these systems, plan to visit the site often to keep up on new assignments or important information.

Evaluate the lecturing style and patterns of one of your current professors by answering the following questions. Then think about how you can use this information to help you take better notes in that professor's class.

Class Name: _____

Is your professor an inductive or deductive lecturer?

_____

How do you know? Give a specific example from your lecture notes.

_____

_____

_____

What kind of cues does your professor give?

_____

_____

_____

How does your professor organize the lectures?

_____

_____

_____

How much overlap is there between your professor's lectures and the textbook used in the class?

_____

_____

_____

What kinds of adjustments might you have to make to this professor's lecturing style?

_____

_____

_____

_____

Matching Your Notes to the Task: Four Methods of Note Taking

Most students have one way that they take notes. They developed their own personal note-taking style through years of experience in high school. However, these students may run into trouble when faced with taking notes in a learning situation that does not match their particular note-taking method. Often students miss key information or get frustrated and take no notes at all. We don't want this to happen to you. So, we will discuss four different methods of note taking that you can use in a variety of classroom situations.

Method One: Cornell Method

Using the Cornell, or split-page method is an effective strategy that will be appropriate in most of your lecture courses. This is most likely the method you will utilize the majority of the time. In the split-page method, you divide your page as shown in Figure 8.2. You can see that a line has been drawn down the left-hand side of the paper, creating a 2- to 3-inch margin. During note taking, take your notes on the wider right-hand side of the paper, and then after class, use the margin to pull out the key points. You should have your lines drawn on several sheets of paper, your paper dated, and several pages numbered before your professor begins to lecture. This method of note taking works well because it allows for self-testing.

SELF-TESTING

Interacting with your notes after the lecture is perhaps the most important phase of note taking. As soon as possible after the lecture, it's important to read over your notes carefully to be sure that you understand all the major concepts presented. This is when you use the 2- to 3-inch margin on the left-hand side of your paper to write in the key points or pose questions. The key points or questions are used to self-test as you study the course material.

In the margin you should:
- Focus on the major points or broad topics
- Get at higher-level thinking by asking "how," "why," or "for example," instead of "what" questions
- Be brief

Creating the self-testing component for your lecture notes as soon after the lecture as possible helps get the information into your memory and helps you remember it better. In addition, when you go through your notes, you can determine if you have questions about what was presented in class. Writing questions or annotating gives you immediate feedback about what you understand and what you need clarification about.

EXAM PREPARATION

When it comes time to prepare for an exam, follow these seven steps to use your annotations or questions to self-test:

1. Read your notes, either to yourself or out loud, trying to get the information fixed in your memory.
2. Fold your paper back, exposing only what you have written in the left-hand column.
3. Ask yourself the questions or explain the concepts.

4. Flip your notes over to see how much of the material you have remembered.

5. If you knew it *accurately* and *precisely*, go on to the next concept. If you had problems, read your notes another time or two and try again.

6. As you learn the concepts, check them off in the margin.

7. When you begin the next study session, review what you know, but concentrate your efforts on what you don't know.

Self-testing by using questions in the margin of your notes should give you confidence as you enter a testing situation. When you self-test, you are monitoring your understanding; therefore, you have a fairly accurate idea of the concepts you know and comprehend very well and those that may still be somewhat unclear or fuzzy.

Nutrition & Digestion   Nov 10

Explain the 3 types of animal diets–give ex.

Animal Nutrition

Animal Diets

- Herbivores–eat plants, algae
  * Ex. Cattle, gorillas, sea urchins

- Carnivores–eat animals (that ate plants)
  * Ex. Lions, snakes, frogs

- Omnivores–eat both plants and animals
  * Ex. Humans, crows, cockroaches

How does food move through the 4 stages of processing?

4 Stages of Food Processing

1. Ingestion–eating (ex. chewing pizza)

2. Digestion–breakdown of food to simple sugars and amino acids

   * Mechanical digestion–physical process such as chewing. Exposes more food molecules

   * Chemical digestion–chem. breakdown of food to smaller molecules

Why must chemical digestion occur?

WHY? 2 reasons

ONE: Polymers must be broken into monomers b/4 cells can absorb

TWO: Most food polymers are diff. than animal polymers so must break down and use amino acids to build new proteins (*see figure 22.3 in text)

3. Absorption– uptake of small molecules into cells lining digestive tract

4. Elimination–disposal of undigested materials

Figure 8.2: Cornell Notes

Method Two: Parallel Notes

When professors use a range of technology—Web notes, PowerPoint presentations, graphs, and visual aids—students tell us that their attention is often divided and that they find it difficult to take notes. One strategy you can use to help you concentrate is parallel notes. First, print out the notes the professor supplies before class and place them in a three-ring binder. As the professor lectures, take your own notes on the blank facing page, following along with the notes the professor supplied and filling in any gaps or added information. After the lecture, create your self testing questions as described in the Cornell method. Figure 8.3 shows parallel notes from a political science class on voter mobilization.

Professor's Notes	Your notes	Self-testing
Impact of Voter Mobilization	Much $ spent on getting out the vote. Over several decades, turnout has declined. In presidential elections has fallen from nearly 65% in the 1960s to just over 50% in the 1990s.	Decline in voting- reasons
• Mobilization matters.		
• What the parties and the campaigns do has an impact on the who and how many people turn out to vote.	Efforts are often only in the states and congressional districts where elections are expected to be close, and are often partisan	
• But you can only mobilize when there is a chance that you can win.	But there are also less partisan efforts designed to boost turnout overall	Partisan vs. non partisan effort
• Turnout is generally low in one-party dominant areas where the general election is noncompetitive.	--Voter participation in the United States is lower than most other well-established democracies.	
	Questions to think about	
	1 Why is turnout lower in the United States than in other advanced democracies?	Would make good essay question!
	2 How have turnout rates been changing for the electorate as a whole and for specific social groups? What are the implications of those trends for the two major political parties?	

Figure 8.3: Parallel Notes

Method Three: Discussion Columns

If your class is based on discussion instead of lecture, we suggest using discussion columns. As Figure 8.4 shows, rather than dividing your paper into a narrow and a wide margin, divide it into three equal columns. In the first column, write the question that is being posed or the theory that is being debated. In the second column, take notes on what the professor has to say about it. In the last column, take notes on what your classmates say.

Then when you are studying, you can evaluate your classmates' comments and decide which are worth studying and which can be ignored. One of our graduate students modified this technique by adding possible test questions or paper topics and text page numbers to help her relate the discussion to her reading in a psychology of creativity class. Figure 8.4 shows how she formatted the notes to follow the flow of conversation.

Question Posed	Professor's comments	Student comments
Must creativity result in a product?		Depends on how you look @ it—whose perspective?
[TQ? Process is more important than product. Defend or refute this statement]	So which is more important—process or product?	Artist—process Public—product
p. 283 creativity outcomes	Does an idea count as a product?	Product. Have to have tangible evidence of creativity
	Good point—anyone expand?	I think that both product and process have to play a role. Process alone can't really cut it.

Figure 8.4: Example of Discussion Notes

Method Four: The T-Method

In classes where the task requires you to summarize or pull together information, the T-method works best. If you know that your exams will consist of essay questions or that you will be asked to think about the information at higher levels, try the T-method. To use it, take notes using the general principles of effective note taking discussed in the chapter, then follow these three steps:

1. Draw a T at the bottom fourth of your last page of notes (you can use the back of the page if you need more room).

2. On the left side of the page, summarize the key points of the lecture.

3. On the right side of the page, create your self-testing component by predicting some test questions about the material.

Figure 8.5 shows the last page of notes from a psychology lecture. The bottom part of the page is used to summarize the day's lecture.

March 3   Page 3/3

3. **Long-term memory**
   (what we usually think of as memory)

• Not currently aware of it

• Permanent storage

• Unlimited capacity

• "Forgetting" occurs because

  a. decay or disuse—no evidence for or against

  b. interference—info. is stored but can't be retrieved

*note: prof will pick up on interference next class

Summary	Questions
Memory consists of 3 systems 1. encoding, 2. storage, 3. retrieval. Information first goes into short-term memory through rehearsal (maintenance or elaborative) where it is either encoded or forgotten quickly (less than 30 sec) Information that is encoded goes into long-term memory	1. What are the three memory systems? Define and describe characteristics. 2. Compare and contrast maintenance and elaborative rehearsal. 3. How does information move from STM to LTM?

Figure 8.5: Example of The T-Method

Note-Taking Myths

We end this chapter by discussing some myths—information that students tend to believe about note taking that isn't necessarily true.

MYTH 1: IF YOU CAN'T KEEP UP WITH THE PROFESSOR, TAPE-RECORD THE LECTURES

The truth is that when students tape lectures, they generally don't listen to the tapes. It's easy to understand why. If you are taking five classes, you hardly have time to do all your reading, studying, and other learning activities, let alone sit and listen to lectures for a second time. In addition, students who tape lectures can become **capricious** about their note taking; they find it much easier to tune out what the professor is saying and will miss information written on the chalkboard or overhead. Our advice to you is to go to class, take the best notes you can, and supplement those notes with information from the text or by forming a study group that has goals that include sharing notes. Unless you have a disability that necessitates recording class lectures, tape-recording your courses simply is not an efficient and active way to learn.

MYTH 2: COPYING A CLASSMATE'S NOTES IS PREFERABLE TO STRUGGLING WITH NOTE TAKING YOURSELF

Think back to sometime in your distant past when you may have actually copied someone's homework. How much did you learn from that experience? Probably not much. You won't learn much from copying someone else's lecture notes either. A better plan is to compare your lecture notes with those of a classmate. This can be a very positive and effective strategy, because you will gain another person's perspective and you just might learn from your classmate ways to take better notes.

MYTH 3: IT'S IMPOSSIBLE TO TAKE NOTES IN A CLASS THAT INVOLVES DISCUSSION

When we have observed students in classes that involve a lot of discussion, we see very little note taking going on. Students seem to think that only information presented by the professor has any merit, so they fail to write down any comments made by their peers. However, if you think about the purpose of classes that involve discussion, you'll realize that the professor's role is to initiate the discussion. It's the students who actually generate the ideas, and these ideas often find their way onto the exam. Using the discussion-columns method described in this chapter should help you record the discussion and make it easier to complete course papers and other tasks.

MYTH 4: IF MY PROFESSOR PROVIDES NOTES ON THE WEB OR HANDS THEM OUT IN CLASS, I DON'T HAVE TO TAKE NOTES

Many students rely solely on their professor's notes and don't interact with their notes or attempt to learn the material until test time. If your professor hands out the notes in class or has you purchase them, we suggest that you print out the notes and take them to class each day. As you listen to the lecture, fill in gaps by adding detail and providing examples. You can also make special note of topics emphasized by the professor. Then, to be sure you understand the concepts in your notes, after each class, use the T-method or parallel notes. If your professor puts notes on the Web after class, attend class and take notes as you normally would. Then, when you get the professor's notes off the Web, you can compare the two sets and fill in any gaps.

Real College

NATE'S NOTES

DIRECTIONS: *Read the following scenario and respond to the questions based on what you have learned in this chapter.*

Nate always considered himself a pretty good note taker. In high school, he would copy down exactly what the teacher wrote on the board and he did just fine on his exams. Now, however, he is having some trouble taking notes in class.

In his history class, the professor never writes anything on the board. She just lectures a mile a minute without even using any notes. Nate is having a hard time getting down everything she says, even though his hand cramps up from writing so much.

In his economics class, the professor uses PowerPoint slides to guide the lectures, but apparently that doesn't help Nate much. For the first exam, Nate printed out and studied the slides but only made a low C on the exam. Many of the exam questions were over topics that were not even covered in class, which Nate finds frustrating.

In his psychology class, Nate doesn't know whether he should even bother taking notes. His professor just seems to be giving examples and telling stories. He finds the class interesting, but he's not sure what he should be getting out of the lectures.

What can Nate do?

1. What advice would you give to Nate?

_____

_____

_____

_____

_____

2. How should he approach note taking in each of his courses?

_____

_____

_____

_____

_____

Add to Your Portfolio

1. Try taking notes in all of your classes using one of the four methods–Cornell method, discussion, parallel notes, or T-method–for one week. First, decide which method will work best in each of your courses based on what you have learned in this chapter.

_____

_____

_____

_____

_____

2. For each method that you have tried, write a paragraph evaluating what you liked and did not like about the methods.

_____

_____

_____

_____

_____

_____

3. How might you modify the methods to suit your own note-taking preferences?

_____

_____

_____

_____

_____

_____

Chapter 9
Active Reading

Read this chapter to answer the following questions:

- Why do you need to warm up before reading and studying?

- What are some strategies for warming up?

- What is the difference between active and passive reading?

- What are some strategies for concentrating on textbook reading?

Self-Assessment

DIRECTIONS: Answer each of the following questions by answering yes or no to give yourself an idea of how actively you read your textbooks.

	Yes	No
Do you have an idea of the concepts that are presented in the chapter before you start to read?	___	___
Do you set some goals prior to reading?	___	___
Do you reflect on what you are going to read?	___	___
Do you try to personalize your reading to help you understand it better?	___	___
Do you write in your textbooks when you read?	___	___
Do you try to put important text information into your own words?	___	___
Do you think about the visual aids in the chapter?	___	___
Do you try to summarize what you have read?	___	___
Do you reflect on ideas while reading?	___	___
Do you understand most of what you have read?	___	___
Do you ask for clarification when you don't understand what you have read?	___	___
Do you keep up with your reading?	___	___

Before reading the chapter, reflect on your responses to the self-assessment. What do you think your strengths are as an active reader? What are your weaknesses? You can get an idea of your strengths by thinking about the questions you answered yes; you can get an idea of your weaknesses by thinking about the questions you answered no.

_____

_____

_____

_____

_____

_____

_____

Before You Begin

WORD WISE

1. **Apathetic** (adj., p. 137) — feeling lack of interest or concern; indifferent.
*The polls found that voters were **apathetic** about the election; thus, there was low voter turnout.*

2. **Galvanize** (v., p.138) — to arouse into action or awareness; to stimulate into action.
*His low grades in chemistry **galvanized** him to change his study habits.*

3. **Proficiency** (n., p. 143) — the quality of having great competence; skillful ability from practice and familiarity.
*Her ability to consistently shoot under par is a testament to her **proficiency** at golf.*

DID YOU KNOW?

Many textbooks try to make it easier for students to identify the key terms in the chapter by pulling them out in the margins and defining them. As a result, students often think that they don't need to pay much attention to them when they read and that they will come back and memorize them when they study. This approach to learning content vocabulary isn't very effective. Even if words are defined for you in the margins, it is still important to put those definitions in your own words as you read the chapter. Remember: Unless you can translate a definition in to your own words, you don't really have a clear understanding of its meaning.

RESEARCH INTO PRACTICE

How Text Headings Impact Comprehension

In this study, researchers asked students to read a text that (a) included headings for each new topic (there were twenty topics in the passage); (b) included headings for only half of the topics; or (c) included no headings at all. Then students summarized the text. The results indicated that students were better able to summarize text when headings were included in the readings than when headings were not included. This means that when the task calls for readers to pay attention to the structure of the topics, students rely heavily on the headings to help them determine what is important to remember from the text. The researchers suggest that headings actually help students organize and process text information. When there are no headings available, students need to make their own judgments about the importance of each topic. The researchers also found that students relied on the position of the topic (those discussed first were considered more important) and the amount of elaboration in the text (those discussed in more detail were considered more important).

This research is relevant for college students because they often do not pay attention to chapter headings or subheadings even when they are obvious in the text. However, the task of preparing for an exam is similar to the task of summarizing in that you need to organize the information topically to remember it better. Therefore, when reading your textbooks, think about the headings and how the information you are reading is related to the topic. By noting how the textbook structures the topics, you will be better prepared to isolate and organize the key ideas.

Source: R. F. Lorch, E. P. Lorch, K. Richey, L. McGovern, and D. Coleman, "Effects of Headings on Text Summarization," *Contemporary Educational Psychology 26* (2001): 171–191.

Warming Up for Reading: Strategies That Work

Reading is something that every college student needs to do every day. But are you getting what you need out of your text reading, or are you just spinning your wheels? Do you find that your first half hour is unproductive because you are not concentrating on what you are doing? Do you close your book after an hour or so and feel as though you have accomplished little? Maybe the reason is that you have not geared up for reading actively.

Picture a track meet at a local college. The athletes pile out of a van just as the first race begins. They throw off their sweats and start running. Would that ever happen? Of course not. Just as an athlete would never run a race or even practice "cold," you should not expect to start reading or studying without warming up in some way. Athletes warm up to get their muscles ready to perform. When you begin to read or study, you need to warm up your brain so that you will be more efficient and productive during that time. This chapter discusses how to become an active reader. But before reading the rest of the chapter, be sure you have read the "Research into Practice" section on page 132 about how textbook headings impact comprehension.

There are several activities to help you gear up for reading. All of these strategies will help you get ready to read so that you will understand and remember more of the information in your texts.

CREATE A GOOD LEARNING ENVIRONMENT

Think about the place where you currently read or study, and ask yourself the following questions: Do you study in a setting that allows you to concentrate and study effectively? Are you constantly distracted by people, noise, or other diversions? Your learning environment can help your progress when reading or studying; a bad setting can hinder your progress. You need to create a place that is free from distractions and allows you to maximize your studying time. The following two factors should be considered.

Noise Level Some students say that they need complete quiet to study—even a clock ticking in the background is enough to distract them. Other students say that they study best in crowded, noisy rooms because the noise helps them concentrate. Some study most successfully when they are in familiar surroundings such as their bedrooms; for others, familiar surroundings make no difference. Some students like quiet music playing; others don't. Many students find that the type of music matters, with instrumental music being less distracting than music with vocals. The point is that you should know the level of noise that is optimal for your own studying. However, as a general rule for all students, television seems to be more of a distraction than music or other background noise, so leave the TV off when you are reading or studying. Also, don't let yourself become distracted by computer games or Internet surfing when you are trying to study.

Your Learning Space Students concentrate better when they read or study in straight-backed chairs, such as desk or kitchen chairs, than on their beds. In addition, the ideal learning space is where the only thing you do in that place is study. If you have a desk, set it up so that you have everything handy—your computer, pens and pencils, paper, calculator, books, notes, and anything else you need to study. If you find that you cannot create an effective learning environment where you live because there are too many distractions, try to find a quiet place on campus to study, such as the library or the student union.

SURVEY YOUR TEXTBOOKS

After establishing a good learning environment, the next step in gearing up is examining each of your textbooks. You only need to use this step the first time you interact with a book. Some textbooks are written and formatted in a way that is very reader-friendly and have some or all of the following features:

• Preview questions and/or an organizer at the beginning of each chapter to help readers focus on what they are about to learn
• Diagrams, pictures, and figures to give readers a better understanding of the topic
• **Bold-faced** or *italicized* words to emphasize key terms
• Summary or review questions at the end of each chapter
• Chapter outlines or guiding maps
• Large margins so that readers have room to write notes as they read

In order to determine if your textbooks are reader-friendly, examine the way they are arranged. Surveying your texts will help you by:

• Familiarizing you with the topics to be covered so that you can activate what you already know
• Increasing your interest in reading the chapters
• Giving you the time you need to gear up for reading effectively
• Allowing you to identify the key topics before you begin to read

PREVIEW YOUR READING ASSIGNMENTS

You have found a quiet place to study, you have all of your studying tools at your fingertips, and you've surveyed your textbooks. Now you're ready to gear up for your required reading by previewing. Previewing doesn't take very long, but just as surveying your entire textbook prepares you to learn the material, previewing before each reading session helps to activate your prior knowledge and builds your interest in the topic. To preview, follow these steps:

Read the Chapter Title The title tells you about the overall topic of the chapter and may clue you in to the author's intent. Reading and reflecting on the title helps you begin to think about what you already know about the topic.

Read the Headings and Subheadings The headings and subheadings tell you about the specific focus of the chapter and may suggest the author's approach to the topic. For example, a subheading in your history text called "The Horrors of War" would introduce very different material than a subheading called "War: Benefits and Advances."

Read the Bold-faced and Italicized Terms These terms clue you in to ideas emphasized in the text and point out new vocabulary or content-specific terms that will be discussed in the chapter.

Note the Typographical Aids Besides bold-faced or italicized words, many texts use graphs, charts, tables, and illustrations to emphasize key ideas. Read these sections to find out what is important in the chapter.

Read the Introduction If your textbook offers chapter introductions, it is a good idea to read these when you preview the chapter, to get an idea of the topic and the scope of information the chapter covers.

Read the Summary If your textbook contains chapter summaries, it is a good idea to read these sections *before* you actually read the chapter. A summary section outlines the key information you should learn when reading the chapter. By reading the summary before the body of the chapter, you will be able to identify the chapter's key points.

Read the End-of-the-Chapter Material This may include study questions, vocabulary lists, or application exercises. These features tell you what is important in the chapter.

Although this might sound like a lot to do before reading, previewing actually only takes a few minutes to accomplish, because you are not getting bogged down in the details of the chapter. Your purpose in previewing is to get a general idea of the concepts that will be covered in the chapter.

DETERMINE YOUR READING PURPOSE

As you preview a chapter, you should begin to think of some questions about the key topics. For example, in previewing the history excerpt "The Great Depression and the New Deal 1929–1939" in Appendix C (which includes an excerpt called "Hard Times in Hooverville"), you might ask yourself what you know about the stock market crash of 1929, events that caused that crash, and how Hoover tried get the United States back on its feet. Some students find it helpful to turn the headings into questions that they will answer when they read the chapter. By asking questions, you are starting to think about the key ideas contained in the text, which will make reading more effective. Jot down your questions and try to answer them as you read.

It is always a good idea to read with a purpose in mind. When you are reading your textbooks, your primary purpose is to learn the information contained in each chapter. But this is a tall order. You probably would have a difficult time if you tried to learn every idea contained in every chapter. What you need to do is figure out which are the chapter's key ideas and focus on them. A good way to help you determine what's important is to use your class syllabus and lecture notes as a guide.

Reality Check

Setting Reading Goals

Many students begin their reading with the sole purpose of plowing through it. If they preview at all, it is just to see how many pages the chapter contains. Setting reading goals and always remembering that you are reading to learn the material will help you stay on track so that you can really concentrate when you read.

Before you read the rest of this chapter, use the skills you have learned about previewing to preview the rest of the chapter. Remember to look at headings, subheadings, and so forth, and also ask yourself questions about your knowledge of the material. Then, consider your current learning environment when responding to these questions.

Where do you currently study? Check all that apply.

____	Bedroom
____	Library
____	Living room
____	Desk
____	Bed
____	Kitchen table
____	No set studying place
____	Other

Which of these best describes your learning environment? Check all that apply.

____	TV on
____	Music playing
____	Complete quiet
____	Roommates/others talking
____	Roommates/others studying
____	Computer on
____	Phone on
____	Other

What are the greatest distractors to your studying?

_____

_____

_____

_____

_____

What changes do you need to make to create a more effective learning environment and to eliminate distractions?

_____

_____

_____

_____

_____

Staying Active During Reading: Text Annotation

If you've ever finished reading a text chapter only to realize that you don't remember anything you just read, chances are you were not reading actively. Because reading textbooks rarely tops any student's list of favorite activities, and also because reading textbooks is one of the most common college tasks, it is important to learn strategies that enable you to understand and remember what you read. If you finish "reading" ten pages of text and can't summarize what you have read, you have just wasted valuable time. It is easy to become **apathetic** when reading, so where do you begin?

PUT AWAY YOUR HIGHLIGHTERS

When asked how they read their textbooks, many students tell us that they try to pull out key ideas by highlighting or underlining during reading. Although this is a popular strategy, in reality, highlighting is a passive activity because students often do not really understand the ideas they are highlighting. Think about it. You can "read," highlight, *and* talk on your cell phone at the same time—but that's not the best way to concentrate or learn. Many students actually put off reading for the purpose of understanding until after they have highlighted the text. In other words, they skim the text looking for important information, highlight entire sections that seem important, and plan to return to those sections later when they study for the exam.

When students highlight their texts, sometimes they are not very selective; often, entire pages are highlighted in bright pink or yellow or blue. Students who highlight most everything are not discriminating about what to mark and will have just as much information to cope with when they begin to study. And they will have to go fishing in a pink or yellow or blue sea in order to find the key points.

On the other hand, some students highlight too little. If these students relied on their highlighting for test reviews, they would not have adequate information and they probably would end up needing to reread the chapters. Our advice is to put away your highlighters because you will want to use strategies that promote greater active involvement in reading and learning.

BEYOND THE CLASSROOM

Many students who work full- or part-time in addition to taking college classes feel a time crunch when it comes to getting reading done. In fact, some students merely skim their texts and rely on class notes for studying. However, textbooks often provide a more complete explanation of material discussed in class and can help clarify the concepts. In addition, professors who assign textbook reading often ask test questions over material that is only contained in the book as a way of checking whether students are doing the reading. Our advice: Unless your professor tells you otherwise, read your text before you go to class.

Active readers gear up to read by previewing, and then are ready to focus on understanding. Some students have trouble concentrating when they read or believe that reading their text is a waste of time because they don't get much out of it. Other students become confused and have trouble determining which ideas are the most important to remember. One way to be sure that you are concentrating on and understanding what you read is to annotate your text. Annotation is an active approach because you are required to write in your books. This might take a bit of adjusting to—most students were not allowed to write in textbooks in high school. But in college, you buy your own books. Be sure you get your money's worth and write, write, write.

WHAT IS ANNOTATION?

In a nutshell, annotation is summing up the information in your text by briefly writing the key ideas in the margin. Unlike highlighting, which promotes passivity, annotation can **galvanize** your comprehension because it requires that you understand what you are reading. It requires you to actively make decisions about what is important because you are putting the ideas into your own words. As shown in the three examples that follow, an annotated piece of text includes key ideas as well as examples, definitions, and other important details about the concepts. You will also see that the information included in the annotations and the way in which it is organized differs depending on the content.

In order to annotate properly, you need to think about what you read before you write. If you find that your mind is wandering or that you are not concentrating, you have to get back on track.

Because you stop reading after a few paragraphs to annotate what you have read, you will be able to reconnect with the reading.

NETWORKING
Taking Notes While Reading

Some students tell us that they like to take notes on their reading using their computers. Although we think it is generally better to take notes directly in the text, this is a pretty good modification of the annotation strategy. Just remember to follow the general annotation guidelines as you make your notes and to note the page numbers in case you need to refer to the text when studying.

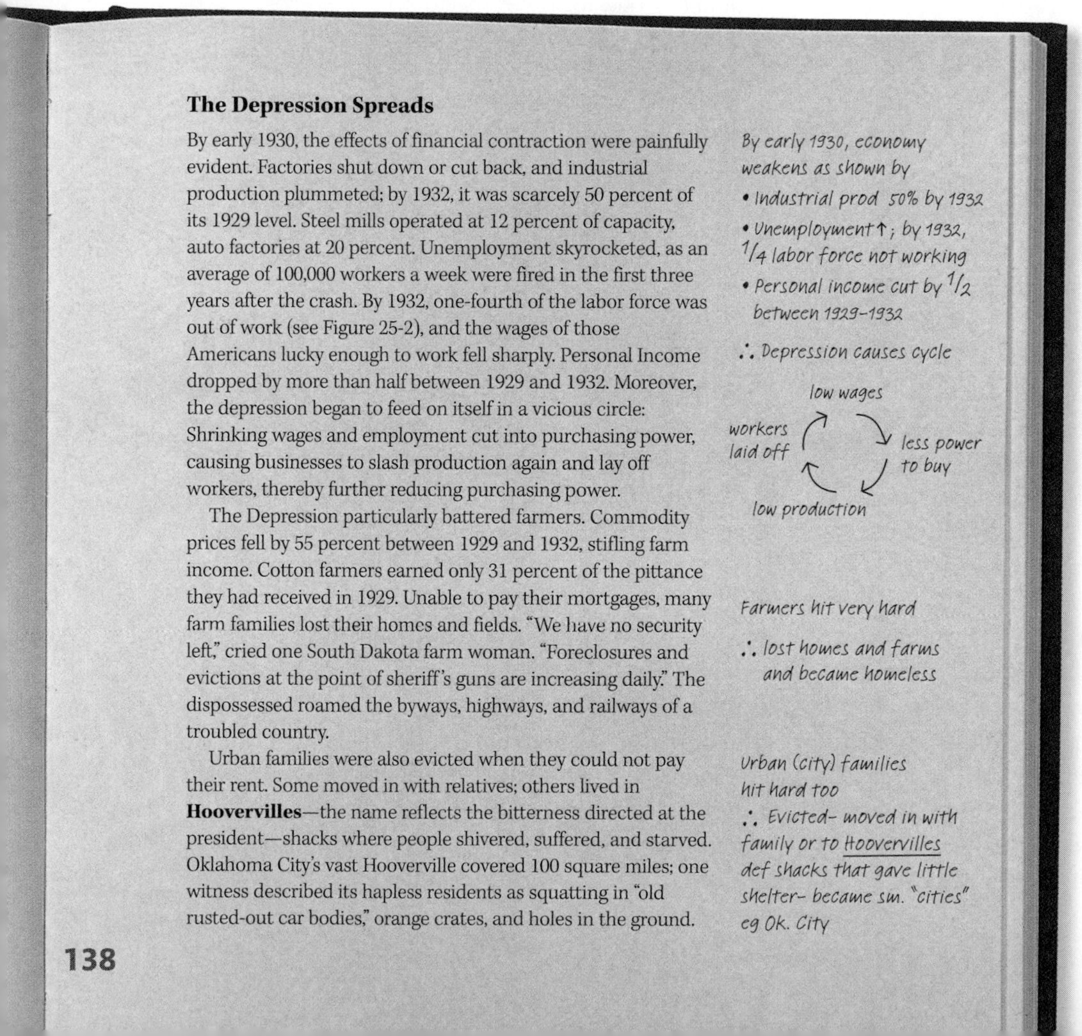

The Depression Spreads

By early 1930, the effects of financial contraction were painfully evident. Factories shut down or cut back, and industrial production plummeted; by 1932, it was scarcely 50 percent of its 1929 level. Steel mills operated at 12 percent of capacity, auto factories at 20 percent. Unemployment skyrocketed, as an average of 100,000 workers a week were fired in the first three years after the crash. By 1932, one-fourth of the labor force was out of work (see Figure 25-2), and the wages of those Americans lucky enough to work fell sharply. Personal Income dropped by more than half between 1929 and 1932. Moreover, the depression began to feed on itself in a vicious circle: Shrinking wages and employment cut into purchasing power, causing businesses to slash production again and lay off workers, thereby further reducing purchasing power.

The Depression particularly battered farmers. Commodity prices fell by 55 percent between 1929 and 1932, stifling farm income. Cotton farmers earned only 31 percent of the pittance they had received in 1929. Unable to pay their mortgages, many farm families lost their homes and fields. "We have no security left," cried one South Dakota farm woman. "Foreclosures and evictions at the point of sheriff's guns are increasing daily." The dispossessed roamed the byways, highways, and railways of a troubled country.

Urban families were also evicted when they could not pay their rent. Some moved in with relatives; others lived in **Hoovervilles**—the name reflects the bitterness directed at the president—shacks where people shivered, suffered, and starved. Oklahoma City's vast Hooverville covered 100 square miles; one witness described its hapless residents as squatting in "old rusted-out car bodies," orange crates, and holes in the ground.

Figure 9.1: Model Annotations of a History Text

Excerpt from D. Goldfield, C. Abbott, V. D. Anderson, J. E. Argersinger, P. H. Argersinger, W. L Barney, and R. M. Weir, *The American Journey, Vol. 2, Fourth Edition* (Upper Saddle River, NJ: Pearson Education, 2007).

Remembering

The Three Processes in Memory

The act of remembering requires three processes: encoding, storage, and retrieval (see Figure 6.1). The first process, **encoding**, involves transforming information into a form that can be stored in memory. For example, if you met someone named Will at a party, you might associate his name with that of the actor Will Smith. The second memory process, **storage**, involves keeping or maintaining information in memory. The final process, **retrieval**, occurs when information stored in memory is brought to mind. Calling Will by name the next time you meet him shows that you have retrieved his name from memory.

Physiological changes must occur during a process called **consolidation**, which allows new information to be stored in memory for later retrieval. These physiological changes require the synthesis of protein molecules (Lopez, 2000). Until recently, conventional wisdom held that the process of consolidation had to occur only once for each item to be memorized. But as we will see later in the chapter, in the section on the cause of forgetting, some seemingly consolidated memories can be induced to disappear (Nader et al., 2000).

3 Memory Processes

1 Encoding—mkg sense of info so that it can be stored in STM or LTM. Transforming information into a form that can be stored in short-term or long-term memory

2 Storage—keeping info in memory. The act of maintaining information in memory

3 Retrieval—getting at info in memory. The act of bringing to mind material that has been stored in memory

Physiological changes happen during consolidation

• A physiological change in the brain that must take place for encoded information to be stored in memory

• Lets new info be stored thru a synthesis of protein

Figure 9.2: Model Annotations of a Psychology Text

Excerpt from S. E. Wood, E. G. Wood, and D. Boyd, *Mastering the World of Psychology* (San Francisco, CA: Pearson, 2004). Allyn and Bacon.

WHY ANNOTATE?

Annotating your text is an effective strategy for several reasons. It is powerful because it encourages you to process the information and think about it as you read. Annotation helps you manage the large volume of information you need to read. Additionally, several underlying processes that promote effective learning are used in annotation. Knowing those processes will help you understand why most students find it a valuable reading strategy. The processes include:

Isolating Information When annotating your texts, you select important information you want to remember. You separate that information and mark it in a way that helps you recall it come exam time.

Reducing Information The material is reduced in each of the annotation examples. This condenses the information you need to study into more manageable amounts. In most texts, annotation helps you reduce the amount of information by more than 50 percent.

**Figure 9.3:
Model Annotations
of a Biology Text**

Excerpt from N. A.
Campbell, J. B. Reece,
and E. J. Simon, *Essential
Biology with Physiology*
(San Francisco, CA:
Pearson, 2004).
Benjamin Cummings.

Proteins Provide Amino Acids for Bulding New Proteins

Protein in the diet serves mainly as a source of amino acids to make the body's own proteins. Dietary protein is broken down in the digestive tract to yield amino acids. In your cells, the amino acids are linked in specific sequences to form the many different proteins specific to your body. Any excess protein in the diet is broken down to extract energy for immediate use or for storage as fat.

Humans can synthesize only 12 of the 20 amino acids commonly used in proteins. The other eight, called **essential amino acids**, must be supplied in the diet. Two additional amino acids are usually synthesized in fairly small amounts, and so are essential for growing children but usually not for adults. Although animal proteins almost always contain sufficient amounts of all of the essential amino acids, many plant proteins are deficient in some, so vegetarians must take steps to avoid protein deficiency. Generally, they need to make sure their diet includes a variety of plants (for example, legumes, grains, and corn) whose proteins collectively provide all of the essential amino acids. Protein deficiency can cause a variety of debilitating conditions, including kwashiorkor, which is seen in some impoverished countries (Fig 21-2).

Proteins

Function=source of amino acids (aa) so body can make own proteins
—Breaks down in digest. tract
—Used 4 energy or stored as fat
Essential Amino Acids (EAA) 8 aa's that must come fm. diet; other 12 are synthesized

—EAA's found in all animal proteind BUT not all veggie proteins: vegetarians must eat a variety of planets
Deficiencey cause illness
(ex) kwashiorkor

Organizing Information If your textbook is reader-friendly and well organized, your annotations can follow the author's organizational patterns if it makes sense to you. However, sometimes your textbooks don't organize information the way you need it. The material may not seem to follow a logical pattern. If such is the case, through careful reading and annotation, you can reorganize the material in a way that is meaningful for you, which will make it easier for you to remember what you have read and to prepare for exams.

Identifying Key Concepts Annotation helps you differentiate between major concepts and supporting ideas. You will have to know something about the major concepts and supporting details for most courses, and by determining what is important, you will know how to focus your studying. Notice how the definitions are underlined and the key points are indented in the annotation examples. Such visual representation helps you make the distinction between key and supporting ideas.

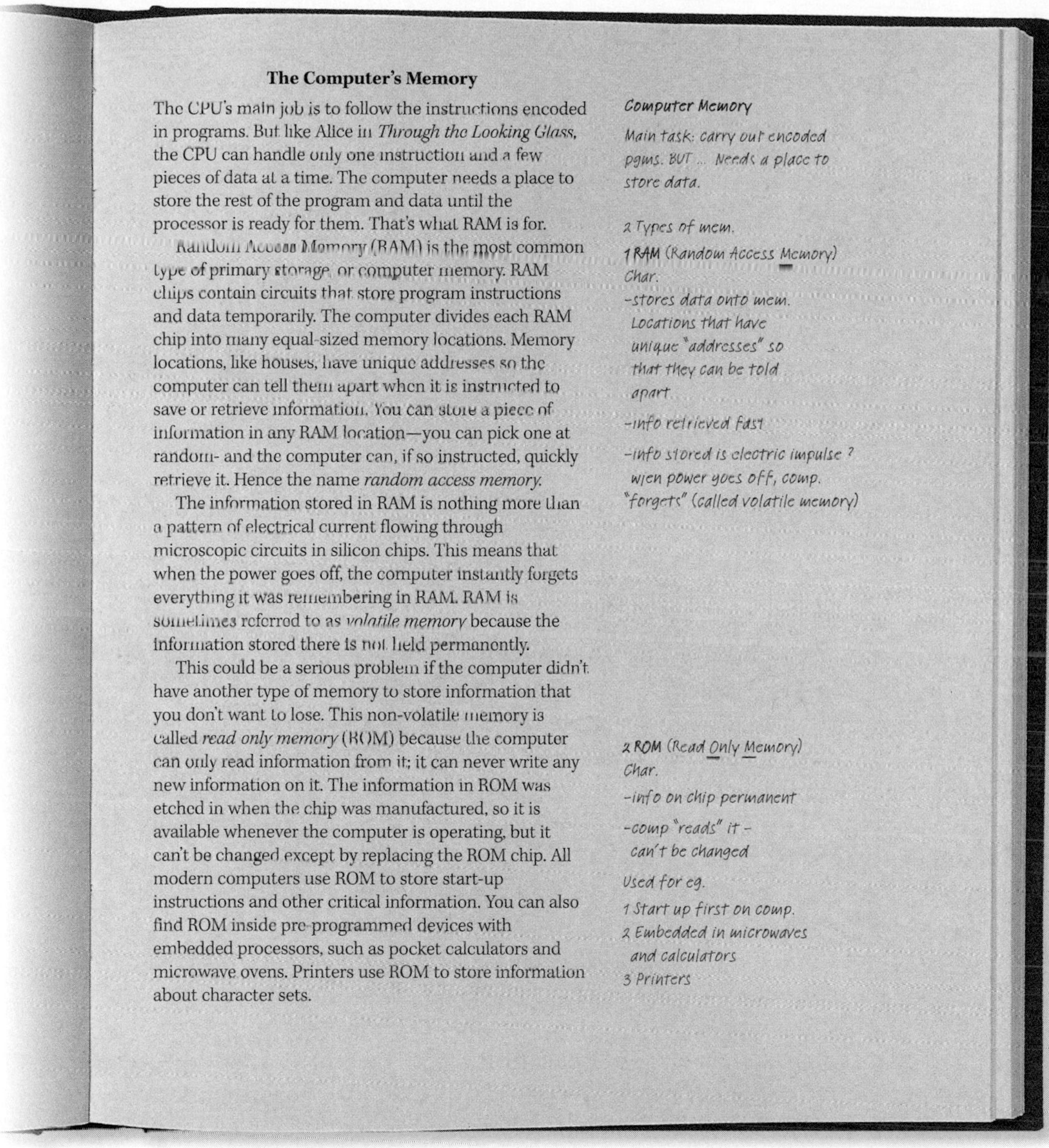

The Computer's Memory

The CPU's main job is to follow the instructions encoded in programs. But like Alice in *Through the Looking Glass*, the CPU can handle only one instruction and a few pieces of data at a time. The computer needs a place to store the rest of the program and data until the processor is ready for them. That's what RAM is for.

Random Access Memory (RAM) is the most common type of primary storage, or computer memory. RAM chips contain circuits that store program instructions and data temporarily. The computer divides each RAM chip into many equal-sized memory locations. Memory locations, like houses, have unique addresses so the computer can tell them apart when it is instructed to save or retrieve information. You can store a piece of information in any RAM location—you can pick one at random—and the computer can, if so instructed, quickly retrieve it. Hence the name *random access memory*.

The information stored in RAM is nothing more than a pattern of electrical current flowing through microscopic circuits in silicon chips. This means that when the power goes off, the computer instantly forgets everything it was remembering in RAM. RAM is sometimes referred to as *volatile memory* because the information stored there is not held permanently.

This could be a serious problem if the computer didn't have another type of memory to store information that you don't want to lose. This non-volatile memory is called *read only memory* (ROM) because the computer can only read information from it; it can never write any new information on it. The information in ROM was etched in when the chip was manufactured, so it is available whenever the computer is operating, but it can't be changed except by replacing the ROM chip. All modern computers use ROM to store start-up instructions and other critical information. You can also find ROM inside pre-programmed devices with embedded processors, such as pocket calculators and microwave ovens. Printers use ROM to store information about character sets.

Computer Memory

Main task: carry out encoded pgms. BUT... Needs a place to store data.

2 Types of mem.
1 RAM (Random Access Memory)
Char:
-stores data onto mem. Locations that have unique "addresses" so that they can be told apart.
-info retrieved fast
-info stored is electric impulse? wjen power goes off, comp. "forgets" (called volatile memory)

2 ROM (Read Only Memory)
Char.
-info on chip permanent
-comp "reads" it – can't be changed
Used for eg.
1 Start up first on comp.
2 Embedded in microwaves and calculators
3 Printers

Figure 9.4: Model Annotations of a Technology Text

Excerpt from C. Bookman, and M. J. Quinn. *Tomorrow's Technology and You* (Upper Saddle River, NJ: Pearson, 2008).

Monitoring Your Learning Because you annotate in your own words, you can monitor your understanding of what you are reading. If you can't put the information into your own words, you immediately know that your comprehension is breaking down.

HOW DO YOU ANNOTATE?

There are two basic guidelines to follow, regardless of the type of text you are annotating. Although you might have to modify these guidelines slightly for special kinds of texts, they will work in a majority of instances.

1. Read First, Then Annotate To help you decide what to annotate, read a section and then think about what would be important if you were going to teach that section to someone else. When students try to read and annotate at the same time, they end up writing either too much or too little. We generally suggest that if your text does not have clearly defined sections, read at least three or four paragraphs before stopping to annotate. Another alternative is to keep reading until the text seems to move to a new topic.

	Your Text States...	Your Annotations Say...
Paraphrasing	Two or more atoms held together by covalent bonds form a **molecule**.	*Molecules— atoms connected by covalent bonds.*
Writing in Your Own Words	Prototypes emerge from our experience with the external world, and new items that might potentially fit within their category are then compared with them. The more attributes new items share with an existing prototype, the more likely they are to be included within the concept.	*Prototypes— a system for organizing concepts into categories based on similar traits. Items with more traits in common are more likely to be included.*

Figure 9.5: Difference Between Paraphrasing and Writing in Your Own Words

2. Write Your Annotations in Your Own Words

Don't copy directly from the book unless you are annotating something that must be learned exactly as it is stated in the book, such as a chemistry or statistics formula. When you are annotating definitions, paraphrase the author's words so that you don't change the meaning of the definition. Otherwise, put all information into your own words. (See the Figure 9.5 for an example of the difference between paraphrasing and writing in your own words.) Keep in mind that stating ideas in your own words is a good way of monitoring whether or not you understand what you have read. Information that is not understood should not simply be skipped over—ask for help from another student or your professor.

WHAT TYPE OF INFORMATION SHOULD YOU ANNOTATE?

It is easy to see in the examples that your annotations will differ depending on the material. This is true when thinking about the amount of information and the way you will mark it in the margins. However, regardless of the content area, you should look for the following types of information whenever you annotate.

Definitions, especially content-specific terms and concepts. Content-specific terms are words you find in that particular subject. For example, *working memory* is a content-specific term in the psychology excerpt. *Glycogen* is a content-specific term from the biology chapter. *Stifling*, from the history appendix, is not a content-specific word. If you did not know the definition for stifling ("...traditional attitudes somewhat *stifling* working women..."), you might look it up in the dictionary, but you would not include it in your annotations.

Examples are important to annotate because they depict specific instances, theories, experiments, cases, and so forth. Text examples often show up on exams, so it is crucial to note them. You should also include personal examples when you can, because relating the information to what you already know will help you remember the information better. If the text does not provide an example but you can think of one that helps you, add that information to your annotations.

Predicted Test Questions are an important consideration. When you read, try to predict some likely test questions about the material. Try to ask higher-level questions that connect your text reading to the class lecture. Higher-level questions require more than just memorization of facts—they require application of the concept.

People, Dates, Places, and Events are important in certain types of courses such as history, social science, and political science. A word of caution, however: This should not be the only type of information you annotate. The type of questions you will be asked in college usually requires you to think at a higher level about the significance of the names, dates, and events. The only reason you annotate such facts is to get a chronology of events. Be sure that you think about how the information fits into the larger context.

Numbered Lists or Characteristics contained in your text should also be annotated. If your text states that there are three major causes of, reasons for, theories of, or factors that contribute to a certain idea, annotate them by numbering them in the margin. In this way, you will connect and learn those ideas together. Reader-friendly texts generally cue you as to how many reasons or characteristics you should annotate, but less friendly texts do not. Even though the text may not be explicit, you should be aware of and number lists.

Relationships Between Concepts, such as causes/effects or comparisons/contrasts, are important to note. When you read your text, look for relationships between concepts, even if the text doesn't explicitly point them out. They will help you reorganize the information in a meaningful way. Identifying relationships between concepts can also help you to predict potential essay questions.

Graphs, Charts, Diagrams, and other visuals are important to annotate. They often contain information that is not anywhere else in the text, or they summarize and condense large amounts of material. In addition, graphs and diagrams can also provide good examples of the concepts discussed in the text.

Studying Your Annotations

When you begin to annotate, you may worry that you have not pulled out the correct information. However, as you continue to use the strategy, you will develop **proficiency** for annotating the important material. And when you have done a good job, studying from your annotations is fairly straightforward. To study your annotations, cover up the text with your hand or a piece of notebook paper. Read your annotations a few times to be sure that you understand the concepts. When you feel comfortable with your understanding and you are certain that your annotations are complete, talk through the major points without looking at them. You should be able to talk about each topic that is annotated, and you should be able to give examples and details as well. If you find that there is a section that you don't know, reread your annotations. If you still don't understand, then reread that section in the text, ask a friend, look at your lecture notes, or ask your professor.

When you talk through your annotations, be sure that you are precise and complete in your explanations. *Preciseness* means that what you are saying is accurate, that the conclusions you are drawing are logical, and that you can see relationships between ideas. *Completeness* means that you know all of the important information, not just the main points. It's also important to know examples, explanations, and, in many cases, details. For example, you should understand the whys and hows of the Great Depression, not just the chronology of events.

Review your annotations a little each day so that when you are ready to study for an exam, you already know a lot of the material. These review sessions are a good time to link your lecture notes, secondary texts, and discussion group notes with your annotations. Pulling everything together as you go along makes studying from your annotations an active approach that is efficient and effective.

Examine the textbooks you are reading this term. Which of the following features do they contain?

	Textbook 1 Subject:	Textbook 2 Subject:	Textbook 3 Subject:	Textbook 4 Subject:	Textbook 5 Subject:
Preview Questions					
Bold-faced Terms					
Summaries					
Diagrams					
Formulas					
Glossaries					
Application Activities					
Large Margins					
Review Questions					
Text Boxes					

List three (3) benefits of using annotation.

_____

_____

_____

List three (3) concerns you have about using annotation.

_____

_____

_____

Self-Assessment

DIRECTIONS: Think about the types of rehearsal strategies you currently use. Answer yes or no for each of the following questions. Do you:

	Yes	No
1. Use notecards, concept maps, or charts to rehearse information?	___	___
2. Select your studying techniques depending on the course tasks?	___	___
3. Create a study plan before each exam?	___	___
4. Connect ideas as you study?	___	___
5. Study with the intent of really learning the information?	___	___
6. Test yourself over the material to monitor what you know?	___	___
7. Use all of your senses when you learn?	___	___

If you answered yes to most of these questions, you probably are on the right track and doing what you need to do in order to study successfully. This chapter details additional rehearsal strategies you could also use. If you answered no to several of the questions, this chapter will help you to rethink how you rehearse information for better studying.

Before reading the chapter, reflect on your responses to the self-assessment. What are you doing that is helping you learn? What do you need to work on?

_____
_____
_____
_____
_____
_____
_____
_____
_____
_____

Before You Begin

WORD WISE

As you read the rest of the chapter, be on the lookout for the following Word Wise vocabulary words.

1. **Premise** (n., p. 159) — a statement or proposition that is assumed to be true and on which a conclusion can be drawn.

*The **premise** of the author's novel is that vampires really exist.*

2. **Insurmountable** (adj., p. 159) — impossible to overcome.

*The suspect was convicted for armed robbery because the evidence against him was **insurmountable**.*

3. **Salient** (adj. p. 164) — obvious or pronounced; prominent.

***Salient** features of effective study strategies would include good organization and a format that allows for self-testing.*

4. **Verbatim** (adv., p. 164) — using exactly the same words; corresponding word for word.

*Carrie wrote down her mother's directions for making the chocolate chip cookies **verbatim** so that they would turn out perfectly.*

DID YOU KNOW?

Did you know that it takes ten to twenty exposures to "know" a word? You may partially understand a word after one viewing, but your depth of understanding and comprehension will increase each time you encounter the new word. This means you will have a richer understanding of the meaning of the word when you hear it or come across it again. This may be why you can't remember many of the words from your elementary school vocabulary lists—to know a word, you need to keep coming back to it.

RESEARCH INTO PRACTICE

Study Time is Not a Prediction of Success

When students put a considerable amount of time into studying and still earn a poor grade, they often don't understand why. Many students assume that the more time they spend studying, the better they will do. However, research indicates that this is not necessarily the case. Professors Plant, Ericsson, Hill, and Asberg examined why the amount of study time is not a good predictor of student success. In this study, college students kept track of the amount of time they studied, where they studied, and the quality of their study time, because the researchers were interested in not only the amount of time students spent studying but also in how they approached studying. The researchers found that those students who engaged in what they called "deliberate practice" had higher GPAs. That is, students who studied in quiet environments and engaged in high-quality studying had greater success than those who reported studying longer. They concluded that it is not the quantity of studying time that matters but the quality of that time.

This study is interesting because it indicates that how you study leads to greater success than how long you study. If you find yourself putting in long studying hours and not reaping the rewards, take a close look at what you are doing and try some of the strategies in *Effective College Learning*.

Source: E. A. Plant, K. A. Ericsson, L. Hill, and K. Asberg, "Why Study Time Does Not Predict Grade Point Average Across College Students: Implications for Deliberate Practice for Academic Performance," *Contemporary Educational Psychology* 30 (2005): 96–116.

Importance of Rehearsal

Just as actors rehearse their lines to remember them, so students must rehearse what they want to learn. Rehearsal means engaging in activities, either written or spoken, that will help you learn information from a variety of sources. You might say the information out loud, write down the information in an organized fashion, or discuss it with a classmate. There are many ways that you can go about rehearsing that we will present throughout the chapter. But first, it is important that you understand what rehearsal is and why it is important to your academic success.

Rehearsal strategies help you organize the concepts that your professor expects you to learn. In Chapter 9, we stressed the importance of engaging your mind before you begin to read by prereading. This warm-up activity, which gets the mind ready for mental exercise, enables you to actively read and annotate. You put the information into your own words and begin to see how the concepts relate. If everything goes well, you understand what you have read. Well, sort of. You

have comprehended it, but you just can't remember all of it. This is where the next step—rehearsal—enters the picture.

Rehearsal helps you to learn and remember the material. If you have ever taken a test and then forgotten the material immediately afterwards, you probably needed more rehearsal. Rehearsal helps you retain what you have learned. You organize the information from your text and lectures, make it meaningful in some way, write it, and then say it to yourself. Rehearsal allows you to use more of your senses in learning, which will help you retrieve—or have access to—the information at exam time. This chapter discusses rehearsal strategies that students will find improve the effectiveness of their studying. But before reading the rest of the chapter, be sure you have read the "Research into Practice" section about how the amount of study time may not predict success

Reality Check

Evaluating Your Approach to Rehearsing

Think about how you currently learn information. If your approach is superficial, your description of what you do may sound something like this: "I read through my book and I look over my notes. When it's time for a test, I keep doing these things until I have the information memorized." If this sounds like you, work on changing your approach. Think about the task and then select the rehearsal strategy that best matches that task. Effective learners are active learners and use writing and talking about the material to go beyond memorization.

Two Types of Rehearsal Strategies

Now that you have an idea of what rehearsal is and why it is important to use rehearsal strategies, let's think about two different types of rehearsal strategies: written strategies and oral strategies. It is important to understand that there is no single best strategy, either written or oral. The best rehearsal strategies are those that work for you in a particular situation. And the best students know and appropriately use a variety of strategies, both written and oral.

Written Rehearsal Strategies

When you use written strategies, you record the important information in an organized fashion. The way you organize depends on the task your professor expects from you, the materials with which you are interacting, and the particular way that you learn best. In other words, because the tasks and materials vary from course to course, the written strategies that work well for you in biology will probably be different from those that work for you in political science. Likewise, what works well for you may not work for the person sitting next to you. Specific written strategies—which we will present and discuss in detail—include concept cards, concept maps, concept charts, questions and answers, and time lines.

CONCEPT CARDS

Of all the rehearsal strategies we will present in this chapter, you are probably most familiar with concept cards. You may have called this strategy "flash cards" if you used it when you were in high school. But there are a few key differences. Like flash cards, concept cards use 3 x 5-inch index cards. As shown in Figure 10.1, you write the key concept that you want to learn on the front of the card. Then you write another word or phrase, called an *organizing*

term, in the top right-hand corner. Using an organizing term is one of the most important elements of making effective concept cards, because it allows you to see how ideas are grouped by the organizing term. In the example concept card for *chyme*, the organizing term is *digestive system,* with the secondary term *stomach*. This suggests that chyme is one of the terms related to the digestive system, and, more specifically, associated with the stomach. Also write the source of the information— the text page, date of the lecture, documentary notes, and so forth—on the front of the card.

On the back of the concept card, write all of the material you want to learn about a particular concept in an organized fashion and in your own words. Notice that the example not only has a definition of chyme but also includes other information that it would be important to know. Because most college professors expect you to go beyond memorization, you should include examples, links to other concepts, and a general synthesis of the key points you need to remember about the concept. Following are some of the major advantages.

Figure 10.1:
Example of a Concept Card

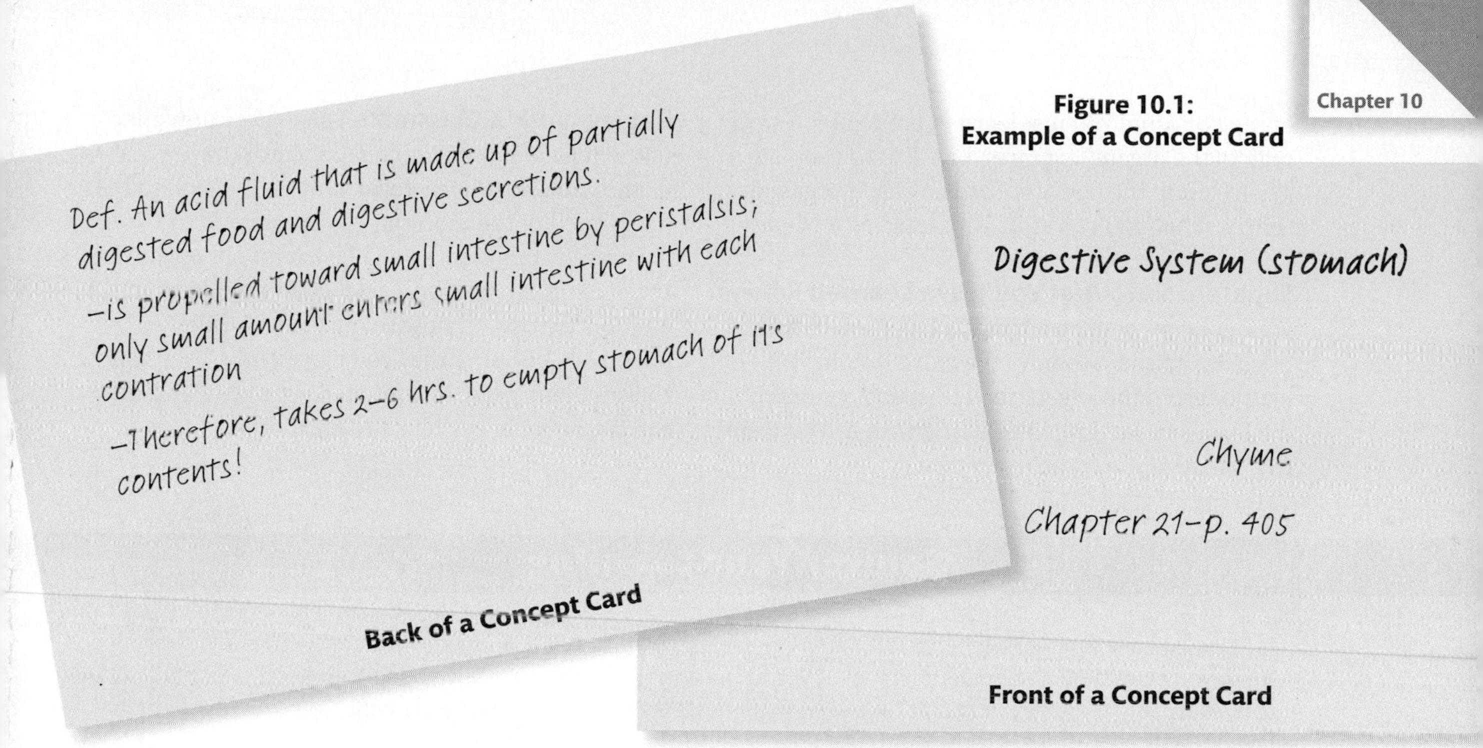

Def. An acid fluid that is made up of partially digested food and digestive secretions.

—is propelled toward small intestine by peristalsis; only small amount enters small intestine with each contration

—Therefore, takes 2–6 hrs. to empty stomach of its contents!

Back of a Concept Card

Digestive System (stomach)

Chyme

Chapter 21–p. 405

Front of a Concept Card

They Can Be Carried Around Easily Keep them in your backpack or pocket, and then pull them out when you have a few minutes to rehearse, such as while you are standing in line at the bookstore or waiting for class to begin. When you rehearse 10 minutes here or 15 minutes there, the additional study time quickly adds up.

They Are Versatile Concept cards work well in classes where you have to learn numerous terms, and if done correctly, can help you to see connections among ideas. For example, when you read and study the biology chapter in the appendix, it's apparent that there are many terms related to the digestive system. Rather than making just one card with a weak definition of the digestive system, you would use *digestive system* as the organizing term and write it in the upper right-hand corner of all the cards relating to the digestive system. Because there are so many parts to the digestive system, you might also want to group your cards better by adding a secondary term. Notice in the example that a specific part of the digestive system is in parentheses (stomach) to further organize the information. For example, you could clip all of your digestive system (stomach) cards together so that you could see how the different terms connect. Concept cards also work well for learning vocabulary, rules, conjugations, and so forth in foreign languages—or in mathematics, statistics, or chemistry where you have to learn and then apply formulas.

HOW DO YOU GO ABOUT STUDYING CONCEPT CARDS?

There are several things that you need to keep in mind when studying concept cards. Rather than just flipping through them, use the elements contained in each card to help you study. If you keep these suggestions in mind, it will make studying your cards effective and efficient.

Organize the Cards Use the organizing term in the upper right-hand corner to group all like terms together.

Start With the Organizing Term Read the key concept on the front of the first card, flip it over to the back, and read the information through a couple of times. Flip the card back over to the front and see how much of the information you can say to yourself without actually looking at it. Turn the card to the back again, and see how much you remembered. Repeat with each concept. Then return to the organizing term. Think about how all of the concepts you just learned are related—not only to the organizing term, but also to each other. Try to group the concept cards by their organizing term so that you can study the topic as a whole.

Separate Out What You Have Learned Review your concept cards each day, using those small pockets of time. Separate the cards you have learned from those you need to spend more time on. Spend more time interacting with the concepts that are giving you the most trouble.

Review with a Classmate Once you know most of the material on your concept cards, have your classmate ask you the term, and then check to see how much of the material you are able to say accurately and precisely. Then exchange roles. (See the section on "Reciprocal Questioning" later in the chapter for tips on how to quiz each other effectively.) Be sure that you can clearly discuss how the smaller concepts relate to larger ones and how the larger concepts relate to each other.

Monitor Your Learning

Students often have a difficult time gauging their level of readiness to take an exam. When you enter a testing situation, you should be able to verbalize what you know and don't know and also be able to accurately predict your grade. Because the rehearsal strategies discussed in this chapter have a self-testing element, you should feel more confident in your test preparedness if you use these strategies. To create awareness about your current practices, answer the following questions and compare your answers with those of your classmates.

Do in-class in groups

1. What do you do after you have read your textbook?

_____

_____

_____

2. How do you know when you are ready for an exam?

_____

_____

_____

3. How do you monitor what you know and what you don't know?

_____

_____

_____

4. How confident are you at test time?

_____

_____

_____

CONCEPT MAPS

Concept maps are visual representations of information and thus are very useful for students who tend to learn visually. A concept map is organized in such a way that it is easy to see the major concept that is being mapped, related concepts, and how everything is connected. See the example concept map below for an example that features theories of crime as an adaptive behavior. Concept mapping works well when it is important to see the relationship between complex concepts, and it works particularly well in the sciences, where many ideas tend to be related and to interact. For example, mapping might work very well to see the relationship among hormones of the endocrine system or the different stages of digestion. Mapping is especially useful for students who like to personalize strategies, because there is no right or wrong way to map. The important thing is that the way ideas are linked together be clearly shown in your concept map. You can hand-draw concept maps in your notebook, or you can use your computer's drawing tools and then print them out to keep in your binder. In fact, maps are such a clear way of showing relationships that textbooks now routinely use them as visual aids. The psychology chapter on memory in Appendix A has two concept maps, both flowcharts (pages 243 and 253) and one that shows relationships (page 244). It is similar to the concept map in Figure 10.2 below.

How Do You Go About Studying Maps? When you study your map, you can rehearse one concept at a time, then cover up everything except the main concept and begin to talk through the information. Talk about all of the related material and then check your accuracy. Focus on how the concepts are related to each other, because that is the major strength of mapping. Rather than viewing ideas one at a time—as is the case with concept cards—mapping enables you to understand how these ideas fit together.

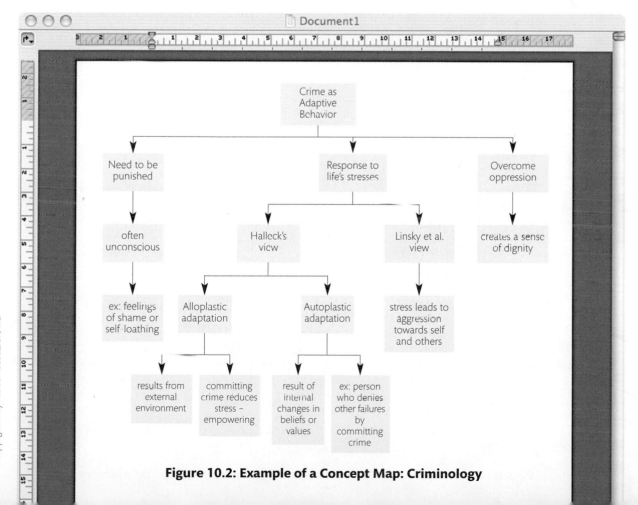

Figure 10.2: Example of a Concept Map: Criminology

CHARTING

Charting is similar to mapping but is useful in different kinds of situations. As shown in the next example, charting helps you synthesize information and is especially helpful when you are asked to compare and contrast ideas. For example, suppose you wanted to chart the four types of computer memory storage from the computer science chapter in the appendix of *Effective College Learning*. Knowing that there was a strong possibility that you might have to explain them and discuss their treatments on your exam would help you select the categories to set up your chart. Note in Figure 10.3 that the four different types of computer memory are on the vertical axis and the three categories are on the horizontal axis. This arrangement makes it easy to compare and contrast the types of memory.

How Do You Go About Studying Charts? You can study your chart by the categories either on the horizontal (across) or vertical (up and down) axis. In fact, it is best to study charts both ways. Using the example of four types of computer memory, you would talk through each, learning how each one works, what it is used for, and examples of when it is appropriate. Then you would study your chart horizontally by comparing and contrasting the four computer memory types in each of the categories— how it works, what it is used for, and some examples of when it is used.

	RAM	ROM	Flash	CMOS
Type	Random Access Memory; volatile (not permanent)	Read Only Memory; non-volatile (permanent)	Similar to RAM but is non-volatile	Complementary metal oxide semiconductor; non-volatile
How it works	RAM chip divides into equal-sized memory locations. Stores only while computer is in use. Must be saved to a hard drive or other storage device for long-term storage.	Information is written when ROM chip is made and cannot be changed or overwritten.	Can be written and erased repeatedly like RAM, but it can keep the information without the flow of electricity.	Low-energy type of RAM that can store small bits of info using battery power.
Used for	It is the most common type of memory. Any information one needs to store temporarily while working on a computer.	Start-up instructions for computers or in preprogrammed electronic devices.	Devices that store data that needs to be changed. Still too expensive for computers but may be the future of RAM.	Storing dates, time, and calendar on PC.
Examples	Word processing, e-mail, accessing program information	Start-up computer information; Pocket calculator; Microwave oven	USB drive; Cell phone; Digital camera	Personal computers; engineering labs

Figure 10.3: Example of a Chart for Technology Types of Computer Memory

QUESTION/ANSWER STRATEGY

Remember the study guides that your high school teachers gave you? These study guides were intended to help focus your thinking for a test, usually by posing a series of questions. The **premise** was that if you could answer the questions on the study guide, you would be able to do well on the test. The question/answer strategy uses a similar premise, except that *you* are the active learner who creates both the questions and the answers. You think about the important information in the text and lectures, pose questions that cover the material, and then answer each of the questions you posed.

In the question/answer strategy as shown in Figure 10.4, you'll see a format that probably looks different from what your previous teachers may have used. Using the question/answer strategy, you write your question on the left-hand side of the paper. The right-hand space, which is wider and longer than the left side, is for answering the question. This format reminds you that the questions you pose should require more than a one-word answer. In fact, even when your exam consists of multiple-choice questions, you will be better prepared if you predict short-answer questions such as those in Figure 10.4 on page 160.

When you are posing your questions, think about Bloom's Taxonomy (discussed in Chapter 7). Try to create questions that focus on the higher levels—questions that typically begin with *why* or

how. By higher level, we mean questions that encourage synthesis of the information to be learned. Try to ask questions that require you to understand the entire concept, not just the small pieces. Most importantly, the questions you write should reflect the kinds of information that your professor expects you to learn.

Figure 10.4 (page 160) shows you the difference between writing primarily memory-level questions and asking higher-level items. (These questions are drawn from the nutrition and digestion chapter in Appendix B.) The questions you pose using the question/answer strategy are more focused than those you predicted during the prereading stage when you were unfamiliar with the important information in the text chapter. For multiple-choice exams that have numerous application and synthesis questions, you would want to write questions that encompass entire concepts. Create as many questions as you need to test yourself on all the relevant material for your exam.

To answer such questions, you would read your text annotations and lecture notes. As with all of the strategies, your question/answer strategy will not be effective if you leave out important information or include information that is wrong or incomplete. You should also be sure to put the material in your own words whenever possible, because this will help you remember it better.

How Do You Go About Studying the Question/Answer Strategy? When you study using the question/answer strategy, fold your paper back so that just the question side is showing. Ask yourself a question, or get someone else to ask you. Then answer it by saying the information out loud. Check to see how much of the material you remembered correctly. If your answer matches what you wrote, repeat the process with the next question. If your answer was incomplete or wrong, read the correct answer several times and try to say it again before moving on to the next question. In addition, because the questions on the exam will most certainly be in random order, don't always begin with your first question and work your way through to the end. Instead, start with the last question, do every other question, or use some

---

BEYOND THE CLASSROOM

Making and using rehearsal strategies may appear to be **insurmountable** tasks for students who must work, raise a family, and go to college at the same time. If this sounds like you, it's especially important to create a study cycle where you are annotating your text for one class and rehearsing and reviewing for another. Some students lose sight of the fact that they don't have to use every strategy for every course. Busy students need to pick and choose their strategies wisely and know how to use them flexibly.

other pattern. In addition, you can use this strategy for a study group. Everyone in the group prepares a set of questions in advance to use in the group meeting.

Questions	Answers
1. Explain the role that amino acids play in nutrition.	1. All proteins are built from 20 different amino acids. – 8 are essential amino acids because the body can't make them. They must be gotten from food. – a source of energy – ex: animal protein (complete) vegetable protein (incomplete)
2. Explain the role that the stomach plays in the digestion of food	2. Stomach walls mix food and gastric juices into acid chyme. – slowly squirts the acid chyme into small intestine – takes 2-6 hours for stomach to empty after a meal – if there is a backflow of acid chyme, it can cause heartburn or acid reflux
3. How do protein deficiencies affect children?	3. This is also called malnutrition and is caused by a lack of consumption of one or more essential amino acids. – It happens mainly in poor countries where there is not enough food. – can cause mental and physical retardation and/or kwashiorkor — a deficiency in blood protein that causes swelling of the belly

Figure 10.4: Example of the Question/Answer Strategy for Science

TIME LINES

Unlike the other strategies we have discussed, time lines are only appropriate in specific situations. Basically, you can use time lines when it is important to know chronology—the order of something that happened over a period of time. For example, you might use time lines in a history course when it's important to know the chronology of the Vietnam conflict, in an art appreciation class when you need to be able to compare and contrast major artistic movements, or in a geology course when you're expected to trace the evolution of the earth's crusts over millions of years. Hence, you can use time lines in many different disciplines, but they do have a very specific function.

Time lines are flexible in that they can be constructed in a variety of ways. The accompanying example in Figure 10.5 shows a time line of events that occurred leading up to the Great Depression, including the stock market crash of 1929. Notice that in this time line, years are grouped together because most of the events that took place did not happen in a specific year—the events happened over a period of time. This is indicated on the time line by using the word "by"—by 1932, for example. Your textbooks may depict other types of time lines to show longer spans of time, like the time line on page 286 in the history excerpt in Appendix C.

In the majority of studying situations, time lines should be supplemented with other strategies such as concept cards, concept maps, or charts. For example, if you were making a time line portraying the events leading up to the Great Depression, you would indicate only the chronology—which events happened when. But that would be insufficient knowledge to have when preparing for an exam. You would need to know why those events happened, what the impact of these events was, and what the details of each event entailed. This information cannot be gleaned from the time line alone.

How Do You Go About Studying Time Lines?

When you are studying time lines, use only your dates as the cue. Talk through the important events, laws, battles, and so forth that occurred on that date. At the same time, use your other strategies to talk through the nature of each of the events, thinking about cause and effect or how one event influenced another. Use newspaper questions—who, what, where, when, why, and how—to be certain that you are fully describing each event. In addition, it's important to understand how events are related, so be sure that you see the big picture as well.

Time Line Chronology of Events Leading Up to the Great Depression	
1923 – 1928	Jobless rates exceed 10% in mass production industries
1920 – 1929	State and local taxes rise faster than personal income
By 1929	Unequal distribution of wealth
	October 29, 1929 – Black Tuesday – Beginning of Depression • US Steel—dropped from $262–$22 • Montgomery Ward—dropped from $138–$4
By 1930	• Factories shut down • Industrial production falls sharply • Unemployment skyrockets
By 1932	• American exports fall by 70% • Personal income drops by more than half • Commodity prices fall by 55%; farmers hit hard, many lose farms and homes • One fourth of labor force out of work
1932	FDR Elected president

Figure 10.5: Example of a Time Line for the Chronology of Events Leading to the Great Depression

Oral Rehearsal Strategies

Oral rehearsal strategies are those that involve speaking in some way, such as talking out loud, to yourself, or to a study partner. Although you might think it odd to talk to yourself as you study and learn, saying information out loud is a powerful tool because it is a form of active learning that keeps you connected with the material. Talking and listening as you study helps you use other senses as well. And remember, the more senses you use when you study, the easier learning will be. Oral strategies work well for students who tend to be auditory learners, meaning they learn better through hearing information than by reading it or writing it. Oral rehearsal also works well for students with test anxiety because once you can verbalize the information, you can be more certain that you understand it. You say the information out loud and then check your accuracy. Like written strategies, the oral strategies you select depend on all the other factors that impact learning—your characteristics, the task, and the text. We believe, however, that "talk-throughs" benefit all students because saying the information out loud will help you recall the information come test time. The specific oral rehearsal strategies that will be presented are reciprocal questioning and talk-throughs.

RECIPROCAL QUESTIONING

Reciprocal questioning involves two learners, one who takes the role of the teacher, and the other who takes the role of the student. The "teacher" asks a question from the question/answer strategy, text annotations, or lecture notes. Most should be questions that elicit higher-level or critical thinking rather than those that promote memorization or one-word answers. The "student" then answers the question, and the "teacher" checks his answer against the written strategy. If the student has answered the question correctly, the teacher asks the next question. If the question was not answered adequately, the teacher gives some hints and tries to guide the student to the answer. In other words, the teacher tries to help the student learn the material

rather than giving the correct response. The same questions should be asked again at the end of the study session.

After all of the questions have been asked and answered—and if necessary reviewed—the two switch roles, with the student becoming the teacher and the teacher becoming the student. The new teacher should be sure that she asks the questions in a different order and adds some new questions.

The examples of good and poor questions on page 163 focus on memory. Notice that the questions in the "Good" column are ones that require critical thinking, synthesis, and analysis, while most of the questions in the "Poor" column require only one-word answers or simple memorization.

Reciprocal questioning can be a powerful strategy for several reasons.

It Brings More Senses into Play You have read the information using the visual sense, you have written important concepts down in an organized fashion using the kinesthetic sense, and you are now hearing the information using the auditory sense. Using more than one sense helps you remember better because it makes you a more active learner.

It Encourages Multiple Perspectives The old adage "two heads are better than one" is true in this situation. One person may be very strong in understanding concept A and the other very knowledgeable about concept B. Pulling the ideas of two people together generally makes for clearer, more precise learning for both.

It Encourages You to Use Your Own Words Because professors rarely write questions that come exactly from the text, it's important to put information in your own words so that you will recognize it in a slightly different form on the test. When you have two people putting it in their own words, you begin to think outside of the textbook,

Good Questions	Poor Questions
I low can you extend the limitations of short-term memory?	What is the capacity of short-term memory?
Explain the three subsystems within long-term memory.	List the three subsystems within long-term memory.
Why is eyewitness testimony often unreliable?	What is the misinformation effect?

and you get another perspective of how the information might be phrased.

It Helps You to Monitor Your Learning When you are asked a question and then provide the answer, you get immediate feedback about your knowledge on that particular topic. This helps you monitor the concepts you know and those on which you need more work.

TALK-THROUGHS

As the name of this strategy suggests, talk-throughs involve saying the information (talking it through) to yourself—either silently or out loud—to monitor your learning. When you talk through the concepts, you become both the student *and* the teacher, because rather than having someone ask you questions or ask you to explain concepts, you fill both roles. Start by making a talk-through list on an index card. As seen in the example in Figure 10.6, a talk-through simply lists, in an organized fashion, the concepts you need to learn and remember. Notice that the supporting ideas are indented so that it is easy to see which ideas are connected in some way. For example, in this talk-through card, it is easy to see that you should know the four main theories of criminal behavior. To create your card, it is often helpful to look at the headings and subheadings

in your text, because they give you the overall picture of the chapter.

After you have made your talk-through card, begin rehearsal by saying what you know about the first major concept. Talk it through, looking back at your written strategies if necessary, including text annotations and lecture notes. In fact, after you have said the information silently or out loud, it is a good idea to go back and read over the information again to be sure that you are rehearsing it completely and precisely. As you learn each piece of information, also be sure that you can make connections between the major concepts and the supporting details. Explain to yourself how the pieces fit together.

4 Theories of Criminal Behavior

1. Modeling
   - Bandura
   - act by learning from how others act
2. Behavior
   - Skinner
   - rewards and punishments
3. Attachment
   - Bowlby
   - based on attachment with parents as a child
4. Self-control
   - Gottfredson & Hirschi
   - a person's ability to control responses and behavior

Figure 10.6: Example of a Talk-Through Card for Criminology

Characteristics of Good Rehearsal Strategies

When you were in high school, you may have used rehearsal strategies without even knowing it. Perhaps you made outlines after you read your text, or put vocabulary words or foreign language terms on index cards. You may have had a family member or friend ask you questions before a test. All of these are examples of rehearsal strategies, some of which are better than others. Use the following guidelines to help you distinguish effective rehearsal strategies from those that are less effective. Effective rehearsal strategies have several **salient** features.

1. THEY ALLOW FOR SELF-TESTING

When you self-test, you rehearse without actually looking at the answer. For example, if you needed to learn the different stages of sleep for a psychology exam, you would want to say the stages to yourself or out loud and then immediately check to see whether you were correct. This process differs greatly from "looking over" or "reading though" information and having no concrete idea of whether you know the material. Effective rehearsal strategies allow you to monitor what you know and allow for the element of self-testing.

2.THEY INCLUDE COMPLETE AND PRECISE INFORMATION

Have you have ever taken a test—particularly a multiple-choice test—where the information seemed "familiar" but you had a difficult time selecting the correct answer? This is probably an instance where you didn't rehearse completely and precisely. Like good text annotations, good rehearsal strategies require you to say or write all the information related to a concept and to see relationships between ideas.

3. THEY ARE ORGANIZED

Effective strategies have some structure to isolate the information in a way that makes sense and helps you remember it. Your brain files information very much like a computer does. That is, concepts are stored in a logical way. Likewise, your rehearsal strategies need to have a logical flow as well.

4. THEY STATE THE IDEAS IN YOUR OWN WORDS

Few professors test you over information from text or lectures **verbatim**. Rather, they paraphrase and synthesize concepts—they put it in their own words. Thus, trying to memorize material straight from the text or lecture will cause problems at test time when the exam questions are written in another way. If after a test you find yourself confused about what the professor is asking and think, "The professor never talked about the information that way in class," you probably need to put the information in your own words as you rehearse and study.

NETWORKING

Building Background Knowledge

You can use the Internet to help you build your background knowledge on the content of your college courses. For one of your classes this semester, choose a topic that interests you and then visit several sites on the Web to find out more about it. Often, getting some additional information helps you understand difficult material (and can even help you become more motivated to learn in the class).

Real College

FRANK'S FRUSTRATION

DIRECTIONS: *Read the following scenario and respond to the questions based on the information you have learned in this chapter.*

Frank is a first-year college student who is frustrated with his performance so far. Halfway into the term, he is particularly discouraged with his inability to see the big picture in some of his courses and is surprised that his classes seem to require him to study in different ways in order to do well. His grades are suffering and Frank is questioning whether he should actually be in college. In high school, Frank simply skimmed the different parts of his texts to answer questions on the study guides that most of his teachers provided. He would memorize the information and do well on almost every exam. But in college, three of his professors expect him to conceptualize information. That is, he has to understand scientific processes in biology, his history professor expects the class "to put information in a historical perspective," and in his literature course he has to think about how character development and use of language relate to the plots in the short stories they are studying. Frank doesn't even know where to start studying for these courses. In high school, he used to put lots of information on index cards and sometimes he would make complex outlines, but those tactics aren't working and he doesn't even know any other study strategies to consider.

What can Frank do?

1. What would your advice to Frank be?

_____

_____

_____

_____

2. What rehearsal and review strategies would you recommend for each of his courses and why?

_____

_____

_____

_____

_____

_____

Add to Your Portfolio

1. Construct a set of 10 questions/answers for a chapter for a course in which you are currently enrolled. Be sure to ask some higher-level questions that begin with the words "how" and "why."

2. Construct one of the following strategies for a course in which you are currently enrolled. Be sure to consider the task before you select your strategy.

- **20 concept cards**   • **1 concept map**   • **1 chart**

3. Write a one-page reflection about one of the strategies you tried. What are the positives and negatives of the strategy? How did you modify it to suit the task and your learning characteristics? Could you adapt this strategy to another course and task? If so, how?

_____

_____

_____

_____

_____

_____

_____

_____

_____

_____

_____

_____

_____

_____

_____

_____

_____

Chapter 11
Reviewing Strategies

Read this chapter to answer the following questions:

- What is the difference between rehearsal and review strategies?

- Why is it important to be able to say material out loud?

- How can study groups promote learning?

- Why is it important to have a specific study plan?

Self-Assessment

DIRECTIONS: Think about the ways you now review your textbooks, lecture notes, and other course materials. Answer yes or no for each of the following questions. Do you review:

	Yes	No
On a daily basis?	——	——
When you have small pockets of time?	——	——
Several days before an exam?	——	——
More than once before an exam?	——	——
At the beginning of each study session?	——	——
At the end of each study session?	——	——
With classmates?	——	——
By questioning yourself over the material?	——	——

If you answered yes to most of these questions, you are probably on the right track and doing what you need to in order to complete the studying process. Read the remainder of the chapter to see what additional reviewing strategies you might use. If you answered no to several of these questions, you might want to rethink how you review as you read the remainder of this chapter.

Before reading the chapter, reflect on your responses to the self-assessment. How are your current studying methods helping you learn? What do you need to work on?

_____

_____

_____

_____

_____

_____

_____

_____

WORD WISE

1. **Arbitrary** (adj., p. 172) — determined by chance or impulse; subject to individual judgment or preference.

*At the last minute, Lucinda and her friends made an **arbitrary** decision to go to the concert rather than watch a movie.*

2. **Allocate** (v., p. 174) — to parcel out or distribute.

*Because Eric had not **allocated** enough time in his schedule to prepare for his exam, he felt very anxious when it came time to take the test.*

3. **Conventional** (adj., p. 175) — customary; conforming to established practice or accepted standards.

*A **conventional** approach for curbing underage drinking is fining establishments who are caught serving those under 21.*

4. **Regimen** (n., p. 180) — a systematic process; a regulated system intended to achieve something beneficial.

*A healthy diet and an exercise **regimen** can lead to weight loss and physical fitness.*

DID YOU KNOW?

It is important to know the difference between content-specific and general vocabulary terms. Content-specific vocabulary terms are words used within an academic subject that describe ideas or concepts particular to that field. For example you don't often hear the word *motherboard* outside the field of computer science. Learning content-specific vocabulary is important to doing well in college courses. General vocabulary terms are those that can be used in many different fields. For example, the word *presumably* could be used in almost any textbook. Knowing the meaning of this word can help you comprehend the text but is not key to understanding the academic field in general. In your own courses, pay particular attention to learning the content-specific terms. You might also want to look up some of the general vocabulary when you sense that it will help your overall comprehension.

RESEARCH INTO PRACTICE

How Procrastination Hinders Success

In this study, Professor C. A. Wolters was interested in determining if students who were effective, motivated learners (what he calls *self-regulated learners*) procrastinated as frequently as other students. In two separate studies, undergraduate students responded to a lengthy questionnaire where they rated how strongly they agreed with statements relating to studying and learning, including items on motivation. The major result of both studies was that self-regulated students procrastinate less than those who are not self-regulated. But perhaps the more relevant implications focused on the planning aspect of self-regulation. The results suggested that students who learned how to set reasonable expectations about the amount of time they needed to complete a task were more successful. Likewise, students who learned to use strategies that helped them plan and regulate their study behaviors—strategies such as making and following a study plan and setting short-term studying goals—decreased their potential to procrastinate. This study draws attention to the important effect that procrastination has in academic success, but it also suggests that students can learn strategies that will help them procrastinate less.

Source: C. A. Wolters, "Understanding Procrastination From a Self-Regulated Learning Perspective," *Journal of Educational Psychology* 95 (2003): 179–187.

Reviewing

In Chapter 10, you learned that rehearsal enables you to learn the information you have read. It not only helps you store the concepts you'll need to learn, but it also helps you to retrieve the material at test time. When you rehearse, you write, say, and listen to the information until you know it very well. You look for connections between ideas and understand how concepts are related. Reviewing, on the other hand, is a way of making sure that the important information has been learned in such a way that it is complete, organized, and precise. It is the step you take after you rehearse. Reviewing ensures that the information will stay fixed in your memory. By reviewing daily, you remember about three times more than if you had not reviewed. Thus, there is a tremendous payoff in review.

You can use reviewing at various times during the studying process. For example, in Chapter 8, which focused on taking effective lecture notes, we emphasized the importance of reviewing notes daily. Getting to class 10 minutes early and using that time to read over your notes is a form of reviewing. This type of review refreshes your memory of what happened in the last class and prepares your mind to receive new information, making it easier to connect ideas. But the kind of reviewing that we focus on in this chapter is generally done as a final phase of studying and test preparation. You review by self-testing to monitor your learning and gain a better understanding of the information you know very well and the information that requires further study through additional rehearsal.

Using Your Talk-Through Card for Reviewing

Talk-through cards, discussed in Chapter 10, can be used as part of verbal rehearsal. In an organized way, list the concepts you want to rehearse and learn as you study the material. Remember that you start with the first concept on the card, rehearse by reading all the information related to that concept a couple of times, and then see whether you can say it without looking at your notes or rehearsal strategies. As you work through your list of key points, you think about connections and relationships between ideas. By the end of your study session, you should have learned at least a portion of the major concepts on your talk-through card. You repeat this same procedure with other concepts in other study sessions until you know and understand each idea.

You can also use your talk-through card to review. Start with the first concept and completely and accurately talk through the key points. If you know all the information related to that concept, check it off and go on to the next. If you have trouble remembering the material, return to your annotations or rehearsal strategies and say the information again. Keep in mind that if rehearsal has been done properly, reviewing should just be a matter of keeping the information retrievable in your memory and seeing which concepts are still giving you problems. You should be able to remember most of the important information and see links between concepts when you are reviewing. At the reviewing stage, the information should already be stored in your memory; you are simply checking to see that you will be able to retrieve it at test time.

The Importance of a Specific Study Plan

We have talked in other chapters about the importance of planning. Rather than having an **arbitrary** approach to test preparation, think about how much time you will spend studying and what you will do during those study sessions. It's particularly important to structure specific study and review sessions as the time for an exam draws closer. That's why we suggest that you develop a Specific Study Plan, or SSP, for each exam you take.

ADVANTAGES OF AN SSP

Perhaps the biggest advantage of an SSP is actually in creating it. It has been our experience that most students benefit more from creating a structured plan than from one that's just in their heads. Creating a plan and clipping it in your daily planner reminds you that you have set aside specific times to rehearse and review and enables you to be ready on test day. The SSP also allows you to evaluate how your plan is working and to modify it if things are not proceeding as you thought they would. Finally, your SSP not only outlines when you will study but also the strategies you will use, requiring you to put more thought into your plan beyond just scheduling the time of your study sessions. For example, it shows when you plan to meet with your study group so that you can prepare in advance.

CONSTRUCTING AN SSP

Construct your study plan about a week or so before the exam. At this point, you are trying to set goals and organize your tasks and studying so that you have enough time to learn the material. If you are not sure about the task for the exam, you will need to find this out before you can construct your SSP. Think about your goals by asking yourself a series of questions:

1. What grade do I want to earn on the exam? (Note: Do not automatically say an A in response to this question. Instead, think about how much time and effort you are willing to invest to earn the grade you desire.)

2. How much time do I need to invest in order to make this grade?

3. Where will I find the extra time? Will I have to give up other activities in order to carve out time to study?

4. What kind of exam is it? Multiple-choice? Essay? What difficulties do I usually have when I take tests of this nature?

5. Do I know the balance of items? Is this a memorization task or will I be expected to answer higher-level questions? What proportion of questions will come from the text and the lectures?

6. What kinds of rehearsal strategies will I need to create because they will work best for this exam?

After you have answered these questions, you are ready to construct your SSP. An SSP outlines what you will do in each particular study session and shows what rehearsal or review strategies you will use, what concepts you will study, and approximately how long each study session will last. Look at Figure 11.1 for an SSP example for a psychology exam covering text chapters and lecture notes. The student in the example has three study sessions (1, 2, and 3) and two specific sessions set aside just to review with her classmates (4 and 6). One session (5) is set aside just for self-testing to get a handle on which concepts may still be problematic. Also note that each study session begins with a review of the information that was rehearsed in the previous session. Each session should also end with a review of what was learned in that session.

SCHEDULING YOUR STUDY TIME

As you construct your SSP and think about the time you will need to rehearse and review the material, remember from the principles discussed in Chapter 2 that you should always allow more time than you think you will need. If you block out 2 hours for a study session to learn a set of concepts and it takes only an hour and a half, you have gained a half hour in which you can do something else. But if you set aside the same 2 hours and it ends up taking you 3 hours to feel comfortable with the concepts, you have lost an hour. Thus, it's important to have some flexibility in your schedule that allows for additional time should you need it.

Session	What I'll do	Strategies I'll use	Reflection and evaluation
#1 Sunday pm: 6:00–7:00	Study all concepts related to remembering	concept cards, maps, lecture notes	Took more than 1 hour (actually 6:00–7:45)
#2 Monday pm: 4:40–6:30	Review remembering; study concepts related to retrieval	talk-through card, concept cards, maps, lecture notes	Too tired to study right after class. Need to plan a different time. zzzzzzz
#3 Tuesday pm: 7:00–9:30	Review remembering and retrieval. Study biology and memory and forgetting.	talk-through card, concept cards, maps, lecture notes	This is a much better study time for me.
#4 Wednesday pm: 7:30–9:00	Review with study group.	question/answer, reciprocal teaching	Great study session Really feel like I am starting to get this stuff!
#5 Thursday pm: 9:00–10:30	Self-test	question/answer, talk-through card	I actually didn't need to use this entire time. I really understand.
#6 Thursday pm: 7:30–9:00	Review with study group.	talk-through card, oral question/answer	I feel ready to go.

EXAM FRIDAY!

Figure 11.1: SSP for an Exam Covering Text Chapters and Lecture Notes

EVALUATING YOUR SSP

When you complete each study session, check it off, evaluate how long it actually took, and determine any specific areas that you might need to return to in your next session.

First, reflect on your overall studying plan. Did you exceed the amount of time you allotted or did you need less time? Did you plan your study sessions for times when you are most alert? Did you study during your planned times or did you miss several sessions?

Think about your learning environment in your evaluation as well. Was the place where you studied conducive to learning? If not, what was distracting you? What changes to the learning environment need to be made to make your study sessions more productive?

After each study session, reflect on the quality of learning. Did you meet your learning goals? Are you prepared for the types of questions your professor will ask about the topics you studied? The answers to these questions will help you as you develop an SSP for the next exam in this course.

DIFFERENT TYPES OF REVIEW

One of the most helpful aspects of the SSP is that it sets aside time to do three different types of review, with each serving a different purpose. The first type targets information that you learned previously, the second focuses on information that you are currently learning, and the third helps you monitor where you are a couple of days before the test.

1. You *begin* each session with a review of what you learned previously. Using your talk-through card as a guide, say what you remember from the earlier study session. If there's material that is still giving you problems, begin the current study session with that. You will find that adding a brief review at the beginning of each study session increases your concentration and your ability to recall the information come exam time. That is because reviewing at the beginning of each session also serves as a warm-up to get you ready to focus on learning.

2. At the *end* of each session, you review only those concepts you concentrated on in that session. This type of review serves as a monitoring device to let you know what you actually remember from the session. If you start this review and find that you are having problems, you can return to those concepts

Reality Check

Allocating Study Time
One of the main difficulties that students have when creating an SSP is figuring out how much time it will take them to prepare for an exam. Think about the last exam you studied for. Did you **allocate** enough time? Did you plan to rehearse and review at several times or did you cram all of your test preparation into one marathon session? How did you perform on the exam? It is important to reflect on how you prepared for your last exam so that you can either change your approach (if you didn't do very well) or stay the course (if you were satisfied with your performance).

immediately and rehearse more. This is the monitoring part of your review, when you discover whether you will need to devote more time to the study session than you originally planned.

3. *A day or two before the test*, you continue to monitor your understanding of all of the concepts you will be tested over. Concentrate the time you have left on the material that you understand least. Many students make the mistake of spending equal amounts of time on everything before an exam, even information that they know fairly well. Learn from their mistakes. The closer the exam, the more you want to concentrate on concepts you don't know well.

STAYING ON TRACK

Setting goals for yourself and making an SSP for each exam helps you stay on track with both rehearsing and reviewing. Note that it is important to focus on learning specific concepts, not on the amount of time you actually have allotted for studying. For Figure 11.1 on page 173, if you were studying for the test outlined in the example, you would want to learn all of the information related to the concept "remembering" in your first study session. It is usually ineffective to go over all the information in each chapter in every study session. Instead, focus on breaking up the concepts to be learned into individual study sessions. Students who plan around time rather than around mastery of the information can easily go into a testing situation unprepared.

Forming Study Groups

One of the best ways to review is to form study groups. Almost everyone can benefit from belonging to a study group at one time or another, but study groups work particularly well for students who learn better auditorily or through discussion and in courses they find problematic. Some students form study groups that meet on a weekly basis to talk about and review what went on in class that week. Other students plan study groups just before an exam as a way of reviewing and perhaps even getting a new or different perspective on what they have learned. Either way, study groups have big advantages if they are conducted appropriately.

Perhaps the biggest advantage of being part of a study group is that it allows you to listen to information in another person's voice, which can provide insights and perspectives that you may not have considered. In a **conventional** course, you listen to your professor's interpretation of the information during lectures, you read the text for another interpretation, and through these two sources, you come up with your own interpretation or meaning. You have listened, read, and written down material, so you have used several of your senses. All of this interaction should help you gain a greater degree of understanding of the material. It stands to reason, then, that by listening to and talking with others who are also trying to understand the course information, you would gain a deeper understanding, be able to remember the concepts better, and subsequently do better on exams.

BEYOND THE CLASSROOM

If you are holding down a job or returning to college after several years, you may find the SSP to be an invaluable strategy. When you are juggling work (even part time), family needs, and your other responsibilities, creating a studying plan that lets you know exactly how much time you will need to prepare can help you find a balance in your busy life. SSPs can also help alleviate some anxiety because if you follow your plan, you will be confident that you will learn the before the exam.

CHARACTERISTICS OF GOOD STUDY GROUPS

It's important to think about the characteristics of *good* study groups. Just meeting with people in the same course does not necessarily make a study group. Productive study groups have the following characteristics:

Everyone Comes Prepared Study groups do not replace studying on your own. Everyone should come to the group prepared to review, pose and answer possible test questions, and ask questions about material they don't understand. If the study group members have to spend all of their time trying to teach a large portion of the course material to someone who didn't even attempt to learn it on her own, most members will not benefit.

Everyone Can Talk Through a Difficult Idea with the Group Divide up the material among the group members. It helps if everyone selects something complex or confusing to discuss. During the study group, each member will lead the discussion on his or her topic. As you are reviewing your understanding of the concept, others who may understand it better than you should be encouraged to offer additional explanations. Don't shy away from discussing information that you don't know very well; it defeats the purpose of the group.

Members of the Group Are Classmates but not Necessarily Friends. Everyone knows what can happen when friends get together to study: Everything goes fine for the first few minutes, but it's easy to get off track. It's much better to have serious students—who all have the goal of doing well—in your study group rather than just recruiting your friends. That's not to say that studying with friends will never work; it's simply harder to study with friends than it is with classmates working toward a common goal.

Meet at a Location That is Conducive to Studying Campus libraries often have study rooms set aside for just this purpose. Such rooms are generally small and soundproof so that normal conversation and discussion can be carried out with ease. If your library doesn't have study rooms, residence halls often have common areas equipped with study rooms. Empty classrooms can also work well, as can a local coffee shop. If your only alternative is to study in someone's room or at someone's home or apartment, remind yourself what the purpose of the session is: to review the course material for a test, not to socialize.

Have Clear Goals and Structure Groups that have a game plan in mind before they come together are generally the most successful. Most groups meet at regular times. We know of a study group in a statistics course that meets weekly to review the week's important ideas and to predict some possible test questions that review those concepts. The group also meets a couple of times right before the exam to review what they know and to predict and solve possible test questions. It doesn't hurt to set some ground rules right from the beginning to prevent difficulties later on. For example, what will happen if someone comes to the group without doing any preparation on his own?

NETWORKING

Virtual Study Groups

Try to set up an online review session prior to an exam in one of your classes. You can review with your classmates by sending questions to one another via e-mail, a class listserv, or a discussion board. Each of you can answer questions posed by the others and provide feedback as to the completeness and accuracy of the answers. You can also plan to "meet" online to use instant messaging as a means of discussing specific concepts.

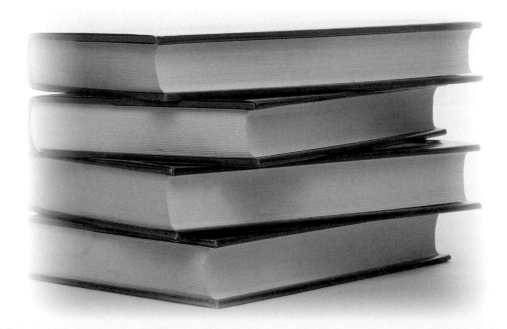

Like annotation and rehearsal, reviewing is an important part of the studying and learning process. To monitor how you are using review strategies in your own studying, answer the following questions.

What are the advantages of saying information out loud as you review?

_____

_____

_____

_____

_____

Are you part of a successful study group? What makes your group successful?

_____

_____

_____

_____

_____

What are the advantages of creating an SSP?

_____

_____

_____

_____

_____

Improving Your Memory Through Reviewing

Reviewing information can help you remember almost three times more than if you did not review. You can maximize the amount you remember, thereby improving your memory, if you keep in mind five basic reviewing principles.

1. ORGANIZE

Research indicates that people tend to remember information the way they have organized it. So the first step you should take as you begin to rehearse and review course material is to be sure that the material is organized, and therefore stored, in an easily retrievable way. Decide how the concepts can be best organized, and then learn them in that way. Remember: You don't have to organize the material the in same way the text does or even in the same way your professor does, but you may find those formats helpful starting points. Create an organization that will work for you.

2. USE IMAGES AND OTHER MNEMONICS WHEN APPROPRIATE

The word *mnemonics* comes from the Greek word for "mindful," and mnemonics are memory devices—little tricks you can use to help you remember specific kinds of information. Even if you are unfamiliar with the term mnemonics, you have probably used them without even knowing it. For example, you may have learned the rhyme "use *i* before *e* except after *c* or in words sounding like *a*, as in *neighbor* and *weigh*." One way you can use mnemonics is to learn a list by taking the first letter of each item you are trying to memorize and making the letters spell something. Your mnemonic device doesn't have to make sense to anyone but you. In fact, the more outrageous the memory device, the easier it generally is to remember. For example, a mnemonic used by physics students to remember the Maxwell relations in thermodynamics is: Good Physicists Have Studied

Under Very Fine Teachers. This helps them remember the order of the variables in the square, in clockwise direction. We will discuss mnemonics in greater detail in Chapter 12.

3. SAY IT RATHER THAN SKIM IT

We have stated more than once that rehearsal is a much more effective way to learn information than rereading. This is true for three reasons. First, few students have time to reread large portions of text. Second, when students reread, they pick up very little additional information. When you say the information, however, you tend to summarize the key points in your own words, which makes verbalization particularly important as you review. If you ask yourself questions (or get someone else to ask them) and then answer the questions, you will remember considerably more than if you simply tried to reread the material. Third, students who only reread get overly dependent on the wording used in the text. If their professor asks questions in even a slightly different way, they often are baffled because they have not thought through the items on their own.

4. PLAN TO HAVE SEVERAL REVIEW SESSIONS

Research indicates that students who read, rehearse, and review in an intensive but short time frame do not do as well as those who distribute their study over time, even when the amount of time engaged in learning is about the same. Therefore, we would expect the student who studied 5 hours spread out over a period of four days prior to an exam to do better than the student who spent 5 hours "studying" the night before an exam. Students who space their learning by using several study sessions to interact with the material tend to get less tired and can concentrate better during studying, thus improving the amount they can recall on test day.

5. OVERLEARN

We add this suggestion to make you aware of the difference between "kinda" knowing something and learning it to the point at which it is almost automatic. When you overlearn something, you know it so well that you don't even have to think about it. We have all overlearned some things as school children—the Pledge of Allegiance, "The Star Spangled Banner," nursery rhymes, the lyrics to popular music. At a sporting event, for example, we stand to sing the National Anthem without having to do much to recall the lyrics. If you could just remember the information for your biology or anthropology exam in the same way! The reason you can remember some information so easily is that you have been exposed to it over and over and over again. You know it so well that it is almost second nature to you. Contrast that with the feeling you have when you have studied but know that you have not grasped the information very well. If you feel as though you "kinda" know the material, you are probably not going to do very well on an exam. By reviewing course information from test to test, you will become more familiar with it. Although you probably will not have overlearned the concepts to the point at which they are second nature to you, reviewing will give you a greater sense of knowing—somewhere between "kinda" and overlearning.

Real College

ENRICO'S EXCUSES

DIRECTIONS: *In the scenario that follows, see if you can help Enrico solve his problems. This scenario is a little different from those in previous chapters in that we ask you to begin to pull together some of the studying issues that have been discussed in* Effective College Learning

By his own admission, Enrico is a slacker. In fact, he prides himself on being a laid-back, low-stress guy. He has been fairly lucky so far in that he at least isn't failing any of his classes. He puts in the minimum amount of work possible to try to maintain what he calls "average" performance. But all of this is starting to wear on him, and on top of that, he's running out of excuses for his parents . . . and he's running out of time. The semester is now two-thirds over, and he finds himself worrying and anxious that he might actually fail his courses this term.

Enrico uses every excuse in the book for not following a study **regimen**: "There's lots of time left." "I have a photographic memory, so I don't have to study and review." "I'll study over the weekend when I have more time." "I don't like this course and the professor is so boring. I'll do better next term when I can take something I like." "I work best under pressure. That's why I study at the last minute." He's even told professors that "the dog ate my homework," and he once told a professor that he missed the 3 p.m. class because "my alarm clock didn't go off."

Enrico has decided to try to turn over a new leaf. His roommate encouraged him to make an appointment at the campus Learning Center where someone might be able to help him move from making excuses to taking positive action to get back on track. Reluctantly, he made an appointment with someone at the Center, and he actually showed up—a little late, but he did make it.

What can Enrico do?

Given what you have read about Enrico, put yourself in the place of the person in the Learning Center assigned to help him.

1. What kind of advice would you give Enrico if it were your job to help him get his studying life together?

_____

_____

2. What strategies would you tell him to use so that he could get on a studying cycle? In particular, how might you encourage him to use daily reviewing as a way of promoting active learning?

_____

_____

3. What "quick start" tips might help Enrico see the light?

_____

_____

Add to Your Portfolio

For the next exam in one of your classes, set goals by answering the following goal-related questions. Then construct an SSP. Remember to set aside time in your SSP for rehearsal and review. Also remember to begin and end each study session with review.

My goals and SSP for the _____ test.

1. What grade do I want to earn on the exam?

2. How much time do I need to invest in order to make this grade?

3. Where will I find the extra time? Will I have to give up other activities in order to carve out time to study?

4. What kind of exam is it? Multiple-choice? Essay? What kinds of problems do I usually have when I take tests of this nature?

5. Do I know the balance of items? Are there more text or lecture questions? Is this a memorization task, or will I be expected to answer higher-level questions?

6. What kinds of rehearsal strategies will work best for this exam? Will I need to begin by reformatting or reconstructing any strategies I have already made?

Session	What I'll do	Strategies I'll use	Reflection and evaluation
1			
2			
3			
4			

Chapter 12
Preparing for and Taking Objective Exams

Read this chapter to answer the following questions:

- What exam preparation strategies work in almost all situations?

- How should I prepare for objective exams?

- How can I use mnemonics to help memorize certain types of information?

- What strategies should I use when I am taking an objective exam?

Self-Assessment

DIRECTIONS: Think about the following questions and answer them honestly. Once you have finished reading this chapter, think about how you can change your current objective exam preparation approach.

1. Taking a multiple-choice test is easy because all I have to do is recognize the correct answer.   **T   F**

2. To study for an objective test, I just memorize all the key terms.   **T   F**

3. It is best to spread out studying time over several days.   **T   F**

4. When I study, I choose one strategy that works and stick with it.   **T   F**

5. Cramming works because I can only get motivated under pressure.   **T   F**

6. Multiple-choice tests can ask application and synthesis questions.   **T   F**

7. To study for exams, I reread the text chapters.   **T   F**

8. When I study, I start with the first concept and work through all of the assigned reading in order.   **T   F**

9. I use mnemonics to help me memorize information.   **T   F**

If you are on the right track in preparing for objective exams, you should have answered False to items 1, 2, 4, 5, 7, and 8 and True for items 3, 6, and 9. Using this information, evaluate how you currently prepare for objective exams. What are you doing that is positive? What behaviors do you need to change? Then read the rest of the chapter to find the most efficient and effective ways to prepare for exams.

_____

_____

_____

_____

_____

_____

Before You Begin

WORD WISE

1. **Assiduous** (adj., p. 187) — constant and diligent; persistent.
*As the author laid out the plot of his new novel, he was **assiduous** in his character development to allow readers to feel that they really know the characters.*

2. **Facilitate** (v., p. 189) — to make easy or easier.
*Because Tonia was a good listener, she could **facilitate** open discussions so that everyone's viewpoint could be heard.*

3. **Relentlessly** (adv., p. 191) — steadily and persistently.
*The infant cried **relentlessly,** and nothing seemed to comfort or sooth him.*

4. **Peruse** (v., p. 194) — to read or examine, usually with great care.
*Lucas loved going to the bookstore to **peruse** the new releases, although he rarely bought anything*

DID YOU KNOW?

Did you know that standardized tests have their own vocabulary? For example, on the SAT vocabulary section, students are not asked to select the definition for a word. Instead, they are asked to select an antonym. Therefore, if you don't know the meaning of *antonym*, you wouldn't know that it means "opposite." Then you probably wouldn't do very well on that section. Words such as *inferences*, *context*, *surmise*, and *tone* pop up on most standardized exams. If you know that you will be taking standardized exams in college (many schools now require students to take "rising junior tests" or competency exams in reading, writing, and mathematics prior to graduation), it's a good idea to learn the vocabulary of standardized testing. It will help you increase your scores.

RESEARCH INTO PRACTICE

Confidence During Test Taking

In this study, Professor L. F. Smith was interested in looking at how confidence levels influenced students' abilities to do well on two quizzes as well as how they perceived their test-taking skills. The participants were 106 undergraduate students who were enrolled in either an introductory statistics or an elementary psychology course. All participants took two measurements of their test-taking skills and two multiple-choice quizzes over course material. As they took the quizzes, they rated their confidence in the correctness of their answers for each of the items on the quiz. The results indicated that confidence was related to students' performance, but perceptions of test-taking skills were not. That is, students' confidence levels influenced how they approached each item on the test, with more confident students actually gaining greater confidence as they progressed through the quiz. Professor Smith also found that confidence was a strong predictor of how well students performed. However, students' perception of their test-taking skills was not related to their performance. This means that some students who thought they had good test-taking skills performed poorly, while some who thought they had weak test-taking skills performed well.

This research is interesting because it suggests that when students feel confident in their knowledge of the content they have studied, they will not only perform better but also increase their confidence as they progress through the exam.

Source: L. F. Smith, "The Effects of Confidence and Perception of Test-taking Skills on Performance," *North American Journal of Psychology* 4 (2002): 37–52.

General Test-Preparation Strategies

Preparing to take an exam begins on the day you begin to read about and listen to topics on which you will be tested. That is, active learners are in a constant state of getting ready to take an exam. They have a difficult time distinguishing when prereading, reading, and taking lecture notes turns into the rehearsal and review that goes into test preparation. That said, we also know that many activities that occur as test time gets closer might be more appropriately labeled as test-preparation strategies.

Although this chapter will focus on the specific strategies that you can use primarily in preparation for objective exams, there are some general test-preparation guidelines that apply to almost any type of exam. We will address these general strategies first because they are "quick starters" that can get you moving in the right direction. Many of these general tips are common sense, but they are tips that students often overlook as they get caught up in exam preparation.

START EARLY

Be sure that you have completed your assigned reading at least several days before the test. Remember that reading and studying are not the same thing. All of your reading should be completed *before* you begin studying.

GET ORGANIZED

Organize all of your studying tools and strategies—notes, text annotations, study strategies—so that you can dig right in. You don't want to interrupt your studying to search for something you need.

DISTRIBUTE YOUR STUDY TIME

Rather than trying to cram all of your studying into one or two days, distribute your time over several days. Spending a total of 6 hours studying, spread over four days, is much more effective than trying to spend 6 hours studying the day before—or even 3 hours a day for two days before the test.

BREAK UP THE WORK

If you begin studying several days in advance, you will be able to break up the information you have to study into chunks of major concepts. In other words, don't sit down to study with the idea in mind that you will study every chapter and every page of notes. Study groups of information that seem to fit together, or at least identify which concepts you want to learn in a particular study session. This helps you stay more focused on the task at hand.

STAY HEALTHY

Eat properly and get enough sleep. Try to remain in a studying routine rather than staying up all night cramming. Eat regular meals, and exercise if that is part of your normal routine. In addition, adequate sleep is crucial to being at the top of your game, especially on the days you take exams. As part of staying healthy, it's also important to monitor your emotional health by evaluating your stress level. When you get too stressed out, it influences other aspects of your performance and becomes a vicious cycle.

SELF-TEST

It's important to have a firm understanding of what you know and what you don't know. Remember that self-testing involves asking yourself questions about the material, saying the information to yourself or to someone else, and then checking to see whether you are correct. It is a crucial part of knowing when you are ready for the exam.

STUDY WITH A CLASSMATE

Studying with another serious-minded student has great benefits, regardless of what kind of test you will have. One of the most successful models for studying with another person is for both individuals to study on their own and then to get together to ask each other questions a day or two before the exam. Both parties can then find out which concepts they know very well and which ones they need to spend more time on.

LOOK AT OLD EXAMS

Talk to others who have previously taken the class. Finding out as much information about the test as possible—whether it's from looking at old exams or by talking to others—is simply a smart thing to do. As long as the professor gives out old exams, it's not cheating; it's being an informed consumer, so to speak. However, if you get the impression that your professor's exams are closely guarded secrets and someone offers you a chance to look at a previously given exam, be careful. Such behavior can lead to academic dishonesty charges. On the other hand, if professors permit students to keep their exams, you can be fairly certain that they will not be giving that same test again. But it's probably also a safe bet that the kinds of questions asked will be similar. When talking with students who have already taken the class with the professor, a good rule of thumb is to find out specifics about the level of questions and grading.

NETWORKING

Online Exams

Many professors now have sample exams online. Check out your professor's Web page or the department Web page to see what is available. In addition, visit the Web site of your textbook publisher. There are often quizzes, sample exams, links to additional information, and chat rooms where you can discuss the text with other students nationwide.

Preparing for and Taking Objective Exams

Objective exams can consist of several different kinds of questions. The most common types are multiple-choice and true/false questions, but matching and fill-in-the-blanks are also objective questions. Another name for this type of question is a *recognition item,* because all of the information is there; your task is to recognize it. For example, when taking multiple-choice tests, you have to recognize which answer out of the four or five choices is correct. For a true/false question, you have to recognize whether the statement is true or false. These items are considered objective because there is only one correct answer, if the test is well written. When you study well and really know the information, the correct answer should be obvious to you.

Preparing for Objective Exams

Because of the precise knowledge required to answer objective items, it is extremely important that two key factors guide your preparation: (1) organization of information and (2) thinking about the information in the way your professor expects.

FACTOR 1: ORGANIZING FOR OBJECTIVE EXAMS

Let's start with an example. Suppose you are in an introductory level psychology course, and every two to three weeks you have a 50-item objective test—always all multiple-choice items. In any given testing period, you have about thirty pages of lecture notes and three or four chapters of information to study. Where do you begin? We have found that the best place to start when you know you will have an objective test is to make a jot list of all of the key concepts from the text and the lectures. Figure 12.1 shows what this jot list might look like for "Memory," the psychology chapter that is in the appendix. Notice that the jot list is not particularly formal. Rather, it simply serves to force you to think about the concepts before you begin to study. One way to come up with your jot list is to use the chapter headings and subheadings as a guide. Unless you make a conscious effort to jot down these concepts, you may leave out important information or simply gloss over concepts that you should spend a significant amount of time on. In addition, if you have been **assiduous** about making talk-through cards for each chapter, you can use your cards rather than making a new jot list. Once you have made your jot list, then you can organize the information that you will need to study.

Chapter 6: Memory

Remembering	Retrieval
3 processes	Serial position effect
3 systems	State dependent memory
Levels of processing model	Context
3 types of memory	Biology and memory
How we remember	Forgetting
Reconstruction	Ebbinghaus
Eye witness testimony	Causes of
Recovering repressed memories	Improving
Flashbulb memories	
Memories and culture	

Figure 12.1: Example of a Jot List

When you organize, you should do the following:

Study by Concept Group together all of your rehearsal strategies related to the overriding concept. (Let's use the memory topic of "remembering" as an example.) You should also know which sections of lecture notes go with this concept.

Look for Overlap Look for overlap between the text and lectures, and focus your studying on the general topic of remembering. This is better than just concentrating on text information at one session and the lecture notes at another.

Narrow Your Focus Focus each study session around a couple of broad concepts, such as "remembering" and "how we remember," rather than simply trying to read through everything you have to learn for the entire test. In other words, one night you might study all the material related to remembering, the next night you might concentrate on retrieval and forgetting. Following this procedure encourages you to think actively and critically.

Use Your Jot List as a Guide Rehearse and self-test the material from each broad concept. Your study schedule might look something like the plan in Figure 12.2. Note that each study session begins with a review and that after all the material is covered, the session ends with self-testing to identify specific areas of weakness.

Know Your Weak Areas Concentrate on any areas of weakness as you and your study partner question each other in one final study session before the exam. Don't waste time by repeatedly talking through what you already know very well.

Review What You're Not Sure Of On the morning of the exam, talk though the couple of ideas that are still giving you difficulty. If you feel confident that you know the material well, don't do anything more.

Session 1—Monday

Focus: Memory

4:30–5:00	Organize all information
5:00–6:00	Self test: Memory systems
6:00–6:45	Eat dinner
7:00–8:00	Review: Memory systems
	Self test: Levels of processing model and the nature of remembering

Session 2—Tuesday

Focus: Retrieval, biology and memory, forgetting

10:00–10:30	Review memory systems, levels of processing, the nature of remembering
10:30–11:30	Self test: Retrieval, biology and memory, forgetting
11:30–12:00	Lunch
12:30–1:50	Biology Class

Figure 12.2: Example of a Study Schedule

FACTOR 2: DETERMINING THE LEVEL OF THINKING REQUIRED

Organizing, both in terms of how you will group the concepts to be learned and how you will structure your study sessions, is crucial to performing well on objective tests. However, organizing won't help you much if you aren't sure about the level of thinking required. On essay tests (which we'll talk about in Chapter 13), you can usually count on having to think critically and to analyze and synthesize information. On objective exams, many students make the mistake of believing that the test

questions are designed solely to see if they have memorized the material. That is, they think the questions don't go beyond asking for facts. Students who fall into this trap can experience grave difficulty and often don't do well. That's why it's important to know the level of thinking that your professor expects. If she expects you to memorize the facts and most of the questions are factual in nature, you would study in one way. If, however, she asks application, synthesis, example, and other types of higher-level questions, you would study another way.

When the Task is Memorization: Mnemonic Devices

Occasionally, you will have a class where your professor only expects you to memorize or gives tests that are primarily memory tasks with a few higher-level questions thrown in just to keep you on your toes. If you find yourself in situations that require mostly memorization, there are some ways to **facilitate** this process through the use of various types of mnemonics.

Mnemonic devices help you stretch your memory, and you most likely already use them. In general, mnemonics encourage the personalization of information so that you have easy access to it at some future date. They are good for learning lists of items or for learning sequences of events or processes. They can be visual to help you create images, or they can be a string of letters or a nonsense sentence—anything that enables you to remember information better. Even if you are unfamiliar with the term *mnemonics*, you have probably used them without even knowing it. For example, you may have learned the rhyme "In 1492, Columbus sailed the ocean blue," or maybe you used "**A r**at **in T**om's **h**ouse **m**ay **e**at **T**om's **i**ce **c**ream," as a way of remembering how to spell *arithmetic*. Almost every elementary school child knows this mnemonic. We realize that some of these techniques may sound strange, but we guarantee that they help stretch your memory under the right circumstances. There are several different types of mnemonics.

ACRONYMS

You can use mnemonics to learn a list by creating an acronym. This means taking the first letter of each item you are trying to memorize and making the letters spell something. Your mnemonic device doesn't have to make sense to anyone but you. In fact, the more outrageous the memory device, the easier it generally is to remember. For example, if you needed to remember the four stages of food processing in the proper order, you could take the first letter of each word to form *IDAE*—Ingestion, Digestion, Absorption, and Elimination. This mnemonic works because you understand that although the mnemonic has the same letters as the word *idea*, the last two letters are simply flip-flopped.

Another way to use acronyms is to think of a common word. Returning to the previous example of the four stages of food processing, you might also remember this information fairly easily by using the acronym IDE↔A, a common word idea. The arrow indicates that the *E* and the *A* are reversed. You could create other mnemonics to help you remember the meaning of each of the four terms.

IMAGERY

Forming images is another powerful way to help you remember when you review. Like other mnemonics, images can be personalized and don't have to make sense to anyone except the person forming the images. Images work best when the information you are trying to learn is concrete rather than abstract. It is difficult to make images for concepts such as courage, democracy, or freedom and it is much easier to make images for ideas such as cell division, the three memory types, or chamber music. Images work well because they give you both verbal and visual labels for things. For example, the three letters d-o-g form a very familiar word. Few people would have trouble understanding this word when they saw it in print. But what would happen if you asked each person who read that word to tell you his or her image of a dog? Would everyone describe *dog* in the same way? Of course not. Your image of a dog would be based on your experience. In the same way, images that you create should be based on past experiences so that they are personalized. This makes it easier for you to remember what the images represent.

Images can also be used to help you remember information from your written rehearsal strategies. (We discussed rehearsal strategies in Chapter 10.) For example, when you construct concept cards for learning in biology, you might visualize how gastric juice mixes with food to form acid chyme by creating an unusual image. If you easily get "pictures in your head," you should sketch them out on your cards and call up the images as you are rehearsing and reviewing. You might even create an image to help you remember more details about IDE↔A, discussed in the previous example.

METHOD OF LOCI

In the loci technique (*loci* is pronounced with a long *o* and *i* and the *c* sounds like an *s*), you image a place that is familiar to you, such as your living room, the street where you live, or your residence hall. Then you walk down this path through your memory. As you proceed, you attach a piece of information you have to learn to different places and objects to help you remember it. Remember that the path markers can be as strange as you want (and the stranger the better), because that will make it easier for you to visualize. One of the authors uses a simplified version of the method of loci to remember who attended certain meetings. She visualizes the room and the table where the meeting was held, starts at one end and mentally walks around the table, visualizing where each person was seated.

When the Task Goes Beyond Memorization: Higher-Level Thinking

Look at the example questions below to get a feel for the difference between memory-level and higher-level questions. Each of the questions in Sets A, B, C, and D is based on one of the chapter excerpts in the appendix of this book. The first example in each set is a memory-level task; the second example is a higher-level question. (The * indicates the correct answer.)

SET A: HISTORY CHAPTER

1. Which of the following is true about minority groups during the Depression?
   a. They kept their jobs because they were paid less money than whites.
   b. More assistance was given to Mexican Americans than was given to African Americans.
   c. African American employment rates were double those of white Americans.*
   d. Whites campaigned for minorities to be given equal consideration for jobs.
2. Overall, the Great Depression
   a. affected all groups of people in the United States as well as in Europe.*
   b. affected the poor to a greater degree than the rich.
   c. was caused mainly by poor government policies.
   d. caused men and women to lose their jobs at equal rates.

SET B: PSYCHOLOGY CHAPTER

1. What are schemas?
   a. pieced-together memories using information that may or may not be accurate.
   b. cues that help you remember a piece of information.
   c. the part of declarative memory that helps you remember facts.

d. frameworks that help you store new memories into information that you already have.*

2. Which of the following is an example of the state-dependent memory effect?
   a. Jamie learns the material for her biology exam when she is sad but takes the exam when she is happy. She does very well on the exam.
   b. Jamie learns the material for her biology exam in the same room where she takes the test. She does poorly on the exam.
   c. Jamie learns the material for her biology exam when she is happy but takes the exam right after she has broken up with her boyfriend. She does well on the exam.
   d. Jamie learns the material for her biology exam when she is depressed. When she takes the exam, she is still depressed. She does well on the exam.*

SET C: BIOLOGY CHAPTER

1. The major functions of the small intestine are to
   a. produce digestive juices and gastric acid.
   b. absorb water and produce necessary bacterium.
   c. aid in chemical digestion and to absorb nutrients.*
   d. store and breakdown food as it leaves the stomach.
2. If you maintain a normal activity level and consume the same amount of calories as your basal metabolic rate, you will
   a. gain weight.
   b. lose weight.*
   c. stay the same.
   d. lose weight but then quickly regain it.

SET D: TECHNOLOGY QUESTIONS

1. What is the difference between RAM and ROM?
   a. RAM is the most common type of memory and ROM is the least common type.
   b. RAM is not stored permanently and ROM is stored permanently.*
   c. RAM is nonvolatile memory and ROM is volatile.
   d. RAM stores only small bits of information while ROM stores lots of information.

2. Why might flash memory be the future of computer memory?
   a. It is less expensive than RAM or ROM memory.
   b. It can store memory like ROM chips but is volatile.
   c. It can store memory like RAM chips but is nonvolatile.*
   d. It is made of metal oxide.

It is fairly easy to see the differences in these sets of questions. The first questions are very straightforward and require little interpretation or thinking beyond the memory level. Studying for an objective test that asked this type of question would be a relatively easy task. But think about the problem you might have if you simply memorized information and then had an exam that asked questions like the second one in each set. You would have a much more difficult time because of thinking about the information in an incorrect way. Even if you studied **relentlessly**, if you only memorized when the task is to somehow go beyond memorization, taking the test would be a struggle.

The point is that you need to be clear about the professor's expectations and the way he tests, what we have called "task" throughout this book. As mentioned earlier, look at old exams, talk to students who have taken a class with the professor, or ask the professor. Whatever you do, have an accurate picture of the kind of test you will have. Then, as you are doing your rehearsal, review, and self-testing, you can frame your studying accordingly.

Reality Check

Thinking About Test Questions
One way to get a feel for the difference between thinking about the information in a factual way and in a more conceptual, higher-level way is to rewrite questions. Using the example questions in Sets A, B, C, and D as a guide, use one of the text excerpts in the appendix to write a factual question. Then write another question that draws from the same information yet taps higher-level thinking. Discuss these questions with a classmate.

DIRECTIONS: Staying motivated when you are preparing for a big test can sometimes be difficult because it is easy to feel overwhelmed. Studying specific concepts at each study session rather than trying to study everything at once is one way to help you maintain motivation. For your next exam, answer the following questions to help you plan your study time.

What major concepts are covered on this test?

_____

_____

_____

_____

_____

How many study sessions will I need to cover this material? How will I divide up the concepts to study?

_____

_____

_____

_____

_____

What can I do to ensure that I will stay on task?

_____

_____

_____

_____

_____

What strategies will be the most efficient and effective for me to use? Why will these strategies work best?

_____

_____

_____

_____

_____

Preparing for Essay Exams

Preparing for essay exams involves different strategies than those used for objective exams. This often comes as a shock, especially to first-year college students who may have had little experience with essay exams in high school—or, if they have had essay exams, they prepared for them in the same way they did for objective exams. As a general rule, essay preparation requires a different type of approach, a different way of thinking, and a different way of organizing.

When we use the term *essay exam*, we are referring to any type of question that requires you to write an extended response. Essay tests would include:
- Traditional multiparagraph responses to questions
- Short-answer, narrowly focused questions that may require you to write a paragraph or two in response
- Identification items that require you to define a term, explain the significance of something, or write several sentences describing a person, place, event, etc.

Sometimes these types of exams are referred to as *recall* tests, because you are asked to recall all of the pertinent information from your memory. Unlike recognition questions (e.g., multiple-choice, true/false) that ask you to recognize the correct information, recall questions require you to remember the information on your own. For this reason, there is a general perception that taking essay exams is more difficult than taking a recognition exam. However, this is not necessarily true. Unlike recognition exams where points are awarded only for correct responses, essay questions are usually graded in such a way that you can receive partial credit even if your response is not entirely complete. Additonally, it could be argued that essay exams are a more accurate reflection of what you have learned about a given topic, because you are able to fully explain what you know in your response.

Students often feel anxious about taking essay exams. This worry may stem from concerns about their ability to answer the questions properly or to remember all the information they have learned. They may also worry about grammar, spelling, or other mechanics of writing. Other students are nervous about their general writing skills because they have not been required to take essay exams before entering college.

Preparing for essay exams differs from preparing for multiple-choice exams. It requires a different way of organizing to recall the information without the clues provided in recognition-type exams. In this chapter, you will learn one of the most effective methods of preparation, which addresses many of the concerns students have about taking essay exams.

PORPE

PORPE is an acronym for Predict, Organize, Rehearse, Practice, and Evaluate.* It is a structured, organized strategy designed by Dr. Michele Simpson to help students prepare for essay or short-answer exams. You begin the PORPE studying process after you have completed your reading, constructed useful study strategies, and have organized your lecture notes. To explain each step of PORPE, in Figure 13.4, we include an example based on a predicted essay question from the history chapter in Appendix C.

*M. L. Simpson, "PORPE: A Writing Strategy for Studying and Learning in the Content Areas," *Journal of Reading* 29 (1986): 407–414.

Step 1: Predict

The first thing you need to do—several days before the test—is predict some broad questions that your professor might include on the exam. Simply put, the better a predictor you are, the better you will do on the exam. But predicting questions can be a tricky business. It has been our experience that when students begin to use PORPE, they either predict questions that are far too broad or way too narrow. For example, predicting a question such as "Discuss the Great Depression" would be too broad because there would be enough information involved to write an entire book. A question such as "What does the term Hooverville mean?" would be too specific for an essay but might make a good identification question. Generally, the fewer the number of questions you are required to answer on an exam, the broader your prediction questions should be. Use the question stems in Figure 13.1 to help you predict your essay.

- Compare and contrast: Present both similarities and differences.
- Analyze: Examine in a systematic way, looking at an entire process.
- Evaluate: Discuss both good points and limitations, with evidence.
- Discuss: Give reasons pro and con, with details.
- Explain: Interpret the reasons.
- Give an example: Give a concrete example from the text or from your own experience.
- Identify: List and describe.
- Justify: Prove or give reasons.
- Trace: Give main points from beginning to end of a particular event.
- Solve: Come up with a solution based on the text or your knowledge.

Figure 13.1: Stems to Help You Predict Your Essay Questions

Keep in mind when predicting that rarely will your specific question be precisely what the professor asks. But once you become a good predictor, there will be considerable overlap between what you predict and the actual questions on the test. The following is an example of a good essay prediction for the history chapter in the appendix of your book.

STEP 1: PREDICT

Predict a question that you think might be asked on the exam.

Q

Discuss the major economic causes of the Great Depression of the 1920s. Then, explain the similarities to the economic crisis of the late 2000s.

Figure 13.2: Sample Predicted Question

Step 2: Organize

After you have predicted several questions, you need to organize the information. Do this three or four days before the test. Most students like to use an outline as a way of organizing so that they can see the key points they want to make and the support they want to provide for each key point. Other organizing strategies, such as concept maps or charts, also work well. When you organize the material, think about both key generalizations and information to support those generalizations. Spend some time organizing your thoughts so that you will study the appropriate material.

As you become more focused and predict specific questions, your outline should be more comprehensive and detailed. To fill in your outline, use the relevant information that you included in your text annotations, rehearsal strategies, and lecture notes. Be sure that you draw from both text and lectures as well as any other sources for which you are responsible. And be sure to make a detailed outline for each of the questions you predict. Figure 13.3 below shows what an outline would look like for the essay question we predicted in Step 1 of PORPE.

STEP 2: ORGANIZE

In an organized fashion, write down the ideas you want to include in your essay.

Four main economic causes of the Great Depression:

1. Unequal distribution of wealth
    a. Richest 0.1% had more than bottom 42%

2. Oligopolies
    a. Prices artificially high
    b. Overproduction of goods (agriculture, coal, etc.)

3. Banks poorly regulated

4. International economic difficulties

    Many of these issues were due to government regulation failures—trade deficits because of policies

Compare to late 2000s
    −causes
    −remedies

Figure 13.3: Sample Organization Format

Step 3: Rehearse

Rehearse each question several times, beginning three or four days before the test. This is the time to commit to memory the information in your outline. Read a question you predicted. Then read your outline slowly and deliberately. "Listen" to what you are saying. Does it make sense? Do you have enough support? Do the ideas flow? After you have read your outline several times, ask yourself the question again. This time, try answering it without looking at the outline. Be sure that you are rehearsing the concepts accurately. If you are not sure of something, immediately return to your outline and read that part through again. (If you are really experiencing problems, you might need to check your text, strategies, or lecture notes to clarify or add support.) Then try to restate the answer to that portion of the question. Always keep in mind that when you rehearse, it's important to also engage in self-testing.

Step 4: Practice

Two days before the test is the time to practice writing out an answer to one of your questions. Write under the same conditions that you will have in class. For example, if you will be required to answer two essay questions in a 50-minute class period, take only 20 minutes to practice one of your questions. That would leave 20 minutes for the second question and 10 minutes to go back and proof your work.

You should also construct your answer so that it is organized in the same way that you will organize it in class. Write in complete sentences, include appropriate examples, and be sure to have an introduction and a conclusion.

STEP 4: ORGANIZE

Figure 13.4 shows a response for the question we predicted in Step 1.

The Great Depression followed a period of record-high stock market gains, easy credit, and poor banking regulation. In many ways, the economic downturn of the late 2000s seems to mirror this combination of factors. The stock market crash in 1929, Black Tuesday, is commonly seen as the beginning of the Great Depression, when investors sold off stock and the nation lost confidence in the economy, which resulted in losses that lasted for years.

Before the crash, the United States experienced a great unequal distribution of wealth. The richest 0.1% of US families had more wealth than the poorest 42%. Workers' salaries had fallen far behind company profits. More than half of all US families were living at or below the poverty level and thus did not have much purchasing power to keep the economy going.

In addition, corporations became more powerful as they consolidated together, creating oligopolies. Because the market was dominated by only a few sellers, those businesses set prices artificially high and did not respond to the purchasing power of the general population. Several industries further complicated the matter by overproduction. For example, agriculture, coal, and textiles produced too many goods, which led to declining prices and staggering debt.

The banking industry saw much growth in the years before the Great Depression, with little government regulation. Once the market crashed, there was a run on the banks when depositors withdrew their funds. The governmental banking policies proved ineffective, and many banks failed, causing an even further spiral.

Governmental policies were also part of the problem. Rather than investing in the banking system, the government failed to act, which many argue deepened the Depression. Additionally, the government imposed high taxes on international trade, which some argue deepened the severity of the Depression worldwide because European markets reduced their imports of American goods. Thus American exports fell by 70%. Moreover, the failure to enforce antitrust laws, failure to regulate banking and the stock market, and reducing the tax rates on the wealthy contributed to the instability of the economy.

The economic crisis of the late 2000s may have been caused by similar problems. The recession came after years of deregulation of businesses, which led to less government oversight and unequal distribution of wealth between executives and workers. Additionally, there was unprecedented stock market and banking expansion that developed into a credit crisis when many of the investments proved unstable. In addition, many people lost their jobs, thus causing an abundance of home foreclosures. However, unlike the Great Depression, the government began taking an active role by trying to secure the banks, limiting company failures, and infusing the economy with a $780 billion stimulus package. Although it is too soon to tell whether these actions will reduce the length or severity of the recession, it is clear that the current government has learned lessons from the Great Depression and is attempting to handle the crisis in a much different manner.

Figure 13.4: Example of an Essay Question

Step 5: Evaluate

Now comes the most difficult part—evaluating your own writing. Immediately after you have finished practicing, read what you have written. After you have finished reading your practice essay, get out your outline and any other materials you have been using to study from, and check for accuracy and completeness. If necessary, you can go back and do some rethinking and reorganizing. You may even want to show your essay to your professor so that he can provide you with feedback. Or, if your campus has a writing center, you may be able to get help with organizing your response.

STEP 5: EVALUATE

As you evaluate, ask yourself the questions posed in Figure 13.5:

- ☐ Is my introduction clear and focused?
- ☐ Are my generalizations complete and precise?
- ☐ Are my examples and supporting information accurate and complete?
- ☐ Do I answer all parts of the question?
- ☐ Do I have a conclusion that relates back to my introduction and overall thesis?

Figure 13.5: Questions to Help You Evaluate Your Essay

BEYOND THE CLASSROOM

We believe that one of the **quintessential** skills you can learn in college is writing. Using components of the PORPE strategy can not only help you prepare for essays, but can also also help you organize a paper, group project, or just about any other writing task you may encounter in college or beyond. Most careers require you to be able to express yourself clearly in writing, and you just may find yourself using some of the elements of PORPE every time you write.

NETWORKING

Critiquing Essays over E-Mail

If you have been working with a classmate this term in a course that requires you to write essay exams, you might try sending your study partner a copy of a practice essay by e-mail. Have your study partner critique your essay by evaluating its strengths and weaknesses. You can do the same for your study partner.

Name at least two differences between preparing for essay exams and multiple-choice exams.

_____

_____

_____

_____

_____

Describe how you currently prepare to take essay exams.

_____

_____

_____

_____

_____

Identify at least two of your greatest challenges when taking essay exams.

_____

_____

_____

_____

_____

Taking Essay Exams

When you are in the actual test-taking situation, you will need to consider these four important factors: (1) how much time you are allotted to write each answer; (2) how you will get started; (3) how you will structure each answer; and (4) the guidelines your professor provides about how she will evaluate or grade your essay. Each of these factors has a bearing on how you will spend your time writing essays in class.

1. TIME ALLOTTED FOR WRITING

Time is usually your biggest enemy when answering essay or short-answer questions. When you are deciding on your approach for taking the exam, think carefully about how you will divide your time. For example, if you have one essay question and five fairly comprehensive identification items to answer, would it be best to spend half of your time on the essay and the other half on the identifications? Or would it be better to spend more time on the essay and less time on the identification items? It's all a give and take, but it's a good rule of thumb to begin with what you know best and feel the most comfortable with. If you know the answers to all the identification questions and feel a bit shaky on how best to approach the essay, start with the IDs and then use the remaining time to do the best job you can on the essay. In addition, consider the point value of each question. If the essay is worth 40 points and each of five IDs is worth 3 points, you will want to spend more time on the essay.

2. GETTING STARTED

The first thing to do after planning out your time is to read the directions. Sometimes professors will ask you to select one essay out of three or two from a certain grouping of questions. Students who neglect to read the directions will end up writing far more than they need to. Then read each question carefully. For longer questions, you might want to underline or annotate the question so that you are sure you have noticed all that it is asking. Then

make a jot list of all of the information you want to include in your essay. This will allow you to organize your thoughts before you begin to write. In addition, if you think of things you need to include as you write, you can add them to your jot list as you go.

Reality Check

Take Time to Review
Do you often run out of time when taking exams? Taking some precious exam time to make a plan of attack for answering questions may seem **counterintuitive**, but you will find that it can help you complete the exam before time is up. When you get your exam, plan to spend about 5 minutes dividing up the tasks and figuring out how long you have for each item. Remember to plan 5 minutes at the end for reviewing your responses. Then stick to your plan as you take your exam.

3. STRUCTURING YOUR ESSAY

Few professors provide students with guidance on how they want essay or short-answer questions structured. As a result, many students will write a paragraph to answer an essay question and a sentence or two to answer a short-answer item. Usually when professors ask you to write an essay, however, they want extended comment; that is, they want you to write considerably more than a paragraph. When you think of an essay, you should plan on writing at least an introductory paragraph, several paragraphs that discuss specific points you think are important to answering the question, and then end with a concluding paragraph. Short-answer questions, as a general rule, are a paragraph or two long and tend to be somewhat less structured than an essay.

If your professor tells you exactly how she wants you to structure your essay, follow exactly what she says. However, if your professor does not provide you with any guidance, the following structure is generally accepted in most disciplines. As you read each of the suggestions below, refer to the sample essay provided in Figure 13.5 earlier in the chapter.

Write an Introductory Paragraph This will outline your thesis and indicate that you understand what the question is asking. By *thesis*, we mean the overall focus of your essay or the argument you will be making. If the question has multiple parts, be sure that your introduction pulls in all of the parts. The first paragraph should not **inundate** the reader with information or be long and involved. But it should be clear and concise and give the reader a picture of your overall points. In addition, if the essay question asks you to argue a point or take a side on as issue, be sure that your introduction clearly states your stance on the topic.

Begin Each Paragraph with a Generalization
Each of your next several paragraphs should begin with a generalization about one of the key points you want to make. Don't worry about following the five-paragraph essay format you may have learned in high school. Instead, use as many paragraphs as necessary to fully answer the question. For example, if your question in political science asks you to discuss political, economic, international policy, and social issues, you would write four paragraphs, one dealing with each of the four issues. For each generalization, you should provide support in the form of events, names, dates, examples, and so forth—specific information that supports your point. Each paragraph should deal with only one key idea. Be careful about including several broad generalizations in the same paragraph. However, also be careful about writing a **litany** of facts without tying them together with generalizations. Whenever possible, have smooth transitions from one idea to the next by using words such as *first*, *second*, *third*, *furthermore*, *in addition to*, *moreover*, and so forth.

Begin with your Strongest Point Once you have an idea of the points your want to make, take a minute to put them in order of importance. In general, it is best to start the body of your essay with your most compelling point rather than saving it for the end of your essay. This works because the reader will be begin to be persuaded by your argument right from the start.

When in Doubt, Leave It Out Unlike objective tests where we encourage you to guess if you have to, for essay exams, follow the "When in doubt, leave it out" rule. If you are not completely sure of something, do not put it in your essay. For example, if you cannot recall the exact year that Black Tuesday occurred, rather than guessing the year, make your statement more general. "In the late 1920s, the stock market experienced a drop known as Black Tuesday." If you have included wrong information in your essay, your professor has no alternative but to deduct points. But if your essay is sound and you have made numerous good points, you might get few or no points taken off if you leave out a bit of information.

Finish with a Short Conclusion End your essay with a concluding paragraph that joins together the points you wanted to make. The conclusion doesn't have to be lengthy, but it should return to your thesis and pull together the most important ideas related to that thesis.

4. EVALUATION GUIDELINES

It's a tall order to write essays within the allotted time frame, have an acceptable structure, and manage to keep the mechanics and grammar errors down to a minimum. That's why it becomes important to know your professor's expectations before you go into the exam situation. For example, how strict will your professor be in considering mechanics, grammar, and usage? If your professor doesn't say anything about his expectations in class, be sure to ask. Most professors do not expect perfection, but they will probably deduct points on a paper that has so many errors that it is difficult to read and understand. The bottom line is to know what your professor expects and then do your best to balance time, structure/content, and grammar/spelling issues.

Identification Items

Identification items ask you to write what you know about specific events, people, laws, dates, and so forth. They differ from essay/short-answer questions in that they are more focused and usually require only a few sentences of explanation. Sometimes you can even write in phrases rather than in full sentences when answering identification questions. However, sometimes your professor expects a full paragraph. To figure out what your professor is expecting, keep these two ideas in mind when preparing for identification items:

1. THINK ABOUT THE TEXT

There are usually many options for identification items. In history, for example, where identification questions are common, every chapter and lecture is filled with material that could be included on a test. So how do you decide which terms are the most important to study? A good place to begin is with your text. If your text provides a listing of key terms or if there is a chapter summary, making sure that you can identify what is in either of those sources is usually your best starting point. Match up those terms with what your professor has spent time on during lectures. Look for overlap, because identification items usually focus on material that has been addressed in a lecture or has been pointed out in the text.

2. THINK ABOUT THE TASK

When responding to identification items, few professors want you to merely define the terms. You have to know the kind of information your professor expects you to include. She may want you to discuss the significance, provide an example, or explain how one concept relates to some other issue or idea. Many students only receive partial credit on short-answer items because they don't include all the information requested by their professors. See Figure 13.6 for an example of an identification item.

ID—"Hooverville"

Response: Hooverville was the name given to shacks built by the homeless during the Great Depression. These shantytowns were called "Hooverville" after President Herbert Hoover, because many felt that he had led the nation into economic turmoil. One Hooverville in Oklahoma City was 100 miles wide.

Figure 13.6: Identification Example

Specialized Exams

Specialized exams differ from essay or multiple-choice exams. They are ones you may not encounter frequently in your college career, but you need to know how to prepare for them when they do come along.

We will discuss three types of specialized exams: (1) problem-solving exams, the most common of the specialized exams; (2) open-book exams; and (3) take-home exams.

Problem-Solving Exams

Several types of courses require you to solve problems, including mathematics, science, engineering, and business courses. Because many students attempt to study for exams of this nature by doing the same problems over and over again, we thought it was important to provide some additional strategies for studying for these types of exams.

PRACTICE PROBLEMS

Working the practice problems as a way of studying for this type of test is certainly a good idea and should be a part of your studying routine. Note that we said "a part of," because if all you do is work the same set of problems over and over again, you will probably not do very well. The important thing to remember is that you have to think about and conceptualize what you are doing. You won't get those exact problems on the exam, so you have to think about the concepts underlying the problems. That's why we suggest that you talk through your problems. Put words to them. As you do a problem, think about and verbalize what you are doing. Annotate formulas using your own words to indicate that you understand the problem. If you can't talk through problems as you solve them, you probably don't understand the concept.

Let's look at an example and talk through some of the thinking that would make it easier to solve the problem. Thinking about math problems in this manner, especially word problems, also lets you know if you understand the reasoning behind your method of solving the problem.

The Problem

Susan begins a 20-mile race at 7:00 a.m., running at an average speed of 10 miles per hour. One hour later, her brother, Jason, leaves the starting line on a motorbike and follows her route at the rate of 40 miles per hour. At what time does he catch up to her?

The Question

What is the problem asking for? You are supposed to solve this problem to find out what time Jason catches up with Susan, so you will need to make sure that the answer you come up with is reflected as time.

The Solution

• *Visualize the problem.*

The diagram below shows that when Jason overtakes her, they have both traveled the same distance.

Susan >>>

Jason   >>>>>>>>>>>>>>>>>>>>>>>>>>>>>>>

	Rate	Time	Distance
Susan	10	t	10t
Jason	40	t – 1	40t

- **What is the basic idea behind the problem?**
  Both are traveling at a constant rate of speed, so we would think about the basic equation as:
  Distance = (Rate)(Time)
  d = rt
- **Explain the variables.**
  Let t equal the number of hours Susan runs until Jason catches her.
  Then $t - 1$ equals the number of hours Jason rides until he catches up. (He leaves 1 hour later, so he travels 1 hour less.)
- **Write and solve the equation.**
  $10t = 40(t - 1)$
  $10t = 40t - 40$
  $-30t = -40$
  $t = -40/-30 = 4/3 = 1\ 1/3$ hours = 1 hour and 20 minutes

The Solution

Remember that the question asked for time. Jason caught up with her 1 hour and 20 minutes after she began the race. Therefore, he would catch up with her at 8:20 a.m. If you wrote "1 hour and 20 minutes" as your answer, you would not receive credit because you did not answer the question that was asked.

MAKE UP A TEST FOR YOURSELF

Think about the types of problems you will be tested on. Put some problems on note cards and then use them as a way of seeing whether you understand the concepts. After you have worked through the problems, shuffle the note cards and work on them again in a different order, concentrating on those that gave you problems.

GET HELP EARLY

Courses such as mathematics, physics, and chemistry tend to be arranged sequentially. That is, the ideas build on one another. If you miss or don't understand something presented in week two of the term, chances are you are going to have trouble with what is presented after that. If you think you are "mathematically challenged," you should arrange to be part of a study group, get a tutor, or make regular appointments to speak with your professor right at the beginning of the term.

Open-Book Exams

Open-book exams allow you access to your text and sometimes even your notes during the examination period. Open-book exams are generally given in the usual class period, which means that you take them under timed conditions. This type of exam is often given in literature courses so that students can have access to specific pieces of text that they have been asked to read and interact with.

When students are told that they will have an open-book exam, they often breathe a sigh of relief. We have even heard students say that they didn't have to study because they were having an open-book test. But it takes just as much effort to adequately prepare for this type of test as it does for the more traditional objective and essay tests.

Organization is the key in preparing for open-book exams. If you are getting ready for an open-book exam, first you have to go through the usual preparation steps of predicting, organizing, rehearsing, practicing, and evaluating. But you have to put extra time into organizing. You should mark information that you might use to support points or pull specific examples from the readings. You will need to have the information you deem important marked in some way so that it is easy to find. For example, you can tab important passages or pages in your text with adhesive notes. Because you are in a timed situation, you must know where things are and have the information organized so that you can find it quickly.

Take-Home Exams

Take-home exams allow you access to your text and notes and put no restrictions on the amount of time you can spend taking the test. The professor gives you the test questions, along with some basic instructions, usually to remind you that you can't get outside assistance to answer the questions. Some professors may even have you sign an academic honesty pledge. When professors give take-home exams, they generally expect a very high level of proficiency and thinking. For example, if they give you a take-home essay exam, they would expect your writing to display synthesis, analysis, and critical thought. They would expect a tremendous amount of support, and a paper virtually free of grammatical and spelling errors. Therefore, you usually have to spend a considerable amount of time working on take-home exams.

Even if you know you will have take-home exams in a course, it is extremely important for you to keep up. Do the reading, attend class, construct rehearsal strategies, and continue to review. Then, when you get your take-home exam from your instructor, you will be ready to organize all the information and spend less time actually taking the test.

Real College

ERICA'S ESSAY

DIRECTIONS: *Read the following scenario and respond to the questions that follow based on what you have learned in this chapter.*

Erica's semester was going quite well—up until this point, that is. Erica had some academic difficulties during her first semester in college, but she had learned from her mistakes, and so far so good. But now it is time for the real test. She knows that an essay exam is rapidly approaching in Dr. Frank's history course, and she is scared. Today is Thursday and the test is next Tuesday. Erica has completed most of the reading. She feels that she is a good memorizer, but she is not very good at pulling ideas together. She is terrified of writing essays, and it doesn't help that Dr. Frank's exams have the reputation of being lethal because his questions are both higher level and have multiple parts. To make things even worse, Erica knows that the essay questions will come from the text and the lectures and that she will be expected to pull text-related information into her essay. Professor Frank has already been very clear about that in class. She knows she needs to prepare for this exam differently than she does for multiple-choice tests, but she is not sure what to do.

What can Erica do?

1. Given the amount of time she has left to study and the kind of exam that she will have, what recommendations would you give to Erica?

2. How should she prepare for and go about taking her history exam so that she can maximize her grade?

Add to Your Portfolio

For your next essay exam, try using the PORPE strategy. Remember that you need to predict, organize, rehearse, practice, and evaluate each essay's effectiveness.

1. In the space below, predict your essay question. Then, on a separate sheet of paper, outline your organizing strategy, and then write your practice essay.

_____

_____

_____

_____

_____

_____

_____

2. Reflect on your experience by writing a paragraph in answer to the following questions: Which PORPE parts of the strategy seemed most beneficial to you? What modifications will you make for the next exam?

_____

_____

_____

_____

_____

_____

_____

Chapter 14
Research, Resources, and Presentations

Read this chapter to answer the following questions:

- How do you use the library and Internet to find resources?

- What processes do you go through when writing up research?

- Exactly what is plagiarism?

- How do you prepare for individual and group presentations?

- How do you use technology as a learning tool?

Self-Assessment

DIRECTIONS: On a scale of 1 to 5, with 1 being "rarely," 3 being "sometimes," and 5 being "most of the time," evaluate your research, writing, and presentation strategies.

	Rarely		Some times		Most of the time
	1	**2**	**3**	**4**	**5**
1. I feel comfortable using my campus library's online databases.					X
2. I choose appropriate research questions.					X
3. I use the campus library to do research for class assignments.			X		
4. I know how to evaluate Internet information.				X	
5. I can organize information for a research project.				X	
6. I write drafts before submitting my final paper.				X	
7. I know how to revise and evaluate my papers.			X		
8. I know what plagiarism is and how to avoid it.					X
9. I know how to do group projects effectively.			X		
10. I know how to give an effective oral presentation.				X	

Now, add up your score. The lowest score you can receive is 10; the highest score is 50. The higher your score, the more effective your research, writing, and presentation skills are. Your score gives you an overall picture of your knowledge of the work involved in research and writing.

Before reading the chapter, reflect on your responses to the self-assessment. What are you doing that is helping you conduct academic research and prepare for class presentations? What do you need to work on?

_____

_____

_____

_____

_____

Before You Begin

WORD WISE

1. **Imperative** (adj., p. 218) — impossible to deter or evade; urgent.
*To stop the spread of the infection, it was **imperative** that the patient begin antibiotic treatment immediately.*

2. **Underutilize** (v., p. 219) — not use to the maximum potential; to underuse.
*Some psychologists believe that humans greatly **underutilize** the brain's potential.*

3. **Honing** (v., p. 223) — perfecting or sharpening; making more intense or effective.
*The mayoral candidate spent countless hours **honing** her acceptance speech.*

DID YOU KNOW?

Learning vocabulary involves using new words in several ways. One effective and fun way to become comfortable with new vocabulary is to play with words—Scrabble, crossword puzzles, online word games. All of these methods can help build a larger vocabulary. One of our favorite sites for word learning is a Web site called *freerice.com*. It is a vocabulary quiz that adapts to your level, and for each question you answer correctly, ten grains of rice are donated by the UN World Food Program to help end world hunger. We love it because you are doing something good for yourself by building your word knowledge and doing something good for humanity as well.

RESEARCH INTO PRACTICE

Writing to Learn

In this study, Drs. Paul and Elder discuss the ways that writing can help people think critically about ideas and learn. Although students often consider writing only as a means to assess learning, Paul and Elder emphasize writing as a way to learn. They state that writing can be a way to test yourself over information because you need to understand it well enough to explain things clearly to a reader. They also view writing as a cyclical concept—you can write to learn but you can also learn when you write. The authors of the study believe that it is **imperative** that college students understand the relationship between writing and learning. In their journal article, they firmly state that "one cannot be a skilled thinker and a poor writer." (42)

The way to become a skilled writer, according to Paul and Elder, is to learn to write reflectively. Reflective writers carry on inner conversations while they write, thinking both about what about they are writing and how the audience might perceive ideas. Thus, they are writing from the reader's point of view. To help the reader understand the issues, reflective writers ask themselves questions while writing: Is my main point clearly stated? Are my points supported and explained fully? Are there examples to help the reader? Have I considered multiple viewpoints?

This topic is important for students, because thinking about writing as a tool for learning brings home the importance of developing the skill of writing well while in college. In fact, like the authors of this article, we believe that learning to write well is a key to learning to learn.

Source: R. Paul and L. Elder, "Critical Thinking . . . and the Art of Substantive Writing, Part I," *Journal of Developmental Education* 29 (2005): 40–42.

218

Researching:
What You Need to Know

In college, you certainly spend a good deal of time engaged in a traditional studying cycle where your task is to take tests over lecture and text information. However, to be successful in college, you also need to know how to locate and synthesize information, because you will be responsible for writing research papers, completing projects, and giving oral presentations. How much writing and presenting you do most likely depends on the number of students in your classes, your major, and how well course content lends itself to these types of tasks. Therefore, the purpose of this chapter is to guide you through the research process from beginning to end. Our purpose is not to teach you how to write or present per se. Rather, we provide you with tips to help you complete your writing and presentation tasks and create an awareness concerning good practices.

Using the Library and Internet to Find Appropriate Resources

In this section, we discuss using both the "bricks and mortar" library and the Internet to conduct research. At some point in your college career, you are likely to have to write a paper that requires you to use resources from both sources. Many college libraries seem intimidating at first, but once you learn how to navigate the library, you will find it an incredibly user-friendly place. Although some college professors may discourage the use of Internet sources in research, we believe that if students learn how to find credible online sources, the Internet complements traditional library resources.

The college library may be one of the most **underutilized** resources on campus—at least for undergraduates. Some students are reluctant to use the library because they are not sure how to get started. College libraries can seem confusing, but with some guidance, you will soon find yourself feeling comfortable there. Libraries house books, government documents, periodicals, and newspapers. They also provide online resources including scholarly articles, newspapers, magazines, and electronic books. The following list offers general advice for library use; however, we strongly suggest finding out about the specific policies and procedures at your own campus library.

Focus Your Research Question When students head into the library with only a fuzzy notion of what they are researching, they quickly become overwhelmed and frustrated. Before you go to the library, take the time to focus your research ideas into a question (or several questions) that can be clearly stated.

Take a Stance Once you have a research question in mind, then it is time to search for materials. Use your library's databases to help you find general ideas of the type of material that is available on your topic. Then you can think about the angle or perspective you want to use when writing your paper.

Use Computerized Searches Most libraries are equipped with a computerized system for conducting searches of their holdings. Although each library seems to work a bit differently, when you conduct a library search, you are looking for three important pieces of information:

1. Call number: This number tells exactly where the resource is and probably works similarly to the system used at your high school library.

2. Location: Many campuses have more than one library, so it is important to note the location of the resource. On our own campus, there is a main library, science library, law library, educational materials library, music library, and map library. Many students become frustrated when they note the call number but not the location and find that they have to trek across campus to another library location to get the resource they need.

3. Status: When you look up a resource, you will also get information about the availability—checked out, on reserve, or available.

Limit Your Searches If your initial search seems to give you too many results, try using the advanced search features that allow you to limit the scope of your search by year, type, author, and so forth.

Ask a Librarian College librarians are there to help, so don't spin your wheels if you are having trouble. If you cannot find what you are looking for, ask for help. They can help you refine your search, locate materials, and direct you to new resources. Most college librarians love to do research, and you will find that they are some of the most helpful people on campus.

Bring Yor ID Card Just like public libraries, college libraries will require you to have a specific card for borrowing privileges. Often, your student ID will also work as your library card, but you usually need to go to the library to set up your account.

Evaluating Internet Information: The SCC Heuristic

Many students turn to the Internet to find material for their research papers. The trouble is that you can find it all on the Web: world-class thinking to pure garbage to blatant lies. Anyone can put up a Web page that looks good. But just because it is well designed doesn't mean that the content is good. To help you evaluate the credibility and quality of online information, use the SCC heuristic—Sourcing, Context, Corroboration—as a general method each time you surf the Web.

Sourcing Who is the author of this information? Is it a noted expert in the field, a high school student doing a report for school, a fan, a business, or an organization? Your answer to this question will tell you a lot about the quality of the information. In general, it is best to trust the information from an authority in the field over a fan or hobbyist.

Context What is the reason for this site to exist? Is it trying to educate, inform, sell a product, or persuade? Although commercial Web sites can sound very persuasive, if they are trying to sell you something, you need to take that into consideration when evaluating the information you find. How current is the information? Because the Web is an ever-changing source of information, in general, the more current the source, the better. Most Web pages tell you the last time the site was updated. If the site has not been updated recently, you might want to visit a more current site.

Corroboration How does the information compare with other Web sites? Corroboration of information deals with the level of agreement the material has with other materials on the topic. Usually there is a good deal of overlap, but if you find a site that is claiming ideas that no one else is discussing, that should send up a red flag. Does the information represent a particular point of view or is it trying to present an unbiased view? Most sites will contain some sort of bias; your job is to figure out what it is. You will need to check out a few sources to help you determine corroboration. Think of corroboration as the step where you pull the ideas from multiple sources together to evaluate the credibility of the information you have gathered.

Research a movie, a video game, or a book by finding five online reviews. Try looking at newspapers, Internet review sites, and other resources you find. Use the SCC heuristic to evaluate the sources and create your argument either for or against seeing the movie, playing the game, or reading the book. Keep in mind that you might find biased opinions on a publisher's or movie studio's Web site.

I am researching the following book, game, or movie:

_____

Use the SCC heuristic to evaluate five Web sites for the credibility of their information.

Web Resource	Sourcing	Context	Corroboration	Notes
1.				
2.				
3.				
4.				
5.				

My recommendation (provide justification, using your sources):

_____

_____

_____

_____

_____

_____

_____

Writing Your Research Paper

Once you have found all of the information necessary to write your paper and you're confident that the references you have chosen are credible and of high quality, you are ready to get started on the writing phase. The writing phase involves much more than just sitting down at your computer and producing a final product in one sitting. Because writing for a college audience may be quite different from your writing experiences in high school, there are several factors you need to keep in mind, as detailed below.

First, keep in mind that college writing is different from other types of writing. These differences are evident both in terms of audience as well as the focus of your papers. For many students, much of the writing they did in high school involved recounting personal experiences, the five-paragraph essay, or the dreaded high school research paper. All of these types of writing are generally very different from the type of research you are expected to do in college. In high school, research papers generally involve selecting a very specific topic, such as the civil rights movement or the relationship between smoking and lung cancer, and writing about it. In these types of papers, you most likely collected information and then summarized and reported what you found.

Second, in college, you will find that the expectations are greater. You will need to write a thesis statement and argue a stance. A thesis statement lets the reader know the main idea of your argument and explains briefly what you will write about. The research paper on the relationship between smoking and lung cancer becomes one that argues for or against banning smoking in restaurants or whether or not secondhand smoke is harmful. In other words, you are writing for an academic audience that expects that you know the facts. You use the facts that you find about smoking and lung cancer, for instance, to support your argument for or against banning smoking in restaurants. Your thesis statement tells your audience right from the beginning the stance you will take; you cite support for your stance as you argue your position. In other words, you are expected to write more than "John Smith found . . ." and "Mary Jones said . . ." You are expected to pull ideas together and think critically about what they mean. An example of a thesis statement for the smoking topic might read: "Because secondhand smoke causes numerous health risks, voters should support the proposition to ban smoking in restaurants."

A New Approach To Writing

Starting the writing process early is of utmost importance. Think back to Chapter 2 where we talked about time management issues. Things always take longer than you think they will; gathering the research will take longer, and the writing will take longer as well. In addition, because a paper in college may be worth a large percentage of your grade, you will want to start early to be sure that you can submit your best work. Moreover, if you start early, you will have time to get help if you need it. Most professors are glad to give you feedback on a work in progress, which can help you improve the quality of your paper. If you wait until the last minute to start, there is a good chance that your evaluation will suffer. The writing process should involve four main stages: organizing, drafting, revising, and evaluating.

1. ORGANIZING.

After you have all of your resources together and you are satisfied that you have the most appropriate support for your argument, you are ready to organize your information. You can organize in any number of ways—on note cards, in an outline form, by creating a map or chart, by color-coding different information by topic—any way that works for you.

The most important part of organizing is not the particular format you use; rather, it is selecting the key points you want to make and then organizing your support around them. For example, if after reading through your sources you find that you are going to present four key arguments as to why smoking should be banned in restaurants, you want to separate your sources so that as you argue each point you will have your references at hand. Many students find that at this stage of writing an outline is the most efficient way to organize. Each main point on the outline is followed by supporting information, examples, and source citations.

2. DRAFTING

After you have organized the information, you are ready to begin writing your first draft. Now is the time when you make sure you have a good thesis statement and that each of the points you want to make is related to and appropriate for your argument. At this stage of your writing, don't worry about getting it perfect. Get your thoughts down, include support for each of your points, and be sure your key points all relate to your thesis statement. Once you have a working draft (and this should take several different writing sessions, especially if your project is fairly lengthy), read what you have written, making notes to yourself in the margins about what you should attend to when you return to your draft. These notes may include information you need to clarify, support you need to add, or connections that don't seem to make sense.

3. REVISING

After you have a respectable first draft, put your paper aside for a day or two. Often, what seemed like a stroke of genius at 1:00 a.m. one day will cause a "What was I thinking?" response two days later. When you return to your draft with a fresh eye, revise by first addressing the notes you made in the margins. At this point, you should be **honing** your content, making sure that you haven't left out important information and that your argument is sound. Check to see that you are sticking to the key points you want to make. That's why organizing and drafting are so important. If you have done a good job of the first two steps, revising should be easier.

Once you are satisfied with your content, it's time to focus on the "flow" of your paper and work on cleaning it up. Keep in mind that you are writing for an academic audience, an audience that expects you to follow conventional mechanics, grammar, and usage rules. In addition, if your professor has given you a specific format to follow or is a stickler for certain details, be sure to take this into consideration as you are nearing completion of the revising process. Moreover, there is no magic number of revisions. Some students write a rough draft and move on to fairly polished final drafts with a few minor edits. For most students, however, it's not that simple. Writing is hard work, and most of us must do a vast amount of revising in order to get it right.

4. EVALUATING

When you have completed the revision process, put your paper aside for another day or so. Then read your paper with a critical eye. Put yourself in the place of the professor who will be grading your work. Then read the questions in Figure 14.1:

☐ Do I have a strong thesis statement that is clear?

☐ Is my paper organized around several key points that relate to my thesis statement?

☐ Do I have adequate support for each of my key points?

☐ Are my resources credible and reliable?

☐ Is my paper free of grammatical errors? (Note that computerized grammar and spell checkers are not foolproof. You must read every sentence yourself.)

☐ Have I followed my professor's guidelines for completing the paper so that I will receive full credit?

Figure 14.1: Questions to Help You Evaluate Your Writing

Citing Your Sources

You will need to find out the citation style required by your professor and be consistent in using the same style throughout your paper. The most common academic citation formats are APA (American Psychological Association) and MLA (Modern Language Association). A campus library usually has a variety of resources, including pamphlets, online tutorials, and reference books to help you figure out academic citation formats.

In addition to using a particular citation format, you also need to know how and when to credit your sources. It is fairly straightforward when you use a direct quote. That is, you lift a sentence or two from one of your sources, put quotes around it, and then provide an indication of the person who authored the source. Within the body of your paper, the citation for a direct quote using APA style would include the author(s) last name(s) and the year of publication and looks something like this:

> "Most tobacco-related cancers come from smoking, but the passive inhalation of secondhand smoke also poses a risk" (Campbell, Reece, & Simon, 2004).

In MLA style, you include the author(s) last name(s) of the author(s) and the page number, and it looks something like this:

> "Most tobacco-related cancers come from smoking, but the passive inhalation of secondhand smoke also poses a risk" (Campbell, Reece, and Simon 54).

You would then give the full citation either on a reference page at the end of the paper or in footnotes, depending on the reference style you are expected to follow. The major problem students have with direct quotes is that their lead-in to the quote may be forced and the thought may flow awkwardly.

The more pressing problem is that students fail to cite their sources when they paraphrase or summarize information. Any thoughts or conclusions that are not exclusively yours must be cited, even if they aren't direct quotes, which brings us to the idea of plagiarism.

Understanding Plagiarism

The *American Heritage College Dictionary* defines *plagiarize* thus: "1. to use and pass off as one's own (the ideas or writings of another). 2. To appropriate for use as one's own passages or ideas from (another)." This definition seems clear and to the point, but the part of this definition that is crucial to understand is that of using the ideas of another. Most students understand that you cannot take someone else's exact words or work and pass it off as your own. However, most cases of plagiarism or academic dishonesty are not because students intentionally copy another's work. They happen because many students do not understand that they cannot use another person's ideas without citing the source (See Figure 14.2). See note on page 225. There are two common ways in which students may plagiarize without consciously realizing it: using the ideas of others and receiving inappropriate assistance.

1. USING THE IDEAS OF OTHERS WITHOUT GIVING CREDIT

In many cases, students fail to give credit to sources when they paraphrase their ideas, believing that they only have to cite direct quotes. It is important to remember that any time you take ideas from someone else or from somewhere else, you must give credit for the idea. A works cited page is not sufficient. You must also cite your sources within your paper to indicate the source for each idea or fact. Some students have developed the habit of cutting and pasting from the Internet, assuming that if it is online then it is okay to use, but Internet information must be cited just like any other information you find. What often happens when students don't give the appropriate credit is that they find themselves before an academic honesty or student judiciary committee with no idea why they have been charged with academic dishonesty.

2. RECEIVING INAPPROPRIATE ASSISTANCE

Another way that students may plagiarize without realizing it is by receiving inappropriate assistance. This can come in the form of help with a paper or a project or even homework assignments where the person giving the help actually does your work. For example, let's assume you were having trouble writing a paper for your English course. You go to the campus writing center for help and a new tutor is assigned to help you. When you begin to discuss your paper with the tutor, she takes your paper and proceeds to rewrite it for you. You retype the paper and turn it in as your own work. Your professor notices that the paper does not read like your usual work and asks if you wrote it. How do you respond? Even though you got what you thought was appropriate help, you could be brought up on academic dishonesty charges in this instance. It's up to you to understand what constitutes appropriate help, so if you are not sure, ask your professor. In this case, the fact that the tutor wrote most of the final paper for you would be viewed as inappropriate.

BEYOND THE CLASSROOM

Now that it is relatively easy to access papers, book reviews, critical essays, and research papers on the Internet, students should know that it is also easy for their instructors to search the Web to be sure that students are submitting their own work. It only takes professors a few minutes to find the source—even when students paraphrase the information. Some campuses purchase software that all faculty can use to check students' papers for plagiarism. You are better off finding credible resources and citing them appropriately than taking a risk.

Figure 14.2: Avoiding Plagiarism

Original Quote	This is plagiarism because it uses almost the exact wording from the text and does not cite the source.	This is plagiarism because it is paraphrased but does not cite the source.	This is cited properly and is not plagiarism.
Brain imaging studies suggest that the general perception that events in REM dreams are stranger and more emotion-provoking than waking experiences is probably true. (Source: S. E. Wood, E. G. Wood, and D. Boyd, *Mastering the World of Psychology* (Boston: Pearson, 2004): 101.	Brain studies suggest that the general perception that events in REM dreams are stranger and more emotion-provoking is true.	Studies on brain imaging suggest a truth to the general perception that events in REM dreams are more emotion filled than waking experiences.	According to Wood, Wood, and Boyd (2004, p. 101) the common perception that the events in REM dreams are more emotion filled than experiences when we are awake is most likely true.

Organizing Oral Presentations

At some point in your college career, you will probably be required to present information to your classmates. Sometimes these oral presentations will be done in conjunction with a written report; sometimes they will not. Additionally, sometimes you will be asked to present the results of a group project to the class. In this section, we discuss how to work effectively in a group and some strategies for effective oral presentations.

WORKING IN GROUPS

Group learning involves sharing your ideas with others and relying on others to get work done. Many students find group work challenging because they are concerned that not all the group members will pull their own weight. However, groups work most effectively when there is trust among members. You have to know that you can count on everyone to give his best effort. Use the following guidelines to help your group decide the best way to get the project done.

Break Down the Tasks At your first group meeting, begin by outlining all of the tasks that need to be completed. Visualize the project from today through your final presentation to the class.

Set Deadlines Have group members put the deadlines in their planners so everyone has a record. Plan to have a group meeting at each deadline so that all group members stay connected with the progress that is being made. Leave yourself some flexibility as you set your deadlines for each task.

Keep in contact Once you have organized meeting times, make a plan to keep in touch with your group via e-mail, phone, chat, or listserv. Having regular contact with your group in between group meetings will help everyone stay on track.

Assign Specific Roles Think about the tasks, deadlines, and the strengths of each group member

> ### Reality Check
>
> #### People Approach Work Differently
> Group work might be difficult for students because people have varying comfort levels with deadlines. Some people like to get things done way ahead of time and others are more last minute. It is a good idea to discuss your own preferences with your group members when you are assigning tasks. Those who like to work ahead can choose the jobs that need to be done first, and those who like to work at the end can take more responsibility for the final tasks.

as you assign tasks to everyone. This is also a good time to establish ground rules. For example, if no one seems to be taking a leadership role, you might want to assign the role on a rotating basis for each group meeting so that each member takes the lead at least once.

Rehearse Plan a time to do a dress rehearsal of your oral presentation. In this rehearsal, you want to make sure that everyone knows what she will be saying and that it fits within your allotted time. Also check that any technology (overheads) and so forth is ready and working. You might want to invite a few people to watch to be sure that they understand the points you are making. In addition, include time to do a group evaluation of your rehearsal and allow time to fix any glitches that may occur.

Set Ground Rules If you work in groups, you are bound to find yourself in a situation where someone doesn't do his share or is difficult to get along with. What usually happens is that other members pick up the slack, especially if everyone in the group will receive the same grade. In an attempt to avoid having to do more than your share, set some ground rules for dealing with difficult individuals. Talk about these ground rules in your first meeting and then follow through if necessary.

CREATING AN INDIVIDUAL PRESENTATION

If your presentation is to be created individually, the first thing to do is to list all of the tasks involved, from conceptualizing the topic to completing the final product. An oral presentation is usually the culmination of a semester's worth of work and cannot be left until the last minute. Use the following steps to help you get it finished on time.

Figure Out the Task Once you have your assignment, ask yourself the following questions: What kind of talk is this—formal, informal, informational, persuasive? Who is the audience? How much time is allotted? What is the purpose of this talk? What do I want the audience to learn from my presentation?

Make a Timeline Once you have listed all of the tasks that need to be done, create a timeline like the one in Figure 14.3 to help yourself visualize completing the project. These deadlines will help you know what is coming up and stay on track.

Date	What's due?
Jan 31	Figure out research question
Feb 6	Complete library searches
Feb 13	Gather library materials
Feb 25	Have all materials read and focus research angle
Mar 3	Write thesis statement
Mar 15	Draft 5-page paper by today
Mar 17	Take paper to writing center for help
Mar 29	Complete outline of 15-minute oral presentation
Apr 3	Make handouts and overheads
Apr 6	Finish paper and practice presentation
Apr 8	PRESENTATION TODAY

Figure 14.3: Example Timeline for a Presentation

Make a Talk-Through Card Use a 3 x 5 note card to outline the key points you will make in your presentation. Remember that your card will not contain the details of each point; rather, it should contain the topics you will discuss in the order you will present them. Talk-through cards work especially well for students who experience public speaking anxiety. Often, these students find themselves less likely to blank out on the information because their reminder is right there in the card.

☐ Rate of speed: Are you speaking too quickly or at just the right pace?

☐ Volume: Are you speaking loudly enough to be heard clearly from the back of the room?

☐ Knowledge of the material: Are you able to give the presentation without merely reading your paper?

☐ Introducing the talk: Have you clearly stated what you will be talking about in the first few sentences? Have you defined important terms?

☐ Transitions between ideas: Can the listener follow your points in the order they are presented?

☐ Conclusion: Have you pulled your ideas together at the end of the presentation?

☐ Time: Have you met the time allotment without going over?

☐ Body language: It is good to move a little as you talk, but are you moving too much so that it is distracting?

Figure 14.4: Criteria for Evaluating Your Presentation

Practice Makes Perfect Before presenting your talk in public, plan to practice a few times. In fact, the difference between a successful and an unsuccessful presentation may hinge on the amount of practice done beforehand. Have a friend or a family member listen for the the criteria outlined in Figure 14.4:

Create Visual Aids It is a good idea to have visual aids to guide the audience as you talk. You might use overheads, posters, or computerized or multimedia presentations. When in doubt of which type of visual aid to use, choose the one that will fit with the assignment and is the least complex. However, note that creating a handwritten poster may not be the best idea, because it is very time-consuming and does not usually provide sufficient information. To avoid suffering technology problems on the day of your presentation, make sure that your format is compatible with the resources in the classroom. Regardless of the type of visual aids you use, be sure that they are large enough to be visible from the back row of the class. In addition, avoid the temptation to over-clutter your visual aids. Stick to one or two font types and use graphic and special effects sparingly. For visual aids, the "less is more" idea generally holds true.

NETWORKING

Computer Presentation Software

Using a computer program such as PowerPoint to create your presentation can help you save time and can be a good guide for you as you present your project. Use your PowerPoint slides as a talk-through, or a way to remind yourself of the topics in the order in which you want to discuss them. Put only enough information on each slide to remind yourself of what you wanted to talk about. Remember to use a large font so the audience can see the slides clearly.

Technology as a Resource for Studying

In addition to using technology to create classroom presentations, many students have found that using a computer can greatly aid in learning and studying for courses. The following list certainly is not exhaustive, and with new technologies coming out every day, we are sure you will find other ways to incorporate technology into your learning and studying. Here are some of the basic ways that students are using technology in learning:

Organizing Lecture Notes Some students like to retype their lecture notes, because typing them on the computer helps them reorganize the information. We know of one student in an art history course who cut and pasted slides of paintings from her professor's Web site (and some from museum Web sites) right into her own notes. That way, she could see the painting as she studied her notes about it.

Creating Maps and Charts There are several software programs that can help you create useful concept maps and charts in a snap. These maps and charts help you organize and synthesize ideas.

Meeting with Virtual Study Groups Students can set up online study groups to meet at designated times before exams. This is a great way to study with others, because the group tends to stay more on task than in a face-to-face study group.

Using Webcasts, Podcasts, or Social Networking Sites A Webcast is a broadcast of information over the Internet. This technology is becoming increasingly utilized on many college campuses. Some colleges are experimenting with offering courses using online Webcasts. Professors may require students to listen to a particular Webcast or Podcast as part of a course assignment. In addition, students may find a wealth of information for research using Webcasts. Some professors are even holding course discussions on social networking sites such as Facebook or Twitter. Plan to check these sites several times each week for updates.

Using Textbook Web Site Material Textbook publishers often have lots of resources available on their Web sites. These can include practice problems, sample quizzes, additional examples, etc. It is always a good idea to use these resources to give you the extra edge.

Researching Information for Papers and Presentations The Internet can be an excellent source of information when researching information for class presentations or papers. As we discussed earlier in this chapter, you need to be careful about the quality of the information you get. You also need to be careful that you do not plagiarize information from the Web.

229

Real College

RACHEL'S RESEARCH PROJECT

DIRECTIONS: *Read the following scenario and respond to the questions based on what you have learned in this chapter.*

Rachel's speech communication class is turning out to be far more work than she was expecting. Not only does she have to give three individual speeches, but she also has to do a group project at the end of the semester. The professor assigned the group members, and she doesn't even know who these people are. He did give them a choice of five topics for which the group must research all sides of the issue and present a 20-minute oral discussion and presentation. In addition, each group member must write a five-page paper arguing his or her stance on the topic. The professor offered very little guidance on how to get started, other than to be careful about using Internet resources and to make sure that the group members were working together. The professor is also giving the class two periods to work on the project during class time so that they can ask questions. Rachel is concerned because every time she has ever worked in a group, she has ended up doing everything!

What can Rachel do?

1. Using what you have learned, help Rachel figure out how to make this group project run smoothly. First, consider how to get started and how to break up the tasks.

_____

_____

_____

_____

_____

2. Second, make a plan for using the two periods of class time efficiently.

_____

_____

_____

_____

_____

Add to Your Portfolio

Take a tour of your campus library to learn how to use its resources. Then select a topic from *Effective College Learning* that you want to know more about, such as motivation, study strategies, or stress management. Use the library to find the following resources about your topic:

1. A book from the *stacks* (this means from the shelves of the library)

_____

_____

2. An online journal article

_____

_____

3. A journal article from the stacks

_____

_____

4. An online newspaper article

_____

_____

Summarize your findings in a one- to two-page report. Remember to cite your sources.

Chapter 15
Flexible Reading and Studying

Read this chapter to answer the following questions:

- What does it mean to be a flexible reader?
- What are some habits that make people read slowly?
- What does it mean to be a flexible studier?
- How do college courses differ from each other?
- How can I modify my strategies to suit different courses and texts?

Self-Assessment

DIRECTIONS: Complete the following chart for each of your courses this term. Think about how you prepare for each class.

	Course 1	**Course 2**	**Course 3**	**Course 4**	**Course 5**
(course name)	_____	_____	_____	_____	_____
1. I read the text before class.	Yes / No	Yes / No	Yes / No	Yes / No	Yes / No
2. I read the text after class	Yes / No	Yes / No	Yes / No	Yes / No	Yes / No
3. My class lecture follows the text.	Yes / No	Yes / No	Yes / No	Yes / No	Yes / No
4. I am responsible for reading multiple texts for this course.	Yes / No	Yes / No	Yes / No	Yes / No	Yes / No
5. I try to study in the same way for each course.	Yes / No	Yes / No	Yes / No	Yes / No	Yes / No
6. I read all of my textbooks at the same rate of speed.	Yes / No	Yes / No	Yes / No	Yes / No	Yes / No
7. I understand the professor's expectations for this course.	Yes / No	Yes / No	Yes / No	Yes / No	Yes / No

The way you have responded to these questions will depend on the tasks involved in your courses. However, the way you prepare and the way you approach reading for class will impact your performance. Think about your responses. Do you see any patterns? For example, did you respond no consistently to a particular item or did you respond no to most of the items for a specific course? Before reading the chapter, reflect on these patterns.

_____

_____

_____

WORD WISE

1. **Residual** (adj., p. 236) — of or relating to something that remains; indicating a remainder.
*Even after Lucy left the room, her strong perfume left a **residual** odor for hours.*

2. **Undermine** (v., p. 242) — to weaken by wearing away; to injure or impair often imperceptivity.
*A lack of sleep can **undermine** one's health.*

3. **Succinct** (adj., p. 242) — clear, precise expression in few words; concise.
*Because James has so many e-mails to answer each day, he always tries to keep his responses **succinct**.*

4. **Vastly** (adv., p. 244) — to an extremely large extent; to a great degree or intensity.
*The FDA's approval of five new medicines will **vastly** improve doctors' options for treating chronic pain.*

DID YOU KNOW?

Did you know that pleasure reading is one of the best ways to improve your vocabulary? Research has shown that students who read widely for pleasure perform better on standardized tests (such as the SAT and ACT), placement tests, and even classroom tests. It really doesn't matter much *what* you read—magazines, novels, newspapers. What *does* matter is that you read widely and dedicate some time each week to reading for fun. Not only does pleasure reading build your vocabulary (the more you read, the more words you are exposed to), but it also improves your reading rate and comprehension.

RESEARCH INTO PRACTICE

Interest, Strategies, Knowledge, and Learning

This study examined the roles of subject matter knowledge (that is, how much background knowledge a student has about a subject), study strategies, and interest on learning in an educational psychology course. Drs. Murphy and Alexander chose educational psychology because they assumed that the students in the study would be relatively unfamiliar with the topics presented in the course but could gain a foundation within a single semester. The researchers asked students questions not only about their knowledge of educational psychology, but also about how knowledge interacts, because this ability to see relationships among ideas is important to learning in the course. They found that students who entered the course with a background in the topic and those who were able to process texts in an interactive way but did not have background knowledge performed well even when they did not have much background in educational psychology. The researchers also measured students' interest and their ability to learn strategically. They found that students became

better learners during the semester as they increased their use of deep-processing strategies and that students who engaged in deeper processing performed better on exams. They also found a relationship between knowledge and interest. That is, the more students knew about the topic, the more they reported being interested in it.

This study is important for college students because it shows that although background knowledge is helpful, having the strategies necessary for course tasks (in this case, the ability to see how knowledge interacts) also plays a significant role in learning and interest. In addition, simply learning more about a topic helped students develop both the necessary skills for the course tasks and the interest throughout one semester. This means that neither learning nor interest is fixed. Each is flexible and can be developed as students learn more about a topic.

Source: P. K. Murphy and P. A. Alexander, "What Counts? The Predictive Powers of Subject-Matter Knowledge, Strategic Processing, and Interest in Domain Performance," *The Journal of Experimental Education* 70 (2002): 197–214.

Flexible Reading

What does the word *flexible* mean to you? You might think of a gymnast able to perform amazing physical feats. Or you might think about a choice: for instance, "Where do you want to have lunch?" "Wherever—I'm flexible." No matter what the context, being flexible means that you are able to adapt to a given situation. You don't often hear the word flexible used when talking about learning and reading, but you should begin to think about becoming more flexible. Most students approach every learning task in the same way. However, flexible learners adapt their approach to learning based on the four factors that impact learning discussed in this text: their characteristics as a learner, the task, the study strategies they select, and the materials they use. Flexible learners modify their approaches to studying and adjust how they study to suit their purpose. They understand that they should study mathematics differently than history and English literature differently than science. As Abraham Maslow, a noted psychologist, once stated, "If the only tool you have is a hammer, you will treat every problem like a nail." Flexible students have lots of "tools" at their disposal from which to pick and choose as the need arises.

Likewise, a flexible reader knows that it is unrealistic to attempt to read everything at the same speed. In other words, you cannot expect to read your chemistry textbook at the same speed at which you read the local newspaper. Your reading rate will vary depending on several factors:
• The easier the material, the faster you will be able to read.
• The more you know about a topic, the faster you can read it.
• The more interest you have in the material, the faster your rate.

The average adult reads about 200 words per minute; that's only about as fast as most people talk. However, the average college student reads about 250 words per minute—a little better, but still not enough to read all of your materials efficiently and effectively given the amount of reading that is required in college, it is to your advantage to increase your reading rate above these averages without sacrificing comprehension.

Increasing your reading rate may mean unlearning some habits you have held since you first learned to read. When you were learning to read difficult material in elementary school, your teacher probably advised you to slow down. Many college students follow the same advice to this very day when they read something difficult. However, if you are already reading at a slow rate and you slow down even further, you might actually be making it harder to comprehend the text.

A student attempting to read the sentence "I have three lab projects and two term papers due next week" who is reading too slowly would read the sentence as individual words instead of phrases: *I/ have/ three/ lab/ projects/ and/ two /term/ papers/ due/ next/ week*.

This student will have a more difficult time with comprehension because he must first recognize each of the individual words, then put the words together into meaningful phrases, and then put those phrases together into a sentence. By then, a good deal of time has passed (in reading terms) and a lot of the comprehension is lost. In this case, reading slower is *decreasing* the ability to comprehend the information. Should you ever slow down when reading difficult material? Well, yes and no. You should slow down to the point of comprehension, but you should not read so slowly that you weaken comprehension. And you should adjust your reading speed according to the type of material you are reading and not fall into the habit of reading everything at the same rate. The key point is this: You adjust your reading rate to the material you are reading; you adjust your studying based on what you are trying to learn.

Habits That Slow Reading

Many students have at least one of several habits that slow their rate of reading speed. They developed these habits when they were children and, therefore, may not even be aware of them. As you read the following, think about your own reading habits, both with your textbooks and with material you read for pleasure.

BACKTRACKING

A person who reads the same words over and over is backtracking. Think about the example sentence used earlier. A person who backtracks would read the sentence as:

I have three/ have three/ lab projects and two/ lab projects/ term papers due next week/ next week.

This habit can dramatically slow both reading and comprehension. Students backtrack when they are not confident that they have understood the reading or when they are not concentrating on what they are reading. If backtracking becomes a habit, students tend to do it no matter what they read, which is why it is one of the toughest habits to break.

To overcome backtracking, you must convince yourself that you understand the information as you read. Backtracking differs from being conscious that you do not understand a particular sentence and need to go back and reread it (which *is* a good strategy for comprehension). People who backtrack do not even realize they are doing it and will backtrack even when they understand the sentence perfectly. One good way to stop this habit is to follow along with a pen or your finger as you read. You won't be able to backtrack unconsciously if you are following your finger, and it will help keep your eyes moving steadily forward. You might also find it helpful to cover up the text with a blank sheet of paper as you read so that you cannot look back without intentionally moving the paper away. Another solution is to be sure to preview the reading. Having an idea about where the chapter is headed will help concentration and, therefore, may also help reduce the tendency to backtrack.

SUBVOCALIZATION

If you say the words to yourself as you read, you are subvocalizing. Subvocalizers may move their lips or say the words under their breath. When you were learning to read, you probably learned to sound out the words, and the teacher asked you to read aloud. Later, when you began to read silently, you were still saying the words in your head. If you have never stopped "saying" the words, you are probably subvocalizing. This habit slows reading rates because you can only speak about 200 words per minute, but most everyone has the ability to read and comprehend at much faster rates.

Luckily, this is a fairly easy habit to break. To overcome subvocalization, put your finger over your lips, and when you feel that they are moving, will yourself to stop. If you are saying the words under your breath, put your hand on your throat as you read. You will feel a vibration if you are subvocalizing, and, again, you can will yourself to stop.

FIXATIONS

Each time your eyes focus on a word or phrase, it is called a *fixation*. Everyone fixates, but some people fixate too often or too long, which can slow down reading. Fixating on every word is also a **residual** habit from when you learned to read. In elementary school, you learned to recognize letters and then words one at a time, which made you fixate often. In fact, you probably needed to stop at every word. However, effective readers do not fixate on every word. Instead, they read groups of words in a single fixation. A person who fixates too often would read the sentence as: *I/ have/ three/ lab/ projects/ and/ two/ term/ papers/ due/ next/ week.*

To overcome fixating too often, a student needs to learn how to include more information in each fixation. There are two main methods to overcoming fixations: the key-word and the phrase word strategies. Some students learn best using the key-word strategy, but others say that they comprehend better using the phrase word strategy. Try out both to see which one works best for you.

1. The Key-Word Strategy One way to break the habit of too many fixations is to use the key-word method. In this strategy, you don't waste your time reading words like *the* or *and*. Instead, you focus on the more meaningful words. As you fixate on the key words, your eyes tend to include the words like *the* without having to fixate on them. A person using the key-word strategy would often read the sentence as: *I have/ three lab* **projects**/ *and two term* **papers**/ *due next week.*

Experiment with this method to see how many times you must fixate in order to get the main idea of a sentence and to prove to yourself that you can comprehend without focusing on every word.

2. The Phrase Word Strategy Another strategy to reduce fixation is phrase word reading. Using this strategy, you go through the passage and stop in the middle of each phrase. When you stop, your eye takes in the entire phrase. It is different from the key-word strategy because you are not looking for specific words; rather, you are taking in larger chunks of information at a time. A person using the phrase word strategy would read the sentence as: *I have* **three lab projects**/ *and two* **term papers**/ *due* **next week.**

Increasing Your Reading Speed

Many companies advertise speed-reading programs that cost several hundred dollars. However, you can increase your reading speed, and sometimes even double it, without spending big bucks. All you need is something interesting to read and some time each day to push yourself to read faster.

The purpose of pushed reading is to increase your overall reading speed. When you practice reading faster, you should never use your textbooks or even novels assigned for class. Repeat: Do not use texts or materials that you will be tested over in your courses. You cannot expect to be able to speed-read a difficult textbook filled with new concepts and comprehend all of the information. In fact, when you speed-read, you can expect to achieve 70 to 80 percent comprehension as you learn to adapt to faster speeds. When you are reading material for an exam, you want 100 percent comprehension. Likewise, if you speed-read a novel from your literature class, you will miss the language that makes the novel a great work. You may grasp the basic plot, but little else. When you are practicing reading faster, use a piece of text that you find enjoyable—the campus newspaper, magazine articles, or a novel you are reading for pleasure.

HOW TO READ FASTER

Just because you currently read slowly doesn't mean that you are doomed to do it for the rest of your life. Reading slowly is a habit, and habits can be broken. In fact, you will probably find that you can dramatically improve your reading speed fairly quickly. The tips that follow give you some suggestions for increasing your rate.

Choose High-Interest Material It is best to push yourself to read faster with material that is familiar and that you enjoy. For example, if you like to read mystery novels, choose one to use for pushed reading.

Practice Every Day To increase your reading rate, you will need to push yourself to read faster every day for at least 10 to 15 minutes. Use your local or school newspaper or anything that will sustain your interest for that amount of time. You might want to choose three or four brief articles and take a short break after each one.

Read at Slightly-Faster-Than-Comfortable Speeds As you read, push yourself to read slightly faster than you usually do. You should be a little uncomfortable reading at this speed and feel that you would prefer to slow down; but you should also sense that you understand what you are reading.

Check Your Comprehension Increasing your reading rate while losing comprehension provides no benefit. Therefore, you need to check your comprehension of the material you are reading. However, because you are changing a habit, it is okay to have comprehension of only 70 to 80 percent of what you read during pushed reading. In fact, if you are comprehending 100 percent, you can probably read faster. To check your comprehension, try to summarize the information. Can you identify all of the key ideas? What about important details and examples? If you find that you are not comprehending the information, slow down a bit.

Try to Read at the Same Time Each Day

Finding 15 minutes to read every day should not be much of a problem, but in order to keep an accurate record of your improvement, you should try to find the time when you are most alert and try to read at that same time every day.

Don't Give Up Because your current reading speed is most likely a result of the habit of reading slowly, improving your reading rate will take a bit of time. You may make some great improvements one week and then see little change the next. Don't worry about the fluctuations in your rate, as long as you are seeing an overall increase. However, if you find that you have gone several weeks without any improvement, make a conscious effort to push yourself even faster. And remember: Most students can almost double their reading rate within six weeks or so, especially if they start out at 250 words per minute or less. That said, keep in mind that your fastest speed is reserved for pleasurable and very easy reading.

HOW QUICKLY SHOULD YOU READ?

Students often ask how quickly they should read. This is not an easy question to answer, because the rate at which you read depends on your purpose and the type of material you are reading. Rather than focusing on a specific reading speed, your goal is to become flexible and to choose a rate based on your purpose. In other words, you should be able to read a magazine or a novel you are reading for pleasure faster than a textbook.

In general, however, you should always strive to read faster than 200 to 250 words per minute because lower speeds can inhibit your comprehension. Otherwise, we are hesitant to give exact numbers. The rate at which you "should" read depends on three factors:

1. How Quickly You Currently Read It would make no sense to tell a student to read at 400 words per minute if she is currently reading at 225 with 70 percent comprehension. Instead, we would tell her to use the pushed-reading strategy to help increase overall reading rate without sacrificing comprehension. In other words, build up your speed a little at time, much like you increase weights in improving your strength. And try to keep in mind that the best way to increase your rate is to do pushed reading every day for 15 minutes

2. Your Purpose for Reading If you are reading to write a paper or to prepare for an exam, you will read at fairly slow speeds because you will want to comprehend everything. This includes reading difficult texts, poetry, technical manuals, textbooks, or literature with which you must take the time to notice and savor the language. If your purpose is to read for pleasure or for general information, you will be able to read more quickly (approximately 300 to 350 words per minute). (Note: If you are reading easy material, you can probably read a bit faster.) This type of reading includes novels, newspapers, magazines, and other reading for enjoyment. If you are scanning material for specific information, you will be able to read at very fast rates (more than 500 words per minute). This type of reading includes dictionaries, catalogs, phone books, and other reference books. Keep in mind, however, that this is not really reading in the true sense of the word.

3. Your Task If you will be tested over the material, take more time to really understand it. It makes no sense to rush through your history text if you are not getting all of the information. If you are reading for pleasure, there may be times when you want to read slowly to enjoy your book and times when you want to use pushed reading to increase your rate. Be sure to leave yourself some time for both.

DIRECTIONS: Read the following article to assess your current reading speed. Use a stopwatch or a watch with a second hand to keep track of your time. When you have completed the reading, record your time and answer the comprehension questions. Use the formula following the passage to determine your reading rate. Time yourself only for reading the passage but not for answering the comprehension questions.

Clean Living on Campus: Does It Work? Substance-Free Dorms

PROUD are the parents whose college-bound children choose to live in "substance-free" or "wellness" dorms. Residents voluntarily commit not to smoke, drink, or use drugs; and in some cases, they eschew loud music and pets too.

Well, not always entirely voluntarily; a good many times, it is really the parents who choose substance-free living, or at least nudge their sons and daughters in that direction. "If your parents are looking over your shoulders when you fill out the housing forms, you want to look good," said George Awkward III, a senior at Washington and Lee University who chose substance-free housing as a freshman but now lives in a regular residence hall. "I thought I would see what it's like, and my mom said, 'You need it.' We kind of made the decision together."

Since the early 1990s, substance-free housing has become de rigueur at dozens of campuses nationwide, from huge state universities like the University of Michigan to Ivy League schools like Dartmouth and small liberal arts colleges like Vassar. Colleges see it as a way to help students avoid not only problems of their own but also secondhand effects like vomit on the floor and the smell of marijuana wafting down the hallway. And it does not hurt that parents love the concept of a nonpartying college life.

But there is something puzzling about the whole idea. Students under 21 are not allowed to drink, most dorms are smoke free, and illegal drugs are, by definition, illegal. Officially, then, every dorm should be substance free. Colleges, if they chose to, could crack down on violators. So is the substance-free movement just a symbolic gesture, or does such housing make a difference in how students live?

As it turns out, it does make a difference.

No one claims that students who live in substance-free housing abstain from smoking, drinking alcohol, or using drugs. But at least, according to one survey, they don't indulge as much as others. A 2001 study of more than 14,000 students nationwide found that, compared with other students, only three-fifths as many residents of substance-free housing reported binge drinking in the previous two weeks.

There were other benefits too. Students in substance-free housing, the study found, were less likely to experience alcohol-related problems, like getting behind in your schoolwork, damaging property, getting into trouble with the police, or riding with a drunken driver.

There is, of course, a chicken-and-egg element to these findings. Students hoping for a college experience that bears some relationship to "Animal House" are not likely to opt for substance-free housing.

But Henry Wechsler, lead author of the study, is a big advocate of such housing and believes it should be available to every student who wants it. "The best bet for students who come into college and want to avoid the secondhand effects of drinking, like having their studying interrupted or having property vandalized, is to request substance-free residences," said Dr. Wechsler, director of College Alcohol Studies at the Harvard School of Public Health.

At the University of Michigan, some 2,600 students, or about 29 percent of those who live in residence halls, choose substance-free housing.

"Sometimes it's parent driven, but a lot of times it's students who drink socially but don't want to live in a climate where there's a lot of drunkenness around them," said Alan Levy, director of housing public affairs at Michigan.

"For most, it's a quality-of-life issue," Mr. Levy said. "For some, like Muslims, there are religious reasons. Still others choose to live in such housing because they, or a family member, had a problem with addiction."

continued on next page

Now that substance-free housing is commonplace, a handful of campuses, including Rutgers, have gone further, offering "recovery" housing for students who have been in treatment for addiction. But even traditional substance-free housing is a good place for students who had drinking or drug problems in high school.

"I was in residential treatment for part of my time in high school," said a junior at Earlham College who asked that his name not be used. "When I got to college, I didn't want to have to worry about having all that stuff in my face. I've been in wellness housing my whole time here. I could handle normal housing now, but I like the people I live with, and there's a very good atmosphere."

Most who choose substance-free housing just want a quieter life than they think they will find in regular college housing. "Drunk people can get pretty obnoxious, and I didn't want all these people going around being really loud," said Dashiell Slootbeck, a Beloit College sophomore who chose a substance-free dorm her freshman year.

Generally, substance-free housing appeals most to freshmen. At Dartmouth, for example, about 400 of the 1,075 incoming freshmen requested it, compared with only about 200 of the 2,200 sophomores, juniors and seniors who live on campus.

Of course, after freshman year, most students can find roommates they know will be compatible in dorms where the culture suits them, or move off campus or into fraternities or sororities.

When substance-free housing was introduced, its residents on many campuses were viewed—by themselves and others—as antisocial grinds. But where such housing has caught on, that perception has largely faded. "We had a floor meeting the first night and the feeling was, we're cool, we live in a substance-free house," said Ugochi Ukegbu, a freshman at Dartmouth.

In financial terms, the housing provides one undeniable benefit to colleges: less property damage. At Vassar, about 350 of the 2,600 students live on wellness corridors—where noise does not flow out from behind closed doors and fish are about the only pets allowed.

Vandalism costs there are substantially lower than on regular floors. According to a 1996 study financed by the United States Department of Education, damage costs were more than twice as much on the regular corridors as on the wellness ones at most of Vassar's dorms; other colleges had similar experiences.

At many campuses, residents of regular dorms, and even those assigned to substance-free housing they did not request, say they are glad the option exists.

"I think it's good that colleges have a wellness choice," said Beatrice Capestany, a freshman who was assigned to the wellness corridor of Vassar's sole remaining all-female dorm, although she did not request it. "My dorm is a really good place to come back home to if I've gone out. It smells a lot nicer than some other dorms, too." On that same wellness corridor, Victoria Ramsey and Kathryn Thomas, both freshmen, could not be more pleased with their choice.

"I don't drink or smoke, and our corridor is clean and quiet," said Ms. Ramsey.

Ms. Thomas added: "I wanted a quiet place for studying. Sometimes it's a refuge, for people who come and stay till they know the party on their floor has died down."

Source: Tamar Lewin, *New York Times* (November 6, 2005): Education Life Supplement.

Add to Your Portfolio

Try out these two activities as a way of increasing your reading rate.

1. For the next week, practice pushing yourself to read faster each day using the strategies you have learned in this chapter. Remember to read at a slightly-faster-than-comfortable pace. Choose something that is of interest to you but is *not* one of your textbooks. Plan to do pushed reading for at least 20 minutes each day, and follow these steps:
   - Use a stopwatch or a watch with a second hand to keep track of your time.
   - When you have completed the reading, record your time.
   - Then, as a comprehension check, think about what you have read. How much can you recall?
   - Think about the factors that influenced your speed. Were you tired, hungry, bored? Was there too much noise or other distractions? Were the conditions just right for pushed reading?

Use the following chart to record your progress.

Source	# of words	Time (minutes and seconds)	Speed in WPM (number of words ÷ time)	Comments

2. Fill in the following chart for your courses this semester to help you determine how to approach studying in that course.

	Course 1	Course 2	Course 3	Course 4	Course 5
What type of course is this? (mathematics, humanities, etc.)					
How is the course structured? (topically, sequentially, chronologically, etc.)					
What are the tasks in this course? (exams, essays, papers, etc.)					
Which learning strategies do I currently use?					
Which learning strategies would be most effective?					

Appendix A

Source: Samuel E. Wood, Ellen Green Wood, & Denise Boyd,
Mastering the World of Psychology, 1/e

Chapter 6
Memory

- Remembering
- The Nature of Remembering
- Factors Influencing Retrieval
- Biology and Memory
- Forgetting
- Improving Memory

Shut up, or I'll cut you," Jennifer's attacker warned her as he held the knife against her throat. Just moments before, Jennifer had screamed as the man grabbed her, threw her down on the bed, and pinned her hands behind her. Now, feeling the pain of the knife's sharp point on her throat, she knew he meant what he said. But she steeled herself to study the rapist—his facial features, scars, tattoos, voice, mannerisms— vowing to herself that she would remember the man well enough to send him to prison.

Hours after her ordeal, Jennifer Thompson viewed police photos of potential suspects, searching for that of her rapist—his pencil-thin moustache, eyebrows, nose, and other features. She then selected a composite photo that looked like the rapist. A week later, she viewed six suspects holding cards numbered 1 to 6. Jennifer looked at suspect number 5 and announced with total confidence, "That's the man who raped me."

The man was Ronald Cotton, who had already served a year and a half in prison for attempted

sexual assault. In court, Thompson was unshakably confident, so sure that this man had raped her. Cotton was nervous and frightened. His alibis didn't check out, and a piece missing from one of his shoes resembled a piece found at the crime scene. But it was the confident, unwavering testimony of the only eyewitness, Jennifer Thompson, that sealed his fate. The jury found him guilty and sentenced him to life in prison, just as Thompson had hoped.

"God knows I'm innocent," said Cotton, and he vowed to prove it somehow.

Remarkably, after Cotton had been in prison for more than a year, a new inmate, Bobby Poole, convicted of a series of brutal rapes, joined him at his work assignment in the kitchen. When Cotton told Poole that he had been convicted of raping Jennifer Thompson, Poole laughed and bragged that Cotton was doing some of his time.

Finally, after Cotton had served 11 years, law professor Richard Rosen heard his story and agreed to help him. Rosen knew that DNA tests could be performed that were far more sophisticated than those that had been available 11 years earlier. It was Cotton's DNA samples that cleared him of the crime. Poole's DNA samples, however, proved that he had raped Thompson.

After being proved innocent and released from prison, Ronald Cotton talked with and forgave Jennifer Thompson, who had falsely accused him. Cotton is now married with a beautiful daughter, Raven. With Thompson's help, he got a six-figure settlement from the state government. (Adapted from O'Neil, 2000.)

Does this case simply reflect the rare and unusual in human memory, or are memory errors common occurrences? This and many other questions you may have about memory will be answered in this chapter.

Remembering

THE THREE PROCESSES IN MEMORY

The act of remembering requires three processes: encoding, storage, and retrieval. The first process, **encoding**, involves transforming information into a form that can be stored in memory. For example, if you met someone named Will at a party, you might associate his name with that of the actor Will Smith. The second memory process, **storage**, involves keeping or maintaining information in memory. The final process, **retrieval**, occurs when information stored in memory is brought to mind. Calling Will by name the next time you meet him shows that you have retrieved his name from memory.

Physiological changes must occur during a process called **consolidation**, which allows new information to be stored in memory for later retrieval. These physiological changes require the synthesis of protein molecules (Lopez, 2000). Until recently, conventional wisdom held that the process of consolidation had to occur only once for each item memorized. But as we will see later in the chapter, in the section on the causes of forgetting, some seemingly consolidated memories can be induced to disappear (Nader et al., 2000).

THE THREE MEMORY SYSTEMS

How are memories stored? According to one widely accepted view, the *Atkinson-Shiffrin model*, there are three different, interacting memory systems, known as sensory, short-term, and long-term memory (Atkinson & Shiffrin, 1968; Broadbent, 1958). We will examine each of these three memory systems.

As information comes in through the senses, virtually everything you see, hear, or otherwise sense is held in **sensory memory**, but only for the briefest period of time. Exactly how long does visual sensory memory last? For a fraction of a second, glance at the three rows of letters shown below and then close your eyes. How many of the items can you recall?

X B D F
M P Z G
L C N H

Most people can recall correctly only four or five of the items when they are briefly presented. Does this indicate that visual sensory memory can hold only four or five items at a time? To find out, researcher George Sperling (1960) briefly flashed 12 items, as shown above, to participants. Immediately upon turning off the display, he sounded a high, medium, or low tone that signaled the participants to report only the top, middle, or bottom row of items. Before they heard the tone, the participants had no way of knowing which row they would have to report. Yet Sperling found that, when the participants could view the letters for}110500 to}12 second, they could report correctly all the items in any row nearly 100% of the time. But the items fade from sensory memory so quickly that during the time it takes to report three or four of the items, the other eight or nine have already disappeared.

Auditory sensory memory lasts about 2 seconds (Klatzky, 1980). You may have the sense that words are echoing in your mind after someone stops speaking to you. This phenomenon is the result of the relatively long time that auditory information remains in sensory memory, compared to visual information. Thus, your brain has much more time to attend to sounds and to move information about them to the next phase of processing.

From sensory memory, information moves to **short-term memory**. Whatever you are thinking about right now is in your short-term memory. Unlike sensory memory, which holds virtually the exact sensory stimulus, short-term memory usually codes information according to sound (Conrad, 1964). The letter T is coded as the sound "tee," not as the shape T. In addition, short-term memory has a very limited capacity—about seven (plus or minus two) different items or bits of information at one time. When short-term memory is filled to capacity, displacement can occur (just as you start to lose things when the top of your desk becomes overcrowded!). In **displacement**, each new incoming item pushes out an existing item, which is then forgotten.

One way to overcome the limitation on the capacity of short-term memory to seven or so bits of information is to use a technique that George A. Miller (1956), a pioneer in memory research, calls *chunking*—organizing or grouping separate bits of information into larger units, or chunks. A *chunk* is an easily identifiable unit such as a syllable, a word, an acronym, or a number (Cowan, 1988). For example, the numbers 5 2 9 7 3 1 2 5 can be chunked as 52 97 31 25, giving short-term memory the easier task of dealing with four chunks of information rather than eight separate bits. Complete *Try It!* 6.1 to get a feeling for the superiority of chunking over trying to memorize individual items one at a time.

Anytime you chunk information on the basis of knowledge stored in long-term memory—in other words, by associating it with some kind of meaning —you increase the effective capacity of short-term memory (Lustig & Hasher, 2002). And when you increase the effective capacity of short-term memory, you are more likely to transfer information to long-term memory. (*Hint*: The headings and subheadings in textbook chapters are labels for manageable chunks of information. You will remember more of a chapter if you use them as organizers for your notes and as cues to recall chapter information when you are reviewing for an exam.)

Items in short-term memory are lost in less than 30 seconds unless you repeat them over and over to yourself. This process is known as **rehearsal**. But rehearsal is easily disrupted. Distractions that are stressful are especially likely to disrupt short-term memory. And a threat to survival certainly does so, as researchers showed when they pumped the odor of a feared predator, a fox, into a laboratory where rats were performing a task requiring short-term memory (Morrison et al., 2002; Morrow et al., 2000).

How long does short-term memory last if rehearsal is prevented? In a series of early studies, participants were briefly shown three consonants (such as H, G, and L) and then asked to count backward by threes from a given number (for example, 738, 735, 732, . . .) (Peterson & Peterson, 1959). After intervals lasting from 3 to 18 seconds, participants were instructed to stop counting backward and recall the three letters. Following a delay of 9 seconds, the participants could recall an average of only one of the three letters. After 18 seconds, there was practically no recall whatsoever. An 18-second distraction had completely erased the three letters from short-term memory.

Allan Baddeley (1990, 1992, 1995) has suggested that *working memory* is a more fitting term than short-term memory. In other words, this memory system is where you work on information to understand it, remember it, use it to solve a problem, or to communicate with someone. Research shows that the prefrontal cortex is the primary area of the brain responsible for working memory (Courtney et al., 1997; Rao et al., 1997).

Some of the information in short-term memory makes its way into **long-term memory**. Long-term memory, the type of memory most people are referring to when they use the word "memory," is each individual's vast storehouse of

---

Try It!

6.1 Chunking

Read the following letters individually at the rate of about one per second and then see if you can repeat them.

N-F L-C-B S-U-S A-V-C R-F-B I

Did you have difficulty? Probably so, because there are 15 different letters. Now try this:

NFL CBS USA VCR FBI

Did you find that five chunks are easier to remember than 15 separate items?

Figure 6.1 Characteristics of and Processes Involved in the Three Memory Systems
The three memory systems differ in what and how much they hold and for how long they store it.
(From Peterson & Peterson, 1959.)

permanent or relatively permanent memories. There are no known limits to the storage capacity of long-term memory, and long-term memories can last for years, some of them for a lifetime. Long-term memory holds all the knowledge you have accumulated, the skills you have acquired, and the memories of your past experiences. Information in long-term memory is usually stored in verbal form, although visual images, sounds, and odors can be stored there, as well.

But how did this vast store of information make its way from short-term memory into long-term memory? Sometimes, through mere repetition or rehearsal, a person is able to transfer information into long-term memory. Your teachers may have used a drilling technique to try to cement the multiplication tables and other material in your long-term memory. Another approach is **elaborative rehearsal**. The goal of this strategy is to relate new information to information already in your long-term memory (Symons & Johnson, 1997). For example, you might remember the French word *maison* (house) by relating it to the English word *mansion* (a type of house). Forming such associations, especially if they are personally

relevant, increases your chances of retrieving new information later. Figure 6.1 summarizes the three memory systems.

There are two main subsystems within long-term memory. The first, **declarative memory** (also called *explicit memory*), stores information that can be brought to mind in the form of words or images and then stated, or declared. **Episodic memory** is the part of declarative memory that holds memories of events as they have been subjectively experienced (Wheeler et al., 1997). It is somewhat like a mental diary, recording the episodes of your life—the people you have known, the places you have seen, and the experiences you have had. **Semantic memory**, the second part of declarative memory, is memory for general knowledge, or objective facts and information. In other words, semantic memory is a mental dictionary or encyclopedia of stored knowledge.

The second subsystem of long-term memory, **nondeclarative memory** (also called *implicit memory*), consists of motor skills, habits, and simple classically conditioned responses (Squire et al., 1993). Acquired through repetitive practice, motor skills include such things as eating with a fork, riding a bicycle, and driving a car. Although acquired slowly,

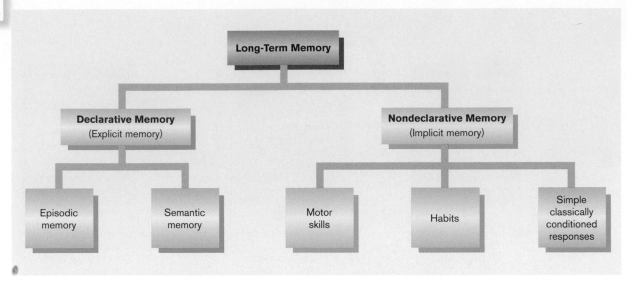

Figure 6.2 Subsystems of Long-Term Memory
Declarative memory can be divided into two parts: episodic memory, which stores memories of personally experienced events, and semantic memory, which stores facts and information. Nondeclarative memory consists of motor skills acquired through repetitive practice, habits, and simple classically conditioned responses.

once learned, these skills become habit, are quite reliable, and can be carried out with little or no conscious effort. Figure 6.2 shows the subsystems of long-term memory.

THE LEVELS-OF-PROCESSING MODEL

Not all psychologists support the notion of three memory systems. Craik and Lockhart (1972) propose instead a **levels-of-processing model**. They suggest that whether people remember an item for a few seconds or a lifetime depends on how deeply they process the information. With the shallowest levels of processing, a person is merely aware of the incoming sensory information. Deeper processing takes place only when the person does something more with the information, such as forming relationships, making associations, attaching meaning to a sensory impression, or engaging in active elaborations on new material. However, the deeper levels of processing that establish a memory also require background knowledge, so that lasting connections can be formed between the person's existing store of knowledge and the new information (Willoughby et al., 2000).

THREE KINDS OF MEMORY TASKS

Psychologists have used three main types of tasks to measure memory retention: recall, recognition, and the relearning method. In **recall**, a person must produce required information by searching memory without the help of **retrieval cues**—the stimuli or bits of information that aid in the retrieval of particular information from long-term memory. Trying to remember someone's name, recalling items on a shopping list, and answering fill-in-the-blank and essay items on exams are all recall tasks. Often, serial recall (recalling items in a certain order) is easier than free recall (recalling items in any order) because in serial recall, each letter, word, or number may serve as a cue for the one that follows. Indeed, research suggests that, in free-recall tasks, order associations are more resistant to distractions than meaningful associations (Howard, 2002).

Recognition is exactly what the word implies. A person simply recognizes something as familiar—a face, a name, a taste, a melody. Recent brain-imaging studies have discovered that the hippocampus plays an extensive role in memory tasks involving recognition, but the degree of hippocampal activity varies for different tasks. When the task is recognizing famous faces, widespread brain activity takes place in both hemispheres, involving the prefrontal and temporal lobes and including the hippocampus and surrounding hippocampal region. Less widespread brain activity is observed during the recognition of recently encoded faces or the encoding of faces seen for the first time (Henson et al., 2002). Studies with monkeys having brain damage limited to the hippocampal region also show that this region is essential for normal recognition tasks (Teng et al., 2000; Zola et al., 2000).

There is yet another way to measure memory retention that is even more sensitive than recognition. With the **relearning method**, or the *savings method*, retention is expressed as the percentage of time saved when material is relearned, compared with the time required to learn the material originally. Suppose it took you 40 minutes to memorize a list of words, and 1 month later you were tested, using recall or recognition. If you could not recall or recognize a single word, would this mean that you had absolutely no memory of anything on the test? Or could it mean that the recall and recognition methods were not sensitive enough to pick up what little information you may have stored? How could a researcher measure a remnant of this former learning? Using the relearning method, a researcher could time how long it took you to relearn the list of words. If it took 20 minutes to relearn the list, this would represent a 50% savings compared to the original learning time of 40 minutes. College students demonstrate the relearning method each semester when they study for comprehensive final exams. Relearning material for a final exam takes less time than it took to learn the material originally.

The Nature of Remembering

MEMORY AS A RECONSTRUCTION

Wilder Penfield (1969), a Canadian neurosurgeon, claimed that experiences leave a "permanent imprint on the brain . . . as though a tape recorder had been receiving it all" (p. 165). Penfield (1975) based this conclusion on observations made while performing more than 1,100 operations on patients with epilepsy. He found that when parts of the temporal lobes were stimulated with an electrical probe, 3.5% of patients reported flashback experiences, as though they were actually reliving parts of their past.

After reviewing Penfield's findings, Ulrich Neisser and other memory researchers (Neisser, 1967) suggested that the experiences the patients reported were "comparable to the content of dreams," rather than the recall of actual experiences (p. 169). Thus, today's memory researchers recognize that memory seldom works like a video cassette recorder, capturing every part of an experience exactly as it happens. Rather a memory is a **reconstruction**—an account pieced together from a few highlights, using information that may or may not be accurate (Loftus & Loftus, 1980). Put another way, remembering "is not so much like reading a book as it is like writing one from fragmentary notes" (Kihlstrom, 1995, p. 341). As a result, memory is quite often inaccurate, and recall is, even for people with the most accurate memories, partly truth and partly fiction.

An early memory researcher, Englishman Sir Frederick Bartlett (1886–1969), suggested that memory is influenced by **schemas**—integrated frameworks of knowledge stored in long-term memory. Schemas aid in processing large amounts of material because they provide frameworks into which people can incorporate new information and experience. For example, if you have taken a course in the past that included discussion of psychoanalytic theory, the information about Freud and other psychoanalysts in Chapter 11 of this book will be easier for you to learn than it will be for students who have no prior knowledge of psychoanalytic theory. Your prior knowledge is organized into schemas that provide "shelves" on which to store the new information.

Schemas can also distort memory, though. When you witness an event, your schemas may cause you to omit some facts about what actually occurred or to add non-factual details. Schema-based distortion can also occur when people alter the memory of an event or an experience in order to fit their beliefs, expectations, logic, or prejudices. The tendency to

Try It!

6.2 Memory Distortion

Read this list of words aloud at a rate of about one word per second. Then close your book, and write down all the words you can remember.

| bed | awake | dream | snooze | nap | snore |
| rest | tired | wake | doze | yawn | slumber |

Now check your list. Did you "remember" the word sleep? Many people do, even though it is not one of the words on the list (Deese, 1959).

distort often causes gross inaccuracies in what people remember. For instance, people often distort memories of their own lives in the positive direction. Bahrick and others (1996) found that 89% of college students accurately remembered the A's they earned in high school, but only 29% accurately recalled the D's. *Try It!* 6.2 demonstrates schema-based memory distortion.

Try It! 6.2 shows that we are very likely to alter or distort what we see or hear to make it fit with what we believe should be true. All the words on the Try It! list are related to sleep, so it seems logical that *sleep* should be one of the words. In experiments using word lists similar to that one, between 40% and 55% of the participants "remembered" the key related word that was not on the list (Roediger & McDermott, 1995). If you "remembered" the word *sleep*, you created a false memory, which probably seemed as real to you as a true memory (Dodson et al., 2000).

EYEWITNESS TESTIMONY

As the story at the beginning of this chapter suggests, eyewitness testimony is highly subject to error. In fact, most memory experts say that it should always be viewed with caution (Loftus, 1979). Nevertheless, it does play a vital role in the U.S. justice system. Says Loftus (1984), "We can't afford to exclude it legally or ignore it as jurors. Sometimes, as in cases of rape, it is the only evidence available, and it is often correct" (p. 24).

Fortunately, eyewitness mistakes can be minimized. Eyewitnesses to crimes often identify suspects from a lineup. If shown photographs of a suspect before viewing the lineup, eyewitnesses may mistakenly identify that suspect in the lineup because the person looks familiar. Research suggests that it is better to have an eyewitness first describe the perpetrator and then search for photos matching that description than to have the eyewitness start by looking through photos and making judgments as to their similarity to the perpetrator (Pryke et al., 2000).

The composition of the lineup is also important. Other individuals in a lineup must resemble the suspect in age and body build and must certainly be of the same race. Even then, if the lineup does not contain the perpetrator, eyewitnesses may identify the person who most closely resembles him or her (Gonzalez et al., 1993). Eyewitnesses are less likely to make errors if a sequential lineup is used, that is, if the participants in the lineup are viewed one after the other, rather than simultaneously (Loftus, 1993a). Some police officers and researchers prefer a "showup"—a procedure that involves presenting only one suspect and having the witness indicate whether that person is the perpetrator. There are fewer misidentifications with a showup, but also more failures in making positive identifications (Wells, 1993).

Eyewitnesses are more likely to identify the wrong person if the person's race is different from their own. According to Egeth (1993), misidentifications are approximately 15% higher in cross-race than in same-race identifications. Misidentification is also somewhat more likely to occur when a weapon is used in a crime. The witnesses may pay more attention to the weapon than to the physical characteristics of the criminal (Steblay, 1992).

Even questioning witnesses after a crime can influence what they later remember. Because leading questions can substantially change a witness's memory of an event, it is critical that the interviewers ask neutral questions (Leichtman & Ceci, 1995). Misleading information supplied to the witness after the event can result in erroneous recollections of the actual event, a phenomenon known as the *misinformation effect* (Kroll et al., 1988; Loftus & Hoffman, 1989). Loftus (1997) and her students have conducted "more than 20 experiments involving over 20,000 participants that document how exposure to misinformation induces memory distortion" (p. 71). Furthermore, after eyewitnesses have repeatedly recalled information, whether accurate or inaccurate, they become even more confident when they testify in court because the information is so easily retrieved (Shaw, 1996). And the confidence eyewitnesses have in their testimony is not necessarily an indication of its accuracy (Loftus, 1993a; Sporer et al., 1995). In fact, eyewitnesses who perceive themselves to be more objective have more confidence in their testimony, regardless of its accuracy, and they are more likely to include incorrect information in their verbal descriptions (Geiselman et al., 2000).

RECOVERING REPRESSED MEMORIES

Perhaps because of the frequency of such cases in novels, on television, and in movies, recent studies have found that many people in the United States believe that unconscious memories of abuse can lead to serious psychological disorders (Stafford & Lynn, 2002). Such beliefs have also been fostered by self-help books such as *The Courage to Heal*, published in 1988, by Ellen Bass and Laura Davis. This best-selling book became the "bible" for sex abuse victims and the leading "textbook" for some therapists who specialized in treating them. Bass and Davis not only sought to help survivors who remembered having suffered sexual abuse, but also reached out to people who had no memory of any sexual abuse and tried to help them determine whether they might have been abused. These authors suggested that "if you are unable to remember any specific instances . . . but still have a feeling that something abusive happened to you, it probably did" (p. 21). They offered a definite conclusion: "If you think you were abused and your life shows the symptoms, then you were" (p. 22). And they freed potential victims of sexual abuse from the responsibility of establishing any proof: "You are not responsible for proving that you were abused" (p. 37).

However, many psychologists are skeptical, claiming that the "recovered" memories are actually false memories created by the suggestions of therapists. Critics point out that numerous studies have shown that traumatic memories are rarely, if ever, repressed (e.g., Bowers & Farvolden, 1996; Merckelbach et al., 2003). Moreover, they maintain that "when it comes to a serious trauma, intrusive thoughts and memories of it are the most characteristic reaction" (p. 359). According to Loftus (1993b), "the therapist convinces the patient with no memories that abuse is likely, and the patient obligingly uses reconstructive strategies to generate memories that would support that conviction" (p. 528). Repressed-memory therapists believe, however, that healing hinges on their patients' being able to recover the repressed memories.

Critics further charge that recovered memories of sexual abuse are suspect because of the techniques therapists usually use to uncover them: hypnosis and guided imagery. As you have learned, hypnosis does not improve the accuracy of memory, only the confidence that what one remembers is accurate.

Can merely imagining experiences lead people to believe that those experiences actually happened to them? Yes, according to some studies. Many research participants who are instructed to imagine that a fictitious event happened do, in fact, develop a false memory of the imagined event (Hyman & Pentland, 1996; Hyman et al., 1995; Loftus & Pickrell, 1995; Worthen & Wood, 2001).

False childhood memories can also be experimentally induced. Garry and Loftus (1994) were able to implant a false memory of being lost in a shopping mall at 5 years of age in 25% of participants aged 18 to 53, after verification of the fictitious experience by a relative. Repeated exposure to suggestions of false memories can create those memories (Zaragoza & Mitchell, 1996).

Critics are especially skeptical of recovered memories of events that occurred in the first few years of life. The hippocampus, which is vital in the formation of episodic memories, is not fully developed then, and neither are the areas of the cortex where memories are stored (Squire et al., 1993). Furthermore, young children, who are still limited in language ability, do not store memories in categories that are accessible to adults. Accordingly, Widom and Morris (1997) found that memories of abuse are better when the victimization took place between the ages of 7 and 17 than when it occurred in the first 6 years of life.

The American Psychological Association (1994), the American Psychiatric Association (1993c), and the American Medical Association (1994) have issued status reports on memories of childhood abuse. The position of all three groups is that current evidence supports the possibilities that repressed memories exist *and* that false memories can be constructed in response to suggestions of abuse. This position suggests that recovered memories of abuse should be verified independently before they are accepted as facts. Taking such a position is critically important. As you saw in *Try It!* 6.2, false memories are easily formed. And, once formed, they are often relied on with great confidence (Dodson et al., 2000; Henkel et al., 2000).

FLASHBULB MEMORIES

We probably all remember where we were and what we were doing when we heard about the tragic events of September 11, 2001. This type of extremely vivid memory is called a **flashbulb memory** (Bohannon, 1988). Brown and Kulik (1977) suggest that a flashbulb memory is formed when a person learns of an event that is very surprising, shocking, and highly emotional. You might have a flashbulb memory of receiving the news of the death or serious injury of a close family member or a friend.

Several studies suggest that flashbulb memories are not as accurate as people believe them to be. Neisser and Harsch (1992) questioned university freshmen about the Challenger disaster the morning after the space shuttle exploded in 1986. When the same students were questioned again 3 years later, one-third gave accounts that differed markedly from those given initially, even though they were extremely confident of their recollections. Further, flashbulb memories appear to be forgotten at about the same rate and in the same ways as other kinds of memories (Curci et al., 2001).

MEMORY AND CULTURE

Sir Frederick Bartlett (1932) believed that some impressive memory abilities operate within a social or cultural context and cannot be understood as a pure process. He stated that "both the manner and matter of recall are often predominantly determined by social influences" (p. 244). Studying memory in a cultural context, Bartlett (1932) described the amazing ability of the Swazi people of Africa to remember the slight differences in individual characteristics of their cows. One Swazi herdsman, Bartlett claimed, could remember details of every cow he had tended the year before. Such a feat is less surprising when you consider that the key component of traditional Swazi culture is the herds of cattle the people tend and depend on for their living. Do the Swazi people have superior memory powers? Bartlett asked young Swazi men and young European men to recall a message consisting of 25 words. The Swazi had no better recall ability than the Europeans.

Among many of the tribal peoples in Africa, the history of the tribe is preserved orally. Thus, an oracle, or specialist, must be able to encode, store, and retrieve huge volumes of historical data (D'Azevedo, 1982). Elders of the Iatmul people of New Guinea are also said to have committed to memory the lines of descent for the various clans of their people stretching back for many generations (Bateson, 1982). The unerring memories of the elders for these kinship patterns are used to resolve disputed property claims (Mistry & Rogoff, 1994).

Barbara Rogoff, an expert in cultural psychology, maintains that such phenomenal, prodigious memory feats are best explained and understood in their cultural context (Rogoff & Mistry, 1985). The tribal elders perform their impressive memory feats because it is an integral and critically important part of the culture in which they live. Most likely, their ability to remember lists of nonsense syllables would be no better than your own.

Studies examining memory for locations among a tribal group in India, the Asur, who do not use artificial lighting of any kind, provide further information about the influence of culture on memory (Mishra & Singh, 1992). Researchers hypothesized that members of this group would perform better on tests of memory for locations than on conventional tasks used by memory researchers. This is because, lacking artificial lights, the Asur have to remember locations so that they can move around in the dark without bumping into things. When the Asur people were tested, they did indeed remember locations better than word pairs.

In classic research, cognitive psychologists have also found that people more easily remember stories set in their own culture than those set in others. In one of the first of these studies, researchers told a story about a sick child to women in the United States and to Aboriginal women in Australia (Steffensen & Calker, 1982). Participants were randomly assigned to groups for whom story outcomes were varied. In one version, the girl got well after being treated by a physician. In the other, a traditional native healer was called in to help the girl. Aboriginal participants better recalled the story with the native healer, and American participants were more accurate in their recall of the story in which a physician treated the girl.

Factors Influencing Retrieval

THE SERIAL POSITION EFFECT

If you were introduced to a dozen people at a party, you would most likely recall the names of the first few individuals you met and the last one or two, but forget many of the names of those in between. The reason is the **serial position effect**—the finding that, for information learned in sequence, recall is better for items at the beginning and the end than for items in the middle of the sequence.

Information at the beginning of a sequence is subject to the **primacy effect**—it is likely to be recalled because it already has been placed in long-term memory. Information at the end of a sequence is subject to the **recency effect**—it has an even higher probability of being recalled because it is still in short-term memory. The poorer recall of information in the middle of a sequence occurs because that information is no longer in short-term memory and has not yet been placed in long-term

memory. The serial position effect lends strong support to the notion of separate systems for short-term and long-term memory (Postman & Phillips, 1965).

ENVIRONMENTAL CONTEXT AND MEMORY

Have you ever stood in your living room and thought of something you needed from your bedroom, only to forget what it was when you got there? Did the item come to mind when you returned to the living room? Tulving and Thompson (1973) suggest that many elements of the physical setting in which a person learns information are encoded along with the information and become part of the memory. If part or all of the original context is reinstated, it may serve as a retrieval cue. That is why returning to the living room elicits the memory of the object you intended to get from the bedroom. In fact, just visualizing yourself in the living room might do the trick (Smith, 1979). (Next time you're taking a test and having difficulty recalling something, try visualizing yourself in the room where you studied!)

Godden and Baddeley (1975) conducted one of the early studies of context and memory with members of a university scuba diving club. Participants memorized a list of words when they were either 10 feet underwater or on land. They were later tested for recall of the words in the same or in a different environment. Words learned underwater were best recalled underwater, and words learned on land were best recalled on land. In fact, when the scuba divers learned and recalled the words in the same context, their scores were 47% higher than when the two contexts were different. More recent studies have found similar context effects (e.g., Bjorklund et al., 2000).

Odors can also supply powerful and enduring retrieval cues for memory. In a study by Morgan (1996), participants were placed in isolated cubicles and exposed to a list of 40 words. They were instructed to perform a cognitive task using the words but were not asked to remember them. Then, back in the cubicle 5 days later, participants were unexpectedly tested for recall of the 40 words. Experimental participants who experienced a pleasant odor during the initial task and again when tested 5 days later had significantly higher recall than control participants who did not experience the odor at either time.

THE STATE-DEPENDENT MEMORY EFFECT

People tend to recall information better if they are in the same internal emotional state as they were when the information was encoded; psychologists call this the **state-dependent memory effect**. Anxiety appears to affect memory more than other emotions. For example, when researchers exposed college students to spiders and/or snakes while they were learning lists of words, the students recalled more words when the creatures were also present during tests of recall (Lang et al., 2001).

Adults who are clinically depressed tend to recall more of their negative life experiences (Clark & Teasdale, 1982) and are likely to remember their parents being unloving and rejecting (Lewinsohn & Rosenbaum, 1987). Moreover, a review of 48 studies revealed a significant relationship between depression and memory impairment. Recognition and recall were more impaired in younger depressed patients than in older ones (Burt et al., 1995). But as depression lifts, the tendency toward negative recall and the memory impairment reverse themselves.

Biology and Memory

BRAIN DAMAGE

Researchers are finding specific locations in the brain that house and mediate functions and processes in memory. One important source of information comes from people who have suffered memory loss resulting from damage to specific brain areas. One especially important case is that of H.M., a man who suffered from such severe epilepsy that, out of desperation, he agreed to a radical surgical procedure. The surgeon removed the part of H.M.'s brain believed to be causing his seizures, the medial portions of both temporal lobes—the amygdala and the **hippocampal region**, which includes the hippocampus itself and the underlying cortical areas. It was 1953, and H.M. was 27 years old.

After his surgery, H.M. remained intelligent and psychologically stable, and his seizures were drastically reduced. But unfortunately, the tissue cut from H.M.'s brain housed more than the site of his seizures. It also contained his ability to use working memory to store new information in long-term memory. Though the capacity of his short-term memory remained the same, and he remembers the events of his life stored well before the operation, H.M. suffers from **anterograde amnesia**. He has not been able to remember a single event that has occurred since the surgery. And though H.M. turned 75 in 2001, as far as his conscious long-term memory is concerned, it was still 1953 and he was still 27 years old.

Surgery affected only H.M.'s declarative, long-term memory—his ability to store facts, personal experiences, names, faces, telephone numbers, and the like. But researchers were surprised to discover that he could still form nondeclarative memories; that is, he could still acquire skills through repetitive practice although he could not remember having done so. For example, since the surgery, H.M. has learned to play tennis and improve his game, but he has no memory of ever having played. (Adapted from Milner, 1966, 1970; Milner et al., 1968.)

Animal studies support the conclusion that the parts of H.M.'s brain that were removed are critical to the functioning of short-term memory (Ragozzino et al., 2002). Moreover, other patients who have suffered similar brain damage show the same types of memory loss (Squire, 1992). Recent research supports the hypothesis that the hippocampus is especially important in forming episodic memories (Eichenbaum, 1997; Gluck & Myers, 1997; Spiers et al., 2001). Semantic memory, however, depends not only on the hippocampus, but also on other parts of the hippocampal region underlying it (Vargha-Khadem et al., 1997). Consequently, many researchers argue that neurological bases for episodic and semantic memory are entirely separate (e.g., Tulving, 2002).

One interesting study (Maguire et al., 2000) suggests that the hippocampus may also support navigational skills by helping to create intricate neural spatial maps. MRI scans revealed that the rear (posterior) region of the hippocampus of

London taxi drivers was significantly larger than that of participants in a matched control group whose living did not depend on navigational skills. In addition, the longer the time spent as a taxi driver, the greater the volume of the posterior hippocampus. Similarly, in many birds and small mammals, the volume of the hippocampus increases seasonally, as navigational skills for migration and spatial maps showing where food is hidden become critical for survival (Clayton, 1998; Colombo & Broadbent, 2000). Moreover, animal studies show that the hippocampus also plays an important role in the reorganization of previously learned spatial information (Lee & Kesner, 2002).

NEURONAL CHANGES IN MEMORY

The first close look at the nature of memory in single neurons was provided by Eric Kandel and his colleagues, who traced the effects of learning and memory in the sea snail *Aplysia* (Dale & Kandel, 1990). Using tiny electrodes implanted in several single neurons in the sea snail, the researchers mapped the neural circuits that are formed and maintained as the animal learns and remembers. They also discovered the different types of protein synthesis that facilitate short-term and long-term memory (Sweatt & Kandel, 1989). Kandel won a Nobel Prize in 2000 for his work. But the studies of learning and memory in *Aplysia* reflect only simple classical conditioning, which forms a type of nondeclarative memory. Other researchers studying mammals report that physical changes occur in the neurons and synapses in regions of the brain involved in declarative memory (Lee & Kesner, 2002).

Most neuroscientists believe that **long-term potentiation (LTP)**—an increase in the efficiency of neural transmission at the synapses that lasts for hours or longer—is the physiological process that underlies the formation of memories (Bliss & Lomo, 2000; Martinez & Derrick, 1996; Nguyen et al., 1994). (To potentiate means "to make potent or to strengthen.") Research demonstrating that blocking LTP interferes with learning supports their hypothesis. For instance, Davis and colleagues (1992) gave rats enough of a drug that blocks certain receptors to interfere with their performance in a maze-running task and discovered that LTP in the hippocampus of the rats was also disrupted. In contrast, Riedel (1996) found that LTP is enhanced and memory is improved when a drug that excites those same receptors is administered to rats shortly after maze training.

HORMONES AND MEMORY

The strongest and most lasting memories are usually those fueled by emotion. Research by Cahill and McGaugh (1995) suggests that there may be two pathways for forming memories—one for ordinary information and another for memories that are fired by emotion. When a person is emotionally aroused, the adrenal glands release the hormones adrenalin (epinephrine) and noradrenaline (norepinephrine) into the bloodstream. Long known to be involved in the "fight or flight" response, these hormones enable humans to survive, and they also help to establish powerful and enduring memories of the circumstances surrounding threatening situations. Such emotionally laden memories activate the amygdala (known to play a central role in emotion) and other parts of the memory system. Emotional memories are lasting memories, and this may be the most important factor in explaining the intensity and durability of flashbulb memories.

Other hormones may have important effects on memory. Excessive levels of the stress hormone *cortisol*, for example, have been shown to interfere with memory in patients who suffer from diseases of the adrenal glands, the site of cortisol production (Jelicic & Bonke, 2001). Furthermore, people whose bodies react to experimenter-induced stressors, such as forced public speaking, by releasing higher-than-average levels of cortisol perform less well on memory tests than those whose bodies release lower-than-average levels in the same situations (Al'absi et al., 2002).

Forgetting

EBBINGHAUS AND THE FIRST EXPERIMENTAL STUDIES ON FORGETTING

Hermann Ebbinghaus (1850–1909) conducted the first experimental studies on learning and memory. He (1885/1964) conducted his studies on memory using 2,300 *nonsense syllables*—combinations of letters that can be pronounced but have no meaning, such as LEJ, XIZ, LUK, and ZOH—as his material and himself as the only participant. He carried out all of his experiments at about the same time of day in the same surroundings, eliminating all possible distractions. Ebbinghaus memorized lists of nonsense syllables by repeating them over and over at a constant rate of 2.5 syllables per second, marking time with a metronome or a ticking watch. He repeated a list until he could recall it twice without error, a point that he called *mastery*.

Ebbinghaus recorded the amount of time or the number of trials it took to memorize his lists to mastery. Then, after different periods of time had passed and forgetting had occurred to some extent, he recorded the amount of time or number of trials needed to relearn the same list to mastery. Ebbinghaus compared the time or trials required for relearning with those of the original learning and then computed the percentage of time saved—the *savings score*. The percentage of savings represented the percentage of the original learning that remained in memory.

Ebbinghaus learned and relearned more than 1,200 lists of nonsense syllables to discover how rapidly forgetting occurs. His famous *curve of forgetting*, which consists of savings scores at various time intervals after the original learning. The curve of forgetting shows that the largest amount of forgetting occurs very quickly, but after that forgetting tapers off. If Ebbinghaus retained information as long as a day or two, very little more of it would be forgotten even a month later. When researchers measured psychology students' retention of names and concepts, they found that the pattern of forgetting was similar to Ebbinghaus's curve. Forgetting of names and concepts was rapid over the first several months, leveled off in approximately 36 months, and remained about the same for the next 7 years (Conway et al., 1991).

THE CAUSES OF FORGETTING

There are many reasons why people fail to remember. Often, however, when people say they cannot remember, they have not actually forgotten. Instead, the inability to remember may be a result of **encoding failure**—the fact that the information never entered long-term memory in the first place. For example, when you do *Try It! 6.3*, you might think you have "forgotten" what a penny looks like.

In your lifetime you have seen thousands of pennies, but unless you are a coin collector, you probably have not encoded the details of a penny's appearance. If you did poorly on the *Try It!*, you have plenty of company. After studying a large group of participants, Nickerson and Adams (1979) reported that few people could reproduce a penny from recall. In fact, only a handful of participants could even recognize a drawing of a real penny when it was presented along with incorrect drawings. (The correct penny is the one labeled A in the *Try It!*)

Decay theory, probably the oldest theory of forgetting, assumes that memories, if not used, fade with time and ultimately disappear entirely. The term *decay* implies a change in the "neural trace" or physiological record, of the experience. According to this theory, the neural trace may decay or fade within seconds, days, or much longer periods of time. Most psychologists now accept the notion of decay, or fading of the neural trace, as a cause of forgetting in sensory and short-term memory but not in long-term memory. There

Try It!

6.3 Penny for Your Memories

On a sheet of paper, draw a sketch of a U.S. penny from memory, using recall. In your drawing, show the direction in which President Lincoln's image is facing and the location of the date, and include all the words on the "heads" side of the penny. Or try the easier recognition task and see if you can recognize the real penny in the drawings below. (From Nickerson & Adams, 1979.)

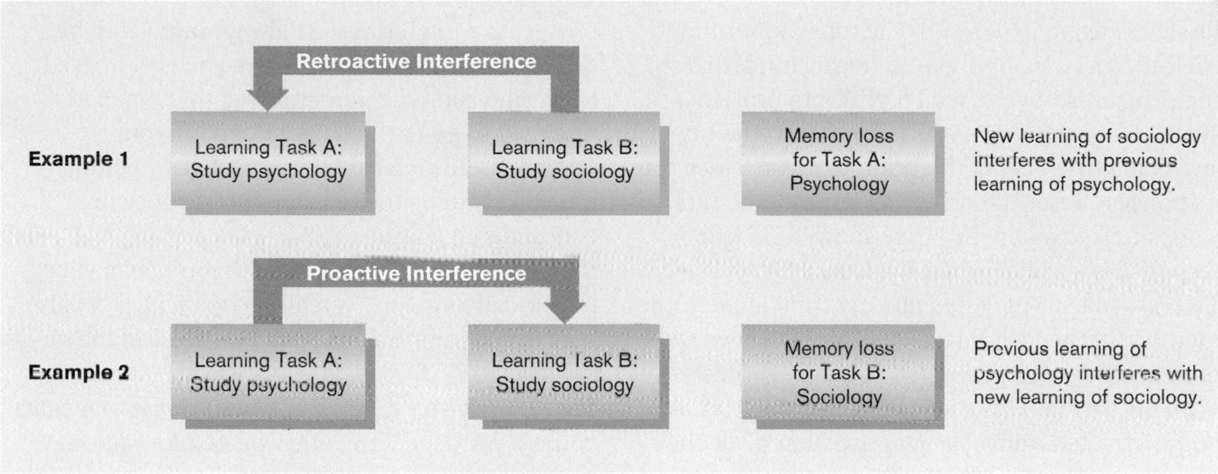

Figure 6.3 Retroactive and Proactive Interference
As shown in Example 1, retroactive interference occurs when new learning hinders the ability to recall information learned previously. As shown in Example 2, proactive interference occurs when prior learning hinders new learning.

does not appear to be a gradual, inevitable decay of the long-term memory trace. In one study, Harry Bahrick and others (1975) found that after 35 years, participants could recognize 90% of their high school classmates' names and photographs—the same percentage as for recent graduates.

A major cause of forgetting that affects people every day is **interference**. Whenever you try to recall any given memory, two types of interference can hinder the effort, as shown in Figure 6.3. *Proactive interference* occurs when information or experiences already stored in long-term memory hinder the ability to remember newer information (Underwood, 1957). For example, Isabel's romance with her new boyfriend, José, got off to a bad start when she accidentally called him Dave, her former boyfriend's name. *Retroactive interference* happens when new learning interferes with the ability to remember previously learned information. The more similar the new learning is to the previous learning, the more interference there is. For example, when you take a psychology class, it may interfere with your ability to remember what you learned in your sociology class, especially with regard to theories (for example, psychoanalytic theory) that are shared by the two disciplines but applied and interpreted differently. To minimize interference, you can

follow a learning activity with sleep and arrange learning time so that you do not study similar subjects back to back.

Recall from earlier in the chapter that *consolidation* is the process by which encoded information is stored in memory. When a disruption in this process occurs, a long-term memory usually does not form. **Consolidation failure** can result from anything that causes a person to lose consciousness—a car accident, intoxication, a blow to the head, a grand mal seizure, or an electroconvulsive shock treatment given for severe depression. Memory loss of the experiences that occurred shortly before the loss of consciousness is called **retrograde amnesia**.

Nader and a team of researchers (Nader et al., 2000) demonstrated that conditioned fears in rats can be erased by infusing into the rats' brains a drug that prevents protein synthesis (such synthesis is necessary for memory consolidation). Rats experienced a single pairing of a tone (the conditioned stimulus) and a foot shock (the unconditioned stimulus). Later, the rats were exposed to the sound of the tone alone (the conditioned stimulus) and showed a fear response of "freezing" (becoming totally immobile as if paralyzed by fright). Clearly, the rats remembered the feared stimulus. Twenty-four hours later, the rats were again exposed to the tone alone, and it elicited fear, causing them to freeze. Immediately, the drug anisomycin, which prevents protein synthesis in the brain, was infused into the rats' amygdala (the part of the brain that processes fear responses). After the drug was infused, the rats were shocked again, but they showed no fear response (freezing) when the tone was sounded. The rats in the study had already consolidated the memory of the fear, but it was completely wiped out after the drug prevented protein synthesis from occurring. This means that fear memories, once activated, must be "reconsolidated," or they may disappear. This finding has positive implications. If fear memories can be activated and then wiped out with drugs that prevent protein synthesis, a new therapy may be on the horizon for people who suffer from debilitating fears (Nader et al., 2000).

Of course, there are occasions when people may prefer to avoid remembering—times when they want to forget. Earlier in the chapter, we discussed the possibility that people may repress memories of traumatic events. But even people who have not suffered severe trauma use **motivated forgetting** to protect themselves from experiences that are painful, frightening, or otherwise unpleasant. With one form of motivated forgetting, known as *suppression*, a person makes a conscious, active attempt to put a painful, disturbing, or anxiety- or guilt-provoking memory out of mind, but the person is still aware that the event occurred. With another type of motivated forgetting— **repression**—unpleasant memories are literally removed from consciousness, and the person is no longer aware that the unpleasant event ever occurred (Freud, 1922). People who have **amnesia** (memory loss) that is not due to loss of consciousness or brain damage have repressed the events they no longer remember.

Prospective forgetting, forgetting to carry out some intended action—such as going to your dentist appointment—is another type of motivated forgetting. People are most likely to forget to do the things they view as unimportant, unpleasant, or burdensome. They are less likely to forget things that are pleasurable or important to them (Winograd, 1988). However, as you probably know,

prospective forgetting isn't always motivated by a desire to avoid something. Have you ever arrived home and suddenly remembered that you had intended to go to the bank to deposit your paycheck? In such cases, prospective forgetting is more likely to be the result of interference or consolidation failure.

Endel Tulving (1974) claims that much of what people call forgetting is really an inability to locate the needed information in memory—as in the *tip-of-the-tongue (TOT) phenomenon* (Brown & McNeil, 1966). Surely you have experienced trying to recall a name, a word, or some other bit of information, knowing what you are searching for almost as well as your own name. You're on the verge of recalling the word or name, perhaps aware of the number of syllables and the beginning or ending letter of the word. It's on the tip of your tongue, but it just won't quite come out.

IMPROVING MEMORY

Organizing material to be learned is a tremendous aid to memory. One way of organizing a textbook chapter is to make an outline; another is to associate important concepts with the psychologists who proposed or discovered them. You can prove the value of organization as a memory strategy by completing *Try It!* 6.4.

Do you still remember the words to songs that were popular when you were in high school? Can you recite many of the nursery rhymes you learned as a child even though you haven't heard them in years? You probably can because of **overlearning**. Research suggests that people remember material better and longer if they overlearn it—that is, if they practice or study beyond the minimum needed to barely learn it (Ebbinghaus, 1885/1964). A pioneering study in overlearning by Krueger (1929) showed substantial long-term gains for participants who engaged in 50% and 100% overlearning (see Figure 6.4). Furthermore, overlearning makes material more resistant to interference and is perhaps the best insurance against stress-related forgetting. So, the next time you study for a test, don't stop studying as soon as you think you know the material. Spend another hour or so going over it, and you will be surprised at how much more you will remember.

Try It!

6.4 Organizing for Memory Improvement

Have a pencil and a sheet of paper handy. Read the following list of items out loud and then write down as many as you can remember.

peas	shaving cream	cookies
toilet paper	fish	grapes
carrots	apples	bananas
ice cream	pie	ham
onions	perfume	chicken

If you organize this list, the items are much easier to remember. Now read each category heading and the items listed beneath it. Write down as many items as you can remember.

Desserts	Fruits	Vegetables	Meat	Toilet Articles
pie	bananas	carrots	chicken	perfume
ice cream	apples	onions	fish	shaving cream
cookies	grapes	peas	ham	toilet paper

Most students have tried cramming for examinations, but spacing study over several different sessions is generally more effective than **massed practice**—learning in one long practice session without rest periods (Glover & Corkill, 1987). You will remember more from less total study time if you space your study over several sessions. Long periods of memorizing make material particularly subject to interference and often result in fatigue and lowered concentration. Also, when you space your practice, you probably create a new memory that may be stored in a different place, thus increasing your chance for recall. The spacing effect applies to learning motor skills as well as to learning facts and information. Music students can tell you that it is better to practice for half an hour each day, every day, than to practice many hours in a row once a week.

Many students simply read and reread their textbook and notes when they study for an exam. Research over many years shows that you will recall more if you increase the amount of recitation you use as you study. For example, it is better to read a page or a few paragraphs and then recite what you have just read. Then continue reading, stop and recite again, and so on. In a classic study, A. I. Gates (1917) tested groups of students who spent the same amount of time in study, but who spent different percentages of that time in recitation and rereading. Participants recalled two to three times more if they increased their recitation time up to 80% and spent only 20% of their study time rereading.

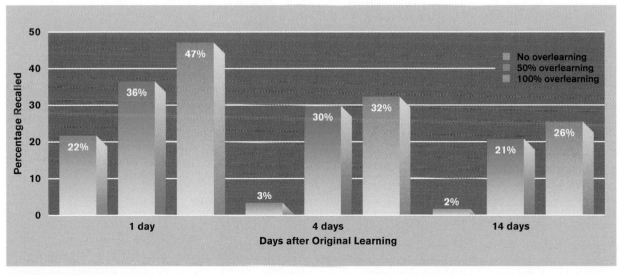

Figure 6.4 Overlearning

When a person learns material only to the point of one correct repetition, forgetting is very rapid. Just 22% is retained after 1 day, 3% after 4 days, and 2% after 14 days. When participants spend 50% more time going over the material, the retention increases to 36% after 1 day, 30% after 4 days, and 21% after 14 days. (Data from Krueger, 1929.)

GLOSSARY

Encoding — Transforming information into a form that can be stored in short-term or long-term memory.

Storage — IThe act of maintaining information in memory.

Retrieval — The act of bringing to mind material that has been stored in memory.

Consolidation — A physiological change in the brain that must take place for encoded information to be stored in memory.

Sensory Memory — The memory system that holds information coming in through the senses for a period ranging from a fraction of a second to several seconds.

Short-term Memory — The memory system that holds about seven (a range from five to nine) items for less than 30 seconds without rehearsal; also called *working memory* because it is the mental workspace for tasks being thought about at any given moment.

Displacement — The phenomenon that occurs when short-term memory is holding its maximum amount of information and each new item entering short-term memory pushes out an existing item.

Rehearsal — The act of purposely repeating information in order to maintain it in short-term memory or to transfer it to long-term memory.

Long-term Memory — The relatively permanent memory system with a virtually unlimited capacity.

Elaborative Rehearsal — A technique used to encode information into long-term memory by considering its meaning and associating it with other information already stored in long-term memory.

Declarative Memory — The subsystem within long-term memory that stores facts, information, and personal life experiences; also called *explicit memory*.

Episodic Memory — (ep-ih-SOD-ik) The part of declarative memory that contains memories of personally experienced events.

Semantic Memory — The part of declarative memory that holds general knowledge; a mental encyclopedia or dictionary.

Nondeclarative Memory — The subsystem within long-term memory that consists of skills acquired through repetitive practice, habits, and simple classically conditioned responses; also called implicit memory.

Levels-of-Processing Model — A model of memory as a single system in which retention depends on how deeply information is processed.

Recall — A measure of retention that requires a person to remember material with few or no retrieval cues, as in an essay test.

Retrieval Cue — Any stimulus or bit of information that aids in the retrieval of a particular memory from long-term memory.

Recognition — A measure of retention that requires a person to identify material as familiar, or as having been encountered before.

Relearning Method — A way of measuring memory retention in terms of the percentage of time saved in relearning material compared with the time required to learn it originally; also called the *savings method*.

Reconstruction — An account that is not an exact replica of a remembered event but has been pieced together from a few highlights, using information that may or may not be accurate.

Schemas — The integrated frameworks of knowledge about people, objects, and events, which are stored in long-term memory and affect the encoding and recall of information.

Flashbulb Memory — An extremely vivid memory of the conditions surrounding one's first hearing the news of a surprising, shocking, or highly emotional event.

```
         Southwest Minn State
        320 North O'Connell St
          Marshall, MN 56258
            507-337-1450

     Barnes & Noble Campus Store

STORE:00210    REG:001    TRAN#:8650
CASHIER.MELISSA M

HOLSCHU/EFFECTIVE
*USED*
2900205750138           N
(1 @ 57.75)                      57.75
LS Tee XL
045171274539            N
(1 @ 21.98)
PROMO New Price
(1 @ 16.48)                      16.48
TOTAL                            74.23
ATM DEBIT                        74.23
   Card#   XXXXXXXXXXXX9889


Amount Saved                      5.50


        www.whywaitforbooks.com

V200.65          08/30/2012  02:27PM
```

```
             CUSTOMER COPY
```

- Without a receipt, a store credit will be issued at the selling price.
- Cash back on merchandise credits or gift cards will not exceed
- No refunds on gift cards, prepaid cards, phone cards, newspapers, or magazines.
- Merchandise must be in original condition.

Fair Pricing Policy

Barnes & Noble College Booksellers comply with local weights & measures requirements. If the price on your receipt is above the advertised or posted price, please alert a bookseller and we will gladly refund the difference.

REFUND POLICY

TEXTBOOKS:

- A full refund will be given in your original form of payment if textbooks are returned during the first week of classes with original receipt.
- With proof of a schedule change and original receipt, a full refund will be given in your original form of payment during the first 30 days of classes.
- No refunds on unwrapped loose leaf books or activated eBooks.
- Textbooks must be in original condition.
- No refunds or exchanges without original receipt.

GENERAL READING BOOKS, SOFTWARE, AUDIO, VIDEO & SMALL ELECTRONICS

- A full refund will be given in your original form of payment if merchandise is returned within 14 days of purchase with original receipt.
- Opened software, audio books, DVDs, CDs, music, and small electronics may not be returned. They can be exchanged for the same item if defective.
- Merchandise must be in original condition.
- No refunds or exchanges without original receipt.

ALL OTHER MERCHANDISE

- A full refund will be given in your original form of payment with original receipt.
- Without a receipt, a store credit will be issued at the current selling price.
- Cash back on merchandise credits or gift cards will not exceed $1.
- No refunds on gift cards, prepaid cards, phone cards, newspapers, or magazines.
- Merchandise must be in original condition.

Fair Pricing Policy

Barnes & Noble College Booksellers comply with local weights & measures requirements. If the price on your receipt is above the advertised or posted price, please alert a bookseller and we will gladly refund the difference.

GLOSSARY Continued

Serial Position Effect — The tendency to remember the beginning and ending items of a sequence or list better than the middle items.

Primacy Effect — The tendency to recall the first items on a list more readily than the middle items.

Recency Effect — The tendency to recall the last items on a list more readily than those in the middle of the list.

State-Dependent Memory Effect — The tendency to recall information better if one is in the same psychological state (mood) as when the information was encoded.

Hippocampal Region — A part of the brain's limbic system, which includes the hippocampus itself (primarily involved in the formation of episodic memories) and its underlying cortical areas (involved in the formation of semantic memories).

Anterograde Amnesia — The inability to form long-term memories of events occurring after a brain injury or brain surgery (although memories formed before the trauma are usually intact).

Long-Term Potentiation (LTP) — A long-lasting increase in the efficiency of neural transmission at the synapses.

Encoding Failure — A breakdown in the process by which information enters long-term memory, which results in an inability to recall the information.

Decay Theory — A theory of forgetting that holds that the neural trace, if not used, disappears with the passage of time.

Interference — Memory loss that occurs because information or associations stored either before or after a given memory hinder the ability to recall it.

Consolidation Failure — Any disruption in the consolidation process that prevents a permanent memory from forming.

Retrograde Amnesia — (RET-ro-grade) A loss of memory affecting experiences that occurred shortly before a loss of consciousness.

Motivated Forgetting — Forgetting through repression in order to protect oneself from a memory that is too painful, anxiety- or guilt-producing, or otherwise unpleasant.

Repression — Removing from one's consciousness disturbing, guilt-provoking, or otherwise unpleasant memories so that one is no longer aware that a painful event occurred.

Amnesia — A partial or complete loss of memory resulting from brain trauma or psychological trauma.

Prospective Forgetting — Forgetting to carry out some action, such as mailing a letter

Overlearning — Practicing or studying material beyond the point where it can be repeated once without error.

Massed Practice — Learning in one long practice session, as opposed to spacing the learning in shorter practice sessions over an extended period.

Appendix B

Source: Teresa Audesirk, Gerald Audesirk & Bruce E. Byers, *Life on Earth, 5/e*

Chapter 21
Nutrition, Digestion, and Excretion

At a Glance

CASE STUDY DYING TO BE THIN

Former supermodel Carré Otis explains, "The sacrifices I made were life threatening. I had entered a world that seemed to support a 'whatever it takes' mentality to maintain abnormal thinness." For many models, performers, and others in the public eye, meeting expectations for thinness is a continuing battle that can lead to eating disorders. At 5 feet 10 inches, Otis once weighed only 100 pounds, giving her a body mass index (BMI) of 14.3. (The World Health Organization considers a BMI below 16 as "starvation.") Now maintaining a healthy weight—at the expense of her modeling career—Otis has become a spokesperson for the National Eating Disorders Association, hoping that she can help others avoid the damage her body suffered.

Otis suffered from two eating disorders, anorexia and bulimia. People with anorexia typically eat very little, and often exercise almost nonstop in an effort to lose still more weight. About half of all anorexics also develop bulimia—binge eating of relatively large amounts of food, followed by self-induced vomiting or overdosing with laxatives to purge the food from their bodies. Anorexics lose muscle mass and often damage their digestive, cardiac, endocrine, and reproductive systems.

Sometimes, the damage proves fatal. In October 2006, Ana Carolina Reston (photo at left), one of Brazil's leading models, was hospitalized for a kidney malfunction. After three weeks in intensive care, she died from multiple organ failure and septicemia (massive infection throughout the bloodstream). At 5 feet 8 inches and 88 pounds, her BMI was only 13.4. Two other extremely thin models, the Uruguayan sisters Luisel and Eliana Ramos, died in 2006 and 2007, respectively, from heart failure probably brought on by anorexia.

Anorexia and bulimia typically strike teenage girls and women in their 20s, who often feel pressured to conform to unrealistic ideals of body size and shape. Because many people with anorexia or bulimia never consult a physician, no one really knows how common these disorders might be. In the United States, health authorities estimate that between 200,000 and a few million people, mostly young women, suffer from anorexia, bulimia, or other eating disorders.

In this chapter, you will learn about the processes of nutrition, digestion, and excretion. As you do, think about how anorexia and bulimia affect the structures and functions of the digestive and urinary tracts. Besides not enough Calories, what specific nutrients might be missing from a "starvation" diet? Why would anorexia and bulimia damage many organs throughout the body? Why are anorexics at risk for heart attacks?

21.1 How Do Animals Regulate the Composition of Their Bodies?

In Chapter 19, we introduced the concept of homeostasis—keeping an organism's body within the narrow range of conditions that allows it to survive and reproduce. Nutrition, digestion, and excretion play crucial roles in homeostasis.

A **nutrient** is any substance that an animal needs but cannot synthesize in its own body, and hence must acquire from its environment as it eats or drinks. Nutrients provide animals with both the materials with which to construct their bodies and the energy to fuel their life processes. An animal may obtain nutrients directly in usable form (for example, water, sodium, or glucose); combined into large, complex molecules such as fats or proteins; or as parts of the bodies of plants or other animals that they eat. **Digestion** is the process whereby an animal physically grinds up and chemically breaks down its food, producing small, simple molecules that can be absorbed into the circulatory system. **Nutrition** is a more comprehensive term that includes taking food into the body, converting it into usable forms, absorbing the resulting molecules from the digestive tract into the circulatory system, and using the nutrients in the animal's own metabolism.

When an animal eats or drinks, it never obtains precisely the right mixture of water, minerals, carbohydrates, fats, and proteins that it needs to build and sustain itself. Some components of its food may be indigestible—hair, bone, and cellulose, for example, cannot be digested by most animals. Other substances in food may be harmful, including toxins produced by many plants. An animal's own metabolism produces carbon dioxide and some highly toxic molecules, such as ammonia, that must be eliminated. Finally, an animal may simply consume too much of otherwise useful substances, such as water, sodium, or potassium. **Excretion** is the disposal of these indigestible, toxic, or surplus materials. There is a great diversity of excretory structures and functions in the animal kingdom. As a general rule, however, indigestible food is expelled from the digestive tract as feces (see section 21.5). Carbon dioxide and, in some animals, ammonia and some other toxic molecules are excreted by the respiratory tract (lungs or gills) or the skin. Surplus minerals and most toxic substances, whether eaten or produced by the animal's own metabolism, are excreted by the urinary tract (see sections 21.6, 21.7, and 21.8).

21.2 What Nutrients Do Animals Need?

Animal nutrients fall into six major categories: lipids, carbohydrates, proteins, minerals, vitamins, and water.

THE PRIMARY SOURCES OF ENERGY ARE LIPIDS AND CARBOHYDRATES

Cells require a continuous supply of energy to stay alive and perform their functions. In animals, energy is provided mostly by three kinds of nutrients: lipids, carbohydrates and, to a lesser extent, proteins. These molecules, or parts of them, are used in glycolysis and cellular respiration, and the energy derived from them is used to produce ATP.

Energy in food can be measured in **calories**, defined as the energy required to raise the temperature of 1 gram of water by 1 degree Celsius. However, this unit is so small—a single Big Mac with cheese contains 700,000 calories—that it is customary to use **Calories** (with a capital C) instead; a Calorie contains 1,000 calories (lowercase c). The unit that you see in the "Nutritional Information" tables on cereal boxes and in fast-food restaurants is the Calorie; a Big Mac, for example, contains 700 Calories. The average human body at rest burns about 1,550 Calories per day (usually somewhat more if you're young and/or male; less if you're older and/or female), and people burn more Calories when exercising than when resting (Table 21-1). In a really fit athlete, vigorous exercise can raise energy consumption from a resting rate of about 1 Calorie per minute to nearly 20 Calories per minute.

LIPIDS INCLUDE FATS, PHOSPHOLIPIDS, AND CHOLESTEROL

Lipids are a diverse group of molecules that includes triglycerides (fats and oils), phospholipids, and cholesterol. Fats and oils are used primarily as a source of energy. Phospholipids are important components of all cellular membranes. Cholesterol is used to manufacture cellular membranes, several hormones including estrogen and testosterone, and bile (which aids in fat digestion).

Animals of some species can synthesize all of the types of lipids they need. Others must acquire specific lipid building blocks, called essential fatty acids, from their food. For example, humans are unable to synthesize linoleic acid, which is required for the synthesis of certain phospholipids. Therefore, we must obtain this essential fatty acid from our diet, mainly from vegetable oils such as safflower or sunflower oil. In most developed nations, obesity is an increasingly serious health problem, so many people rightly try to limit the amount of fat in their diets. However, a truly fat-free diet would be lethal.

Fats Store Energy in Concentrated Form

Humans and most other animals store energy primarily as fat. When an animal eats more Calories than it uses, most of the excess carbohydrates, fats, or proteins are converted to fat for storage. Fats have two major advantages as energy-storage molecules. First, they contain more than twice as much energy per unit weight as either carbohydrates or protein (about 9 Calories per gram for fats compared with about 4 Calories per gram for carbohydrates and proteins). Second, lipids are hydrophobic; that is, they do not dissolve in water. Fat deposits, therefore, do not cause water to accumulate in the body. For both these reasons, fats store more calories with less weight than do other molecules.

Minimizing weight allows an animal to move faster and farther (important for escaping predators, hunting prey, and migrating) and to use less energy for movement (important when food supplies are limited). For example, ruby-throated hummingbirds migrate across the Gulf of Mexico in the fall. Obviously, the open ocean doesn't provide anything for a hummingbird to eat. Therefore, a ruby-throat that weighs 2 to 3 grams in early summer puts on about 2 grams of fat before

migrating. If it stored carbohydrate or protein instead, it would have to gain almost 6 grams to provide the same amount of energy. It probably could barely fly, and certainly couldn't make it across the Gulf before collapsing from exhaustion.

Because people evolved under the same food constraints as other animals did, we have a strong tendency to eat when food is available, even if we aren't really hungry. In addition, foods that are high in fat and sugar usually taste the best. Many people now have access to almost unlimited, high-calorie food, and have jobs that do not require much exercise. Under these circumstances, we often need considerable willpower to avoid becoming overweight.

DYING TO BE THIN Continued

In her efforts to lose weight, Ana Reston ate almost nothing but tomatoes and apples for several months. These foods contain virtually no fat, so she would have lacked essential fatty acids, damaging her cell membranes.

		Time to "Work Off"			
Activity	Calories/Hour	500 Calories (Cheeseburger)	300 Calories (Ice Cream Cone)	70 Calories (Apple)	40 Calories (1 Cup Broccoli)
Running (6 mph)	700	43 min	26 min	6 min	3 min
Cross-country skiing (moderate)	560	54 min	32 min	7.5 min	4 min
Roller skating	490	1 hr 1 min	37 min	8.6 min	5 min
Bicycling (11 mph)	420	1 hr 11 min	43 min	10 min	6 min
Walking (3 mph)	250	2 hr	1 hr 12 min	17 min	10 min
Frisbee® playing	210	2 hr 23 min	1 hr 26 min	20 min	11 min
Studying	100	5 hr	3 hr	42 min	24 min

Table 21-1 Approximate Energy Consumed by a 150-Pound Person Performing Different Activities

CARBOHYDRATES ARE A SOURCE OF QUICK ENERGY

Carbohydrates include simple sugars, as well as longer chains of sugars called polysaccharides. The simple sugar glucose is the primary source of energy for most cells, but the typical diet contains little glucose. During digestion, glucose is derived from the breakdown of more complex carbohydrates, such as sucrose and starch.

Animals, including humans, store the carbohydrate **glycogen**—a large, highly branched chain of glucose molecules—in the liver and muscles. Glycogen provides much of the energy used during exercise, but people typically store less than a pound of it, the equivalent of less than 2,000 Calories. Therefore, marathon runners can go about 20 miles before their glycogen is used up. The expression "hitting the wall" describes the extreme fatigue that long-distance runners experience when their supply of glycogen is gone.

PROTEINS PROVIDE AMINO ACIDS FOR BUILDING NEW PROTEINS

Protein in the diet serves mainly as a source of amino acids to make the body's own proteins. Dietary protein is broken down in the digestive tract to yield amino acids. In your cells, the amino acids are linked in specific sequences to form the many different proteins specific to your body. Any excess protein in the diet is broken down to extract energy for immediate use or for storage as fat.

Humans can synthesize only 12 of the 20 amino acids commonly used in proteins. The other eight, called **essential amino acids**, must be supplied in the diet. Two additional amino acids are usually synthesized in fairly small amounts, and so are essential for growing children but usually not for adults. Although animal proteins almost always contain sufficient amounts of all of the essential amino acids, many plant proteins are deficient in some, so vegetarians must take steps to avoid protein deficiency. Generally, they need to make sure their diet includes a variety of plants (for example, legumes, grains, and corn) whose proteins collectively provide all of the essential amino acids. Protein deficiency can cause a variety of debilitating conditions, including kwashiorkor, which is seen in some impoverished countries (Fig. 21-2).

MINERALS ARE ELEMENTS REQUIRED BY THE BODY

The term "mineral" has very different meanings in geology and in nutrition. In geology, a mineral is a homogeneous, usually crystalline, element or compound, such as the beautiful crystals often displayed in natural history museums. In nutrition, a **mineral** is specifically a chemical element (not a compound) required for proper bodily function (Table 21-2). Because animals cannot manufacture elements, minerals must be obtained through the diet, either from food or dissolved in drinking water. Essential minerals include calcium, magnesium, and phosphorus, which are major constituents of bones and teeth. Others, such as sodium and potassium, are essential for muscle contraction and the conduction of nerve impulses. Iron is used in the production of hemoglobin, and iodine is found in hormones produced by the thyroid gland. In addition, trace amounts of several other minerals, including zinc, copper, and selenium, are required, typically as parts of enzymes.

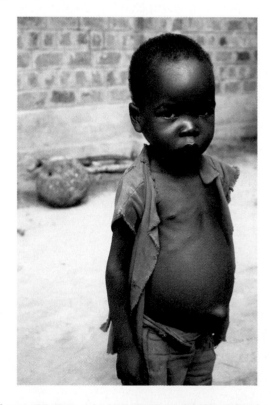

Figure 21-2 Kwashiorkor Symptoms of kwashiorkor, caused by protein deficiency, include a swollen abdomen and emaciated arms and legs.

Mineral	Dietary Sources	Major Functions in Body	Deficiency Symptoms
Calcium	Milk, cheese, green vegetables, legumes	Bone and tooth formation Blood clotting Nerve impulse transmission	Stunted growth Rickets, osteoporosis Convulsions
Phosphorus	Milk, cheese, meat, poultry, grains	Bone and tooth formation Acid-base balance	Weakness Demineralization of bone Loss of calcium
Potassium	Meats, milk, fruits	Acid-base balance Body water balance Nerve function	Muscular weakness Paralysis
Chlorine	Table salt	Formation of gastric juice Acid-base balance	Muscle cramps Apathy Reduced appetite
Sodium	Table salt	Acid-base balance Body water balance Nerve function	Muscle cramps Apathy Reduced appetite
Magnesium	Whole grains, green leafy vegetables	Activation of enzymes in protein synthesis	Growth failure Behavioral disturbances Weakness, spasms
Iron	Eggs, meats, legumes, whole grains, green vegetables	Constituent of hemoglobin and enzymes involved in energy metabolism	Iron-deficiency anemia (weakness, reduced resistance to infection)
Fluorine	Fluoridated water, tea, seafood	Strengthening teeth and probably bone	High frequency of tooth decay
Zinc	Widely distributed in foods	Constituent of enzymes involved in digestion	Reduced growth rate Small sex glands
Iodine	Seafish and shellfish, dairy products, many vegetables, iodized salt	Constituent of thyroid hormones	Goiter (enlarged thyroid)
Chromium	Fruits, vegetables, whole grains	Metabolism of sugar and fats	Reduced glucose tolerance Elevated insulin in blood

Table 21-2 Minerals, Sources, and Functions in Humans

VITAMINS PLAY MANY ROLES IN METABOLISM

Vitamins are a diverse group of organic compounds that animals require in very small amounts. The body cannot synthesize most vitamins (or cannot synthesize them in adequate amounts), so they are normally obtained from food.

Convenience foods—doughnuts, soda, and French fries, for example—usually contain lots of Calories but not many vitamins. The vitamins considered essential in human nutrition are listed in Table 21-3. These vitamins are often grouped into two categories: water soluble and fat soluble.

Vitamin	Dietary Sources	Functions in Body	Deficiency Symptoms
Water Soluble B-complex			
Vitamin B$_1$ (thiamin)	Milk, meat, bread	Coenzyme in metabolic reactions	Beriberi (muscle weakness, peripheral nerve changes, edema, heart failure)
Vitamin B$_2$ (riboflavin)	Widely distributed in foods	Constituent of coenzymes in energy metabolism	Reddened lips, cracks at corner of mouth, lesions of eye
Niacin	Liver, lean meats, grains, legumes	Constituent of two coenzymes in energy metabolism	Pellagra (skin and gastrointestinal lesions; nervous mental disorders)
Vitamin B$_6$ (pyridoxine)	Meats, vegetables, whole-grain cereals	Coenzyme in amino acid metabolism	Irritability, convulsions, muscular twitching, dermatitis, kidney stones
Pantothenic acid	Milk, meat	Constituent of coenzyme A, with a role in energy metabolism	Fatigue, sleep disturbances, impaired coordination
Folic acid	Legumes, green vegetables, whole wheat	Coenzyme involved in nucleic and amino acid metabolism	Anemia, gastrointestinal disturbances, diarrhea, retarded growth, birth defects
Vitamin B$_{12}$	Meats, eggs, dairy products	Coenzyme in nucleic acid metabolism	Pernicious anemia, neurological disorders
Biotin	Legumes, vegetables, meats	Coenzymes required for fat synthesis, amino acid metabolism, and glycogen formation	Fatigue, depression, nausea, dermatitis, muscular pains
Others			
Choline	Egg yolk, liver, grains, legumes	Constituent of phospholipids, precursor of the neurotransmitter acetylcholine	None reported in humans
Vitamin C (ascorbic acid)	Citrus fruits, tomatoes, green peppers	Maintenance of cartilage, bone, and dentin (hard tissue of teeth); collagen synthesis	Scurvy (degeneration of skin, teeth, gums, blood vessels; epithelial hemorrhages)
Water Soluble			
Vitamin A (retinol)	Beta-carotene in green, yellow, and red vegetables; retinol added to dairy products	Constituent of visual pigment; maintenance of epithelial tissues	Night blindness, permanent blindness
Vitamin D (ascorbic acid)	Cod-liver oil, eggs, dairy products	Promotes bone growth and mineralization; increases calcium absorption	Rickets (bone deformities) in children; skeletal deterioration
Vitamin E (tocopherol)	Seeds, green leafy vegetables, margarines, shortenings	Antioxidant, prevents cellular damage	Possibly anemia
Vitamin K (tocopherol)	Green leafy vegetables; product of intestinal bacteria	Important in blood clotting	Bleeding, internal hemorrhages

Table 21-3 Vitamins, Sources, and Functions in Humans

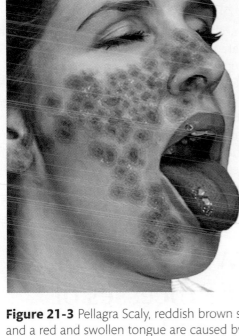

Figure 21-3 Pellagra Scaly, reddish brown skin lesions and a red and swollen tongue are caused by a deficiency of niacin, a B vitamin.

Water-Soluble Vitamins Water-soluble vitamins include vitamin C and the eight compounds that make up the B-vitamin complex. These substances dissolve in the water of the blood plasma and are excreted by the kidneys, so they are not stored in the body in any appreciable amounts. Water-soluble vitamins generally work together with enzymes to promote essential chemical reactions in the body's cells.

Because each vitamin participates in several metabolic processes, a deficiency of a single vitamin can have wide-ranging effects (see Table 21-3). For example, deficiency of niacin, a B vitamin, causes pellagra, associated with cracked, scaly skin as well as digestive and nervous system disorders . In 1996, the U.S. Food and Drug Administration (FDA) ordered folic acid, another B vitamin, to be added to grain foods such as bread, pasta, and rice. The addition of folic acid has reduced the incidence of neural tube defects (serious birth defects of the brain and spinal cord linked to folic acid deficiency in pregnant women) by about 20%. Researchers believe that supplementing food with folic acid has also contributed to a decline in both stroke and heart disease.

Fat-Soluble Vitamins The fat-soluble vitamins are A, D, E, and K. Vitamin A is used to produce the light-capturing molecule in the retina of the eye, and vitamin A deficiency can cause poor night vision or, in severe cases, blindness. Vitamin D is important for bone formation. Several recent studies have found a high incidence of vitamin D deficiency in the United States, including in urban adolescents, postmenopausal women (who may suffer more bone fractures as a result), and African Americans. People with dark skin are at particular risk because vitamin D is synthesized in skin exposed to sunlight, and dark pigmentation reduces the penetration of sunlight to the cells beneath that synthesize vitamin D. Pediatricians are seeing an alarming increase in rickets, particularly in African American children, as a consequence of vitamin D deficiency. Vitamin E is an *antioxidant*, which may help to protect the body against damaging substances that are formed as cells use oxygen to produce high-energy molecules such as ATP. Vitamin K helps regulate blood clotting.

Fat-soluble vitamins can be stored in body fat and may accumulate in the body over time. For this reason, some fat-soluble vitamins (vitamin A, for example) may be toxic if excessive amounts are eaten.

DYING TO BE THIN Continued

People with anorexia usually don't eat a nutritionally balanced diet. Vitamin deficiencies are very common. If their diets lack the essential amino acids, they will suffer from deficiencies of protein metabolism. If anorexics fail to ingest enough of the right minerals, they can develop severe imbalances of sodium, potassium, calcium, and magnesium in their blood and extracellular fluid, which can result in nervous and cardiac disorders.

THE HUMAN BODY IS ABOUT TWO-THIRDS WATER

Water is a crucial part of both the structure and physiology of all animals. For example, water is the principal component of saliva, blood, lymph, extracellular fluid, and the cytoplasm within each cell. Most metabolic reactions occur in a watery solution, and water directly participates in the hydrolysis reactions that break down proteins, carbohydrates, and fats into simpler molecules. As we will see later in this chapter, the kidneys excrete wastes dissolved in the water of urine.

The average adult human requires about 10 cups (2.5 liters) of water per day, but this need can increase dramatically with exercise, high temperatures, or low humidity, as water evaporates from sweat and from our lungs when we breathe. Although people can often survive for weeks without food, death occurs in a few days without water, because we lose so much every day. Water intake occurs mostly through eating and drinking. There is enough water in the typical diet for about half of the usual daily requirement, with the rest obtained by drinking fluids.

NUTRITIONAL GUIDELINES HELP PEOPLE OBTAIN A BALANCED DIET

Most people in the United States are fortunate to live amidst an abundance of food. However, the amazing diversity of foods in a typical U.S. supermarket and the easy availability of fast food can lead to poor nutritional choices. To help people make informed choices, the U.S. government has recently placed nutritional guidelines called "My Pyramid" on an interactive Web site. Another source of information is the nutritional labeling required on commercially packaged foods. These labels provide complete information about Calorie, fiber, fat, sugar, and vitamin content. Also, most fast-food chains provide nutritional information about their products.

ARE YOU TOO HEAVY?

A simple way to determine whether your weight is likely to pose a health risk is to calculate your body mass index (BMI). The BMI takes into account your weight and height to arrive at an estimate of body fat. This simple calculation assumes that you have an average amount of muscle, so it does not apply to bodybuilders or marathon runners. The formula is as follows: weight (in kilograms)/height2 (in meters), but you can calculate your BMI by multiplying your weight (in pounds) by 703, then dividing by your height2 (in inches). Or, simply type "BMI" on your favorite Internet search engine, and you will find many sites that calculate it for you. A BMI between 18.5 and 25 is considered healthy. People with anorexia usually have a BMI of 17.5 or lower. Unless you are a bodybuilder and have far more muscle than average, a BMI between 25 and 30 indicates that you are probably overweight and a BMI over 30 indicates that you are probably obese. "Health Watch: Obesity and the Brain–Gut Connection" on p. 408 explores some potential future treatments for obesity.

21.3 What Are the Major Processes of Digestion?

Animals eat the bodies of other organisms, but these organisms may resist becoming food. Plants, for example, support each cell with a wall of indigestible cellulose. Animals may be covered with indigestible fur, scales, or feathers. In addition, the complex lipids, proteins, and carbohydrates in food cannot be used directly. These nutrients must be broken down before they can be used by the cells of the animal that has consumed them; after being broken down, they are recombined into new molecules. Animals have various types of digestive tracts, each finely tuned for a unique diet and lifestyle. Amid this diversity, however, all digestive systems must accomplish certain tasks:

• **Ingestion** The food must be brought into the digestive tract through an opening, usually called a mouth.

• **Mechanical Breakdown** In most animals, food must be physically broken down into smaller pieces. The particles produced by mechanical breakdown provide a large surface area for attack by digestive enzymes.

• **Chemical Breakdown** The particles of food must be exposed to digestive enzymes that break down large molecules into smaller subunits.

- **Absorption** The small molecules must be transported out of the digestive tract and into the body cells. In a few animals, the small molecules may be absorbed directly into the body cells.
- **Elimination** Indigestible materials must be expelled from the body.

21.4 What Types of Digestive Systems Are Found in Non-Human Animals?

The animal kingdom displays a remarkable diversity of digestive systems, ranging from digestion inside single cells in sponges, to relatively simple sacs in jellyfish and anemones, through an array of tubular digestive systems with two openings in animals as different as earthworms, insects, and humans.

IN SPONGES, DIGESTION OCCURS WITHIN INDIVIDUAL CELLS

Sponges are the only animals that rely exclusively on individual cells to digest their food. As you might suspect, this limits their food to microscopic organisms or particles. Sponges circulate seawater through pores in their bodies. Fringes of plasma membrane on specialized collar cells filter microscopic organisms from the water and ingest the prey by phagocytosis. Because the food is so small, mechanical breakdown, which is essential in most digestive systems, is unnecessary. Rather, phagocytosis encloses the food in a small sac called a food vacuole, which basically serves as a temporary, miniature stomach. The vacuole fuses with other sacs called lysosomes, which contain digestive enzymes, and the food is then digested within the vacuole into smaller molecules that can be absorbed into the cell cytoplasm. Undigested remnants of food remain in the vacuole, which eventually expels its contents back into the seawater.

JELLYFISH AND THEIR RELATIVES HAVE DIGESTIVE SYSTEMS CONSISTING OF A SAC WITH A SINGLE OPENING

In most other animals, digestion takes place in a chamber within the body where enzymes break down chunks of food. One of the simplest of these chambers is found in cnidarians, such as sea anemones, *Hydra*, and jellyfish. These animals possess a digestive sac with a single opening for ingesting food and ejecting wastes. This opening is generally referred to as the mouth, but it also serves as the anus. The animal's stinging tentacles capture its prey, which is then moved into the digestive sac where enzymes break it down. Cells lining the cavity absorb the nutrients and engulf small food particles. The undigested remains are eventually expelled through the mouth.

MOST ANIMALS HAVE DIGESTIVE SYSTEMS CONSISTING OF A TUBE WITH SEVERAL SPECIALIZED COMPARTMENTS

Most animal species, including worms, mollusks, arthropods, and vertebrates, have a digestive system that is principally a one-way tube through the body. It begins with a mouth and ends with an anus. Such digestive systems usually consist of a series of specialized regions that process food in an orderly sequence, first grinding it up, then breaking it down with enzymes, absorbing the nutrient molecules into the circulatory system, and finally excreting the undigested wastes. This orderly processing in a tube allows the animal to eat more frequent meals than does a saclike digestive system.

The earthworm, which continuously ingests soil as it burrows, is a good example. A tubular digestive system is essential to its way of life. Soil and bits of vegetation enter the mouth and pass through the pharynx and the esophagus to the crop, a thin-walled storage organ. The crop collects the food and gradually passes it to the gizzard. There, bits of sand and muscular contractions grind the food into smaller particles. The food then travels to the intestine, where enzymes digest it into simple molecules that can be absorbed by the cells lining the intestine and, ultimately, into the circulatory system. Indigestible material passes out through the anus.

Different species of animals show a remarkable diversity of digestive tracts. There are specializations for capturing and ingesting food, such as the slender bills and long tongues of hummingbirds, the sharp canines and meat-slicing molars of tigers, and the pincers of lobsters and ants. The digestive tracts of carnivores tend to be short and simple, because meat is fairly easy to digest. Herbivores, however, often have chambers housing bacteria that digest the abundant cellulose found in plants, because the herbivores themselves cannot produce cellulose-digesting enzymes. Some animals, such as spiders, inject enzymes into their prey, so that the prey is actually digested outside of the spider's body and the spider slurps up the resulting liquid diet.

21.5 How Do Humans Digest Food?

Like most other animals, humans have a tubular digestive tract with several compartments in which food is broken down—first physically and then chemically (Fig. 21-4). Nearly everything of nutritional value is extracted and absorbed into the circulatory system. Digesting and absorbing food requires coordinated action from the various structures of the digestive system.

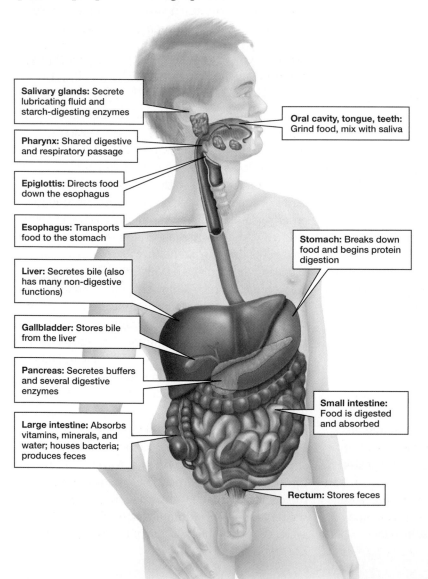

Salivary glands: Secrete lubricating fluid and starch-digesting enzymes

Pharynx: Shared digestive and respiratory passage

Epiglottis: Directs food down the esophagus

Esophagus: Transports food to the stomach

Liver: Secretes bile (also has many non-digestive functions)

Gallbladder: Stores bile from the liver

Pancreas: Secretes buffers and several digestive enzymes

Large intestine: Absorbs vitamins, minerals, and water; houses bacteria; produces feces

Oral cavity, tongue, teeth: Grind food, mix with saliva

Stomach: Breaks down food and begins protein digestion

Small intestine: Food is digested and absorbed

Rectum: Stores feces

Figure 21-4 The human digestive system The digestive system includes both the digestive tube, consisting of the oral cavity, pharynx, esophagus, stomach, small intestine, and large intestine; and organs such as the salivary glands, liver, gallbladder, and pancreas, which produce and store digestive secretions. QUESTION: Why is the stomach both muscular and expandable?

BREAKDOWN OF FOOD BEGINS IN THE MOUTH

You take a bite, you salivate, and you begin chewing. This begins both the mechanical and chemical breakdown of food. In humans and other mammals, the mechanical work is done mostly by teeth. In adult humans, 32 teeth of varying shapes and sizes tear, cut, and grind food into small pieces .

While the food is being pulverized by the teeth, the first phase of chemical digestion begins as three pairs of salivary glands pour saliva into the mouth. Saliva has many functions. It contains the digestive enzyme amylase, which begins the breakdown of starches into sugar. Saliva also contains a bacteria-killing enzyme and antibodies that help to guard against infection. It lubricates food to facilitate swallowing and dissolves some food molecules, such as acids and sugars, carrying them to taste buds on the tongue. The taste buds bear sensory receptors that help to identify the type and the quality of the food.

THE PHARYNX CONNECTS THE MOUTH TO THE REST OF THE DIGESTIVE SYSTEM

With the help of the muscular tongue, the food is manipulated into a mass and pressed backward into the **pharynx**, a muscular cavity connecting the mouth with the esophagus. The pharynx also connects the nose and mouth with the larynx, which leads to the trachea, the tube that conducts air to the lungs. This arrangement occasionally causes problems, as anyone who has ever choked on a piece of food can attest. Normally, however, the swallowing reflex (triggered by food entering the pharynx) elevates the larynx, so that a flap of tissue called the epiglottis blocks off the opening to the larynx and guides food into the esophagus.

THE ESOPHAGUS CONDUCTS FOOD TO THE STOMACH

Swallowing forces food into the **esophagus**, a muscular tube that propels the food from the mouth to the stomach. Muscles surrounding the esophagus produce a wave of contraction that begins just above the swallowed food and progresses down the esophagus, forcing the food toward the stomach. This muscular action, called

peristalsis, occurs throughout the digestive tract, and is so effective that a person can actually swallow while upside-down. Mucus secreted by cells that line the esophagus helps to protect the lining from abrasion and lubricates the food during its passage.

THE STOMACH STORES AND BREAKS DOWN FOOD

The human stomach is an expandable muscular sac capable of holding as much as a gallon of food and liquids. The stomach has three primary functions. First, it stores food and releases it gradually into the small intestine at a rate suitable for proper digestion and absorption. Second, the stomach assists in the mechanical breakdown of food. Its muscular walls produce a variety of churning movements that break up large pieces of food. The third function of the stomach is to break food down chemically.

Glands in the stomach lining secrete hydrochloric acid, a protein called pepsinogen, and mucus. The hydrochloric acid gives the fluid in the stomach a pH of 1 to 3 (about the same as lemon juice). This kills many microbes that are inevitably swallowed along with food. Pepsinogen is the inactive precursor of a protein-digesting enzyme called pepsin. The stomach's acidity converts pepsinogen to pepsin, which then begins digesting the proteins in food. Why not just secrete pepsin in the first place? The glands secrete pepsinogen because pepsin would digest the very cells that manufacture it before it ever got into the stomach. Finally, mucus coats the stomach lining and serves as a barrier to self-digestion. The protection, however, is not perfect, so the cells lining the stomach must be replaced every few days.

Food in the stomach is gradually converted to a thick, acidic liquid called **chyme**, which consists of partially digested food and digestive secretions. Peristaltic waves (about three per minute) propel the chyme toward the small intestine. A ring of muscle at the lower end of the stomach allows only about a teaspoon of chyme to enter the small intestine with each contraction. It takes 2 to 6 hours, depending on the size of the meal, to empty the stomach completely.

Although digestion begins in the stomach, almost no absorption of nutrients occurs there. Only a few substances, including water, alcohol, and some other drugs, can enter the bloodstream through the stomach wall.

MOST DIGESTION OCCURS IN THE SMALL INTESTINE

The **small intestine** is about 1 inch in diameter and 10 feet long in a living human adult. The small intestine digests food into small molecules and absorbs these molecules into the bloodstream. The first role of the small intestine—digestion—is accomplished with the aid of secretions from three sources: the liver, the pancreas, and the cells of the small intestine itself.

The Liver and Gallbladder Provide Bile The

liver has many functions, including storing glycogen and detoxifying many poisonous substances. Its role in digestion is to produce **bile**, a complex mixture of bile salts, other salts, water, and cholesterol. Bile is stored in the gallbladder (see Fig. 21-4) and released into the small intestine through a tube called the bile duct. Although they help in the digestion of lipids, bile salts are not enzymes. Rather, much like dish detergent, bile salts have a hydrophobic part that interacts with fats and a hydrophilic part that dissolves in water. As a result, bile salts disperse chunks of fat into microscopic particles, exposing a large surface area to attack by lipid-digesting enzymes produced by the pancreas.

The Pancreas Secretes Digestive Substances

The **pancreas** consists of two major types of cells. One type produces hormones that help to regulate blood sugar, and the other produces a digestive secretion called pancreatic juice. About a quart of **pancreatic juice** is released into the small intestine each day. This secretion contains water, sodium bicarbonate, and several digestive enzymes that break down carbohydrates, lipids, and proteins. Sodium bicarbonate (the active ingredient in baking soda) neutralizes the acidic chyme in the small intestine, producing a slightly basic pH. In contrast to the stomach's digestive enzymes, which require an acidic pH, pancreatic digestive enzymes require a slightly basic pH to function properly.

The Intestinal Wall Completes Digestion and Absorbs Nutrients The wall of the small intestine

contains cells that complete the digestive process and absorb the small molecules that result. Digestive enzymes are actually embedded in the plasma membranes of the cells that line the small intestine, so the final phase of digestion occurs as the nutrient is being absorbed into the cell. As in the stomach, the small intestine is protected from digesting itself by mucus, which is secreted by specialized cells in its lining.

DYING TO BE THIN Continued

When someone with bulimia vomits, the contents of the stomach erupt back through the esophagus, pharynx, and mouth. These structures do not have the thick mucous layer that protects the stomach, so the stomach acid burns away the cells of their linings. Further, the acid dissolves the enamel of the teeth, so that prolonged bulimia can lead to significant tooth loss.

MOST ABSORPTION OCCURS IN THE SMALL INTESTINE

The small intestine is the major site of nutrient absorption into the blood. The small intestine has numerous folds and projections, giving it an internal surface area about 600 times greater than a smooth tube of the same length. Finger-like projections called **villi** (singular, villus) cover the entire surface of the intestinal wall. Villi, which range from 0.5 to 1.5 millimeters in length, give the intestinal lining a velvety appearance to the naked eye. Each individual cell of a villus bears a fringe of microscopic projections called **microvilli**. Collectively, these projections of the small intestine wall give it a surface area of more than 2,700 square feet (about 250 square meters)—almost the size of a tennis court.

Contractions of the circular muscles of the intestine slosh the chyme back and forth, bringing nutrients into contact with the absorptive surface of the small intestine. Within each villus is a network of blood capillaries and a single lymph capillary, called a lacteal . Most nutrients, including water, simple sugars, amino acids, vitamins, and minerals, pass through the cells lining the small intestine and enter the capillaries. The breakdown products of fat (glycerol and fatty acids), however, take a different route. After diffusing into the cells lining the small intestine, they are resynthesized into fats, coated with protein, and then released as particles into the extracellular fluid within the villi. These particles are far too large to enter the blood capillaries, but they can pass through the lacteal wall. Suspended in lymph, the particles move from the lacteals through other lymph vessels, and are eventually delivered to the bloodstream when the lymph vessels empty into the veins (see pp. 382–384).

THE LARGE INTESTINE ABSORBS WATER, MINERALS, AND VITAMINS, AND FORMS FEECES

The **large intestine** in a living human adult is about 5 feet long and 3 inches in diameter. The large intestine has two parts. For most of its length it is called the **colon**; its final 6-inch compartment is called the **rectum**. The leftovers of digestion flow from the small intestine into the colon: a mixture of water, minerals, indigestible fibers (mostly cellulose, from the cell walls of vegetables and fruits), and small amounts of undigested fats and proteins. The colon contains a flourishing bacterial population that lives on these nutrients. These bacteria synthesize vitamin B12, thiamin, riboflavin, and, most importantly, vitamin K, which would otherwise be deficient in a typical diet. Cells lining the large intestine absorb these vitamins as well as water and minerals.

After absorption is complete, the result is the semisolid **feces**, consisting mostly of indigestible wastes and bacteria (about one-third of the dry weight of feces). The feces are transported by peristaltic movements until they reach the rectum, where expansion of this chamber stimulates the urge to defecate.

DIGESTION IS CONTROLLED BY THE NERVOUS SYSTEM AND HORMONES

When you eat, your body coordinates the events that convert food into nutrients circulating in your blood. The secretions and muscular activity of the digestive tract are regulated by both nerves and hormones.

Sensory Signals Initiate Digestion The sight, smell, taste, and sometimes just the thought of food generate signals from the brain that act on many parts of the digestive tract. For example, nerve impulses stimulate the salivary glands and cause the stomach to begin secreting acid and mucus. As food moves through the digestive tract, its bulk stimulates local nervous reflexes that cause peristalsis.

Hormones Help Regulate Digestive Activity
There are at least a couple of dozen hormones that control appetite, satiation, and digestion. Here, we discuss only four major hormones, all secreted by the digestive system. These enter the bloodstream, circulate through the body, and act on specific receptors within the digestive tract. Like most hormones, they are regulated by negative feedback. For example, nutrients in chyme such as amino acids and peptides from protein digestion stimulate cells in the stomach lining to release the hormone *gastrin* into the bloodstream. Gastrin travels back to the stomach cells and stimulates further acid secretion, which promotes protein digestion. When the stomach contents become sufficiently acidic, gastrin secretion is inhibited, which in turn inhibits further acid secretion.

In response to chyme, the cells of the small intestine release secretin and *cholecystokinin*. These hormones stimulate the release of digestive fluids into the small intestine: bicarbonate and digestive enzymes from the pancreas and bile from the liver and gallbladder. *Gastric inhibitory peptide*, produced by cells of the small intestine in response to fatty acids and sugars in chyme, stimulates the pancreas to release insulin, which stimulates many body cells to absorb sugar. Gastric inhibitory peptide (as its name suggests) also inhibits both acid production and peristalsis in the stomach. As a result, it slows the rate at which chyme is pumped into the small

281

intestine, providing additional time for digestion and absorption to occur.

A host of other hormones also regulate appetite, the sensation of fullness, and the rate at which food is metabolized. Some of these offer hope for controlling weight gain and obesity, as we discuss in the "Health Watch: Obesity and the Brain–Gut Connection."

21.6 What Are the Functions of Urinary Systems?

We may load our digestive tracts with pepperoni pizza, hot fudge sundaes, and coffee, but our cells must remain bathed in a precisely regulated solution of salts and nutrients. The digestive system is relatively unselective, so that any molecule that *can* be absorbed into the circulatory system through the small intestine *is* absorbed, whether the molecule is useful or toxic, needed immediately or already available in excess. How does the animal body, then, maintain homeostasis, fine-tuning and precisely regulating its internal environment? The skin, digestive tract, and respiratory system all play a role. However, eliminating harmful substances and excess nutrients while retaining useful substances is primarily the domain of the urinary system.

Whether we consider flatworms, fishes, or people, all urinary systems function similarly. First, the blood or other body fluids are filtered, with water and small dissolved molecules moving from the blood into the urinary system. Next, nutrients are selectively reabsorbed back into the blood. Often, highly toxic substances that must be removed very quickly are actively secreted from the blood into the urinary system. Finally, wastes and excess nutrients, dissolved in variable amounts of water, are excreted from the body.

21.7 What Types of Urinary Systems Are Found in Non-Human Animals?

There are nearly as many types of urinary systems (in invertebrates, these are usually called excretory systems) as there are phyla of animals. In a few, such as sponges, individual cells merely dump their wastes into the surrounding water. Most animals, however, have complex urinary systems, often under nervous and hormonal control, that precisely regulate which substances are excreted and which are kept in the body's fluids. These mechanisms ensure that the internal chemical composition of the animal remains fairly constant, despite enormous changes in its diet or living conditions. Here, we discuss only two of the many types of excretory systems in invertebrates.

FLAME CELLS FILTER FLUIDS IN FLATWORMS

The freshwater flatworm lives in streams. Because it constantly absorbs water by osmosis, it must excrete the water or else it will explode. Therefore, the major function of its excretory system is to regulate water balance. The flatworm's excretory system consists of a network of tubes that branch throughout the body. At intervals, the branches end blindly in single-celled bulbs called flame cells. Water and dissolved substances are filtered from the body into the bulbs, where a cluster of beating cilia (that reminded their discoverers of the flickering flame of a candle) produces a current that forces the fluid through the tubes. Within the tubes, more wastes are added and some nutrients are reabsorbed. The resulting solution is expelled through pores in the body surface. Flatworms also have a large surface area through which many cellular wastes leave by diffusion.

NEPHRIDIA FILTER FLUIDS IN EARTHWORMS

Earthworms, mollusks, and several other invertebrates have simple filtering structures called *nephridia* (singular, nephridium) that resemble the

Obesity and the Brain–Gut Connection

In 2006, medical experts estimated that about 65% of American adults were overweight; about half of these were obese (defined as a body mass index of more than 30—that's a 5-foot 6-inch woman weighing about 185 pounds, or a 5-foot 10-inch man weighing about 210 pounds). Overweight people have traditionally been told to eat less and exercise more. While that's good advice, it clearly isn't stemming the rise in obesity in the United States and many other countries around the world. And obesity isn't just a matter of personal health or fitting into airline seats. In the United States, every year, obesity is estimated to cost more than $100 billion in medical expenses and reduced productivity on the job, and to contribute to 300,000 deaths.

For at least the past half-century, diet books have appeared on bookshelves with depressing frequency, each claiming to be the answer to the prayers of the overweight. Diet pills have been around for decades, too, but most either have little long-term effect or are dangerous. Many overweight people diet strenuously for a few weeks, lose a few pounds, and find themselves a few months later just as heavy as before. Can anything really be done?

Maybe soon, something can be. Researchers have discovered a bewildering array of hormones that are produced by the digestive tract and act on the brain, influencing appetite, satiation, and metabolism. In 1994, Jeffrey Friedman of Rockefeller University discovered a hormone, synthesized by fat cells, that travels to the brain and suppresses appetite. Perhaps optimistically, Friedman called the hormone leptin, after a Greek word meaning thin. Many people hoped that a simple injection of leptin would suppress appetite in overweight people, so they could comfortably eat less and lose weight. No such luck. It turns out that obese people make plenty of leptin, more than lean people do, but their brains don't respond to it.

Since then, researchers have found additional eating-related hormones, some of which look a lot more promising than leptin. Two of these hormones, with opposing effects on appetite and satiation, are ghrelin and peptide YY (often called PYY) (Fig. E21-1). When the stomach has been empty for a few hours, it churns out ghrelin, which travels to the brain and stimulates hunger. After a meal, ghrelin levels drop dramatically. Food in the intestines causes PYY to be produced, which travels to the brain to reduce hunger. Unfortunately, in dieters and overweight people, both ghrelin and PYY act in ways that make dieting hard and eating easy. Ghrelin levels increase when people diet and lose weight, which makes them feel hungrier and hungrier. Obese people also generally produce less PYY after a meal, so they don't feel full even though they've eaten enough food.

These two hormones are attractive targets for weight control. In 2006, researchers at the Scripps Research Institute successfully vaccinated rats against ghrelin. The vaccines caused the rats to produce antibodies that bind ghrelin, so it can't get to the brain and stimulate hunger. The vaccinated rats ate normally, but gained less weight than control rats, indicating that their metabolism might have increased. Also in 2006, Nastech Pharmaceutical Company started clinical trials of a PYY nasal spray in people. When sprayed into the nose, PYY apparently penetrates to the brain and reduces appetite.

Will these new treatments help people to lose weight and keep it off? Or will other pathways in the body compensate for too much PYY or not enough ghrelin? Appetite, metabolism, and satiation are controlled by complex, interacting mechanisms, and it's too early to tell if treatments targeting ghrelin and PYY will work. Nevertheless, someday biomedical science may solve enough of the puzzle of weight gain and weight loss to produce effective treatments. For hundreds of millions of people around the world, that day can't come soon enough.

filtering structures that we will examine in vertebrate kidneys. The earthworm body is composed of repeating segments, and nearly every segment contains its own pair of nephridia. Fluid fills the body cavity that surrounds the earthworm's internal organs. This fluid collects both wastes and nutrients from the blood and tissues. The fluid is moved by cilia into a narrow, tubelike portion of the nephridium. Here, salts and other dissolved nutrients are absorbed back into the blood, leaving water and wastes behind. The resulting urine is stored in an enlarged bladder-like portion of the nephridium and is excreted through an excretory pore in the body wall.

21.8 How Does the Human Urinary System Work?

Urinary systems of all vertebrates, including humans, face major challenges. Urine formation begins by filtering the blood. Size, however, is the only criterion for filtration—anything small enough to fit through the pores of the filter will leave the blood and enter the urinary system. Therefore, not only wastes, but also water and nutrients that the body cannot afford to lose, are filtered out. In humans and many other vertebrates, the kidneys have evolved complex internal structures and metabolic abilities that eliminate wastes while retaining most of the water and nutrients.

THE HUMAN URINARY SYSTEM PRODUCES, TRANSPORTS, AND EXCRETES URINE

The **kidneys** are organs in which the fluid portion of the blood is collected and filtered. From this fluid, water and important nutrients are then reabsorbed into the blood. The remaining fluid, called **urine**—consisting of toxic substances, cellular waste products, excess vitamins, salts, some hormones, and water—stays behind to be excreted from the body. The rest of the urinary system channels and stores urine until it is eliminated from the body.

THE URINARY SYSTEM IS CRUCIAL FOR HOMEOSTASIS

The urinary system of humans and other vertebrates helps maintain homeostasis in the body in several ways. These include:

- Regulating blood levels of minerals and other ions such as sodium, potassium, chloride, and calcium.
- Regulating the water content of the blood.
- Maintaining the proper pH of the blood.
- Retaining important nutrients such as glucose and amino acids in the blood.
- Eliminating cellular waste products such as urea. When amino acids are used in cells as a source of energy or for the synthesis of new molecules, ammonia (NH_3) is produced as a by-product. Ammonia is very toxic. In mammals, the liver converts ammonia to urea, a far less toxic substance. In the kidneys, urea is filtered from the blood and ultimately excreted in the urine.

THE URINARY SYSTEM CONSISTS OF THE KIDNEYS, URETER, URINARY BLADDER, AND URETHRA

Human kidneys are paired organs located on either side of the spinal column, slightly above the waist. Each is approximately 5 inches long, 3 inches wide, and 1 inch thick. Blood enters each kidney through a renal artery. After the blood has been filtered, it exits through a renal vein. The kidneys produce urine that leaves each kidney through a narrow, muscular tube called the **ureter**. Using peristaltic contractions, the ureters transport urine to the **urinary bladder**. This hollow, muscular chamber collects and stores the urine. During urination, contraction of the bladder forces the urine out of the body through the **urethra**, a single narrow tube about 1.5 inches long in women and about 8 inches long in men.

URINE IS FORMED IN THE NEPHRONS OF THE KIDNEYS

Each kidney contains a solid outer layer where urine forms and an inner chamber that collects urine and funnels it into the ureter. The outer layer of each kidney contains about a million tiny individual tubes, called **nephrons**, which filter the blood, process the filtered fluid, and form urine. Each nephron has three major parts: (1) the **glomerulus**, a dense knot of capillaries from which fluid is filtered from the blood and collected into (2) a surrounding cuplike structure, called **Bowman's capsule**, which funnels the fluid into (3) a long, twisted **tubule**. The Bowman's capsule channels fluid into the **proximal tubule**. The fluid then moves through the **loop of Henle** and the **distal tubule**. Different portions of the tubule selectively modify the fluid as it travels through them. In the tubule, nutrients are selectively reabsorbed from the fluid back into the blood, while wastes and some of the water are left behind to form urine. Additional wastes are also secreted into the tubule from the blood. Finally, the distal tubules of multiple nephrons drain into a **collecting duct**, which conducts urine into the renal pelvis, a hollow, funnel-like structure in the center of the kidney that connects with the ureter.

Blood is Filtered by the Glomerulus

Urine formation starts with the process of **filtration**. Blood enters each nephron by an arteriole that branches from the renal artery. Within the cup-shaped portion of the nephron—Bowman's capsule—the arteriole branches into numerous capillaries that form the mass of the glomerulus. The walls of these capillaries are extremely permeable to water and small dissolved molecules, but blood cells and most proteins are too large to be filtered out, so they remain in the blood. Blood pressure within the capillaries drives water and dissolved substances from the blood out through the capillary walls. The resulting watery fluid, called the **filtrate**, is collected in Bowman's capsule, beginning its journey through the rest of the nephron.

The Filtrate is Converted to Urine in the Tubules of the Nephron

The filtrate collected in Bowman's capsule contains a mixture of wastes, essential nutrients, and a lot of water. In fact, in the average adult human, 8 quarts (about 7.5 liters) of fluid are filtered into the nephrons *every hour*. When you consider that a human has only a little over 5 quarts (about 5 liters) of blood, and only a little over 3 quarts (about 3 liters) of that is water, you can appreciate how important it is for the kidneys to reclaim almost all of the water that is filtered. Normally, a person produces only about 1.5 quarts (1.5 liters) of urine each day, so more than 99% of the water is returned to the blood.

Overall, therefore, the nephrons must restore the nutrients and most of the water to the blood while retaining wastes for elimination. This task is accomplished by two processes: tubular reabsorption and tubular secretion.

Tubular Reabsorption Moves Water and Nutrients from the Nephron to the Blood From Bowman's capsule, the filtrate passes through the proximal tubule, which is surrounded by capillaries. Most of the water and nutrients in the filtrate move from the proximal tubule into the capillaries in a process called **tubular reabsorption**. The cells of the proximal tubule actively transport salts and other nutrients, such as amino acids and glucose, out of the tubule and into the surrounding extracellular fluid. The nutrient molecules then diffuse from the extracellular fluid into the adjacent capillaries. Water follows the nutrients out of the tubule and into the capillaries by osmosis. Wastes such as urea remain in the tubule and become more concentrated as water leaves.

Tubular Secretion Moves Wastes from the Blood into the Nephron In **tubular secretion**, wastes such as hydrogen ions, potassium, ammonia, and many drugs are moved from the capillaries into the nephron. Typically, the cells of the distal tubule actively transport wastes from the surrounding extracellular fluid into the tubule. Lowering the concentration of wastes in the extracellular fluid produces a concentration gradient so that the wastes passively diffuse out of the capillaries.

Why bother with tubular secretion, when these wastes are mostly small molecules that can enter the nephron by filtration anyway? Because many of these wastes, such as acid and ammonia, are extremely toxic, even the rapid filtration of the blood into Bowman's capsule cannot remove them from the blood fast enough. Tubular secretion speeds up the process of ridding the body of these dangerous substances.

Urine Becomes Concentrated in the Collecting Ducts

Finally, in the collecting ducts, **concentration** of urine may occur through the removal of water. When mammals (including humans) and birds need to conserve water, they can produce urine that has a higher concentration of dissolved materials than their blood has.

Urine can become concentrated because there is a concentration gradient of salts and urea in the extracellular fluid that surrounds the nephrons and the collecting ducts. (The concentration gradient is created and maintained by the loops of Henle.) As filtrate travels through the collecting ducts to the renal pelvis, it passes through areas of increasingly concentrated extracellular fluid. As the difference in concentration between the filtrate and the surrounding fluid increases, water leaves the filtrate by osmosis and is carried off by the surrounding capillaries. The filtrate in the collecting duct, now called urine, can become as concentrated as the surrounding fluid, which may be four times as concentrated as blood. The urine remains concentrated because the rest of the excretory system is fairly impermeable to water, salts, and urea.

NEGATIVE FEEDBACK REGULATES THE WATER CONTENT OF THE BLOOD

Maintaining the proper volume of water in the body is a key function of the urinary system, as we have seen, but the appropriate amount of water to retain changes continually as conditions change. The kidneys, therefore, must reabsorb more water when a person is perspiring heavily and less water when the person has just drunk a lot of water.

The amount of water reabsorbed into the blood is controlled by negative feedback. One of these feedback mechanisms is based on the amount of *antidiuretic hormone* (ADH) circulating in the blood. This hormone (secreted by the pituitary gland) allows more water to be reabsorbed from the urine. It does so by increasing the permeability of the distal tubule and the collecting duct to water. The release of ADH is regulated by receptor cells in the brain that monitor the concentration of the blood and by receptors in the heart that monitor blood volume.

Let's look at an example. A lost traveler staggers through the hot desert, perspiring heavily and losing water with every breath. As he becomes dehydrated, his blood volume falls, and the osmotic concentration of his blood rises, triggering release of ADH by the pituitary gland. The ADH increases the permeability of the distal tubule and the collecting duct, thereby increasing the reabsorption of water. Water is returned to the blood, leaving urine that is more concentrated than the blood.

Eventually, our traveler finds an oasis and overindulges in the cool, clear water of a spring. His blood volume rises and its osmotic concentration falls, triggering a decrease in his ADH output. Reduced ADH makes his distal tubules and collecting ducts less permeable to water, so less water is reabsorbed from them. He will now produce urine that is more dilute than the blood. In extreme cases, urine flow may exceed 1 quart (about 1 liter) per hour. As the proper water level in his blood is restored, the increased osmotic concentration of the blood and decreased blood volume will again stimulate some ADH release, thus maintaining homeostasis by keeping the blood water content within narrow limits.

21.7 WHAT TYPES OF URINARY SYSTEMS ARE FOUND IN NON-HUMAN ANIMALS?

In the invertebrate flatworm, wastes and excess water are filtered from the body fluids into tubules. Cilia on flame cells move the fluids through the tubules and expel them through pores in the body surface. In the earthworm, nephridia (which resemble individual nephrons) filter fluid that bathes the organs and blood vessels, storing excess water and wastes, which are excreted through pores.

21.8 HOW DOES THE HUMAN URINARY SYSTEM WORK?

The urinary system of vertebrates (including humans) helps maintain homeostasis in the body in several ways, including (1)regulating the blood levels of important minerals and other ions; (2) regulating the water content of the blood by negative feedback involving antidiuretic hormone (ADH), produced in the pituitary gland of the brain; (3) maintaining proper pH of the blood; (4) retaining important nutrients; and (5) eliminating cellular waste products such as urea.

The urinary system of humans and other vertebrates consists of kidneys, ureters, bladder, and urethra. Kidneys produce urine, which is conducted by the ureters to the bladder, a storage organ. Urine passes out of the body through the urethra.

Each kidney contains more than a million individual nephrons in its outer layer. Urine formed in the nephrons enters collecting ducts that empty into the renal pelvis, from which it is funneled into the ureter. Each nephron is served by an arteriole that branches from the renal artery. The arteriole further branches into a mass of capillaries called the glomerulus. There, water and dissolved substances are filtered from the blood by pressure. The filtrate is collected in the cup-shaped Bowman's capsule and conducted along the tubular portion of the nephron. During tubular reabsorption, nutrients are actively pumped out of the filtrate through the walls of the tubule. Nutrients then enter capillaries that surround the tubule, and water follows by osmosis. Some wastes remain in the filtrate; others are pumped into the tubule by tubular secretion. The tubule forms the loop of Henle, which creates a salt concentration gradient surrounding it. After completing its passage through the tubule, the filtrate enters the collecting duct, which passes through the concentration gradient. Final passage of the filtrate through this gradient via the collecting duct concentrates the urine.

Thinking Through the Concepts

Suggested answers to end-of-chapter and figure-based questions can be found at the end of the text.

FILL-IN-THE-BLANK

1. A substance that an animals needs to build or operate its body, but that it cannot synthesize itself, is called a(n) _____. _____ is the process of physically and chemically breaking down food into molecules that can be absorbed into the circulatory system. Indigestible material, waste products of cellular metabolism, toxic substances, and substances eaten in excess of the body's needs are eliminated through _____, which occurs in the _____, _____, _____, and _____ (major organs or organ systems of the body).

2. The primary sources of energy for animals are _____ and _____. Organic molecules needed in very small amounts that an animal cannot synthesize itself (in sufficient quantities) are called _____. _____ are important components of bone, teeth, and the dissolved materials in the blood and extracellular fluid.

3. Amino acids and fatty acids that the body requires but cannot synthesize are called _____.

4. Digestion includes five major processes: _____, _____, _____, _____, and _____.

5. Most animals have a tubular digestive tract. The major cavities of the human digestive tract are the _____, _____, _____, stomach, _____, and _____.

6. Glands in the stomach wall produce three major secretions: _____, _____, and _____.

7. Enzymes from the _____ empty into the small intestine; this gland also produces an acid-neutralizing buffer called _____. The small intestine also receives _____ from the liver and gallbladder; this secretion, although not an enzyme, is important in the digestion of _____ (type of nutrient).

8. In humans, urine is produced in tiny tubules of the kidney, called _____. Blood is first filtered into the beginning of the tubules, the _____. The filtrate is then processed through tubular absorption and secretion. Finally, it is concentrated in the _____. Urine is stored in the _____ and leaves the body through the _____.

9. If you begin to dehydrate, a gland called the _____ releases the hormone _____, which causes your kidneys to reabsorb water and produce concentrated urine.

Review Questions

1. List six general types of nutrients, and describe the role of each in nutrition.

2. List and describe the function of the three principal secretions of the stomach.

3. List the substances secreted into the small intestine, and describe the origin and function of each.

4. Describe the structural and functional adaptations of the human small intestine that ensure good digestion and absorption.

5. Control of the human digestive tract involves messages that coordinate activity in one chamber with those taking place in subsequent chambers. List the coordinating events you discovered in this chapter in the appropriate order, beginning with tasting, chewing, and swallowing a piece of meat and ending with residue that enters the large intestine. What initiates each process?

6. What are the major functions of the urinary system in any animal?

7. Describe the processes of filtration, tubular reabsorption, and tubular secretion.

Appendix C

Source: D. Goldfield, C. Abbott, V. Anderson, J. E. Argersinger, P.H. Argersinger, W. L. Barney, and R. M Weir., *The American Journey, Vol. 2, 4/e*

Chapter 25
The Great Depression and the New Deal 1929 - 1939

Chapter Outline

Hard Times in Hooverville
Crash!
The Depression Spreads
"Women's Jobs" and "Men's Jobs"
Families in the Depression
"Last Hired, First Fired"
Protest

Herbert Hoover and the Depression
The Failure of Voluntarism
Repudiating Hoover: The 1923 Election

Launching the New Deal
Action Now!
Creating Jobs
Helping Some Farmers
The Flight of the Blue Eagle
Critics Right and Left

Consolidating the New Deal
Weeding Out and Lifting Up
Expanding Relief
The Roosevelt Coalition and the Election of 1936

The New Deal and American Life
Labor on the March
Women and the New Deal
Minorites and the New Deal
The New Deal: North, South, East, and West
The New Deal and Public Activism

Ebbing of the New Deal
Challenging the Court
More Hard Times
Political Stalemate

Good Neighbours and Hostile Forces
Neutrality and Fascism
Edging Toward Involvement

Conclusion

KEY TOPICS

- The Great Depression
  The Worldwide Collapse

- Hoover's Voluntary remedies

- FDR's New Deal

- The New Deal and organized labor, minorities, women, and farmers

- FDR's Democratic coalition of reformers, labor, urban ethnic groups, white southerners, westerners, and African Americans

- The faltering of the New Deal

- Diplomacy in the Great Depression

My mother had two small babies on her hands. When I became sickly, Grandmother Joseta took me home with her, and I never returned to my parents. . . . My grandmother's house was located on the "American" side of town, but there was nothing they could do about it because she was there before anybody else. . . . My grandmother worked very hard; I grew up in the Depression.

When it was time for me to go to school I was assigned to [the] Mexican side of town. We were segregated; [the] Anglo children were sent to Roosevelt and the Mexican children who lived closer to Roosevelt [still] had to go down to Harding. I'll admit, there was a lot of discrimination in those years.

During the Depression my grandmother sewed piecework for the WPA. My dad helped out when he could [and] Uncle Ernesto also worked. He used to dig graves.

The Depression years were very, very hard. I remember seeing the people passing on their way to California. . . . It hurt me to see the people in their rickety old cars, their clothes in tatters, escaping from the drought and the dust bowls.

Oral Testimony,
Carlotta Silvas Martin

On April 27 [1933], according to the *New York Times*, Paul Schneider, aged forty-four, a sick and crippled Chicago school teacher, shot himself to death. His widow, left with three children, stated that he had not been paid for eight months. . . . Less than a month after Paul Schneider's discouragement drove him to suicide, the militant action of Chicago teachers—patient no more . . . resulted in the payment of $12,000,000 due them for the last months of 1932. Their pay for the five months of 1933 is still owed them. Five hundred of them are reported to be in asylums and sanitariums as a result of the strain. . . .

These are the conditions facing teachers fortunate enough to be employed. What of the unemployed? . . . "We are always hungry," wrote [one unemployed teacher]. "We owe six months' rent. . . . We live every hour in fear of eviction. . . . My sister, a typist, and I . . . have been out of work for two years. . . . We feel discouraged . . . and embittered. We are drifting, with no help from anyone."

Eunice Langdon,
The Nation, August 16, 1933

I am sitting in the city free employment bureau. It's the women's section. We have been sitting here now for hours. We sit here every day, waiting for a job. There are no jobs. . . .

. . . [W]e don't talk much. . . . There is a kind of humiliation. . . . We look away from each other. We look at the floor.

Meridel LeSueur,
"Women on the Breadlines," 1932

Dear Mrs. Roosevelt,

I am now 15 years old and in the 10th grade. I have always been smart but I never had a chance as all of us is so poor. I hope to complete my education, but I will have to quit school I guess if there is no clothes can be bought. (Don't think that we are on the relief.) Mother has been a faithful servant for us to keep us together. I don't see how she has made it.

Mrs. Roosevelt, don't think I am just begging, but that is all you can call it I guess. . . . Do you have any old clothes you have throwed back. You don't realize how honored I would feel to be wearing your clothes.

Your friend,
M.I.
Star Route One
Albertville, Ala.
January 1, 1936

"Carlotta Silvas Martin: A Mexican American Childhood during the Depression" and "Meridel LeSueur: The Despair of Unemployed Women," both from Susan Ware, *Modern American Women: A Documentary History* (New York: McGraw-Hill Higher Education, 2002), pp. 162–165, 145–146, respectively; Eunice Langdon, "The Teacher Faces the Depression," *Nation* 137 (August 16, 1933): 182–187; Letter to Eleanor Roosevelt, January 1, 1936, www.newdeal.feri.org/eleanor/mi0136.htm.

Carlotta Silvas Martin, Eunice Langdon, and Meridel LeSueur convey some of the trauma of the Great Depression, but no one voice can capture its devastating effect on Americans. The American economy utterly collapsed, leaving millions of people jobless, homeless, or in continual fear of foreclosure, eviction, even starvation. Men, women, children everywhere saw their families and dreams shattered and felt the sting of humiliation as they stood in bread lines or begged for clothes or food scraps. The winter of 1932–1933 was particularly cruel: unemployment soared and stories of malnutrition and outright starvation made headlines in newspapers throughout the nation.

Natural disaster accompanied economic crisis in the drought-stricken states of the Great Plains, forcing families to leave their farms. They packed up their meager belongings and took to the road to escape the darkened skies of the "Dust Bowl" in search of anything better.

The election of Franklin D. Roosevelt, however, lifted spirits and hopes of jobless Americans throughout the nation. They enthusiastically responded to his **New Deal**, taking jobs, as did Carlotta's grandmother, with such programs as the Works Progress Administration (WPA). In unprecedented numbers, they also wrote to both FDR and Eleanor Roosevelt, asking for advice and for assistance for everything from a month's rent money to tide them over to old clothes to wear to school, as did the 15-year-old girl from Alabama. And they also wrote to thank the president and first lady for their compassionate support and leadership. Throughout all such letters ran a common theme: the belief among poor and unemployed Americans that for the first time there were people in the White House who were interested in their welfare.

The collapse hit hardest those industries dominated by male workers, leaving mothers and wives with new roles as the family breadwinners, sometimes straining family relationships and men's sense of purpose and respect. Some families drifted apart, while others coped simply by making do. As Carlotta Silvas noted, her "dad helped out when he could."

Race and ethnicity further complicated the problems of joblessness and relief. Southern states routinely denied African Americans relief assistance, as did southwestern states for Hispanic Americans. The New Deal failed to overcome most of the traditional attitudes and practices that targeted women and minorities and reinforced local prejudice and segregation. For Carlotta Silvas, that meant walking farther to school—a daily journey that she remembered throughout her life.

Hard times, then, both united and divided the

American people. Franklin and Eleanor Roosevelt and the programs of the New Deal brought fresh hope and connected Americans to the White House as never before. And although the federal activism of the 1930s achieved neither full recovery nor systematic reform, it restored confidence to many Americans and permanently transformed the nation's responsibility for the welfare of its citizens. By the end of the decade, President Roosevelt was no longer worried that the economy—indeed the whole of society—teetered on the edge of catastrophe; his gaze now fixed abroad, where even more ominous developments, he believed, threatened the nation's future and security.

Hard Times in Hooverville

The prosperity of the 1920s ended in a stock-market crash that revealed the flaws honeycombing the economy. As the nation slid into a catastrophic depression, factories closed, employment and incomes tumbled, and millions lost their homes, hopes, and dignity. Some protested and took direct action; others looked to the government for relief.

CRASH!

The buoyant prosperity of the New Era, more apparent than real by the summer of 1929, collapsed in October, when the stock market crashed. During the preceding two years, the market had hit record highs, stimulated by optimism, easy credit, and speculators' manipulations. But after peaking in September, it suffered several sharp checks, and on October 29, "Black Tuesday," panicked investors dumped their stocks, wiping out the previous year's gains in one day. Confidence in the economy disappeared, and the slide continued for months, and then years. The market hit bottom in July 1932. Much of the paper wealth of America had evaporated, and the nation sank into the **Great Depression.**

The Wall Street crash marked the beginning of the depression, but it did not cause it. The depression stemmed from weaknesses in the New Era economy. Most damaging was the unequal distribution of wealth and income. Workers' wages and farmers' incomes had fallen far behind industrial productivity and corporate profits; by 1929, the richest 0.1 percent of American families had as much total income as the bottom 42 percent. With more than half the nation's people living at or below the subsistence level, there was not enough purchasing power to maintain the economy.

A second factor was that oligopolies dominated American industries. By 1929, the 200 largest corporations (out of 400,000) controlled half the corporate wealth. Their power led to "administered prices," prices kept artificially high and rigid rather than determined by supply and demand. Because it did not respond to purchasing power, this system not only helped bring on economic collapse but also dimmed prospects for recovery.

Weaknesses in specific industries had further unbalanced the economy. Agriculture suffered from overproduction, declining prices, and heavy debt; so did the coal and textile industries. Increased mechanization in key industries had resulted in significant unemployment even during the 1920s. Banking presented other problems. Poorly managed and regulated, banks had contributed to the instability of prosperity; they now threatened to spread the panic and depression.

International economic difficulties spurred the depression as well. Shut out from U.S. markets by high tariffs, Europeans had depended on American investments to manage their debts and reparation payments from the Great War. The stock market crash dried up the flow of American dollars to Europe, causing financial panics and industrial collapse and making the Great Depression global. In turn, European nations curtailed their imports of American goods and defaulted on their debts, further debilitating the U.S. economy. American exports fell by 70 percent from 1929 to 1932 (See Global Perspectives, "The Worldwide Collapse").

Government policies also bore some responsibility for the crash and depression. Failure to enforce antitrust laws had encouraged oligopolies and high prices; failure to regulate banking and the stock market had permitted financial recklessness and irresponsible speculation. Reducing tax rates on

CHRONOLOGY

1929 Stock market crashes.

1932 Farmers' Holiday Association organizes rural protests in the Midwest.

Reconstruction Finance Corporation is created to assist financial institutions.

Bonus Army is routed in Washington, D.C.

Franklin D. Roosevelt is elected president.

1931 Japan invades Manchuria.

1933 Adolf Hitler comes to power in Germany.

Emergency Banking Act is passed.

The United States recognizes the Soviet Union.

Agricultural Adjustment Administration (AAA) is created to regulate farm production.

National Recovery Administration (NRA) is created to promote industrial cooperation and recovery.

Federal Emergency Relief Act provides federal assistance to the unemployed.

Civilian Conservation Corps (CCC) is established to provide work relief in conservation projects.

Public Works Administration (PWA) is created to provide work relief on large public construction projects.

Civil Works Administration (CWA) provides emergency winter relief jobs.

Tennessee Valley Authority (TVA) is created to coordinate regional development.

1934 Securities and Exchange Commission (SEC) is established.

Indian Reorganization Act reforms Indian policy.

Huey Long organizes the Share-Our-Wealth Society.

Democrats win midterm elections.

1935 Supreme Court declares NRA unconstitutional.

Italy attacks Ethiopia.

National Labor Relations Act (Wagner Act) guarantees workers' rights to organize and bargain collectively.

Social Security Act establishes a federal social insurance system.

Banking Act strengthens the Federal Reserve.

Revenue Act establishes a more progressive tax system.

Resettlement Administration is created to aid dispossessed farmers.

Rural Electrification Administration (REA) is created to help provide electric power to rural areas.

Soil Conservation Service is established.

Emergency Relief Appropriation Act authorizes public relief projects for the unemployed.

Works Progress Administration (WPA) is created.0

Huey Long is assassinated.

1936 Supreme Court declares AAA unconstitutional.

Roosevelt is reelected president.

Hitler remilitarizes the Rhineland.

Roosevelt sails to South America as part of Good Neighbor Policy.

Sit-down strikes begin.

1937 Chicago police kill workers in Memorial Day Massacre.

FDR tries but fails to expand the Supreme Court.

Farm Security Administration (FSA) is created to lend money to small farmers to buy and rehabilitate farms.

National Housing Act is passed to promote public housing projects.

"Roosevelt Recession" begins.

1938 Congress of Industrial Organizations (CIO) is founded.

Germany annexes Austria.

Fair Labor Standards Act establishes minimum wage and maximum hours rules for labor.

Roosevelt fails to "purge" the Democratic Party.

Republicans make gains in midterm elections.

Munich agreement reached, appeasing Hitler's demand for Sudetenland.

Kristallnacht, violent pogrom against Jews, occurs in Germany.

the wealthy had also encouraged speculation and contributed to the maldistribution of income. Opposition to labor unions and collective bargaining helped keep workers' wages and purchasing power low. The absence of an effective agricultural policy and the high tariffs that inhibited foreign trade and reduced markets for agricultural products hurt farmers. In short, the same governmental policies that shaped the booming 1920s economy also led to economic disaster.

State and local fiscal policies also pointed to economic problems for the 1930s. The expansion of public education and road construction led to higher property taxes in communities throughout the nation. Indeed, state and local taxes rose faster than personal incomes in the 1920s.

But the crash did more than expose the weaknesses of the economy. Business lost confidence and refused to make investments that might have brought recovery. Instead, banks called in loans and restricted credit, and depositors tried to withdraw their savings, which were uninsured. The demand for cash caused banks to fail, dragging the economy down further. And the Federal Reserve Board prolonged the depression by restricting the money supply.

THE DEPRESSION SPREADS

By early 1930, the effects of financial contraction were painfully evident. Factories shut down or cut back, and industrial production plummeted; by 1932, it was scarcely 50 percent of its 1929 level. Unemployment skyrocketed and, by 1932, one-fourth of the labor force was out of work. Personal income dropped by more than half between 1929 and 1932. Moreover, the depression began to feed on itself in a vicious circle: Shrinking wages and employment cut into purchasing power, causing business to slash production again and lay off workers, thereby further reducing purchasing power.

The depression particularly battered farmers. Commodity prices fell by 55 percent between 1929 and 1932, stifling farm income. Unable to pay their mortgages, many farm families lost their homes and fields. "We have no security left," cried one South Dakota farm woman. "Foreclosures and evictions at the point of sheriff's guns are increasing daily." The

dispossessed roamed the byways, highways, and railways of a troubled country.

Urban families were also evicted when they could not pay their rent. Some moved in with relatives; others lived in **Hoovervilles**—the name reflects the bitterness directed at the President—shacks where people shivered, suffered, and starved.

Soup kitchens became standard features of the urban landscape, with lines of the hungry stretching for blocks. But charities and local communities could not meet the massive needs, and neither the states nor federal government had welfare or unemployment compensation programs. To survive, people planted gardens in vacant lots and back alleys and tore apart empty houses or tapped gas lines for fuel. In immigrant neighborhoods, social workers found a primitive "communism" in which people shared food, clothing, and fuel.

"WOMEN'S JOBS" AND "MEN'S JOBS"

The depression affected wage-earning women in complex ways. Although they suffered 20 percent unemployment by 1932, women were less likely than men to be fired. Gender segregation had concentrated women in low-paid service, sales, and clerical jobs that were less vulnerable than the heavy industries where men predominated. But while traditional attitudes somewhat insulated working women, they also reinforced opposition to female employment, especially that of married women. As one Chicago civic organization complained, "They are holding jobs that rightfully belong to the God-intended providers of the household." Nearly every state considered restricting the employment of married women. Many private employers, especially banks and insurance companies, fired married women. Despite such hostility, the proportion of married women in the workforce increased in the 1930s as women took jobs to help their families survive, and about one-third of working married women provided the sole support for their families.

FAMILIES IN THE DEPRESSION

"I have watched fear grip the people in our neighborhood around Hull House," wrote Jane Addams as the depression deepened in 1931 and family survival itself seemed threatened. Divorce

The Worldwide Collapse

The Wall Street crash did not immediately provoke widespread alarm at home or abroad. One French observer commented that an "abscess" had been "lanced." British commentators dismissed it as an isolated event and predicted continuing prosperity. President Hoover remained confident well into 1930, even telling a group of religious leaders requesting relief for the unemployed, "You have come sixty days too late. The depression is over."

Still, the stock market collapse did have consequences: It made European borrowing more difficult, especially hurting Germany's failing economy. Without loans from the United States, Germany defaulted on its war debts and faced near bankruptcy. Moreover, the United States accounted for 40 percent of the world's manufactured goods—twice the figure for Germany and England combined in 1929. When the United States slid into depression, the global repercussions were staggering.

The international crisis required global cooperation, but the world's nations responded with various forms of economic nationalism. The United States rejected its role as the lender of the last resort for destitute countries and constructed trade barriers by passing the Smoot-Hawley tariff in 1930. Within months Canada, Mexico, France, Spain, and New Zealand raised their tariffs against American goods. World trade came to a standstill; its volume plummeted by two-thirds between 1929 and 1933.

As the depression deepened, world leaders pointed to external causes and turned to conventional solutions. In the United States, Herbert Hoover claimed that "the hurricane that swept our shores was of European origin" and affirmed the need to balance the budget in hard times. French leaders blamed British monetary policies and blasted the United States for "exporting unemployment" through "mechanization" that replaced workers with machines. The French also regarded a balanced budget as inviolable. In Britain, however, the socialist prime minister, Ramsay MacDonald, faulted capitalism for the collapse, adding "we are not on trial, it is the system under which we live." Britain provided unemployment insurance and public relief. But even the socialist prime minister refused to unbalance the budget to meet the needs of all the jobless. The Japanese finance minister also objected to increased spending for the unemployed. By 1932, the international crisis had worsened, and the United States and Germany had unemployment rates of 25 and 40 percent, respectively. The German banking system had collapsed in 1931, and the depression helped facilitate the political success of the Nazi Party in 1932. Jobless Germans looted stores and coal yards for food and fuel. As in the United States, working women were targeted as a cause of the depression. One German newspaper declared that "Germany will perish if the women are working and the men are unemployed."

The shockingly high rates of unemployment throughout the world created unprecedented conditions of poverty and despair. And although Americans did not leap from windows during the collapse of the stock market, suicide rates went up in both Germany and the United States during the 1930s. Cases of malnutrition were found in New York, Budapest, and Vienna, among other cities, and relief agencies everywhere were overwhelmed by the needs of the jobless. People lost jobs and homes, creating Hoovervilles in the United States, bidonvilles ("tin cities") in France, and the Hungry Mile in Australia. The Great Depression had indeed become global, and, without international cooperation, the unemployed looked to their governments for solutions and support.

declined because it was expensive, but desertion increased, and people postponed marriage. Birthrates fell. Husbands and fathers, the traditional breadwinners, were often humiliated and despondent when laid off from work. A social worker observed in 1931, "Like searing irons, the degradation, the sheer terror and panic which loss of job brings, the deprivation and the bitterness have eaten into men's souls."

The number of female-headed households increased sharply. Not only did some women become wage earners, but their traditional role as homemakers also gained new significance. To make ends meet, many women sewed their own clothing and raised and canned vegetables, reversing the trend toward consumerism.

Some parents sacrificed their own well-being to protect their children. One witness described "the uncontrolled trembling of parents who have starved themselves for weeks so that their children might not go hungry." But children felt the tension and fear, and many went without food. In New York City, 139 people, most of them children, died of starvation and malnutrition in 1933. Boys and girls stayed home from school and church because they lacked shoes or clothing; others gave up their plans for college. As hope faded, family conflicts increased. The California Unemployment Commission concluded that the depression had left the American family "morally shattered. There is no security, no foothold, no future."

"LAST HIRED, FIRST FIRED"

The depression particularly harmed racial minorities. With fewer resources and opportunities, they were less able than other groups to absorb the economic pain. African Americans were caught in a double bind, reported a sociologist at Howard University in 1932: They were "the last to be hired and the first to be fired." Black unemployment rates were more than twice the white rate, reflecting increased job competition and persistent racism. In Atlanta, white citizens paraded with banners denouncing the hiring of black workers "Until Every White Man Has a Job."

Racism also limited the assistance African Americans received. Religious and charitable organizations often refused to care for black people. Local and state governments set higher relief eligibility requirements for black people than for white people and provided them with less aid. One Memphis resident saw the result of such policies: "Colored men and women with rakes, hoes, and other digging tools, with buckets and baskets, digging around in the garbage and refuse for food." In 1931, African-American women in Harlem joined together as the Harlem Housewives League to challenge New York City's race-based unequal distribution of relief. An African-American social worker described the despair and poverty of Harlem's residents: "Packed in damp, rat-ridden dungeons, they existed in squalor not too different from that of Arkansas sharecroppers."

Hispanic Americans also suffered. As mostly unskilled workers, they faced increasing competition for decreasing jobs paying declining wages. They were displaced even in the California agricultural labor force, which they had dominated. By the mid-1930s, they made up only a tenth of the state's migratory labor force, which increasingly consisted of white people who had fled the South and the Great Plains.

Economic woes and racism drove nearly half a million Mexican immigrants and their American-born children from the United States. Local authorities in the Southwest, with the blessing of the Department of Labor, urged all Mexicans, regardless of their citizenship status, to return to Mexico and free up jobs and relief assistance for white Americans. To intimidate Mexican residents, the U.S. Immigration Service conducted several raids, rounding up people and demanding immediate proof of citizenship. In 1931, a Los Angeles official announced that tens of thousands of Mexicans "have been literally scared out of southern California."

PROTEST

Bewildered and discouraged, most Americans reacted to the crisis without protest. Influenced by traditional individualism, many blamed themselves for their plight. But others did act, especially to protect their families. Protests ranged from small desperate gestures like stealing food and coal to more dramatic deeds. In Louisiana, women seized a train to call attention to the needs of their families; in New Jersey, in the "bloodless battle of Pleasantville," 100 women held the city council hostage to demand assistance.

Communists, socialists, and other radicals organized more formal protests. Communists led the jobless into "unemployment councils" that staged hunger marches, demonstrated for relief, and blocked evictions. Mothers facing eviction in Chicago told their children: "Run quick and find the Reds." Socialists built similar organizations, including the People's Unemployment League in Baltimore. However, local officials often suppressed their protests. In 1932, police fired on the Detroit Unemployment Council as it marched to demand food and jobs, killing four marchers and wounding many more.

Rural protests also broke out. Again, communists organized some of them, as in Alabama, where the Croppers' and Farm Workers' Union mobilized black agricultural laborers in 1931 to demand better treatment. In the Midwest, the Farmers' Holiday Association, organized among family farmers in 1932, stopped the shipment of produce to urban markets, hoping to drive up prices. A guerrilla war broke out as farmers blocked roads and halted freight trains, dumped milk in ditches, and fought bloody battles with deputy sheriffs. In Iowa, farmers beat sheriffs and mortgage agents and nearly lynched a judge conducting foreclosure proceedings.

Herbert Hoover and the Depression

The Great Depression challenged the optimism, policies, and philosophy that Herbert Hoover had carried into the White House in 1929. The president took unprecedented steps to resolve the crisis but shrank back from the interventionist policies activists urged. His failures, personal as well as political and economic, led to his repudiation and to a major shift in government policies.

THE FAILURE OF VOLUNTARISM

Hoover fought the economic depression more vigorously than any previous president, but he believed that voluntary private relief was preferable to federal intervention. The role of the national government, he thought, was to advise and encourage the voluntary efforts of private organizations, individual industries, or local communities. After the crash, he tried to apply this voluntarism to the depression.

Hoover obtained pledges from business leaders to maintain employment and wage levels. But most corporations soon repudiated these pledges, slashed wages, and laid off workers. Hoover himself said, "You know, the only trouble with capitalism is capitalists; they're too damn greedy." Still, he rejected government action.

Hoover also depended on voluntary efforts to relieve the misery caused by massive unemployment. He created the President's Organization for Unemployment Relief to help raise private funds for voluntary relief agencies. Charities and local authorities, he believed, should help the unemployed; direct federal relief would expand government power and undermine the recipients' character. He vetoed congressional attempts to aid the unemployed.

The depression rendered Hoover's beliefs meaningless. Private programs to aid the unemployed scarcely existed. Company plans for unemployment compensation covered less than 1 percent of workers, revealing the charade of the welfare capitalism of the 1920s. Private charitable groups like the Salvation Army, church associations, and ethnic societies quickly exhausted their resources. By 1931, the director of Philadelphia's Federation of Jewish Charities conceded, "Private philanthropy is no longer capable of coping with the situation." Tens of thousands of Philadelphians, he noted, had been reduced to "the status of a stray cat prowling for food. . . . What this does to the innate dignity of the human soul is not hard to guess."

Nor could local governments cope, and their efforts declined as the depression deepened. New York City provided relief payments of $2.39 a week for an entire family, and other cities much less. By

1932, more than 100 cities made no relief appropriations at all, and the commissioner of charity in Salt Lake City reported that people were sliding toward starvation. Only eight state governments provided even token assistance.

As the depression worsened, Hoover adopted more activist policies. He persuaded Congress to cut taxes to boost consumers' buying power, and he increased the public works budget. The Federal Farm Board lent money to cooperatives and spent millions trying to stabilize crop prices. Unable to control production, however, the board conceded failure by late 1931. More successful was the Reconstruction Finance Corporation (RFC). Established in January 1932, the RFC lent federal funds to banks, insurance companies, and railroads so that their recovery could "trickle down" to ordinary Americans.

But these programs satisfied few Americans. "While children starve," cried Pennsylvania's governor, Hoover "intends to let us have just as little relief as possible after the longest delay possible." Far more action was necessary, but Hoover remained committed to voluntarism and a balanced budget. Hoover's ideological limitations infuriated Americans who saw him as indifferent to their suffering and a reactionary protector of privileged business interests—an image his political opponents encouraged.

REPUDIATING HOOVER: THE 1932 ELECTION

Hoover's treatment of the **Bonus Army of 1932** symbolized his unpopularity and set the stage for the 1932 election. In 1932, unemployed veterans of World War I gathered in Washington, demanding payment of service bonuses not due until 1945. Hoover refused to meet with them, and Congress rejected their plan. But 10,000 veterans erected a shantytown at the edge of Washington and camped in vacant public buildings. Hoover decided to evict the veterans, but General Douglas MacArthur exceeded his cautious orders and on July 28 led cavalry, infantry, and tanks against the ragged Bonus Marchers. The troops cleared the buildings and assaulted the shantytown, dispersing the veterans and their families and setting their camp on fire.

This assault provoked widespread outrage. "What a pitiful spectacle is that of the great American Government, mightiest in the world, chasing unarmed men, women, and children with army tanks," commented the *Washington News*. The administration tried to brand the Bonus Marchers as communists and criminals, but subsequent investigations refuted such claims.

In the summer of 1932, with no prospects for victory, Republicans renominated Hoover. Confident Democrats selected Governor Franklin D. Roosevelt of New York, who promised "a new deal for the American people." Born into a wealthy family in 1882, FDR had been educated at Harvard, trained in the law, and schooled in politics as a state legislator, assistant secretary of the navy under Wilson, and the Democratic vice presidential nominee in 1920. In 1921, Roosevelt contracted polio, which paralyzed him from the waist down. His struggle with this ordeal gave him greater maturity, compassion, and determination. His continued involvement in politics, meanwhile, owed much to his wife, Eleanor. A social reformer, she became a Democratic activist, organizing women's groups and campaigning across New York. In a remarkable political comeback, FDR was elected governor in 1928 and reelected in 1930.

The 1932 campaign gave scant indication of what Roosevelt's New Deal might involve. The Democratic platform differed little from that of the Republicans, and Roosevelt spoke in vague or general terms. Still, observers found clues in Roosevelt's record in New York, where he had created the first state system of unemployment relief and supported social welfare and conservation. More important was his outgoing personality, which radiated warmth and hope in contrast to Hoover's gloom.

FDR carried every state south and west of Pennsylvania. It was the worst rout of a Republican candidate ever (except in 1912, when the party had split). Yet Hoover would remain president for four more months, and in those four months, the depression worsened, with rising unemployment, collapsing farm prices, and spreading misery. The final blow came in February 1933, when panic struck the banking system. Nearly 6,000 banks had already failed, robbing 9 million depositors of their savings. Desperate Americans rushed to withdraw their funds from the remaining banks, pushing them to the brink. With the federal government under Hoover immobilized, state governments shut the banks to prevent their failure.

Launching the New Deal

In the midst of this national anxiety, Franklin D. Roosevelt pushed forward an unprecedented program to resolve the crises of a collapsing financial system, crippling unemployment, and agricultural and industrial breakdown and to promote reform.

ACTION NOW!

On March 4, 1933, Franklin Delano Roosevelt became president and immediately reassured the American people. He insisted that "the only thing we have to fear is fear itself—nameless, unreasoning, unjustified terror, which paralyzes needed efforts to convert retreat into advance." And he promised "action, and action now!" Summoning Congress, Roosevelt pressed forward on a broad front. In the first three months of his administration, the famous Hundred Days of the New Deal, the Democratic Congress passed many important laws (see the Overview table, "Major Laws of the Hundred Days").

Roosevelt's program reflected a mix of ideas, some from FDR himself, some from a diverse group of advisers, including academic experts dubbed the "brain trust," politicians, and social workers. It also incorporated principles from the progressive movement, precedents from the Great War mobilization, and even plans from the Hoover administration. Above all, the New Deal was a practical response to the depression. FDR had set its tone in his campaign when he declared, "The country needs, and, unless I mistake its temper, the country demands bold, persistent experimentation. . . . Above all, try something."

FDR first addressed the banking crisis. On March 5, he proclaimed a national bank holiday, closing all

remaining banks. Congress then passed his Emergency Banking Act, a conservative measure that extended government assistance to sound banks and reorganized weak ones. Prompt government action, coupled with a reassuring **fireside chat** over the radio by the president, restored popular confidence in the banks. When they reopened on March 13, deposits exceeded withdrawals. "Capitalism," said Raymond Moley of the brain trust, "was saved in eight days." In June, Congress created the **Federal Deposit Insurance Corporation (FDIC)** to guarantee bank deposits up to $2,500.

The financial industry was also reformed. The Glass-Steagall Act separated investment and commercial banking to curtail risky speculation. The Securities Act reformed the sale of stocks to prevent the insider abuses that had characterized Wall Street, and in 1934 the **Securities and Exchange Commission (SEC)** was created to regulate the stock market. Two other financial measures in 1933 created the Home Owners Loan Corporation and the Farm Credit Administration, which enabled millions to refinance their mortgages.

CREATING JOBS

Roosevelt also provided relief for the unemployed. The Federal Emergency Relief Administration (FERA) furnished funds to state and local agencies. Harry Hopkins, who had headed Roosevelt's relief program in New York, became its director and one of the New Deal's most important members. FERA spent over $3 billion before it ended in 1935, and by then Hopkins and FDR had developed new programs that provided work rather than just cash. In the winter of 1933–1934, Hopkins spent nearly $1 billion to create jobs for 4 million men and women through the Civil Works Administration (CWA). The Public Works Administration (PWA) provided work relief on useful projects to stimulate the economy through public expenditures. Directed by Harold Ickes, the PWA spent billions from 1933 to 1939 to build schools, hospitals, courthouses, dams, and bridges.

One of FDR's personal ideas, the Civilian Conservation Corps (CCC), combined work relief with conservation. Launched in 1933, the CCC employed 2.5 million young men to work on reforestation and flood-control projects, build roads

GLOBAL PERSPECTIVES

MAJOR LAWS OF THE HUNDRED DAYS

Law	Objective
Emergency Banking Act	Stabilized the private banking system
Agricultural Adjustment Act	Established a farm recovery program based on production controls and price supports
Emergency Farm Mortgage Act	Provided for the refinancing of farm mortgages
National Industrial Recovery Act	Established a national recovery program and authorized a public works program
Federal Emergency Relief Act	Established a national system of relief
Home Owners Loan Act	Protected homeowners from mortgage foreclosure by refinancing home loans
Glass-Steagall Act	Separated commercial and investment banking and guaranteed bank deposits
Tennessee Valley Authority Act	Established the TVA and provided for the planned development of the Tennessee River Valley
Civilian Conservation Corps Act	Established the CCC to provide work relief on reforestation and conservation projects
Farm Credit Act	Expanded agricultural credits and established the Farm Credit Administration
Securities Act	Required full disclosure from stock exchanges
Wagner-Peyser Act	Created a U.S. Employment Service and encouraged states to create local public employment offices

and bridges in national forests and parks, restore Civil War battlefields, and fight forest fires.

HELPING SOME FARMERS

Besides providing relief, the New Deal promoted economic recovery. In May 1933, Congress established the Agricultural Adjustment Administration (AAA) to combat the depression in agriculture caused by crop surpluses and low prices. The AAA subsidized farmers who agreed to restrict production. The objective was to boost farm prices to parity, a level that would restore farmers' purchasing power to what it had been in 1914. In the summer of 1933, the AAA paid southern farmers to plow up 10 million acres of cotton and midwestern farmers to bury 9 million pounds of pork.

Agricultural conditions improved. Farm prices rose from 52 percent of parity in 1932 to 88 percent in 1935, and gross farm income rose by 50 percent. Not until 1941, however, would income exceed the level of 1929, a poor year for farmers. Moreover, some of the decreased production and increased prices stemmed from devastating droughts and dust storms on the Great Plains. The AAA itself harmed poor farmers while aiding larger commercial growers. As southern planters restricted their acreage, they dismissed tenants and sharecroppers, and with AAA payments, they bought new farm machinery, reducing their need for farm labor.

The Supreme Court declared the AAA unconstitutional in 1936, but new laws established the farm subsidy program for decades to come.

Increasing mechanization and scientific agriculture kept production high and farmers dependent on government intervention.

THE FLIGHT OF THE BLUE EAGLE

The New Deal attempted to revive American industry with the National Industrial Recovery Act (NIRA), which created the National Recovery Administration (NRA). The NRA sought to halt the slide in prices, wages, and employment by suspending antitrust laws and authorizing industrial and trade associations to draft codes setting production quotas, price policies, wages and working conditions, and other business practices. The codes promoted the interests of business generally and big business in particular, but Section 7a of the NIRA guaranteed workers the rights to organize unions and bargain collectively—a provision that John L. Lewis of the United Mine Workers called an Emancipation Proclamation for labor.

Hugh Johnson became director of the NRA. He persuaded business leaders to cooperate in drafting codes and the public to patronize participating companies. The NRA Blue Eagle insignia and its slogan "We Do Our Part" covered workplaces, storefronts, and billboards. Blue Eagle parades marched down the nation's main streets and climaxed in a massive demonstration in New York City.

Support for the NRA waned, however. Corporate leaders used it to advance their own goals and to discriminate against small producers, consumers, and labor.

Businesses also violated the labor rights specified in Section 7a. Defiant employers viewed collective bargaining as infringing their authority. Employers even used violence to smother unions. The NRA did little to enforce Section 7a, and Johnson, strongly probusiness, denounced all strikes. Workers felt betrayed. Roosevelt tried to reorganize the NRA, but the act remained controversial until the Supreme Court declared it unconstitutional in 1935.

CRITICS RIGHT AND LEFT

The early New Deal did not end the depression. Recovery was fitful and uneven; millions of Americans remained unemployed. Nevertheless, the New Deal's efforts to grapple with problems, its successes in reducing suffering and fear, and Roosevelt's own skills carried the Democratic Party to victory in the 1934 elections. But New Deal policies also provoked criticism, from both those convinced that too little had been achieved and those alarmed that too much had been attempted.

Despite the early New Deal's probusiness character, conservatives complained that the expansion of government activity and its regulatory role weakened the autonomy of American business. They also condemned the efforts to aid nonbusiness groups as socialistic, particularly the "excessive" spending on unemployment relief and the "instigation" of labor organizing. These critics attracted little popular support, however, and their selfishness antagonized Roosevelt.

More realistic criticism came from the left. In 1932, FDR had campaigned for "the forgotten man at the bottom of the economic pyramid," and some radicals argued that the early New Deal had forgotten the forgotten man. Communists and socialists focused public attention on the poor, especially in the countryside. In California, communists organized Mexican, Filipino, and Japanese farm workers into the Cannery and Agricultural Workers Union; in Arkansas and Tennessee, socialists in 1934 helped organize sharecroppers into the Southern Tenant Farmers Union, protesting the "Raw Deal" they had received from the AAA. Both unions encountered violent reprisals. This terrorism, however, created sympathy for farmworkers.

Even without the involvement of socialists or communists, labor militancy in 1934 pressed Roosevelt. The number of workers participating in strikes leaped from 325,000 in 1932 (about the annual average since 1925) to 1.5 million in 1934.

Rebuffing FDR's pleas for fair treatment, employers moved to crush the strikes, often using complaisant police and private strikebreakers. In Minneapolis, police shot 67 teamsters, almost all in the back, as they fled an ambush arranged by employers; in Toledo, company police and National Guardsmen attacked autoworkers with tear gas, bayonets, and rifle fire; in the textile strike, police

AMERICAN VIEWS

The Commissioner of the Bureau of Indian Affairs on the New Deal for Native Americans.

John Collier, refomer and social worker, served as commissioner of the Bureau of Indian Affairs (BIA) from 1933 until 1945. During his tenure, he radically transformed the agency—long known to be corrupt and hostile to Native Americans– into an organization committed to the preservation of tribal cultures and the restoration of Indian lands. Like other New Dealers, Collier attempted to use the power of the federal government to protect those who had no political power or economic influence—in this case Native Americans.

Collier was extraordinarily successful in promoting the restoration of tribal rights and autonomy and helped ensure that future generations of Indians could reclaim their lands. Yet he was frustrated by Congress' unwillingness to fund the programs he believed necessary for a genuine New Deal for Native Americans. In his 1938 annual report, he calls for greater economic support, arguing that it would be a good investment for the nation. Most important, even as he acknowledges that real changes have occurred since 1933, he points out that there is still much to be done to achieve political autonomy and economic self-sufficiency for American Indians.

- How did Collier describe the treatment of Native Americans, and why did white Americans regard Indians as a "problem" to be eliminated?
- What were the new goals of the Bureau of Indian Affairs?
- How did Collier regard the role of land in Native American society? Why?
- What was the greatest challenge Collier saw for Native Americans in 1938?

For nearly 300 years white Americans, in our zeal to carve out a nation made to order, have dealt with the Indians on the erroneous, yet tragic, assumption that the Indians were a dying race—to be liquidated. We took away their best lands; broke treaties, promises; tossed them the most nearly worthless scraps of a continent that had once been wholly theirs. But we did not liquidate their spirit. The vital spark which kept them alive was hardy. So hardy, indeed, that we now face an astounding and heartening fact. Actually, the Indians, on the evidence of federal census rolls of the past eight years, are increasing almost twice the rate of the population as a whole.

With this fact before us, our whole attitude toward the Indians has necessarily undergone a profound change. Dead is the centuries-old notion that the sooner we eliminate this doomed race, preferably humanely, the better. . . . No longer can we naively talk of or think of the "Indian problem."

We, therefore, define our Indian policy somewhat as follows: So productively to use the moneys appropriated by the Congress for Indians as to enable them, on good, adequate land of their own, to earn decent livelihoods and lead self-respecting, organized lives in harmony with their own aims and ideals, as an integral part of American life. This will not happen tomorrow; perhaps not in our lifetime; but with the revitalization of Indian hope due to the actions and attitudes of this government during the last few years, that aim is a probability, and a real one. . . .

So intimately is all of Indian life tied up with the land and its utilization that to think of Indians is to think of land. The two are inseparable. Upon the land and its intelligent use depends the main future of the American Indian.

The Indian feels toward his land, not a mere ownership but a devotion and veneration befitting that what is not only a home but a refuge. . . . Not only does the Indian's major source of livelihood derive from the land but his social and political organizations are rooted in soil.

Since 1933, the Indian Service has made a concerted effort—an effort which is as yet but a mere beginning—to help the Indian to build back his landholdings to a point where they will provide an adequate basis for a self-sustaining economy, a self-satisfying social organization.

Source: John Collier. Annual Report of the Secretary of the Interior for the Fiscal Year Ended June 30, 1938. From www.historymatters.gmu.edu.

killed six picketers in South Carolina, and soldiers wounded another 50 in Rhode Island. Against such powerful opponents, workers needed help to achieve their rights. Harry Hopkins and other New Dealers realized that labor's demands could not be ignored.

Four prominent individuals mobilized popular discontent to demand government action to assist groups neglected by the New Deal. Representative William Lemke of North Dakota, an agrarian radical leader of the Nonpartisan League, called attention to rural distress. Lemke objected to the New Deal's limited response to farmers crushed by the depression. In his own state, nearly two-thirds of the farmers had lost their land through foreclosures.

Francis Townsend, a California physician, proposed to aid the nation's elderly, many of whom were destitute. The Townsend Plan called for a government pension to every American over the age of 60, provided that the recipient retired from work and spent the entire pension. This scheme promised to extend relief to the elderly, open jobs for the unemployed, and stimulate economic recovery. Over 5,000 Townsend Clubs lobbied for government action to help the elderly poor.

Father Charles Coughlin, a Catholic priest in the Detroit suburb of Royal Oak, threatened to mobilize another large constituency against the limitations of the early New Deal. Thirty million Americans listened eagerly to his weekly radio broadcasts, which mixed religion with anti-Semitism and demands for social justice and financial reform. Coughlin had condemned Hoover for assisting banks but ignoring the unemployed, and initially he welcomed the New Deal as "Christ's Deal." But after concluding that FDR's policies favored "the virile viciousness of business and finance," Coughlin organized the National Union for Social Justice to lobby for his goals. With support among lower-middle-class, heavily Catholic, urban ethnic groups, Coughlin posed a real challenge to Roosevelt's Democratic party.

Roosevelt found Senator Huey P. Long of Louisiana still more worrisome. Alternately charming and autocratic, Long had modernized his state with taxation and educational reforms and an extensive public-works program after his election as governor in 1928. Moving to the Senate and eyeing the White House, Long proposed more comprehensive social-welfare policies than the New Deal had envisaged. In 1934, he organized the Share-Our-Wealth Society. His plan to end poverty and unemployment called for confiscatory taxes on the rich to provide every family with a decent income, health coverage, education, and old-age pensions. Long's appeal was enormous. Within months, his organization claimed more than 27,000 clubs and 7 million members.

These dissident movements raised complex issues and simple fears. Their programs were often ill-defined or impractical and some of the leaders, like Coughlin and Long, approached demagoguery. Nevertheless, their popularity warned Roosevelt that government action was needed to satisfy reform demands and ensure his reelection in 1936.

Consolidating the New Deal

Responding to the persistence of the depression and political pressures, Roosevelt in 1935 undertook economic and social reforms that some observers have called the Second New Deal. The new measures shifted government action more toward reform even as they still addressed relief and recovery. Nor did FDR's interest in reform simply reflect cynical politics. He had frequently championed progressive measures in the past, and many of his advisers had deep roots in reform movements.

WEEDING OUT AND LIFTING UP

"In spite of our efforts and in spite of our talk," Roosevelt told the new Congress in 1935, "we have not weeded out the overprivileged and we have not effectively lifted up the underprivileged." To do so, he developed "must" legislation. One of the new laws protected labor's rights to organize and bargain collectively. The Wagner National Labor Relations Act, dubbed "Labor's Magna Carta," guaranteed workers the right to organize unions and prohibited employers from adopting unfair labor practices, such as firing union activists and forming company unions.

Social Security Of greater long-range importance was the Social Security Act. The law was a compromise, framed by a nonpartisan committee of business, labor, and public representatives and then weakened by congressional conservatives. It provided unemployment compensation, old-age pensions, and aid for dependent mothers and children and the blind.

The conservative nature of the law appeared in its stingy benefit payments, its lack of health insurance, and its exclusion of more than one-fourth of all workers, including many in desperate need of protection, such as farm laborers and domestic servants. Moreover, unlike in other nations, the old-age pensions were financed through a regressive payroll tax on both employees and employers rather than through general tax revenues. Thus the new system was more like a compulsory insurance program.

Despite its weaknesses, the Social Security Act was one of the most important laws in American history. It provided, Roosevelt pointed out, "at least some measure of protection to the average citizen and to his family against the loss of a job and against poverty-ridden old age." Moreover, by establishing federal responsibility for social welfare, it inaugurated a welfare system that subsequent generations would expand.

Money, Tax, and Land Reform Another reform measure, the Banking Act of 1935, increased the authority of the Federal Reserve Board over the nation's currency and credit system and decreased the power of the private bankers whose irresponsible behavior had contributed to the depression and the appeal of Father Coughlin. The Revenue Act of 1935, passed after Roosevelt assailed the "unjust concentration of wealth and economic power," provided for graduated income taxes and increased estate and corporate taxes.

The Second New Deal also responded belatedly to the environmental catastrophe that had turned much of the Great Plains from Texas to the Dakotas into a Dust Bowl. Since World War I, farmers had stripped marginal land of its native grasses to plant wheat. When drought and high winds hit the plains in 1932, crops failed, and nothing was left to hold the soil. Dust storms blew away millions of tons of topsoil, despoiling the land and darkening the sky a thousand miles away. Families abandoned their farms in droves. Many of these poor "Okies" headed for California, their plight captured in John Steinbeck's novel, *The Grapes of Wrath* (1939).

In 1935, Roosevelt established the Resettlement Administration to focus on land reform and help poor farmers. This agency initiated soil erosion projects and attempted to resettle impoverished farmers on better land, but the problem exceeded its resources. Congress moved to save the land, if not its people, by creating the Soil Conservation Service in 1935.

EXPANDING RELIEF

If reform gained priority in the Second New Deal, relief remained critical. With millions still unemployed, Roosevelt pushed through Congress in 1935 the Emergency Relief Appropriation Act, authorizing $5 billion—at the time the largest single appropriation in American history—for emergency public employment. Roosevelt created the Works Progress Administration (WPA) under Hopkins, who set up work relief programs to assist the unemployed and boost the economy. Before its end in 1943, the WPA gave jobs to 9 million people (more than a fifth of the labor force) and spent nearly $12 billion. Three-fourths of its expenditures went on construction projects that could employ manual labor: the WPA built 125,000 schools, post offices, and hospitals; 8,000 parks; nearly 100,000 bridges; and enough roads and sewer systems to circle the earth 30 times. The WPA laid much of the basic infrastructure on which the nation still relies.

The WPA also developed work projects for unemployed writers, artists, musicians, and actors. The Federal Art Project hired artists to teach art in night schools, prepare exhibits at museums, and paint murals on post office walls. The Federal Theatre Project organized theatrical productions and drama companies that in four years played to 30 million Americans. The Federal Music Project hired musicians to collect and perform folk songs. These WPA programs allowed people to use their talents while surviving the depression, increased popular access to cultural performances, and established a precedent for federal support of the arts.

The National Youth Administration (NYA), another WPA agency, gave part-time jobs to students, enabling 2 million high school and college students to stay in school, learn skills, and do productive work.

THE ROOSEVELT COALITION AND THE ELECTION OF 1936

The 1936 election gave Americans an opportunity to judge FDR and the New Deal. Conservatives alarmed at the expansion of government, business people angered by regulation and labor legislation, and wealthy Americans furious with tax reform decried the New Deal. But they were a minority. Even the presidential candidate they supported, Republican Governor Alf Landon of Kansas, endorsed much of the New Deal, criticizing merely the inefficiency and cost of some of its programs.

The programs and politicians of the New Deal had created an invincible coalition behind Roosevelt. Despite ambivalence about large-scale government intervention, the New Deal's agricultural programs reinforced the traditional Democratic allegiance of white southerners while attracting many western farmers. Labor legislation clinched the active support of the nation's workers. Middle-class voters, whose homes had been saved and whose hopes had been raised, also joined the Roosevelt coalition.

So did urban ethnic groups, who had benefited from welfare programs and appreciated the unprecedented recognition Roosevelt's administration gave them. FDR named the first Italian American to the federal judiciary, for example, and appointed five times as many Catholics and Jews to government positions as the three Republican presidents had during the 1920s. African Americans voted overwhelmingly Democratic for the first time. Women, too, were an important part of the Roosevelt coalition, and Eleanor often attracted their support as much as Franklin did.

This political realignment produced a landslide. Roosevelt polled 61 percent of the popular vote and the largest electoral vote margin ever recorded, 523 to 8. Roosevelt's political coalition reflected a mandate for himself and the New Deal; it would enable the Democrats to dominate national elections for three decades.

The New Deal and American Life

The landslide of 1936 revealed the impact of the New Deal on Americans. Industrial workers mobilized to secure their rights, women and minorities gained increased, if still limited, opportunities to participate in American society, and southerners and westerners benefited from government programs they turned to their own advantage. Government programs changed daily life, and ordinary people often helped shape the new policies.

LABOR ON THE MARCH

The labor revival in the 1930s reflected both workers' determination and government support. Workers wanted to improve their wages and benefits as well as to gain union recognition and union contracts that would allow them to limit arbitrary managerial authority and achieve some control over the workplace.

The Second New Deal helped. By guaranteeing labor's rights to organize and bargain collectively, the Wagner Act sparked a wave of labor activism. But if the government ultimately protected union rights, the unions themselves had to form locals, recruit members, and demonstrate influence in the workplace.

At first, those tasks overwhelmed the American Federation of Labor (AFL). Its reliance on craft-based unions and reluctance to organize immigrant, black, and women workers left it unprepared for the rush of industrial workers seeking unionization. More progressive labor leaders saw that industry-wide unions were more appropriate for unskilled workers in mass-production industries. Forming the Committee for Industrial Organization (CIO) within the AFL, they campaigned to unionize workers in the steel, auto, and rubber industries, all notoriously hostile to unions. AFL leaders tried to make the CIO disband and then in 1937 expelled its unions. The militants reorganized as the separate **Congress of Industrial Organizations**. (In 1955, the two groups merged as the AFL-CIO.)

The split roused the AFL to increase its own organizing activities, but it was primarily the new CIO that put labor on the march. It inspired workers previously neglected by organized labor. The CIO's interracial union campaign in the Birmingham steel mills, said one organizer, was "like a second coming of Christ" for black workers, who welcomed the union as a chance for social recognition as well as economic opportunity. The CIO also employed new and aggressive tactics, particularly the sit-down strike, in which workers, rather than picketing outside the factory, simply sat inside the plant, thereby blocking both production and the use of strikebreakers.

The CIO won major victories despite bitter opposition from industry and its allies. The issue was not wages but labor's right to organize and bargain with management. Sit-down strikes paralyzed General Motors in 1937 after it refused to recognize the United Auto Workers. GM tried to force the strikers out of its Flint, Michigan, plants by turning off the heat, using police and tear gas, threatening strikers' families, and obtaining court orders to clear the plant by military force. But the governor refused to order National Guardsmen to attack, and the strikers held out, aided by the Women's Emergency Brigade. After six weeks, GM signed a contract with the UAW. Chrysler soon followed suit. Ford refused to recognize the union until 1941, often violently disrupting organizing efforts.

Steel companies also used violence against unionization. In the Memorial Day Massacre in Chicago in 1937, police guarding a plant of the Republic Steel Company fired on strikers and their families, killing ten people as they tried to flee. A Senate investigation found that Republic and other companies had hired private police to attack workers seeking to unionize, stockpiled weapons and tear gas, and corrupted officials. Federal court orders finally forced the companies to bargain collectively.

New Deal labor legislation, government investigations and court orders, and the federal refusal to use force against strikes helped the labor movement secure basic rights for American workers. Union membership leaped from under 3 million in 1932 to 9 million by 1939, and workers won higher wages, better working conditions, and more economic democracy.

WOMEN AND THE NEW DEAL

New Deal relief programs had a mixed impact on working women. Formal government policy required equal consideration for women and men, but local officials flouted this requirement. Women on relief were restricted to women's work—more than half worked on sewing projects, regardless of their skills—and were paid scarcely half what men received. WPA training programs also reinforced traditional ideas about women's work; black women, for example, were trained to be maids, dishwashers, and cooks. Although women constituted nearly one-fourth of the labor force, they obtained only 19 percent of the jobs created by the WPA, 12 percent of those created by the FERA, and 7 percent of those created by the CWA. The CCC excluded women altogether. Still, relief agencies provided crucial assistance to women during the depression.

Other New Deal programs also had mixed benefits for women. Despite demands by the League of Women Voters and the Women's Trade Union League for "equal pay for equal work and equal opportunity for equal ability regardless of sex," many NRA codes mandated lower wage scales for women than for men. But by raising minimum wages, the NRA brought relatively greater improvement to women, who were concentrated in the lowest-paid occupations, than to male workers. The Social Security Act did not cover domestic servants, waitresses, or women who worked in the home, but it did help mothers with dependent children.

Still more significant, the Social Security Act

reflected and reinforced prevailing notions about proper roles for men and women. The system was based on the idea that men should be wage earners and women should stay at home as wives and mothers. Accordingly, if a woman worked outside the home and her husband was eligible for benefits, she would not receive her own retirement pension. And if a woman had no husband but had children, welfare authorities would remove her from work-relief jobs regardless of whether she wanted to continue to work, and would give her assistance from the Aid to Dependent Children (ADC) program, which was also created under the Social Security Act. These new programs, then, institutionalized a modern welfare system that segregated men and women in separate spheres and reaffirmed the then popular belief that the success of the family depended on that separation.

Women also gained political influence under the New Deal. Molly Dewson, the director of the Women's Division of the Democratic party, exercised considerable political power and helped to shape the party's campaigns. Around Dewson revolved a network of women, linked by friendships and experiences in the National Consumers' League, Women's Trade Union League, and other progressive reform organizations. Appointed to many positions in the Roosevelt administration, they helped develop and implement New Deal social legislation.

Eleanor Roosevelt was their leader. Described by a Washington reporter as "a cabinet member without portfolio," she roared across the social and political landscape of the 1930s, pushing for women's rights, demanding reforms, traveling across the country, writing newspaper columns and speaking on the radio, developing plans to help unemployed miners in West Virginia and abolish slums in Washington, and lobbying both Congress and her husband. Indeed, Eleanor Roosevelt had become not merely the most prominent first lady in history but a force in her own right and a symbol of the growing importance of women in public life.

MINORITIES AND THE NEW DEAL

Although Roosevelt deplored racial abuses, he never pushed for civil rights legislation, fearing to antagonize southern congressional Democrats whose support he needed. For similar reasons, many New Deal programs discriminated against African Americans. In addition, racist officials discriminated in allocating federal relief. Atlanta, for instance, provided average monthly relief checks of $32.66 to white people but only $19.29 to black people.

Nonetheless, disproportionately poor and unemployed African Americans did benefit from the New Deal's welfare and economic programs. W.E.B. DeBois affirmed that the New Deal sharpened their sense of the value of citizenship by making clear the "direct connection between politics and industry, between government and work, [and] between coting and wages." And key New Dealers campaigned against racial discrimination. Eleanor Roosevelt prodded FDR to appoint black officials, wrote articles supporting racial equality, and flouted segregationist laws. Harry Hopkins and Harold Ickes also promoted equal rights. Ickes, a former president of Chicago's NAACP chapter, insisted that African Americans receive PWA relief jobs in proportion to their share of the population and ended segregation in the Department of the Interior, prompting other cabinet secretaries to follow suit. As black votes in northern cities became important, pragmatic New Dealers also began to pay attention to black needs.

African Americans themselves pressed for reforms. Civil rights groups protested discriminatory policies, including the unequal wage scales in the NRA codes and the CCC's limited enrollment of black youth. African Americans demonstrated against racial discrimination in hiring and their exclusion from federally financed construction projects.

In response, FDR took more interest in black economic and social problems. He prohibited discrimination in the WPA in 1935, and the NYA adopted enlightened racial policies. Roosevelt also appointed black people to important positions, including the first black federal judge.

The New Deal improved economic and social conditions for many African Americans. Black illiteracy dropped because of federal education projects, and the number of black college students and graduates more than doubled, in part because the NYA provided student aid to black colleges. New

Deal relief and public health programs reduced black infant mortality rates and raised life expectancy rates. Conditions for black people continued to lag behind those for white people, and discrimination persisted, but the black switch to the Roosevelt coalition reflected the New Deal's benefits.

Native Americans also benefited from the New Deal. The depression had imposed further misery on a group already suffering from poverty, wretched health conditions, and the nation's lowest educational level. Many New Deal programs had limited applicability to Indians, but the CCC appealed to their interests and skills. More than 80,000 Native Americans received training in agriculture, forestry, and animal husbandry, along with basic academic subjects. CCC projects, together with those undertaken by the PWA and the WPA, built schools, hospitals, roads, and irrigation systems on reservations.

New Deal officials also refocused government Indian policy. Appointed commissioner of Indian affairs in 1933, John Collier prohibited interference with Native American religious or cultural life, directed the Bureau of Indian Affairs to employ more Native Americans, and prevented Indian schools from suppressing native languages and traditions.

Collier also persuaded Congress to pass the Indian Reorganization Act of 1934, often called the Indians' New Deal. The act guaranteed religious freedom, reestablished tribal self-government, and halted the sale of tribal lands. It also provided funds to expand Indian landholdings, support Indian students, and establish tribal businesses. White missionaries and business interests attacked Collier's reforms as atheistic and communistic. And not all Native Americans supported Collier's reforms, asserting that he, too, stereotyped Indians and their culture, and labeling his efforts as "back-to-the-blanket" policies designed to make Native American cultures historical commodities (see American Views: "The Commissioner of the Bureau of Indian Affairs on the New Deal for Native Americans").

Hispanic Americans received less assistance from the New Deal. Relief programs aided many Hispanics in California and the Southwest but ignored those who were not citizens. Moreover, local administrators often discriminated against Hispanics, especially by providing higher relief payments to Anglos. Finally, by excluding agricultural workers, neither the Social Security Act nor the Wagner Act gave Mexican Americans much protection or hope. Farm workers remained largely unorganized, exploited, and at the mercy of agribusinesses.

THE NEW DEAL: NORTH, SOUTH, EAST, AND WEST

"We are going to make a country," President Roosevelt declared, "in which no one is left out." And with that statement, along with his belief that the federal government must take the lead in building a new "economic constitutional order," FDR ensured that his New Deal programs and policies fanned out throughout the nation, bolstering the stock market and banking in New York, constructing public housing for poor white and African-American families in most major cities, and building schools, roads, and bridges in every region of the United States.

The New Deal in the South The New Deal's agricultural program boosted farm prices and income more in the South than any other region. By controlling cotton production, it also promoted diversification; its subsidies financed mechanization. The resulting modernization helped replace an archaic sharecropping system with an emergent agribusiness. The rural poor were displaced, but the South's agricultural economy advanced.

The New Deal also improved southern cities. FERA and WPA built urban sewer systems, airports, bridges, roads, and harbor facilities. Whereas northern cities had already constructed such facilities themselves— and were still paying off the debts these had incurred—the federal government largely paid for such modernization in the South, giving its cities an economic advantage.

Federal grants were supposed to be awarded to states in proportion to their own expenditures, but while southern politicians welcomed New Deal funds, they refused to contribute their share of the costs. Nationally, the federal proportion of FERA expenditures was 62 percent; in the South, it was usually 90 percent and never lower than 73 percent.

Federal money enabled southern communities to balance their budgets, preach fiscal orthodoxy, and maintain traditional claims of limited government. Federal officials complained about the South's "parasitic" behavior, and even southerners acknowledged the hypocrisy of the region's invocation of state's rights. "We recognize state boundaries when called on to give," noted the *Houston Press*, "but forget them when Uncle Sam is doing the giving."

The federal government had a particularly powerful impact on the South with the **Tennessee Valley Authority (TVA)**, launched in 1933. Coordinating activities across seven states, the TVA built dams to control floods and generate hydroelectric power, produced fertilizer, fostered agricultural and forestry development, encouraged conservation, improved navigation, and modernized school and health systems. Its major drawback was environmental damage that only became apparent later. Over a vast area of the South, it provided electricity for the first time.

The New Deal further expanded access to electricity by establishing the Rural Electrification Administration (REA) in 1935. Private companies had refused to extend power lines into the countryside because it was not profitable consigning 90 percent of the nation's farms to drudgery and darkness. The REA revolutionized farm life by sponsoring rural nonprofit electric cooperatives. By 1941, 35 percent of American farms had electricity; by 1950, 78 percent.

The New Deal in the West The New Deal also changed the West. Westerners received the most federal money per capita in welfare, relief projects, and loans. Western farmers and cattle raisers were saved by federal payments, and even refugees from the Dust Bowl depended on relief assistance and medical care in federal camps.

The Bureau of Reclamation, established in 1902, emerged as one of the most important government agencies in the West. It built huge dams to control the western river systems, promote large-scale development, and prevent flooding, and it produced cheap hydroelectric power and created reservoirs and canal systems to bring water to farms and cities. By furnishing capital and expertise, the government subsidized and stimulated western economic development, particularly the growth of agribusiness.

Westerners welcomed such assistance but rarely shared the federal goals of rational resource management. Instead, they often wanted to continue to exploit the land and resented federal supervision as colonial control. In practice, however, the government worked in partnership with the West's agribusinesses and timber and petroleum industries.

THE NEW DEAL AND PUBLIC ACTIVISM

Despite Hoover's fear that government responsibility would discourage local initiative, the 1930s witnessed an upsurge in activism. New Deal programs, in fact, often encouraged or empowered groups to shape public policy and social and economic behavior. Moreover, because the administration worried about centralization, some federal agencies fostered what New Dealers called "grassroots democracy." The AAA set up committees that ultimately included more than 100,000 people to implement agricultural policy and held referendums on crop controls; local advisory committees guided the various federal arts projects; federal management of the West's public grasslands mandated cooperation with associations of livestock raisers.

At times, local administration of national programs enabled groups to exploit federal policy for their own advantage. But federal programs often allowed previously unrepresented groups to contest traditionally dominant interests. Often seeing greater opportunities for participation and influence in federal programs than in city and state governments, community groups campaigned to expand federal authority. In short, depression conditions and New Deal programs actually increased citizen involvement in public affairs.

Ebbing of the New Deal

After his victory in 1936, Roosevelt committed himself to further reforms. "I see one-third of a nation ill-housed, ill-clad, ill-nourished," he declared in his second inaugural address. "The test of our progress is not whether we add more to the abundance of those who have much; it is whether we provide enough for those who have too little." But determined opponents, continuing economic problems, and the president's own misjudgments blocked his reforms and deadlocked the New Deal.

CHALLENGING THE COURT

Roosevelt regarded the Supreme Court as his most dangerous opponent. During his first term, the Court had declared several important measures unconstitutional. FDR complained that the justices held "horse-and-buggy" ideas about government that prevented the president and Congress from responding to changes.

Emboldened by the 1936 landslide, Roosevelt decided to restructure the federal judiciary. In early 1937, he proposed legislation authorizing the president to name a new justice for each one serving past the age of 70. His goal was to appoint new justices more sympathetic to the New Deal.

His Court plan led to a divisive struggle. The proposal was perfectly legal: Congress had the authority, which it had used repeatedly, to change the number of justices on the Court. But Republicans and conservative Democrats attacked the plan as a scheme to "pack" the Court and subvert the separation of powers among the three branches of government and even many liberals expressed reservations about the plan or FDR's lack of candor in proposing it.

The Court itself undercut support for FDR's proposal by upholding the Social Security and Wagner acts and minimum-wage legislation. Moreover, the retirement of a conservative justice allowed Roosevelt to name a sympathetic successor. Congress rejected Roosevelt's plan.

Roosevelt's challenge to the Court hurt the New Deal. It worried the public, split the Democratic Party, and revived conservatives. Opponents promptly attacked other New Deal policies, from support for unions to progressive taxation. Henceforth, a conservative coalition of Republicans and southern Democrats in Congress blocked FDR's reforms.

MORE HARD TIMES

A sharp recession, beginning in August 1937, added to Roosevelt's problems. As the economy improved in 1936, Roosevelt decided to cut federal expenditures and balance the budget. But private investment and employment remained stagnant, and the economy plunged. A record decline in industrial production canceled the gains of the preceding two years, and unemployment leaped from 7 million to 11 million within a few months.

In 1938, Roosevelt reluctantly increased spending. His decision was based on the principles of the British economist John Maynard Keynes. As Marriner Eccles of the Federal Reserve Board explained, the federal government had to serve as the "compensatory agent" in the economy—it would use deficit spending to increase demand and production when private investment declined, and would raise taxes to pay its debt and cool the economy when business activity became excessive. New appropriations for the PWA and other government programs revived the faltering economy, but neither FDR nor Congress would spend what was necessary to end the depression. Only the vast expenditures for World War II would bring full recovery.

POLITICAL STALEMATE

The recession interrupted the momentum of the New Deal and strengthened its opponents. In late 1937, their leaders in Congress issued a "conservative manifesto" decrying New Deal fiscal, labor, and regulatory policies. Holding seniority in a Congress malapportioned in their favor, they blocked most of Roosevelt's reforms. None of his must legislation passed a special session of Congress in December. In 1938, Congress rejected tax reforms and reduced corporate taxes.

The few measures that passed were heavily amended. The Fair Labor Standards Act established maximum hours and minimum wages for workers but authorized so many exemptions that one New Dealer asked "whether anyone is subject to this bill."

To protect the New Deal, Roosevelt turned again to the public, with whom he remained immensely popular. In the 1938 Democratic primaries, he campaigned against the New Deal's conservative opponents. But FDR could not transfer his personal popularity to the political newcomers he supported. Roosevelt lost further political leverage when the Republicans gained 75 seats in the House, seven in the Senate, and 13 governorships.

With Roosevelt in the White House and his opponents controlling Congress, the New Deal ended in political stalemate.

Good Neighbors and Hostile Forces

Even before FDR's conservative opponents derailed the New Deal, the president felt their impact in the area of foreign policy. Isolationists in Congress counseled against any U.S. involvement in world affairs and appealed to the growing national disillusionment with America's participation in the Great War to support their position.

Responding to the spreading popular belief that World War I had been fought to protect the fortunes of financiers and munitions makers, Republican Senator Gerald Nye established a committee in 1934 to investigate the origins of U.S. involvement in what many Americans now termed the European War. For two years, the Nye Committee sensationally exposed the greed of big business and intimated that President Woodrow Wilson had gone to war to save profits for capitalists—and not democracy for the world. Jobless and homeless Americans reacted angrily to the committee's findings, and public sentiment against fighting another foreign war hardened. Moreover, Roosevelt himself believed that the gravity of the nation's economic depression warranted a primary focus on domestic recovery, and in the early years of his presidency, took few international initiatives.

The actions he did take related directly to salvaging America's desperate economy. As the depression worsened in 1933, American businesses searched for new markets throughout the world, and key business leaders informed FDR that they would welcome the opportunity to expand trade to the Soviet Union. Moscow was also eager to renew ties to the United States, and President Roosevelt extended formal recognition of the Soviet Union in November 1933.

Enhancing trade opportunities and rescuing the economy from the damage wrought by high tariffs figured prominently in Roosevelt's policies in the Western Hemisphere. In large measure, Roosevelt merely extended the Good Neighbor policy begun by his predecessor. Still, the Great Depression strained U.S.-Latin American relations, sending economic shock waves throughout Central and South America and, in several instances, helping propel to power ruthless dictators who ruled with iron fists and U.S. support. Moreover, although FDR continued the policy of military nonintervention, his displeasure with the 1933 election of a radical as president of Cuba led him to support a coup there that resulted in the coming to power of the infamous dictator Fulgencio Batista. The Batista era lasted until he was overthrown by Fidel Castro in 1959.

In 1936, FDR broke new ground by becoming the first U.S. president to sail to South America. He also worked to encourage trade by reducing tariffs. Between 1929 and 1933, the volume of trade worldwide had collapsed by 40 percent and American exports had plummeted by 60 percent. Secretary of State Cordell Hull finalized trade agreements with numerous Latin American nations that allowed "most favored nation" status and resulted in sharply increasing U.S. exports to its southern neighbors. Good neighbors were also good trading partners.

NEUTRALITY AND FASCISM

Outside the hemisphere, during his first term as president, Roosevelt generally followed the policy of avoiding involvement in Europe's political, economic, and social problems. But the aggressive actions of Adolf Hitler in Germany ultimately led Roosevelt to a different position, and in the latter part of the decade, he faced the task of educating the American public about the fascist danger that was spreading in Europe.

Hitler came to power in 1933, shortly before FDR entered the White House. As the leader of the National Socialist Workers Party, or Nazis, Hitler established a **fascist government**—a one-party dictatorship closely aligned with corporate interests, committed to a "biological world evolution," and determined to establish a new empire, the Third Reich. He vowed to eliminate Bolshevik radicalism and purify the German "race" through the elimination of those he deemed undesirable, especially targeting Jews, the group Hitler blamed for most, if not all, Germany's ills.

Others aided the spread of fascism. Italian leader Benito Mussolini, who had assumed power in 1922 and envisaged emulating the power and prestige of the Roman Empire, brutally attacked Ethiopia in 1935. The following year, a young fascist military officer, Francisco Franco, led an uprising in Spain, and with the assistance of Italy and Germany, successfully ousted the Spanish Republic and its loyalist supporters by 1939 to create an authoritarian government. Meanwhile, Hitler implemented his plan of conquest: he remilitarized the Rhineland in 1936, and in 1938 he annexed Austria.

The aggressive actions of Germany and Italy failed to eclipse American fears of becoming involved in another European war. Congress passed four Neutrality Acts designed to continue America's trade with its world partners but prohibit the president from taking sides in the mounting European crisis.

Appeasement and More Neutrality After
annexing Austria, Hitler pushed again in 1938 when he demanded the Sudetenland from Czechoslovakia. Meeting in Munich in September 1938, the leaders of England and France abandoned their security obligations to the Czechs, yielding the Sudetenland to Hitler in exchange for a weak promise of no more annexations.

In America, too, the sentiment was for peace at all costs, and isolationism permeated the halls of Congress. Indeed, Hitler himself did not regard the

¬United States as a threat to his expansionist plan. Hitler held FDR in low esteem and denounced America as a racially mixed nation of intellectual inferiors.

Isolationism compounded by anti-Semitism and by the divisions among leaders of the American Jewish community combined to ensure that the United States would not become a haven for Jews suffering under Nazi brutality. News of Nazi atrocities against Austrian Jews in 1938 shocked the American press, and Hitler's violent pogrom, known as *Kristallnacht* ("Night of the Broken Glass"), conducted against Jews throughout Germany in November 1938, added fresh proof of Nazi cruelty. Although the United States recalled its ambassador from Berlin to protest the pogrom, it did not alter its restrictive immigration-quota system to provide refuge for German Jews.

As Europe edged closer to war, the relationship between the United States and Japan, periodically tense in the twentieth century, became more strained. The United States regarded Japan's desires for empire as threatening but also needed Japan as a trading partner, especially in the economically depressed 1930s. Consequently, in September 1931, when Japan seized Manchuria, the United States did little more than denounce the action. Again in 1937, after Japanese troops attacked Chinese forces north of Beijing and outright war began between Japan and China, the United States merely condemned the action.

EDGING TOWARD INVOLVEMENT

After the Munich agreement, President Roosevelt moved away from domestic reform toward preparedness for war, fearful that conflict in Europe was unavoidable and determined to revise the neutrality laws. In his State of the Union address in January 1939, FDR explained that America's neutrality laws might "actually give aid to an aggressor and deny it to the victim." By the fall of that year, he had won support for eliminating the prohibition on arms sales and adding armaments to the list of cash-and-carry items—a revision that would enable the United States to provide important assistance to Britain and France in the winter of 1939-1940. Hitler's defiance of the Munich agreement, overrunning Prague, by March 1939, merely anticipated his next move toward Poland and also convinced the British and the French that war was imminent.

Conclusion

The Great Depression and the New Deal mark a major divide in American history. The depression cast doubt on the traditional practices, policies, and attitudes that underlay not only the nation's economy but also its social and political institutions and relationships. The New Deal brought only partial economic recovery. However, its economic policies, from banking and securities regulation to unemployment compensation, farm price supports, and minimum wages, created barriers against another depression. The gradual adoption of compensatory spending policies expanded the government's role in the economy. Responding to the failures of both private organizations and state and local governments, the federal government assumed the obligation to provide social welfare. "Better the occasional faults of a Government that lives in a spirit of charity," Roosevelt warned, "than the constant omission of a Government frozen in the ice of its own indifference."

Roosevelt expanded the role of the presidency and made the federal government, rather than state or local governments, the focus of public interest and expectations.

Roosevelt and the New Deal also revitalized the Democratic Party, drawing minorities, industrial workers, and previously uninvolved citizens into a coalition with white southerners that made the Democrats the dominant national party.

Political constraints explain some of the New Deal's failures. Conservative southern Democrats and northern Republicans limited its efforts to curtail racial discrimination or protect the rural and urban poor. But Roosevelt and other New Dealers were often constrained by their own vision, refusing to consider the massive deficit spending necessary to end the depression or not recognizing the need to end gender discrimination. But if the New Deal

did not bring the revolution its conservative critics claimed, it did change American life.

By the end of the 1930s, FDR cautiously led the nation toward war—this time against an enemy far more threatening than the Great Depression. Ironically, only then would President Roosevelt end the depression that had ravaged the nation for nearly a decade.

Summary

Hard Times in Hooverville The prosperity of the 1920s ended in a stock market crash that revealed the flaws in the economy. As the nation slid into a catastrophic depression, factories closed, employment and incomes tumbled, and millions lost their homes, hopes, and dignity. Some protested and took direct action; others looked to the government for relief. The stock market crash of 1929 marked the beginning of the Great Depression but did not cause it. Contributing factors were the uneven distribution of wealth and income; industries dominated by oligarchies; overproduction in agriculture and other industries; declining prices; government policies; and European debts.

Herbert Hoover and the Depression President Hoover took unprecedented steps to resolve the growing economic crises, but he believed that voluntary private relief was preferable to federal intervention. The scope of the depression overwhelmed anything that private individuals and agencies could manage; Hoover blundered by refusing to admit a more activist approach was needed. The Reconstruction Finance Corporation lent funds that could "trickle down" to the public. The treatment of the Bonus Army symbolized Hoover's unpopularity and set the stage for the election of Franklin D. Roosevelt.

Launching the New Deal In the midst of national anxiety, Franklin D. Roosevelt pushed forward an unprecedented program to resolve the crisis of a collapsing financial system, crippling unemployment, and agricultural and industrial breakdown and to promote reform. After initially addressing the banking crisis, the New Deal went on to establish relief agencies and promote economic recovery. The New Deal achieved successes and attracted support but it also had limitations and generated criticism that suggested the need for still greater innovations.

Consolidating the New Deal In 1935 Roosevelt undertook additional economic and social reforms. Labor's right to organize and bargain collectively was addressed, the path-breaking Social Security Act was passed, and the Works Progress Administration was created. The administration also responded to the environmental crises that had turned the Great Plains into a dustbowl and driven the "Okies" to California. The 1936 election gave Americans an opportunity to judge the New Deal and Roosevelt. Political realignment resulted: Former Republican constituents voted Democratic and produced a landslide victory for the president.

The New Deal and American Life The election of 1936 revealed the impact the New Deal had on Americans. Industrial workers mobilized to secure their rights; women and minorities gained increased, if still limited, opportunities to participate in American society; and Southerners and Westerners benefited from government programs like the TVA that they turned to their own advantage. Government programs changed daily life, and ordinary people often helped shape the new policies.

Ebbing of the New Deal After his 1936 election, Roosevelt committed himself to further reforms, but his misjudgment blocked some efforts and deadlocked others. Regarding the Supreme Court as an adversary, Roosevelt attempted to restructure the federal judiciary; his attempt to "pack" the court hurt the New Deal. A 1937 recession caused by the New Deal's lack of aggressiveness caused the administration to adopt Keynesian economic theories and have the government use deficient spending to increase demand and production.

Good Neighbors and Hostile Forces While isolationists in Congress counseled against involvement in foreign affairs, fascism was spreading in Europe and Asia. In his first term Roosevelt followed a policy of neutrality; after the Munich crisis, Hitler's intentions toward the world and Germany's Jewish citizens had become more defined and threatening. America's relationship with Japan continued to deteriorate; by 1939, the "epidemic of world lawlessness" was edging the United States toward involvement.

REVIEW QUESTIONS

1. What were the international consequences of the stock market crash in 1929? How did world leaders respond to the global depression? With what results?

2. Why did President Hoover's emphasis on voluntarism fail to resolve the problems of the Great Depression in the United States?

3. Describe the relief programs of the New Deal. What were they designed to accomplish? What were their achievements and their limitations?

4. What were the major criticisms of the early New Deal? How accurate were those charges?

5. How did the policies of the New Deal shape the constituency and the prospects of the Democratic Party in the 1930s?

6. Describe the conflict between management and labor in the 1930s. What were the major issues and motivations? How did the two sides differ in resources and tactics, and how and why did these factors change over time?

7. How did the role of the federal government change in the 1930s? What factors were responsible for the changes?

WHERE TO LEARN MORE

Center for New Deal Studies, Roosevelt University, Chicago, Illinois. The center contains political memorabilia, photographs, papers, and taped interviews dealing with Franklin D. Roosevelt and the New Deal; it also sponsors an annual lecture series about the Roosevelt legacy.

Herbert Hoover National Historic Site, West Branch, Iowa. This 186-acre site contains the birthplace cottage and grave of Herbert Hoover as well as his presidential library and museum, which contains a reconstruction of Hoover's White House office. www.nps.gov/heho; www.hoover.archives.gov

Labor Museum and Learning Center of Michigan, Flint, Michigan. Exhibits trace the history of the labor movement, including the dramatic "Sit-Down Strike" of 1936–1937.

Franklin D. Roosevelt Home and Presidential Library, Hyde Park, New York. The Roosevelt home, furnished with family heirlooms, and the spacious grounds, where FDR is buried, personalize the president and provide insights into his career. The nearby library has displays and exhibitions about Roosevelt's presidency, and the Eleanor Roosevelt Wing is dedicated to her career. www.fdrlibrary.marist.edu

Eleanor Roosevelt National Historic Site, Hyde Park, New York. These two cottages, where Eleanor Roosevelt worked and, after 1945, lived, contain her furniture and memorabilia. Visitors can also watch a film biography of ER and tour the grounds of this retreat where she entertained personal friends and world leaders. www.nps.gov/elro

Civilian Conservation Corps Interpretive Center, Whidbey Island, Washington. This stone and wood structure, built as a CCC project, now houses exhibits and artifacts illustrating the history of the CCC.

Bethune Museum and Archives National Historic Site, Washington, D.C. This four-story townhouse was the home of Mary McLeod Bethune, a friend of Eleanor Roosevelt and the director of the New Deal's Division of Negro Affairs, and the headquarters of the National Council of Negro Women, which Bethune founded in 1935. Exhibits feature the contributions of black activist women and activities of the civil rights movement.

U.S. History Documents CD-ROM

For primary sources related to this chapter, refer to the document CD-ROM.

www.prenhall.com/goldfieldFor study resources related to this chapter, visit the *Companion Website*™.

Appendix D

Source: George Beekman & Michael J. Quinn,
Tomorrow's Technology and You, 8/e

Chapter 2
Hardware Basics

"**What's one** and **one** and **one** and **one** and **one** and **one** and **one** and **one** and **one** and **one**?" "**I don't know**," said Alice. "I lost count." "**She can't do addition**," said the Red Queen.

—Lewis Carroll, in *Through the Looking Glass*

THE COMPUTER'S MEMORY

The CPU's main job is to follow the instructions encoded in programs. But like Alice in *Through the Looking Glass*, the CPU can handle only one instruction and a few pieces of data at a time. The computer needs a place to store the rest of the program and data until the processor is ready for them. That's what RAM is for.

Random access memory (RAM) is the most common type of primary storage, or computer memory. RAM chips contain circuits that store program instructions and data temporarily. The computer divides each RAM chip into many equal-sized memory locations. Memory locations, like houses, have unique addresses so the computer can tell them apart when it is instructed to save or retrieve information. You can store a piece of information in any RAM location—you can pick one at random—and the computer can, if so instructed, quickly retrieve it. Hence the name random access memory.

The information stored in RAM is nothing more than a pattern of electrical current flowing through microscopic circuits in silicon chips. This means that when the power goes off, the computer instantly forgets everything it was remembering in RAM. RAM is sometimes referred to as volatile memory because information stored there is not held permanently.

This could be a serious problem if the computer didn't have another type of memory to store information that you don't want to lose. This **nonvolatile memory** is called **read-only memory (ROM)** because the computer can only read information from it; it can never write any new information on it. The information in ROM was etched in when the chip was manufactured, so it is available whenever the computer is operating, but it can't be changed except by replacing the ROM chip. All modern computers use ROM to store start-up instructions and other critical information. You can also find ROM inside preprogrammed devices with embedded processors, such as pocket calculators and microwave ovens. Printers use ROM to hold information about character sets.

Other types of memory are available; most are seldom used outside of engineering laboratories. There are two notable exceptions:

• *Complementary metal oxide semiconductor (CMOS)* is a special low-energy kind of RAM that can store small amounts of data for long periods of time on battery power. CMOS RAM stores the date, time, and calendar in a PC. (CMOS RAM is called *parameter RAM* in Macintoshes.)
• *Flash memory* chips, like RAM chips, can be written and erased rapidly and repeatedly. But unlike RAM, flash memory is nonvolatile; it can keep its contents without a flow of electricity.

How It Works 2.4 Memory

Memory is the work area for the CPU. In order for the CPU to execute instructions or manipulate data, these instructions or data must be loaded into memory. Think of memory as millions of tiny storage cells, each of which can contain a single byte of information. Like mailboxes in a row, bytes of memory have unique addresses that identify them and help the CPU keep track of where things are stored. Personal computers contain a large amount of random access memory (RAM) and a small amount of read-only memory (ROM).

A typical personal computer has from 256 megabytes (millions of bytes) to 2 gigabytes (billions of bytes) of RAM. The CPU can store (write) information into RAM and retrieve (read) information from RAM. The information in RAM may include program instructions, numbers for arithmetic, codes representing text characters, digital codes representing pictures, and other kinds of data. RAM chips are usually grouped on small circuit boards called **single in-line memory modules (SIMMs)** and **dual in-line memory modules (DIMMs)** and are plugged into the motherboard. RAM is volatile memory, meaning that all the information is lost when power to the computer is turned off.

Personal computers also have a small amount of ROM. Information is permanently recorded on the ROM, meaning the CPU can read information from the ROM, but cannot change its contents. On most computer systems, part of the operating system is stored in ROM. Programs stored in ROM are called firmware.

Digital cameras, cell phones, pagers, portable computers, handheld computers, PDAs, and other digital devices use flash memory to store data that needs to be changed from time to time. Data flight recorders also use it. Flash memory is still too expensive to replace RAM and other common storage media, but it may in the future replace disk drives and memory chips.

It takes time for the processor to retrieve data from memory—but not very much time. The *access time* for most memory is measured in *nanoseconds (ns)*—billionths of a second. Compare this with hard disk access time, which is measured in *milliseconds (ms)*—thousandths of a second. Memory speed (access time) is another factor that affects the computer's overall speed.

BUSES, PORTS, AND PERIPHERALS

In a desktop computer, the CPU, memory chips, and other key components are attached to the motherboard. Information travels between components on the motherboard through groups of wires called **system buses**, or just **buses**. Buses typically have 32 or 64 wires, or data paths; a bus with 32 wires is called a 32-bit bus because it can transmit 32 bits of information at a time, twice as many as an older 16-bit bus. Just as multilane freeways allow masses of automobiles to move faster than they could on single-lane roads, wider buses can transmit information faster than narrower buses. Newer, more powerful computers have wider buses so they can process information faster.

Buses connect to storage devices in **bays**—open areas in the system box for disk drives and other devices. Buses also connect to **expansion slots** (sometimes just called *slots*) inside the computer's housing. Users can customize their computers by inserting special-purpose circuit boards (called *expansion cards*, or just *cards*) into these slots. Buses also connect to external buses and **ports**—sockets on the outside of the computer chassis. The back of a computer typically has a variety of ports to meet a variety of needs. Some of these ports—where you might plug in the keyboard and mouse, for example—are connected directly to the system board. Others, such as the monitor port, are generally attached to an expansion card. In fact, many expansion cards do little more than provide convenient ports for attaching particular types of peripherals.

In portable computers, where size is critical, most common ports go directly to the system board. Because portable computers don't have room for full-sized cards, many have slots for **PC cards**—credit-card-sized cards that contain memory, miniature peripherals, and additional ports. (When these cards were first released, they were known as PCMCIA cards. One writer humorously suggested that this stood for "People Can't Memorize Computer Industry Acronyms" though the unfortunate acronym actually means "Personal Computer Memory Card International Association." Thankfully, the name was shortened to the simpler PC card.)

Slots and ports make it easy to add external devices, called peripherals, to the computer system so the CPU can communicate with the outside world and store information for later use. Without peripherals, CPU and memory together are like a brain without a body. Some peripherals, such as keyboards and printers, serve as communication links between people and computers. Other peripherals link the computer to other machines. Still others provide long-term storage media.

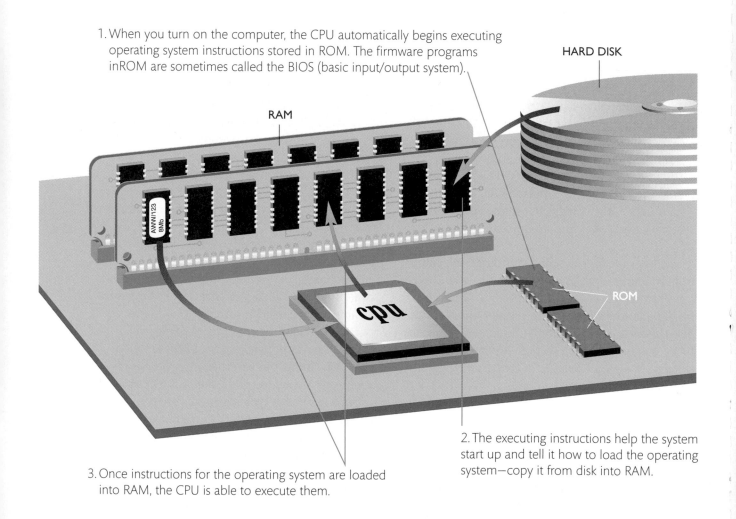

1. When you turn on the computer, the CPU automatically begins executing operating system instructions stored in ROM. The firmware programs inROM are sometimes called the BIOS (basic input/output system).

HARD DISK

RAM

ROM

cpu

2. The executing instructions help the system start up and tell it how to load the operating system—copy it from disk into RAM.

3. Once instructions for the operating system are loaded into RAM, the CPU is able to execute them.

Tomorrow's Processors

The only thing that has consistently **grown faster** than hardware
in the last 40 years is **human expectation**.

—Bjarne Stroustrup, AT&T Bell Labs, designer of the C++ programming language

Many research labs are experimenting with alternatives to today's silicon chips. For example, IBM researchers have developed plastic chips that are more durable and energy efficient than silicon chips. Intel, Motorola, and AMD are working with the U.S. government to develop new laser etching technology called **extreme ultraviolet lithography (EUVL)** that could reduce chip size and increase performance radically. Motorola researchers have created chips that combine silicon with gallium arsenide, a semiconductor that conducts electricity faster than silicon and emits light that can be used for information applications; the research should soon produce chips that are much faster than any currently available. IBM and Motorola researchers are making progress producing chips based on carbon rather than silicon. Carbon-based nanoscale processors would be much smaller and consume far less electricity than conventional silicon-based microprocessors. Scientists at HP Labs are experimenting with an alternative to transistors made out of nanowires only 100 atoms in diameter.

Researchers are pursuing other radical research technologies, too. Superconductors that transmit electricity without heat loss could increase computer speed a hundredfold. Unfortunately, superconductor technology generally requires a supercooled environment, which isn't practical for most applications. A more realistic alternative is the **optical computer**, which transmits information in light waves rather than in electrical pulses. Optical computers outside research labs are currently limited to a few narrow applications, such as robot vision. But when the technology is refined, general-purpose optical computers may process information hundreds of times faster than silicon computers do.

Some of the most revolutionary work in computer design involves not what's inside the processors, but how computers are put together. One example is IBM's Blue Gene supercomputer. The Blue Gene architecture is designed around small, simple processors, each capable of handling eight threads of instructions simultaneously. The processors don't have power-hungry embedded caches, but they do have built-in memory to improve speed. The network of processors is self-heading; it detects failed components, seals them off, and directs work elsewhere. The first computer in the Blue Gene series, Blue Gene/L, is already in operation at Lawrence Livermore National Laboratory, where it is being used for nuclear weapons–related research. Blue Gene/L is currently the fastest computer in the world. The eventual goal is to create a system with one million processors, capable of executing one quadrillion (1,000,000,000,000,000) instructions per second—300,000 times faster than today's PCs!

Get Ready for the Real Bionic Man *by E. J. Mundell*

Powerful microprocessors make possible the development of sophisticated new tools. In this April 2006 article, HealthDay writer E. J. Mundell reports that primitive bionic hands, limbs, and eyes already exist.

The cyborgs are coming. Human-machine hybrids, they will carry 100-pound loads over long distances; develop artificial arms, hands, and legs; and scan their surroundings with powerful bionic eyes.

But don't worry—the science whizzes who designed them say ordinary humans have nothing to fear.

"Integrating machines with human life is part of the natural progression of technology," says Homayoon Kazerooni, a professor of mechanical engineering and director of the Robotics and Human Engineering Laboratory at the University of California, Berkeley.

His team astounded the scientific world in 2004 after it introduced BLEEX, a wearable robotics system with its own set of legs. BLEEX tracks the wearer's every movement as it helps him or her carry enormous loads for miles without tiring.

The device, designed right now for industrial or military use, is in the fine-tuning stage at this point, Kazerooni says.

"It's a 'lower-extremity exoskeleton,'" he says. "It looks like another person walking right behind you, with its own sensors and onboard computer. It simply walks behind you and takes the load."

Kazerooni was just one of several bionics experts convened for a special press conference Monday in San Francisco, part of the annual Experimental Biology 2006 meeting.

Many Americans over 40 have vivid memories of the original bionic man, TV's Col. Steve Austin. In those days, making a person "better, stronger, faster" by incorporating machinery into or outside his or her body was the stuff of the future.

But Kazerooni points out that bionics—using technology to extend the body's potential—actually has a very longhistory.

"You use glasses, and they help you to see better; you carry a cell phone to communicate with people," he points out. "It was always there. But now, it's becoming more organic, more integrated—we already have artificial hips, remember."

His lab is just one of many across the country doing this kind of work. Also on Monday's panel was William Craelius, the Rutgers University researcher who created Dextra, the first multifinger artificial hand.

Dextra works on the premise that muscles and nerves at the point of amputation still "remember" the missing hand and work as if it were still there. Craelius, an associate professor of biomedical engineering at Rutgers, points out that much hand movement originates higher up the wrist and arm anyway.

"The assumption is that the brain and residual [arm] muscles are intact," Craelius says. Dextra's built-in computer picks up data from sensors lying next to the stump end of the arm and translates that to simple movements—such as grasping—in the artificial hand. "There are certain patterns that we associate with different grasps," Craelius says.

There are limitations, however, and Craelius says, "We're still decades away from reproducing the dexterity of the human hand. But this model can open doors, turn keys, that sort of thing."

Then there's the bionic eye.

Daniel Palanker, the Stanford University physicist whose team designed the optical device, explains that it is intended for people who've lost their retinas, usually through degenerative diseases such as retinitis pigmentosa or age-related macular degeneration.

Those diseases kill off the retina's photoreceptors, and the bionic eye seeks to replicate that lost activity. It consists of a wallet-sized portable computer, a tiny solar-powered battery implanted in the eye, and a light-sensing chip half the size of a grain of rice, also implanted in the eye. The final component is a tiny video camera mounted on virtual-reality style infrared goggles.

When everything's working right, this machinery stimulates cells in the retina to perceive images, just as the now-defunct photoreceptors used to do. Initial trials in rats suggest a bionic eye is feasible, and the researchers are hoping someday to achieve 20/80 vision capability—enough to read large print and recognize faces.

Other innovations covered by the panel include an artificial wrist that's proven a godsend for patients crippled by arthritis, and super-accurate computer simulations of real-life human movement—essential to the development of new prosthetics.

Kazerooni says his lab is currently fine-tuning the BLEEX exoskeleton and plans to roll out its final version soon, for use by healthy individuals.

"But we're also looking for partners—engineers, physicians, scientists—to make this device available for people who have a limited ability to walk," he says. "That's our next step—to design these for people like post-stroke patients, or even people with short-term disability, such as a broken leg. If we get the right resources, it won't take more than three years to create such a device."

So forget The Terminator, bionics is nothing to be scared of, he says.

"If you have a firefighter who's carrying major equipment, we want to make his life a little bit easier and help him avoid injuries. Or a guy working in an auto-assembly line. It's all about making human life better."

Discussion Questions

1. Is there a significant difference between a pair of glasses and an artificial retina, or between an artificial hip and a lower-extremity exoskeleton?

2. What are the potential benefits and risks of advanced bionic devices containing embedded microprocessors?

3. If advanced bionic devices are conceivable, do you think their development is inevitable?

Credits

The publisher would like to thank the following for their kind permission to reproduce their photographs:

Page 2: Gary Conner/PhotoEdit, Inc.; **11:** Bubbles Photolibrary/Alamy Images; **14:** Corbis; **15:** Dex Images/Corbis; **18:** Moodboard/Corbis RF; **27:** Cindy Charles/PhotoEdit, Inc.; **34:** Corbis Super RF/Alamy; **44:** Superstock; **50:** Taxi/Getty Images; **52:** Ceredigion Pix/Alamy; **57:** Corbis; **62:** Photodisc Red/Getty Images; **64:** Radius Images/Alamy; **71:** Mylife Photo/Alamy; **80:** Superstock; **93:** Peter M. Fisher/Corbis; **96:** Brownie Harris/Corbis; **105:** Creatas Images/Jupiter Images/Getty Images; **108:** Michael Newman/PhotoEdit, Inc.; **115:** David Frazier/Photolibrary.com; **130:** Masterfile RF; **125:** KPS/ Masterfile; **148:** Michael Prince/Corbis; **150:** Rachel Epstein/PhotoEdit, Inc.; **153:** Jamie Grill/ JGI/ Blend Images/Getty Images RF; **154:** Stone/Getty Images; **168:** Kate Mitchell/Corbis; **172:** Michael Newman/PhotoEdit, Inc.; **180:** The Image Bank/Getty Images; **182:** David Deas/DK Stock/Getty Images; **193:** Andrew Bannister/Gallo Images/Corbis; **198:** Steve Dunwell/The Image Bank/Getty Images; **210:** Gary Conner/PhotoEdit, Inc.; **214:** Stone/Getty Images; **216:** David Young-Wolff/PhotoEdit, Inc.; **227:** ColorBlind Images/Iconica/Getty Images; **230:** Photodisc Red/Getty Images; **232:** Somos Images/Corbis RF; **243:** Insadco Photography/Alamy; **272:** General Board of Global Ministries, The United Methodist Church; **265:** A.D.A.M. Inc.

All other images © Dorling Kindersley
For further information see: www.dkimages.com

Chapter 15: Tamar Lewin, from "DOES IT WORK? SUBSTANCE-FREE DORMS; Clean Living on Campus." From The New York Times, November 6, 2005, copyright © 2005 The New York Times. All rights reserved. Used by permission and protected by the Copyright Laws of the United States. The printing, copying, redistribution, or retransmission of the material without express written permission is prohibited.

Appendix A: Wood et al., *Mastering the World of Psychology*, pp. 149–167, © 2004. Reproduced by permission of Pearson Education, Inc.

Appendix B: Excerpts, pp. 394–407, Tables 21.1, p. 396, 21.2, p. 398, 21.3, p. 399, and Fig. 21.9, p. 403 from *Life on Earth*, 5th by Teresa Audersirk, Gerald Audersirk, and Bruce E. Byers. Copyright © 2009 by Pearson Education, Inc. Reprinted by permission.

Appendix C: Goldfield, David; Abbott, Carl E.; Anderson, Virginia DeJohn; Argersinger, Jo Ann E.; Argersinger, Peter H.; Barney, William; Weir, Robert, *The American Journey: Combined Volume*, 4th edition, © 2007, pp. 774–783. Reprinted by permission of Pearson Education, Inc., Upper Saddle River, NJ.

Appendix D: Beekman, George; Quinn, Michael J., *Tomorrow's Technology and You*, 8th Edition, © 2007, pp. 53–57. Reprinted by permission of Pearson Education, Inc., Upper Saddle River, NJ.

Index